1 MONTH OF
FREE
READING

at
www.ForgottenBooks.com

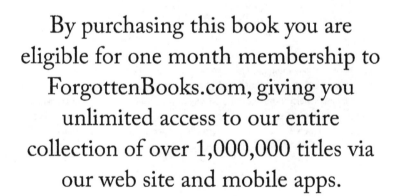

By purchasing this book you are eligible for one month membership to ForgottenBooks.com, giving you unlimited access to our entire collection of over 1,000,000 titles via our web site and mobile apps.

To claim your free month visit:
www.forgottenbooks.com/free960312

ISBN 978-0-260-62451-2
PIBN 10960312

Forgotten Books is a registered trademark of FB &c Ltd.
Copyright © 2018 FB &c Ltd.
FB &c Ltd, Dalton House, 60 Windsor Avenue, London, SW19 2RR.
Company number 08720141. Registered in England and Wales.

For support please visit www.forgottenbooks.com

INSURANCE COMMISSIONER'S REPORT

STATE OF NORTH CAROLINA,
INSURANCE DEPARTMENT,
RALEIGH, April 1, 1918.

To His Excellency, THOS. W. BICKETT,
Governor of North Carolina.

DEAR SIR:—As Insurance Commissioner, it becomes my duty to submit to you, as required by law, a report of the Insurance Department, embodying a statement of the work for the past year, as well as the condition of all companies and associations supervised by the Commissioner as shown by the reports filed with him. The report filed herewith covers the fiscal year ending April 1, 1918.

DEPARTMENT

The Department was formed in 1899, and has fully demonstrated the wisdom of its creation. Its value to the State and her citizens increases each year. The increase of the insurance business in the State calls for more work, for a proper supervision, as well as for the collection of revenue due the State from insurance companies and their representatives.

REVENUE

The revenue collected and paid into the State Treasury by this Department has increased each year, until there was collected and paid in for the past fiscal year $415,468.16.

The gradual increase of the revenues collected from insurance companies through this Department and paid into the State Treasury is more clearly shown by a comparison with the amount ($84,879.28) collected for the fiscal year ending April 1, 1899, the year prior to the formation of the Department.

The amount collected by the Department and paid into the State Treasury each year since its formation is as follows:

For the first fiscal year 1899-00 ....$	91,973.49
For the fiscal year 1900-01	91,072.92
For the fiscal year 1901-02	132,034.03
For the fiscal year 1902-03	153,667.12
For the fiscal year 1903-04	174,633.60
For the fiscal year 1904-05	197,402,23
For the fiscal year 1905-06	205,124.07
For the fiscal year 1906-07	215,331.56
For the fiscal year 1907-08	224,680.58

For the fiscal year 1908-09.........................$ 234,469.63
For the fiscal year 1909-10......................... 246,566.89
For the fiscal year 1910-1-1........................ 270,300.08
For the fiscal year 1911-12......................... 285,040.50
For the fiscal year 1912-13......................... 319,389.67
For the fiscal year 1913-14......................... 344,546.28
For the fiscal year 1914-15......................... 352,047.20
For the fiscal year 1915-16......................... 348,780.90
For the fiscal year 1916-17......................... 372,044.12
For the fiscal year 1917-18......................... 415,468.16

  Total......................................$ 4,674,573.08

Under the old law, prior to the organization of this Department, tain fees were allowed to the Secretary of State as compensation for supervision of insurance companies. These fees are now paid into State Treasury, and amount to more than double the whole cost of Department, including salaries and every other expense.

Of course, these taxes collected make a good showing, but the amo saved to the citizens of the State by proper supervision really brings n benefit to them and in the end makes a decidedly greater total than revenues collected. In the opinion of many the State should not col from insurance companies more than is necessary to finance the In: ance Department; but the Commissioner has always held, and ins that the companies should pay their pro rata part of the cost of run the Government—no more, and no less.

SUPERVISION

The collection of the licenses, taxes, and fees from insurance compa above referred to is an important matter, and adds very materially to State's revenue; but by far the most important work of the Departm and that of greatest benefit to the citizens of the State is the pr supervision of insurance companies, associations, and societies, as we their representatives operating in the State. The great improvemen the practices of the companies and their agents show the work ac plished in this respect. This supervision takes in:

1. *The admission and regulation of all companies doing or propo to do any kind of insurance in the State.*—There are about four hun companies, associations, and societies doing the following classes o surance: Life, health, accident, casualty, fire, marine, credit, burgl plate-glass, liability, steam-boiler, automobile, etc.

2. *Fire Marshal.*—The Commissioner is also *ex officio* fire marshal, has charge of the investigation of all suspicious fires, and the prosecu of those supposed to be responsible for them. There have been man these investigations and prosecutions which have been very benefici

their results. A number of convictions are obtained each year and the deterrent effect is especially good. The average convictions each year are from 15 to 20. This is a fine record when it is remembered that it is more difficult to convict for burning than perhaps for any other crime. There can be no question but that these convictions obtained, as well as the vigorous prosecutions conducted even where no conviction followed, have had a good effect and are materially reducing fires in the State.

3. *Building and Inspection Laws.*—The Commissioner is charged with the enforcement of the building and inspection laws. This involves not only having inspections made throughout the State by men sent from the Department, but also in seeing that the work is kept up and the laws enforced by the officers of the different cities and towns. The State Building Code and its enforcement in the different cities and towns in the State is not only greatly improving the fire conditions and liability to conflagrations in our cities and towns, but is having a fine effect in the education of our people as to the advantage of better and safer buildings and the protection they afford against the destruction by fire of property throughout the State. The Legislature of 1915 provided that the license fees collected from fire insurance companies should be used for this purpose. This gave a sufficient sum and has enabled the Commissioner to start out upon different lines of fire prevention and lay a broader foundation for a great and effective work along this line in the State. There is some complaint because of lack of funds for the enforcement of the law passed by the Legislature of 1915 in regard to forest fires. It might be well for this General Assembly to consider the advisability of restoring this work to the Fire Marshal Department of the Insurance Department, as it was prior to the enactment of this law.

4. *Exits and Fire-escapes.*—Under chapter 637, Public Laws 1909, the Insurance Commissioner is given supervision over and charged with the enforcement of the law in regard to sufficient exits and proper fire-escapes for buildings in the State where people congregate. This is a most important law and one that has called for considerable thought and work from the Insurance Commissioner and his deputies; over 1,000 fire-escapes having been erected under their direction. It is to be greatly regretted that so many of our public buildings, especially theaters, dormitories, and school buildings, should be so erected that it is impossible to arrange for an absolutely safe escape of the inmates in case of fire. Of course, the Commissioner has endeavored to do what he could in the way of having buildings already erected put in proper shape, but some provision should be made so that plans for new buildings of this character must be passed upon by the Insurance Commissioner or some expert in his Department to secure not only the safety of the building itself, but especially of the inmates, from fire.

5. *Publication of Statements.*—The Commissioner is required to make an abstract of the financial statements filed with him by the different companies operating in the State; to collect the fees for the publication of the same and have them published in the newspapers of the State.

6. *Firemen's Relief Fund.*—The Commissioner is also required to collect from insurance companies operating in the State the taxes for the benefit of our firemen and to distribute these taxes among the firemen of 90-odd towns of the State, or all the cities and towns complying with the law. This fund amounts annually to over $9,000. Under the law a tax of one-half (½) of 1 per centum is collected on the premiums received in the city or town by foreign fire insurance companies and constitute the Firemen's Relief Fund of that city or town.

7. *Complaints and Violations.*—It is also the duty of the Insurance Commissioner to seek out and prosecute all violations of the insurance law, to look into all complaints made to him by the citizens of the State, and to give them such information as they may desire at his hands in regard to companies and associations under his supervision, and such aid as they may need in any controversy or misunderstanding. The work and correspondence in these matters take practically the time of a first-class man.

8. *Approval of Contracts.*—Under the law the Insurance Commissioner must approve all insurance contracts issued in the State, and every company, association, or society is required to submit to the Insurance Commissioner for his approval all applications for as well as contracts of insurance, with clauses modifying the same, before it is lawful to offer them in the State. While this involves a considerable amount of work, largely technical, it is a very valuable law, and certainly helpful in regard to the character of the contracts of insurance issued in the State.

9. *Rate-making Bureaus and Associations.*—These associations and bureaus of practically every class of insurance are subject to the inspection and examination of the Insurance Commissioner, and it requires much labor of a technical and painstaking character to keep in touch with the various rules, regulations, and rates promulgated. Under the law every company must file with the Insurance Department the schedules and rules on which they base their rates, and fire companies must not only do this, but furnish each owner of property with each rate made (or changed), in detail.

10. *Insurance on State Buildings and Inspections Thereof.*—Under the law the Insurance Commissioner is charged with placing all insurance upon the different State properties, as well as the inspection of the State institutions and buildings, not only as to their safety from fire, but as to the safety of the inmates in case of fire. This is a most important duty,

4

as it involves not only the protection of the property of the State but of the lives of the inmates in the State institutions, most of whom are helpless, especially in case of fire. Sufficient attention has not heretofore been paid in this State to the character of State buildings erected, as to the protection of the buildings from fires and the safety of their inmates in case of fire and its attendant panics.

11. *Building and Loan Associations.*—The Commissioner is now charged with the supervision of building and loan associations, and the great work being done by these associations, the organization of new associations almost continually, as well as the suggestion that these associations as Land and Loan Associations can be adapted to and be made of great benefit to the farmers of the State as well as to those living in cities and towns who have received their benefits, makes this a most important part of the work of the Department.

12. *Investment and Promotion Companies.*—The looking after these companies calls for prompt and intelligent work, that our citizens may not be imposed upon or defrauded, for such companies and their representatives are usually very active. The small fund allowed for use by the Insurance Commissioner for seeking out and prosecuting violations of the insurance laws is used up in that work. A special allowance should be available for violations by investment and promotion companies. Vigorous prosecutions against these would save thousands of dollars each year to our people.

COMPANIES ADMITTED

The following companies and associations were admitted to do business in the State during the year:

LIFE

Citizens Mutual	Maryland Assurance
George Washington.	Morris Plan
Life and Casualty	

FIRE (MUTUAL)

Alamance Farmers	Michigan Millers
Middlesex	Stanly Mutual

FIRE (STOCK)

Columbian	Northwestern Fire and Marine
Home Fire (Utah)	Norwegian Assurance
Marquette National	Palmetto Fire
National (Denmark)	

RECIPROCAL OR INTER-INSURERS

Consolidated Underwriters	Southern Lumber Underwriters
National Lumber Manufacturers	Western Reciprocal Exchange

UNDERWRITERS' AGENCIES

Fire and Marine Underwriters   London Underwriters

MISCELLANEOUS

American Automobile

INVESTMENT

Bankers Trust and Title   Durham Morris Plan Company

FRATERNALS

Norfolk and Western (Relief Dept.)   Independent Love and Union

STOPPED BUSINESS

The following companies or associations either did not renew their license at the close of the year 1917, or ceased to do business in the State during the past year:

LIFE

Home Mutual Life, Accident and   Merchants Life
  Health   Eastern Relief Association
Mutual Christian Burial Aid

FIRE

Aachen and Munich   International Re-Assurance
Balkan National   Liberty Insurance Association
Cologne   Munich
First Bulgarian   Newark Fire Underwriters
Frankona   Peoples National
Georgia Fire Underwriters Prussian National
Hamburg-Bremen   Nord-Deutsch
Hamburg Assurance   South German

During the year the following companies made changes in name as indicated below.

German-American Insurance Co. to Great American Insurance Co.
German Alliance Insurance Co. to American Alliance Insurance Co.
Germania Fire Insurance Co. to National Liberty Insurance Co. of America.
Germania Underwriters to Washington Underwriters.
Germania Life Insurance Co. to Guardian Life Insurance Co. of America.

COMPANIES LICENSED

The following companies were admitted to do business in the State under the general insurance laws, where they had not been already admitted, and were licensed for the year ending April 1, 1918:

LIFE COMPANIES

Ætna Life
Atlantic Life
American Central
American National
Business Mens Mutual
Columbian National Life
Connecticut Mutual Life
Durham Life
Equitable Life Assurance
Fidelity Mutual Life
Gate City Life and Health
Guardian Life of America
George Washington
Home Life of New York
Home Security Life
Imperial Mutual Life and Health
Jefferson Standard Life
LaFayette Mutual Life
Life Insurance Company of Virginia
Life and Casualty
Manhattan Life
Maryland Life
Maryland Assurance
Massachusetts Mutual Life
Metropolitan Life
Michigan Mutual Life
Missouri Life
Morris Plan Life

Mutual Benefit
Mutual Life
National Life of America
National Life of Vermont
New England Mutual Life
New York Life
N. C. Mutual and Provident
Northwestern Mutual Life
Ohio National Life
Pacific Mutual Life
Pan-American Life
Penn Mutual Life
Philadelphia Life
Phœnix Mutual Life
Provident Life and Trust
Prudential of America
Reliance Life
Reserve Loan Life
Security Mutual Life
Southern Life and Trust
State Life
Standard Life
State Mutual of Massachusetts
Travelers Life
Union Central Life
United Life and Accident
Union Mutual Life and Health
Volunteer State Life

MUTUAL OR ASSESSMENT LIFE COMPANIES

Afro-American Mutual
Catawba Benevolent
Citizens Mutual
Cumberland Mutual Life and Health
Cumulative Coffin Company

International Mutual
Mutual Christian Burial Aid
Toilers Mutual
Winston Mutual Life

FIRE AND FIRE AND MARINE COMPANIES

STOCK

Ætna
Agricultural
American Alliance
American Eagle
American of Newark
American Central
Alliance
Atlantic
Atlas

Automobile
British America
Boston
Caledonian
Camden
Carolina
Citizens of Missouri
Columbia
Commercial Union Assurance

Commercial Union

Commonwealth

Concordia

Connecticut Fire

Continental

County

Dixie

Equitable Fire and Marine

Equitable of South Carolina

Fidelity-Phenix

Fire Association of Philadelphia

Fireman's Fund

Firemen's of Newark

Franklin of Pennsylvania

Georgia Home

Great-American

Glens Falls

Girard Fire and Marine

Globe and Rutgers

Granite State

Hanover

Hartford

Home of New York

Insurance Co. of North America

Liverpool & London & Globe

London Assurance

London and Lancashire

Massachusetts Fire and Marine

Mechanics

Mechanics and Traders

Milwaukee Mechanics

Nationale of Paris

National

National Liberty

National Union

Netherlands Fire and Life

Newark Fire

New Hampshire

Niagara

North British and Mercantile

North Carolina Home

North Carolina State

Northern Assurance

North River

Northwestern National

Norwich Union

Old Colony

Orient

Palatine

Pennsylvania

Petersburg Savings and Insurance

Phenix of Paris

Phœnix of Hartford

Phœnix of London

Piedmont

Providence-Washington

Queen of America

Rhode Island

Royal

Royal Exchange Assurance

St. Paul Fire and Marine

Scottish Union and National

Security Insurance

Southern Stock

Southern Underwriters

Springfield Fire and Marine

Standard

Sun Insurance Office

Svea Fire and Life

Underwriters of Rocky Mount

Underwriters of Greensboro

Union Assurance

Union of Paris

United States

Virginia Fire and Marine

Westchester

Western Assurance

Yorkshire

REINSURANCE ONLY

Abeille

Century

Columbian

Eagle

First Reinsurance

Fire Reassurance

First Russia

Home of Utah

Imperial

International

Inter-State

Independence

Jakor

Marquette National

Mercantile Insurance of America

Moscow

Norwegian Assurance

National of Denmark

Norske Lloyd
Northern of Moscow
Northwestern Fire and Marine
Palmetto
Peoples National
Paternelle
Rossia
Russian
Salamandra

Second Russian
Skandia
Skandinavia
Sterling
Swiss National
Swiss Reinsurance
Union and Phenix Espagnol
Warsaw

MUTUALS

Alamance Farm Mutual
Arkwright Mutual
Baltimore Mutual
Blackstone Mutual
Cabarrus County Mutual
Cotton and Woolen Manufacturers
· Mutual
Davidson County Mutual
Farmers Douglass Mutual
Farmers Mutual of Edgecombe
  County
Farmers Mutual
Firemen's Mutual
Fitchburg Mutual
Gaston County Farmers Mutual
Hardware Mutual
Hope Mutual
Indiana Lumbermen's Mutual
Industrial Mutual
Keystone Mutual·
Lumbermen's Mutual

Lumber Mutual
Manton Mutual
Michigan Millers Mutual
Methodist Mutual
Mecklenburg Farmers Mutual
Merchants Mutual
Mercantile Mutual
Millers Mutual
Middlesex Mutual
Narragansett Mutual
National Mutual
Pennsylvania Lumbermen's Mutual
Philadelphia Manufacturer's Mutual
Rowan Mutual
Rubber Manufacturers Mutual
Southern Mutual Furniture
Stanly Mutual
State Mutual
Union County Farmers Mutual
What Cheer Mutual

RECIPROCAL OR INTERINSURANCE EXCHANGES

Consolidated Underwriters
Druggist· Indemnity Exchange
Individual Underwriters
Lumber Underwriters
Lumber Manufacturers
Lumbermen's Underwriters· Alliance
Mfrs. Lumbermen's Underwriters
Mfg. Woodworkers Underwriters

Millers Indemnity Underwriters
National Lumber Manufacturers
Reciprocal Exchange
Southern Lumber Underwriters
Utilities Indemnity Exchange
Warners Inter-Ins. (Gro. Dep.)
Western Reciprocal Underwriters

UNDERWRITERS' AGENCIES

Ætna Underwriters
Atlanta Home Underwriters
Colonial Underwriters
Delaware Underwriters
Exchange Underwriters
Fire and Marine Underwriters
Georgia Fire Underwriters
Globe Underwriters

Home Underwriters
London Underwriters
New York Underwriters
Philadelphia Underwriters
Rochester Underwriters
Sun Underwriters
Washington Underwriters

MISCELLANEOUS COMPANIES

Ætna Casualty and Surety
Ætna Life (Accident)
American Automobile
American Credit Indemnity
American National Life (Accident)
American Surety
Columbian National Life (Accident)
Continental Casualty
Employers' Liability
Fidelity and Casualty
Fidelity and Deposit
General Accident
Georgia Casualty
Hartford Accident and Indemnity
Hartford Steam-boiler
Lloyds Plate-glass
London Guarantee and Accident
Maryland Casualty
Massachusetts Bonding and Insurance

Metropolitan Casualty
National Surety
National Casualty
National Life of America (Acci
New Amsterdam Casualty
New York Plate-glass
North American Accident
Ocean Accident and Guarantee
Pacific Mutual Life (Accident)
Provident Life and Accident
Preferred Accident
Reliance Life (Accident)
Royal Indemnity
Standard Accident
Travelers (Accident)
Travelers Indemnity Company
United States Casualty
U. S. Fidelity and Guaranty

LIVE STOCK COMPANIES

Western Live Stock Company, Peoria Ill.

TRUST AND INVESTMENT COMPANIES

American Trust Company
Asheville Morris Plan Company
Bankers Trust and Title
Branch Banking and Trust Company
Citizens Savings and Loan
Citizens Bank and Trust Company
Community Savings and Loan
Durham Morris Plan Company

High Point Morris Plan Compa
New Bern Banking and Trust (
Raleigh Savings Bank and Trus
Rocky Mount Savings and Trust
Southern Real Estate and Trust
Wachovia Bank and Trust
Wilson Morris Plan Company

FRATERNAL ORDERS OR SOCIETIES

A. C. L. Relief Department
Benefit Association of All Railway
    Employees
Ben Hur Supreme Tribe
Brothers' and Sisters' Aid Society
Brothers' and Sisters' Union of
    America
District Household of Ruth, No. 10
Eastern Star
Fraternal Mystic Circle
Funeral Benefit Association of U. S.
Grand Court of Calanthe
Grand United Order Abraham

Grand United Order of Brothers
    Sisters of Love and Charity
Grand United Order O. F. (col.)
Household of David.
Independent Order of Good Sam
    tans, No. 1
Independent Order of Good Sam
    tans, No. 10
Independent Order of G. S. and 1
Independent Order St. Luke
Independent Order of J. R. Gidd
    and Jollifee Union
Independent Order Brith Sholor

Independent Order of True Reformers

Jr. O. U. A. M.

Knights of Gideon Mutual Society

Knights of Columbus

Knights of the Guiding Star of the East

Knights of Pythias, Supreme Lodge

Knights of Pythias (col.)

Lincoln Benefit Society

Loyal Order of Moose

Masons 'Annuity

Masonic Benefit Fund (col.)

Masonic Mutual Life

Modern Brotherhood of America

Modern Woodmen of America

Mutual Life and Indemnity

N. C. Camp Patriotic Order Sons of Am^{e}ric^a

Norfolk and Western Relief Department

Oasis and Omar Temples 'Widows' Fund

Order of the Golden 'Seal

Order United Commercial Travelers

Patriotic Order Sons of America

Pink Hill Fraternal

Peoples Ind. Order True Reformers

Raleigh Union Society

Red Men's Benefit

Royal Arcanum

Royal Fraternal Association

Royal Knights King David

Sons and Daughters of Peace

The Maccabees

Travelers Protective Association

United Order of J. R. Giddings and Jollifee Union

Woodmen of the World, Sovereign Camp

Woodmen Circle, Supreme Forest

Wise Men of North Carolina

Women's Benefit Association of the Maccabees

Woman's Union Burial Association

CHARTERS

Under the law enacted several years ago, all charters for insurance companies and associations are now issued by the Honorable Secretary of State upon the approval of the Insurance Commissioner. This saves considerable time to the Legislature and expense in its work, and subjects all charters to the critical examination of the official who is presumed to have the technical knowledge of the business, and is responsible for their supervision after they are licensed.

During the year ending April 1, 1918, the Commissioner has examined, approved, and certified to the Honorable Secretary of State articles of incorporation for the following companies and associations:

LIFE

Citizens Mutual Life

FIRE

Alamance Farmers Mutual Fire

North Carolina State Fire

Stanly Mutual

TRUST AND INVESTMENT

Bankers Trust and Title Company

Charlotte Morris Plan Company

Raleigh Morris Plan Company

Winston-Salem Morris Plan Company

FRATERNALS

Grand United Order Tent Sisters of North Carolina

Gates Mutual Burial Association

Knights of King Solomon

RECOMMENDATIONS AND NEW LEGISLATION

It is not thought necessary to give in full a statement of the reco
mendations of the Commissioner to the last General Assembly or the la
enacted in response to such recommendations, but it is no doubt well
call your attention to some of these recommendations and new laws.

Standard Fire Policy.—It has always been thought desirable to hav
"Standard Fire Policy," and the form commonly known as the N
York Standard was used in this State until 1915, when the Legislatι
adopted as the North Carolina Standard Fire Policy the form that ν
recommended by the National Convention of Insurance Commissione
After its adoption, at the insistence of some of the states, a few chanι
were made in this policy, and the policy as changed was adopted in N
York and other states. It is, therefore, desirable that the North Ca
lina standard form as now adopted and used in the State should
amended so as to include the changes referred to above. The new staι
ard fire policy is an improvement upon the old form and has worked ν
in this State.

Whole-family Insurance by Fraternal Societies.—The bill adopted
allow whole-family protection by fraternal societies in this State was
the form recommended by the National Convention of Insurance Co
missioners, and seems to be working well in the State, but it may p
haps be desirable to make one or two minor changes in the same in orι
to provide fully for the protection of the children insured under this l
by different societies when they reach the age at which they can beco
regular members of the society.

Increase of Capital by a Stock Dividend and Transfer of Stock.—C
North Carolina insurance laws provide that there can be no change
the charter of a domestic insurance company or in the amount of ι
capital stock without the approval of the Insurance Commissioner. T
is the law, also, in New York, and possibly one or two other states. I
action of the Union Central Life Insurance Company of Ohio, a forei
life insurance company doing business in this State, in increasing th
capital stock from $100,000 to $2,000,000 by stock dividends would
mind us that some provision is necessary in our law to prevent sυ
action as this, by which a company with a disregard for the rights of
policyholders in this State is willing to place burdens upon them to
borne in years to come. There is no disposition to interfere with ι
domestic companies of other states, but the Commissioner believes tł
the citizens of this State who become policyholders in such a life insι
ance company should be protected by a provision in our law requiri
that such action shall meet with the approval of the proper official
this State, unless the action is required to be passed upon and approν

by the proper official in the home state of the company. The Commissioner is also of the opinion that proper action should be taken in regard to the transfer of stock to prevent such a transfer of the stock and management of a life insurance company to irresponsible parties as will enable the company to be "looted" and the rights of its policyholders trampled upon, as was attempted with the Pittsburg Life and Trust Company not long since.

Workmen's Compensation.—For several years the Commissioner in his annual reports and recommendations to the General Assembly has strongly urged the enactment in this State of a Workmen's Compensation Law, but so far such action has not been taken, largely because of the fact that our people have not been educated to know the value and importance of such a law in the industrial progress of our State. Such a law has been enacted in a large number of states and is proving entirely satisfactory to both the employers and employees. The Commissioner would strongly urge that you, as Governor of this State, in your recommendations to the next General Assembly, shall bring this matter to their attention, to the end that it may receive such a consideration as it deserves at their hands.

Fire Protection for State Institutions.—It is made the duty of the Commissioner to inspect annually all of the State property and to place such an amount of insurance thereon as can be purchased with an annual appropriation of $10,000. This only enables the Commissioner to carry about 30 per cent of the value of the State property, and the Commissioner believes that it would be well for the Legislature to provide by an appropriation for the carrying of at least 50 per cent of the value of the State property, this being the amount that was originally protected when the appropriation was first made.

The last Legislature not only made a decidedly forward step in the protection of the State property by providing that all of the new buildings to be erected out of the $3,000,000 bond issue should be fireproof, but provided that $40,000 of this amount should be used under direction of the Commissioner for improving the fire conditions of the State institutions so as to protect the property as well as the inmates from fire. The improvements called for are being made as rapidly as possible and are certainly very desirable in view of the fact that State institutions are being burned and the lives of their inmates lost by fires throughout the country, and within the last few months the matter has been brought close to us by the destruction in Columbia, S. C., of a state institution and the death of twenty-odd helpless inmates.

Lightning Rods.—The last Legislature, realizing that lightning rods of approved make, when properly installed, were a great protection to our people, and that this protection was being lost largely by the general distrust of our citizens as to the business and its character, undertook to remedy this condition by providing that every person who sold or erected a lightning rod should be licensed by this department and that only approved rods should be used. No doubt much good has been accomplished so far by this law; but the statute is in such shape as not to provide the proper machinery for its enforcement, and the Commissioner believes that the law should be redrawn so as to make it more easily enforceable and more efficient in its service.

Building and Loan Associations.—This class of associations supervised by this Department continue to make progress and enlarge the scope of their work and usefulness to the citizens of our State, but it is evident that some provision must be made by which the Commissioner may be better prepared to provide for examinations and such other work as will enable him to keep in close touch with the condition of the different associations and their methods. It is wonderful the amount of good that is being done by these associations in building up our cities and towns and provding homes for their citizens, and it is worthy of note that the benefits go largely to the class of citizens who could not procure homes in other ways. While the many calls for investments by the Government in these war times to a certain extent hampers the work of these associations, yet the plan of the Government, as shown in War Savings Certificates and Thrift Stamps, being largely copied after the plan of building and loan associations, is educating our people in thrift and in the use of building and loan methods, and will ultimately prove of great educational value in the work of building and loan associations.

When the business was placed under the supervision of my Department in 1904, the report showed 41 associations doing business in the State, with assets of $5,542,988.51, of which amount $2,427,065.65 were loaned out in the State for the purpose of building homes. My forthcoming report of 1917 business will show 145 associations with assets of $17,774,915.62, with $16,845,109.53 loaned out in the State to build homes, and receipts for the year $11,659,530.13. Profits paid out during the year, $497,563.26, and undivided profits $1,093,777.13. The average interest rate earned is .05993, and the average expense ratio .032457. This is a fine and gratifying showing when it is remembered that the business of building and loan associations is not one that accumulates money to be held, but is continually not only receiving money but paying it out in matured shares. During the time referred to (1904-1917) the building and loan associations in this State have paid back to their shareholders $27,134,392.30.

INSURANCE RATES

In his recommendation to the last General Assembly the Insurance Commissioner had this to say in regard to this subject, and also included it in his last report:

"Rate-making Bureaus and Associations.—These associations and bureaus of practically every class of insurance are subject to the inspection and examination of the Insurance Commissioner, and it requires much labor of a technical and painstaking character to keep in touch with the various rules, regulations, and rates promulgated. Under the law every company must file with the Insurance Department the schedules and rules on which they base their rates, and fire companies must not only do this, but furnish each owner of property with each rate made (or changed), in detail."

The matter of fire insurance rates is still (and perhaps will ever be) a disturbing problem. Under our law the Insurance Commissioner has the supervisory powers set out in both the New York and Massachusetts laws on this subject. While the fire insurance rates in North Carolina are yet lower than those in any state in this section or similarly situated, there have been two increases of rates by the companies since the last Legislature. In July, 1917, an increase of 10 per cent was proposed on all *unprofitable classes;* but because of the objection of the Commissioner was not put into effect until November 1, 1917. Again, on March 29, 1918, a like increase was made to cover all other classes. The companies insist that the increases are necessary because of the great increase in operating expenses largely on account of the war. There is no doubt of a considerable increase in operating expenses, which must of course be taken care of. The companies are faring well in this State in a reduction of losses, and the old question, of course, arises as to how far the local conditions are to govern and to what extent the rates must be based upon the conditions and results throughout the whole country.

THE REDUCTION OF FIRE WASTE

Under the law of our State the Insurance Commissioner is *ex officio* Fire Marshal, and what is commonly known as the Fire Marshal Law and Building Code is embraced in three different laws on the statute books of the State.

1. A bill along the line of the regular Fire Marshal bill is chapter 58, Public Laws of 1899. (Revisal 1905, secs. 4815-4823.)

2. A bill known as "Fire Waste Bill" is practically a building code, and is embraced in chapter 506, Public Laws of 1905. (Revisal 1905, secs. 2981-3011.)

3. The bill for proper exits and fire escapes is chapter 637, Public Laws of 1909.

These laws should be combined and codified, as they would then be rendered easier for examination and construction.

The Insurance Commissioner is charged with seeing that the requirements of these statutes are carried out. He is given large power and much discretion. The spirit of the law is to protect life and property. The law requires that each incorporated city and town in the State shall have a chief of fire department, and prescribes certain duties that he must perform.

The people of the State and fire insurance companies are at last awaking to the importance, yea, necessity of cutting down the fire waste. That there is room for this is shown by the heavy loss ratio in this country as compared with that in European countries. With immensely better equipped fire departments to put out fires when once started, our loss is, yet, several times as great. This clearly shows that the fight must be made in preventing rather than in putting out fires. The public as well as the companies are certainly being aroused to a realization of what can be accomplished by safer building, better equipment, and the necessary care in looking after the building and its equipment. Of course there are losses intentionally brought about by the assured for gain or an enemy for revenge or malice. These are largely preventable by the companies and their representatives. The losses through malice constitute a comparatively small proportion and are lessened by the retardant effect of strict laws vigorously enforced. The burning for gain must be reduced or stopped by a proper vigilance and thorough efficiency of companies and agents against over-insurance and the reckless placing of risks. If there is no over-insurance then there is no profit in burning nor inducement for burning from malice. Of course, the Fire Marshal Department can by efficient service greatly aid in reducing incendiary fires. Conviction for burning and vigorous prosecutions, even where no verdict is obtained, greatly reduce this class of fires and prove of great benefit to the people as well as the companies.

REDUCTION OF FIRE WASTE

We consider in North Carolina that the reduction of fire waste covers the loss of life and property and that both can be worked together to great advantage. In this way those who feel that property can and should be covered by insurance, may respond to an appeal to save life, while those who feel that few lives are lost by fires may be reached by an appeal on account of the loss of property, as they so frequently see property destroyed by fire. Women and children are especially reached by an appeal on account of the loss of life. In fact, they readily see that they furnish a large majority of those who suffer in this way. The fact that so many people believe that fires must happen and do not realize that at least two-thirds of them are preventable, makes it hard to arouse the public generally to the necessity of their prevention.

The work naturally divides itself into two calsses: (1) The prevention of fires; (2) the putting out of fires. Each must be stressed and worked, but it is easier to arouse the average city or town to the necessity of being prepared to put out fires than to attempt to prevent them. In our work we have appeared before the governing bodies of cities and towns spending from $10,000 to $30,000 for the annual up-keep of their fire department, to say nothing of its purchase cost, and have had them look at us as if they thought we were beside ourselves in proposing that they should employ a regular inspector at a cost of $1,000 or $1,500, to see that their buildings were properly erected and kept in good condition so as to prevent fires. It is hard for the average man to realize that anything can be accomplished in the prevention of fires, much less how much can be done with proper work along this line.

EDUCATIONAL WORK

We treat the enforcement of all the laws for the reduction of fire waste—in fact everything connected with it—in an educational way. They are all used as teachers or text-books. We find it decidedly best to show the citizen, whether male or female, adult or child, business or professional man, official or private citizen, the reason of the thing, the advantage of the work, rather than simply to enforce the law because we have the power to do so.

PUTTING OUT FIRES

While we lay great stress upon the prevention of fires, we do not by any means underestimate the importance of being prepared to put out fires when they start, or in any way minimize this work. We take up with each city and town in the State the importance of the necessary fire apparatus and trained firemen, and furnish them all the aid and information that they desire in properly equipping their department and training their firemen. We pay especial attention not only to the fire department and its equipment and training, but also to the water supply and the arrangements for sending in alarms in case of fires.

PREVENTION OF FIRES

For our convenience and as a help to the work we divide our work and workers in fire prevention into seven (7) classes. While, of course, each class and its workers will frequently mix with and overlap the other, yet the division enables us to keep in closer touch with the needs and the progress along the different lines.

1. *State Building Code.*—Our State Building Code, while not as perfect as it might be, is well adapted to the needs of our State, and certainly is elastic in its adaptation to use in the large city or the small town. It covers the erection of buildings and the manner in which they are kept, and calls for a building inspector and an electrical inspector, both of whom are under the general supervision of the Insurance Commissioner. Each city or town must lay off a fire district and is given the right to elect a building inspector and also an electrical inspector. If they elect a building inspector and not an electrical inspector, then the building inspector becomes *ex officio* electrical inspector. If they fail to elect either, then the chief of the fire department becomes *ex officio* building and electrical inspector. The Code provides for a fire district and forbids the erection of frame buildings therein. The law being a State one, cannot be waived by local authorities.

2. *Inspections.*—Under our law an inspection must be made of all premises in the fire district quarterly, and of all premises outside of the fire district at least once a year. The building inspector is charged with the duty of making these inspections. The Insurance Commissioner also has the authority to make these, and in fact any inspections, with his deputies, either with or without the local inspector. Reports are required of these inspectors, which are required to be followed up and the deficiencies corrected.

3. *Prosecutions.*—Under the law the Insurance Commissioner is charged with the investigation of all suspicious fires. It is made his duty to investigate them fully and where the evidence justifies it to conduct vigorous prosecutions, employing counsel to aid the State solicitor, and doing whatever in his opinion is necessary. The building inspectors in cities and towns and the sheriffs for territory outside of the cities and towns must make report of every fire to the Insurance Commissioner, and render him whatever aid he desires in all investigations.

4. *Fire Prevention Expert.*—The Department employs a fire prevention expert, who is a trained fireman and well qualified to pass upon the necessity and value of all fire apparatus and its use, and to instruct the firemen in handling fire apparatus and making inspections. This expert visits all cities and towns and frequently spends several days in organizing and training the firemen.

5. *Proper Ordinances.*—We give much attention to educating the officials of cities and towns as well as their citizens in a knowledge of our laws and the reasons for their enactment and strict enforcement. This work brings fine results, but we do not stop here. We frame and present for their adoption ordinances covering every phase of fire prevention

not found fully covered in our State Code, such as the handling and storage of explosives and oils, use of fireworks, anti-shingle roof, disposition of ashes and trash, etc.

We have advocated and had adopted ordinances for free water for private fire protection in hydrants, stand-pipes and automatic sprinklers. This costs the city nothing, as less water is necessary in putting out fires in this way, to say nothing of the big fires and even conflagrations nipped in the bud. The results from the use of automatic sprinklers in stopping fires in their incipiency is such that cities and towns should not only encourage their installation by free water, but make their use in the fire district and in all large buildings compulsory. To install them is in the end the cheapest thing, to say nothing of their safety. The reduction in insurance rates will soon pay for them.

6. *Electrical Expert and Inspector.*—The Department has and uses a State Electrical Inspector. It is his business to visit all cities and towns, make inspections, and see that the local inspectors are performing their duties and carrying out the law in regard to the proper installation of all electrical apparatus and wiring. A wonderful improvement has been made in the electrical work and conditions in the State through the use of this expert.

7. *Educational Work.*—As stated before, all work of this Department is done along educational lines, and we spare no efforts to use everything that is calculated to bring about a better knowledge of the work and how conditions can be improved. We follow up this work especially along the following lines:

(a) P*amphlets and Leaflets.*—We print large quantities of fire prevention literature and scatter it over the State. We are always preparing, not only general literature, but such as is suited to character of hazards and special occasions, as holidays, Christmas and Fourth of July, Fire-Prevention Days, Clean-up Weeks, the beginning of winter and the opening of spring. An attempt is made to have the literature cover every phase of safety for life and property, and to arouse the people to an understanding of the conditions. It is sent out free in such quantities as may be needed, the only condition being that it will be used.

(b) *Signs.*—We also print and distribute signs calling for care and caution in the various ways for the prevention of fires and accidents. These signs are distributed free to the railroads, manufacturing plants, and in fact all who will use them.

(c) *Press.*—An attempt is made to use to the fullest extent the press of the State in an educational work for the reduction of fire waste in the loss of life and property. A bulletin is issued each week and sent to every paper in the State and a page of plate matter is sent out monthly to each paper in the State that will use it. At one time this plate mat was used by over 150 newspapers, representing a circulation of o 250,000. The matter for these bulletins and plate page is all prepared the Department, and recently the Commissioner has employed a pub ity man who will relieve him of the burden of this work.

(d) *Addresses.*—An attempt is made to reach the people thro addresses. The Commissioner, his deputies and two women, emplo for this purpose, make addresses throughout the State wherever opportunity can be found, especially at community fairs and assembl on special occasions.

(e) *Schools.*—The Department attempts to reach the teachers a children of the public and private schools and colleges throughout State. This is done through addresses, fire prevention books and lite ture, and the law has authorized the Commissioner, in conjunction w the Superintendent of Public Instruction, to prepare a text-book on prevention for use in the schools of the State.

(f) *Officials.*—The Department, of course, keeps in close touch w the different municipalities of the State and all officials, and finds g erally a hearty coöperation on their part.

(g) *Associations.*—The Fire Prevention Association, and, in fa every association in the State, is visited and furnshed with literat for the use of their members, and talked to on the subject of fire a accident prevention.

(h) *Women's Clubs.*—The Department realizes the advantage of t efforts of the women of the State, and attempts to reach them throu their clubs with literature, addresses, etc. The State meeting of t Federation of Women's Clubs has adopted a resolution promising hearty coöperation in the work of the Department, and is active in t work.

(i) *Institutes.*—The Commissioner arranges for the Department to represented at the teachers' summer schools and all teachers' and far ers' institutes held throughout the State, and by addresses and a distrib tion of literature and coöperation in different ways arouses them to realization of what they can do in the saving of life and property.

(j) *Movies and Slides.*—The Department has equipped itself with moving-picture machine with films and slides, and is now using th great educational agent in this work and to accompany the address delivered throughout the State with illustrations that will tend to ma them more effective.

(k) *State and County Fairs.*—The Department puts on regul exhibits at our State and county fairs of pictures and special placarc and uses the occasion for a general distribution of literature gotten o by the Department.

(*l*) *Firemen's and Electrical Institutes.*—The Department holds annually two institutes—one for firemen and the other for electrical inspectors. These institutes are well attended by the officers of fire departments, city officials, electrical inspectors, contractors, and supply men. Through addresses and papers by experts and general discussions they are made intensely practical and both interesting and valuable to the interested parties. This results in uniformity and a great improvement in both classes of work throughout the State.

(*m*) *North Carolina Safety League.*—The Commissioner has arranged for the organization and work of Safety Leagues throughout the State, and will send out to them constitutions and by-laws with such literature for fire and accident prevention as they will distribute. It is proposed to organize a Safety League in every school or in every community in North Carolina. At the last meeting of the Federation of Women's Clubs these leagues federated or joined with the various women's clubs and will thus have their active coöperation and support.

Our men and women are taking hold of different classes of conservation work as necessary to aid in winning this war. The prevention of fire waste and its attendant loss of life and property furnishes one of the broadest and most effective fields for real conservation. It is most important to press this work at this time because of its patriotic conservation value and because there never was and will not be again, certainly for a century, such an opportunity to bring it home to our people in all of its educational and effective value.

SAFETY FIRST

The Commissioner would not be satisfied in attaching this letter to his report if it did not contain an appeal for "Safety First." In this great crisis of our country's history, as she is engaged in the world-wide war for civilization, liberty, and religion, the call is for all, each one, to do everything to help win the war, especially along conservation lines. The "Fire Waste" is an unpardonable fault. There is no excuse for its loss of life and property, amounting in this State alone to over three hundred lives and four million dollars of property values annually. It is from five to ten times as great as like losses in European countries. It is largely—certainly two-thirds—due to ignorance and carelessness, and can be easily avoided and should be.

In all of our official and private appeals for conservation to win the war, no field has been found more open for effective work along broader lines. The opportunity should be readily embraced, especially when it is seen that there never was such a chance, and perhaps will not be in a century, to arouse our people to a realization of how inexcusable this waste is and what it means in a loss of efficiency, and educate them to proper observance of such thoughts and actions as will stop the loss o life and property.

How long will our American people continue to "build to burn" an have their buildings, especially hotels, theaters, school buildings, an even homes, a menace to the lives of our men, women, and children There is no excuse, as in the end it is cheaper, even in money cost, t erect a better class of buildings, as a protection against fire and for th safety of the inmates.

The expense of the investigation of fires and the enforcement of th fire-waste or building law is now paid from a special fund made up o the annual licenses collected of fire insurance companies doing busines in the State. During the past year there has been collected for thi fund $35,988.84, and expended, in accordance with the provisions of th law, $26,143.38, as follows:

Salaries	$ 14,272.88
Traveling and other expenses......................	6,370.06
Expenses of courts and attorneys....................	1,311.19
Publicity, furniture, maps, and supplies.............	4,189.25
	$ 26,143.38

VIOLATIONS

The insurance laws are made for the protection of our citizens an do not impose upon them burdens or unnecessarily harass them. The provide that no insurance company, association, or society can do busi ness in this State unless their application is passed upon and they ar licensed by the Insurance Commissioner. It is also provided that eacl and every agent of these companies shall be licensed by the Commis sioner so that the State and her citizens know what companies th agents represent and what companies are responsible for their act: The Insurance Commissioner is also required to look after all violation of the insurance laws.

It is not proposed by the law to curtail the right or liberty of an citizen, but provide for his protection. This is most important, as an company or association that will withhold from the State the lega licenses and taxes will, when an opportunity occurs, not hesitate t defraud her citizens. The violations of the law have lessened, no doub brought about largely by the law passed by the General Assembly o 1915, requiring that any citizen taking out insurance in an unlicense company should retain 5 per cent of the premium to be paid and pay i over to the Insurance Commissioner.

Under this head your attention and that of the people of the State i called to the supervision of investment companies under section 480 and what is commonly known as the "Blue Sky" Law, section 4805a. These laws apply principally to foreign corporations, and the former, section 4805, calls for only a small supervision of domestic companies. Thousands and thousands of dollars have been saved to our citizens in the restriction of the sale of stock of foreign corporations, and recent attempts to evade this law by forming domestic corporations would seem to call for the application of both laws to domestic corporations, at least where they propose to sell stock by agents.

FIREMEN'S RELIEF FUND

The General Assembly of North Carolina at their session in 1907 created a "Firemen's Relief Fund," as set forth in chapter 831, Public Laws 1907. Under this law each fire insurance company, corporation, or association doing a fire business in the State was required to report to the Insurance Commissioner the premiums received by it in each city and town that met the requirements of the law in regard to fire equipment and observance of the building laws, and the companies were also required to pay to the Insurance Commissioner one-half of 1 per cent upon the amount of the premiums in each city and town, to go to this fund for the relief of the firemen of that city or town. A board of trustees was created in each city and town to receive and disburse the funds in accordance with the provisions of the law. In obedience to this law the Commissioner has collected for the "Firemen's Relief Fund" as follows:

On premiums during 1907	$ 6,805.19
On premiums during 1908	5,940.91
On premiums during 1909	7,113.66
On premiums during 1910	7,864.84
On premiums during 1911	7,672.02
On premiums during 1912	8,949.61
On premiums during 1913	8,758.02
On premiums during 1914	9,519.42
On premiums during 1915	9,447.83
On premiums during 1916	11,024.85
On premiums during 1917	12,547.97

These amounts have been disbursed among the cities and towns in accordance with the premiums collected by fire insurance companies therein.

This law is a proper recognition of the value of the firemen and their work. The amount collected is comparatively small, and the question has been raised as to whether this tax should not be paid by the domestic companies also, as they get the benefit of the firemen's work. It has also

been suggested that in view of the fact that at least 40 per cent
property in our cities and towns is not covered by insurance, the
should also contribute to this fund.

No insurance company, association, or order can do business
State unless licensed by the Insurance Commissioner after he is sa
as to their methods of business and financial standing.   Each of
companies doing business in the State is required to file on or
March 1st of each year an annual statement showing its financia
dition as of the preceding December 31st.   The Commissioner fur
the blanks upon which these statements are made out and filed, an
give the condition in such detail that he can readily, as required b
audit them and prepare abstracts to be published in some newspa
the State, and to be filed with the clerk of the Superior Court i
county.   This is done for the information of the people of the
and that they may not only see them published in the press, b
find a copy on file in the office of the clerk of the Superior Co
their county, as well as in the publications and records of the Ins
Department.   The statements published in this report are those fil
the year ending December 31, 1917, and with the statistical table
give much information to those desiring to be informed as to the
cial condition of companies and societies doing business in this
In a large number of cases this information is all that is desire
other and fuller information, not only in regard to the financial
tion of the companies, but their general standing and methods, c
obtained on application to the Commissioner.

FINANCIAL

All licenses, taxes, and fees required of insurance companies, as
tions, and orders doing business in the State are payable to the Inst
Commissioner.   During the past year the Commissioner has col
and paid to the Honorable State Treasurer:

For taxes on gross receipts..........................$359,798.73
For licenses from companies........................ 25,281.95
For fees and licenses for agents.................... 30,387.48

Total paid Treasurer $415,468.16
For publication annual statements in newspapers.....   2,646.00
For investigation of fires........................... 35,988.84

Total $454,103.00

CONCLUSION

The Commissioner desires to bear testimony to and express his appreciation of the aid rendered to him by the solicitors, sheriffs, chiefs of fire departments, building inspectors, and other officers throughout the State, as well as to the efficient help rendered by the deputies and employees in his Department.

Respectfully submitted,

Insurance Commissioner.

STATISTICAL TABLES

RELATING TO FIRE, MARINE AND INLAND INSURANCE COMPANIES

(NOTE.—These figures were compiled prior to the Department's audit of the companies' statements.)

TABLE No. I—INCOME.

SHOWING THE INCOME OF FIRE, MARINE AND INSURANCE COMPANIES (LICENSED TO DO BUSINESS IN THIS STATE) FOR YEAR ENDING DECEMBER 31, 1917.

NORTH CAROLINA COMPANIES.

Name of Company	Fire Premiums, Including Perpetuals	Marine and Inland Premiums	Interest, Dividends, and Rents	From Other Sources	Total Income	Income Over Disbursements	Disbursements Over Income
Atlantic	$ 100,270.63	$	$ 12,771.15	$ 23,195.56	$ 136,237.34	$ 30.33	$
Cabarrus	2,287.41		101.05		2,388.46	357.35	
Carolina	26,610.00		7,134.61	4,000.00	37,744.61	10,636.82	
Dixie	341,762.72		50,718.98	1,998.00	394,479.70	116,720.21	
Farmers Mutual (Raleigh)	71,814.88			1,630.32	73,445.20	10,702.86	
Farmers Mutual (Edgecombe Co.)	1,741.82				1,741.82	78.36	
Gaston City Farmers Mutual	2,952.91		153.52		3,106.43		657.82
Hardware Mutual	10,389.22		611.15		11,000.37	4,846.62	
Mecklenburg Farmers	1,466.28			405.71	1,871.99	916.31	
North Carolina Home	146,132.27		19,749.84	640.00	166,522.11	25,821.08	
Piedmont	138,140.43		38,817.67	30,000.00	206,958.10	55,319.83	
Rowan Mutual	2,851.59				2,851.59		977.52
Southern Mutual Furniture	4,733.68		13.11	2.59	4,749.38	988.11	
Southern Stock	120,278.79		17,800.15	113.65	138,192.59	36,738.43	
Southern Underwriters	133,568.69		18,649.24		152,217.93	30,545.83	
State Mutual	5,108.79		37.50	1,316.50	6,462.79		79.81
Underwriters (Rocky Mount)	31,020.79		6,152.99		37,173.78	6,235.34	
Underwriters of Greensboro	88,037.94		11,830.88		99,868.82	23,962.52	
Union City Farmers Mutual	5,703.74				5,703.74		261.87
Totals	1,234,872.58		184,541.84	63,302.33	1,482,716.75	323,900.00	1,977.02

COMPANIES OF OTHER STATES (STOCK).

(ii)

Company							
American Eagle	483,63.00	43,036.82	176,449.40	1,319,430.30	2,022,679.52	3,391,904.24	173,032.25
Automobile	1,871,265.47	3,316,930.81	100,902.31	1,140,883.87	6,429,982.46	968,865.76	
Boston	2,693,742.02	4,415,963.92	333,798.80	1,42.40	7,460,997.14	655,054.76	
Camden	2,394,240.25	455,033.55	178,982.80	109,326.09	3,137,582.69	390,425.12	
Citizens of	240,245.05	5,906.37	23,056.41	349,456.04	618,263.87		
Columbia	204,949.89	475,873.11	48,544.00	166.72	524,583.83	40,315.13	
	851,023.89	46,390.54	19,763.04	37,153.19	308,261.66	100,162.45	
Commercial Union (New York)	1,353,148.39	515,768.50	51,009.02		902,032.91	159,486.02	
Commonwealth	1,711,8.63	3,962.19	135,366.28	27,050.16	2,031,333.33	145,637.41	
Concordia			103,876.10	144,272.92	1,963,798.84	392,894.25	
Continental	4,520,641.83	774,197.12	282,210.71	57,559.58	5,634,609.24	1,331,417.55	1,490,467.50
	10,498,972.81	1,037,238.59	1,778,165.16	140,349.27	13,454,725.83	61,941.17	
Eagle	260,714.06		38,468.38	1,266.41	300,448.85	165,588.95	
Equitable Fire and Marine	568,690.16	295,921.56	31,199.62	42,478.13	642,367.91	190,209.80	
	503,847.59		64,711.68	258.00	864,738.83		
Equitable (South Carolina)	201,531.64	881,745.12	22,113.08	115.00	223,759.72	69,336.03	
Fidelity-Phenix	8,743,83.69	*661,167.10	970,611.61	32,305.59	10,628,446.01		
First Reinsurance	615,947.89	19,068.76	94,539.06	144,025.93	1,515,679.98	145,833.48	
Fire Association of Philadelphia	6,017,720.99		477,025.57	1,033,524.87	7,547,340.19	1,983,069.59	
Firemen's Fund	5,491,502.93	*8,686,241.75	548,814.22	25,579.53	14,752,138.43	3,867,347.03	287,093.14
Firemen's (Newark)	3,302,363.44	169,536.80	392,983.18	264,183.26	4,129,066.68	258,165.17	
Franklin	819,149.14	225,680.11	101,587.14	219,105.90	1,365,522.29	562,411.33	
Georgia Home	237,053.43		29,642.93	180,427.15	447,123.51	2,906.37	
Germania	3,825,821.51	778,174.06	369,823.72	731.25	4,974,540.54	273,826.99	282,052.99
Girard Fire and Marine	1,036,189.74		97,700.18	9,928.88	1,143,818.80		
Glens Falls	2,679,376.87	1,110,117.48	309,267.70	114,262.52	4,213,024.57	723,275.10	
Globe and Rutgers	9,387,069.01	9,370,534.36	739,293.08	91,648.50	19,588,544.95	8,351,028.59	
State	853,683.81	427,355.04	47,123.27	1,186.95	901,994.03	145,092.53	
American	12,181,504.21	629,355.75	1,200,045.32	23,176.70	13,832,081.27	2,592,282.87	
Hanover	3,251,505.17		239,924.81	1,947.33	4,122,733.06	868,053.27	
Hartford	23,264,807.62	2,344,859.64	1,094,240.29	5,353.35	26,709,260.90	5,178,145.24	
Home of New York	23,308,716.24	1,743,024.51	1,776,114.47	377,966.42	27,205,821.64	4,847,708.20	
Home of Utah	122,380.66		82,919.77	45,620.49	250,920.92	31,805.13	
Imperial	535,293.06		33,194.36		568,487.42	104,012.25	
Insurance Company of North America	8,694,852.68	11,356,625.02	1,009,355.80	47,925.83	21,1 8,762.33	5,037,594.12	
International	7,888,413.93	820,145.88	133,092.75	372,983.56	8,394,490.29	4,465,413.67	
Interstate	368,989.77		27,490.53	9,150.00	405,630.30	37,633.16	
Massachusetts Fire and Marine	560,281.59		60,764.72	1,095.52	1,442,287.71	242,463.04	
Marquette National	277,985.23		55,114.68		333,099.91	24,801.14	
Mechanics	594,634.19		65,282.94	11,951.97	671,869.10	98,565.00	
Mechanics and Traders	756,943.65		67,421.55	65,438.66	889,803.86	158,783.34	

*Life and Miscellaneous.

TABLE No. I—INCOME.

SHOWING THE INCOME OF FIRE, MARINE AND INLAND COMPANIES (LICENSED TO DO BUSINESS IN THIS STATE) FOR YEAR ENDING DECEMBER 31, 1917.

COMPANIES OF OTHER STATES (STOCK)—CONTINUED.

Name of Company	Fire Premiums, Including Perpetuals	Marine and Inland Premiums	Interest, Dividends, and Rents	From Other Sources	Total Income	Income Over Disbursements	Disbursements Over Income
Mercantile Insurance Company of America	$ 1,130,142.02	$ 404,934.40	$ 125,668.70	$ 448.52	$ 1,661,193.64	$ 196,910.77	$
Milwaukee Mechanics	2,644,442.83	55,728.93	203,330.35	190,146.03	3,093,648.14	707,124.16	
National	10,869,735.84	529,867.56	680,607.53	53,523.92	12,133,734.85	1,963,527.71	
National Union	3,301,688.42	517,521.22	189,762.86	12,183.21	4,021,155.71	1,034,714.34	
Newark	1,306,607.61	177,727.72	97,104.80	143.77	1,582,183.90	147,663.50	
New Hampshire	3,329,489.40	95,991.65	307,049.47	3,103.20	3,735,633.72	519,423.27	
Niagara	4,663,937.85	578,441.86	390,177.61	4,325.11	5,636,882.43	1,152,656.95	
North River	2,862,053.43	3,390.16	208,915.36	73,067.89	3,147,426.84	438,914.70	
Northwestern National	405,851.71		38,392.03	404,485.80	848,729.54	180,906.75	
Northwestern Fire and Marine	3,352,058.21	396,190.63	322,576.59	12,568.15	4,083,393.58	583,090.99	
Old Glory	667,377.07	546,735.04	69,681.78	200,006.85	1,483,800.74	342,456.94	
Orient	1,644,449.75	410,703.86	158,102.21	913.20	2,214,169.02	328,092.96	
Palmetto	126,573.90	99,286.53	4,802.42		230,662.85	67,984.64	
Pennsylvania	4,446,338.56		349,307.90	25,455.17	4,821,101.63	226,790.76	
Petersburg Savings and Insurance	132,771.33		7,305.54	917,413.87	1,057,490.74	761,696.96	
Phoenix (Hartford)	6,504,401.25	1,276,586.39	852,344.42	17,402.38	8,650,734.44	1,757,419.44	
Providence-Washington	2,958,559.60	2,498,416.53	249,583.62	18,903.73	5,725,463.48	743,371.12	
Queen of America	5,306,850.11	2,243,352.09	462,959.06	4,802.60	8,017,963.86	857,605.63	
Rhode Island	1,230,572.41		67,886.31	310.48	1,298,769.20	273,441.59	
St. Paul Fire and Marine	6,423,997.15	3,927,348.24	508,918.07	11,778.50	10,872,241.96	1,499,466.57	
Security	3,008,740.80		200,557.33	107,876.09	3,317,174.22	529,249.31	
Springfield Fire and Marine	7,494,442.42	172,899.58	511,332.41	2,509.59	8,181,184.00	1,493,957.50	
Standard	667,694.39		59,531.71	275,158.73	1,002,384.83	255,031.16	
Sterling	624,039.09	28,929.02	89,412.54	7,574.65	749,955.30	245,843.97	
United States	3,955,985.61	813,364.34	383,344.03	134,691.33	5,287,385.31	752,035.20	
Virginia Fire and Marine	954,701.23		83,266.61	134.18	1,038,102.02	201,039.29	
Westchester	5,333,140.72	567,130.95	296,051.32	544,019.70	6,740,342.69	1,458,108.47	
Totals	263,001,266.62	72,953,564.26	22,509,248.89	9,684,832.40	368,148,912.17	72,328,973.84	2,232,645.88

(iv)

COMPANIES OF OTHER STATES (MUTUAL.)

Arkwright Mal	2,396,390.39	109,844.89	760.00	2,506,995.28	454,722.22	4,674.45
Baltimore Mutual	88,577.55	4,470.62	9,692.50	102,740.67		
Blackstone Mutual	1,326,039.82	73,901.84	3.25	1,399,944.91	250,821.58	
l ... Underwriters	1,483,066.77	22,252.47	188,392.59	1,693,711.83	277,554.07	
...n and Woolen	651,544.63	29,149.59	1,292,241.94	1,972,936.16	177,265.79	
Druggists ... ity	149,644.01	2,271.03		151,915.04	13,650.62	
Firemen's Mutual	1,892,223.58	107,476.03	5,708.00	2,005,407.61	388,887.29	
...ng Mutual	240,097.25	10,878.82		250,976.07	30,192.29	
Hope Mutual	708,551.63	33,976.51	2,352.10	744,880.24	135,930.68	
Indiana Lumbermen's Mutual	577,022.34	39,766.03		616,788.37	142,441.61	
l ... al Underwriters	405,731.80	25,301.90	31,000.00	462,033.70	94,092.08	13,584.73
Industrial M	400,773.61	20,726.41	144.20	421,644.22	50,109.60	
Keystone ...	437,736.45	17,148.98		454,885.43		
...ber ...	58,273.14	2,079.27	887.28	61,239.69		
Lumber Manufacturers Interinsurance	297,570.62	10,057.41	83,179.82	390,807.85	1,648.90	72,020.65
Lumber Mutual	650,141.95	49,011.14	29,030.31	728,183.40	161,507.95	
...s Mutual	901,559.84	37,496.00	16,689.56	955,745.40	131,460.46	
... ars	983,105.92	38,763.10	115.21	1,021,984.23	193,949.60	
Mon Mutual	413,587.38	15,590.73	15.00	429,193.11	61,122.98	
...Mg Lumbermen's Underwriters	993,180.81	40,582.24		1,033,763.05	92,961.22	
...g Underwriters	217,440.65	7,119.49	90.53	224,650.67	13,200.74	
Merchants M	709,380.44	41,720.76	6.00	751,107.20	120,947.95	
...le Mutual	319,381.77	20,827.74	204.63	340,414.14	59,632.70	
...ex Mal	205,264.11	25,314.63	90,000.00	320,578.74	96,198.71	
Man Millers Mutual	941,084.38	74,879.34	396,091.78	1,412,065.50	242,338.33	
Millers Mutual	263,298.18	23,864.22		287,162.40	99,325.51	
Millers Indemnity Underwriters	235,114.54	2,484.16	22,964.08	260,562.78	175,800.60	
N ...	121,056.37	6,303.34	25.00	127,384.71	13,721.13	
N ... al Mal	148,742.24	6,543.24		155,285.48	26,785.30	
National Lumber	149,186.59	3,723.28	55,000.00	207,909.87	42,661.28	
Penn Lumbermen's ... Mal	603,863.88	40,281.88	15,012.35	659,158.11	80,660.58	
...s Mutual	682,074.90	32,931.82	3,161.16	718,167.88	143,596.61	
Reciprocal Exchange	561,021.98	26,000.09		587,022.07	131,927.90	
Rubber ... Mutual	619,483.89	29,021.21	286.25	648,791.35	157,190.98	1,887.83
... ther U ...	76,570.04	1,284.61	1,854.76	79,709.41		
Utilities ... ity Exchange	224,650.85	419.88	52,501.10	277,571.83	61,573.89	
Wrn ... al Underwriters	184,693.43	885.90	2,663.08	188,242.41		
What Cheer Mutual	730,905.16	34,406.90	1,630.00	766,942.06	140,750.15	28,839.04
...s Interinsurers (Grocers' Dept.)	126,105.31	2,416.19	73,210.56	201,532.06	110,079.12	
als	22,174,138.20	1,071,173.69	2,374,713.04	25,620,024.93	4,374,776.42	121,006.70

TABLE No. I—INCOME.

SHOWING THE INCOME OF FIRE, MARINE AND INLAND COMPANIES (LICENSED TO DO BUSINESS IN THIS STATE) FOR YEAR ENDING DECEMBER 31, 1917.

COMPANIES OF ... IN COUNTRIES.

Name of Company	Fire Premiums, Including Perpetuals	Marine and Inland Premiums	Interest, Dividends, and Rents	From Other Sources	Total Income	Income Over Disbursements	Disbursements Over Income
Abeille	$ 332,199.60	$	$ 23,512.62	$ 3,933.54	$ 359,645.76	$ 68,435.81	$
	2,266,244.94	49,378.64	122,581.45	2,351.91	2,440,556.94	18,817.88	
Balkan N ...	1,679,990.32		63,734.45	250.00	1,743,974.77		379,899.37
British ...	1,347,412.19	48,756.85	68,171.06	98,500.00	1,562,840.10	282,653.10	
	1,573,792.47	102,921.78	107,934.66	1,742.50	1,786,391.41	271,709.73	
... Union Assurance	305,857.31	8,629.34	29,255.60		343,742.25	50,900.44	
He ...	7,140,661.89	1,320,046.74	307,858.82	383,365.36	9,241,932.81	940,048.63	
First ...	2,425,383.17		77,473.62		2,502,856.79	560,088.81	
Hamburg-Bremen	1,945,806.50		70,654.65		2,016,461.15	413,628.74	
	703,147.64		68,430.51	2,238.96	773,917.11		287,800.72
Jakor ...	4,103,686.36	1,054,353.18	144,302.38	87,472.14	4,335,460.88	399,056.10	
...ol and London and Globe	9,203,784.03		554,329.17	25,816.15	10,838,282.53	526,084.51	
London Assurance	2,284,113.04	2,254,337.83	177,630.26	197,870.59	4,913,951.72	1,036,332.99	
London and	2,557,552.66	573,893.78	205,787.79	80,901.34	3,418,135.57	497,763.82	
	2,776,448.92		91,687.59		2,868,136.51	564,938.01	
...l (Denmark)	565,972.83	171,327.76	14,675.39	831,778.40	1,588,754.38	1,281,179.53	
... (Rus)	498,299.40		30,044.11	6,077.48	534,420.99	141,447.45	
Nord-Deutsche	555,227.38		43,112.52	40,678.62	639,018.52	129,943.95	
Norske Ll yd	469,591.65	2,582,463.67	98,081.51	56,624.98	3,206,766.81	752,339.28	
	2,141,929.49		30,490.28	500,000.00	2,672,419.77	1,253,771.51	
North British and ...	5,757,318.85	620,341.20	350,258.02	5,281.88	6,733,199.95	963,526.73	
Northern (Moscow)	4,046,117.94	103,461.56	239,865.89	53,723.48	4,437,168.87	155,457.24	
Norwegian Assurance	1,435,853.58		47,951.91		1,483,805.49	515,730.45	
N ... h Union	390,402.94		7,097.24	504,107.88	901,608.06	684,798.08	
	2,259,617.98	447,086.48	125,789.22	4,727.26	2,837,220.94	416,833.07	
Phix Fire	1,168,929.57		42,999.21		1,211,928.78	279,853.87	
a...ne (London)	498,299.40		26,086.58	142.41	524,528.39	121,840.74	
Phoenix (London)	2,286,769.02		116,021.86	18,742.97	2,421,533.85	423,420.18	
	2,959,813.65	319,813.95	153,955.63	66,368.19	3,499,951.42	332,136.30	
...	7,469,548.88	4,586,003.88	304,346.99	16,882.06	12,376,781.81	1,953,590.20	
...al	8,508,701.00	3,065,312.32	743,104.52	516,148.20	12,833,266.04	2,141,999.53	

Royal Exchange Assurance	1,814,878.72	964,879.20	130,965.60	1,510.53	2,912,234.05	331,169.97	---
...ian	2,146,202.97	---	78,269.28	---	2,224,472.25	367,709.12	---
Salamandra	4,103,746.73	175,398.31	153,967.67	1,236.63	4,258,951.03	365,973.89	---
Scottish Union and National	3,031,359.90	---	285,183.08	5,559.57	3,497,500.86	679,485.19	---
Second ...an	1,492,157.92	---	63,611.33	---	1,555,769.25	174,070.98	---
Skandia	1,157,546.95	---	61,150.19	102,575.00	1,321,272.14	360,898.44	---
Scandinavia	1,441,925.86	241,186.54	31,326.28	475,000.00	2,189,438.68	1,287,790.12	---
Sun Insurance	2,903,719.98	---	201,007.33	227,437.55	3,332,164.86	447,408.72	---
Svea Fire and Life	1,303,311.03	---	59,604.43	209,323.56	1,572,239.02	447,908.72	---
Swiss ...ial	2,710,711.54	---	92,320.54	---	2,802,432.08	310,028.16	---
Swiss Reinsurance	1,224,156.34	---	70,648.87	656.00	1,295,461.21	178,736.22	---
Union ...	886,429.65	---	61,721.41	58,170.48	1,006,321.54	275,063.83	---
Union (Paris)	695,561.97	---	34,561.34	440.53	730,563.84	116,788.48	---
Union ...al Phenix Espag ol	1,953,023.61	---	64,391.10	100,489.36	2,117,904.07	475,743.37	---
Warsaw ...	840,721.16	---	31,990.26	---	872,711.42	250,475.41	---
...n Assurance	1,748,161.87	1,903,973.27	119,458.09	213,882.96	3,985,476.19	906,735.84	---
...e	901,244.01	35,188.34	34,411.99	203,037.32	1,173,881.66	450,451.97	---
Total	112,006,734.81	20,628,759.62	6,151,814.30	5,105,045.79	143,892,354.52	24,604,740.11	667,700.09

APi TI N.

N ...th Carolina Companies	1,234,872.58	72,953,564.26	184,541.84	63,302.33	1,482,716.75	323,900.00	1,977.02
...s of ...r States (...k)	263,001,266.62	---	22,509,248.89	9,684,832.40	368,148,912.17	72,328,973.84	2,232,645.88
...s of other S...s (mutual)	22,174,138.20	---	1,071,173.69	2,374,713.04	25,620,024.93	4,374,776.42	121,006.70
...s of foreign countries	112,006,734.81	20,628,759.62	6,151,814.30	5,105,045.79	143,892,354.52	24,604,740.11	667,700.09
Grand ...	398,417,012.21	93,582,323.88	29,916,778.72	17,227,893.56	539,144,008.37	101,632,390.37	3,023,329.69

SHOWING THE DISBURSEMENTS OF FIRE, MARINE AND INLAND COMPANIES (LICENSED TO DO BUSINESS IN THIS STATE) FOR YEAR ENDING DECEMBER 31, 1917.

NORTH ██A COMPANIES.

Name of Company	Fire Losses	Marine and Inland Losses	Interest or Dividends	Commissions or Brokerage	Salaries of Officers and Other Employees	Insurance Department Fees and Taxes	All Other Disbursements	Total Disbursements
Atlantic	$ 36,746.46	$	$ 37,500.00	$ 32,750.92	$ 14,946.87	$ 513.78	$ 13,748.98	$ 136,207.01
██s ██ Mal	2,264.25				282.75	42.62	156.19	2,745.81
██a	5,869.51		5,000.00	2,905.21	5,504.96	236.31	7,591.80	27,107.79
Dixie	107,980.47		29,853.00	61,071.87	38,332.86	3,628.62	36,892.67	277,759.49
██ Mual (Raleigh)	44,601.00				17,070.52	258.36	812.46	62,742.34
Farmers ██ Mal	707.50				305.75	10.00	639.39	1,662.64
██n ██y ██s M	3,053.59				557.75	57.04	95.87	3,764.25
██e Mual ██ M	3,417.00				1,839.12	251.61	645.12	6,153.75
Mecklenburg ██ ██e	466.67				354.65	50.82	83.54	955.68
North	63,497.39		12,000.00	18,041.31	17,811.76	3,478.40	25,861.17	140,690.03
Piedmont	59,380.79		10,000.00	21,573.68	12,189.36	1,131.34	47,363.10	151,638.27
██n Mual ██ I	3,173.50				475.00	46.60	134.01	3,829.11
Southern Mal	2,024.35				752.50	190.50	793.92	3,761.27
Southern Stock	34,998.92		8,400.00			206.57	57,848.67	101,454.16
Southern ██s	44,909.62		12,000.00		273.46	256.68	64,232.34	121,672.10
██te Ml	1,791.75		4,120.00	1,013.64	234.00	123.97	3,379.24	6,542.60
██ ██s W M	13,125.96		6,000.00	10,355.46	388.35	719.03	2,229.64	30,933.44
██s of ██o Ml	30,964.81				180.25	91.75	38,669.49	75,906.30
██n Gity ██s	1,502.00				359.41	52.40	4,051.80	5,965.61
	460,476.44		124,873.00	147,712.09	111,859.32	10,846.40	305,729.40	1,161,496.65

COMPANIES OF ██R STA██ES (STOCK).

Company								
American Eagle	168,600.22	11,338.40	160,000.00	30,785.83	40,512.75	10,000.16	1,774,474.41	2,195,711.77
Automobile	499,888.92	996,532.39	100,000.00	797,131.25	341,874.20	34,032.85	268,619.61	3,038,078.22
Boston	1,223,428.33	2,154,703.46	240,000.00	1,173,986.92	420,931.32	87,887.40	1,191,203.95	6,492,141.38
Camden	1,136,267.98	118,074.54	105,000.00	733,281.73	113,018.16	37,542.87	239,342.65	2,482,527.93
Citizens of Missouri	115,155.31	229.96	27,000.00	81,317.53	136.46		3,999.49	227,838.75
Columbia	77,550.83	321,923.47		113,203.69	16,692.93	16,304.40	16,144.21	484,268.70
Columbian	390,178.01	1,001.06		64,940.53	19,953.19	3,803.84	40,849.76	208,099.21
Commercial Union (New York)	747,490.86		20,000.00	198,306.33	53,787.96	16,747.52	63,527.07	742,546.89
Commonwealth	704,633.66	211,115.66	225,000.00	399,819.37	154,952.72	30,404.46	116,912.85	1,885,695.92
Concordia		47.50	60,238.48	449,443.75	112,997.57	32,875.05	210,668.58	1,570,904.59
Connecticut	1,850,962.77	211,120.07	225,000.00	1,178,126.41	413,382.48	93,163.04	331,436.92	4,303,191.69
Continental	4,561,050.75	164,614.94	1,200,000.00	2,330,354.93	883,985.45	224,124.09	5,581,063.17	14,945,193.33
County	137,270.80		20,000.00	40,240.53	3,853.48	9,824.05	27,318.82	238,507.68
Eagle	265,008.08		11,250.00	171,975.45	14,939.78	2,901.14	10,704.51	476,778.96
Equitable Fire and Marine	220,935.28	101,142.35	50,000.00	266,586.97	11,742.11	163.69	23,958.63	674,529.03
Equitable (South Carolina)	70,112.65	159,827.03	15,000.00	27,573.90	22,403.95	1,553.12	17,780.07	154,423.69
Fidelity-Phenix	3,916,574.61	*59,022.14	500,000.00	2,079,633.27	774,163.10	180,716.25	3,304,624.89	10,915,539.15
First Reinsurance	872,729.24			369,907.41	29,847.43	956.91	37,383.37	1,369,846.50
Fire Association of Philadelphia	2,853,662.68	12,447.10	300,000.00	1,237,410.19	553,841.00	128,886.14	478,023.49	5,564,270.60
Firemen's Fund	2,436,310.68	3,881,009.20	390,000.00	2,562,445.18	763,256.31	213,908.61	637,861.42	10,884,791.40
Firemen's (Newark)	1,833,081.82	6.93	300,000.00	809,793.38	251,790.38	84,864.16	591,364.84	3,870,901.51
Franklin	257,326.83	103,245.33	50,000.00	282,084.22	28,220.80	374.32	81,859.46	803,110.96
Georgia Home	124,149.87			51,451.38	31,314.91	7,643.53	229,657.45	444,217.14
Germania	1,842,974.41	336,310.92	235,000.00	936,750.06	326,771.48	91,578.35	1,488,208.31	5,257,593.53
Girard Fire and Marine	337,847.79		60,000.00	253,424.54	93,362.44	16,468.45	108,888.59	869,991.81
Glens Falls	1,373,623.02	450,433.82	185,000.00	778,098.54	289,626.40	61,166.79	351,800.90	3,489,749.47
Globe and Rutgers	3,502,205.40	4,037,979.35	251,992.00	2,667,232.53	300,543.67	88,173.35	389,390.06	11,237,516.36
Granite State	414,935.77		20,000.00	187,634.60	51,220.78	16,036.45	67,073.90	756,901.50
Great American	5,556,172.64	205,059.30	620,000.00	2,580,058.99	1,079,037.69	202,389.43	997,080.35	11,239,798.40
Hanover	1,361,328.76	261,796.48	100,000.00	873,807.62	235,644.85	62,326.38	359,775.70	3,254,679.79
Hartford	10,632,229.18	826,634.28	800,000.00	4,945,722.70	1,847,120.54	440,389.44	2,039,019.52	21,531,115.66
Home of New York	10,252,601.37	736,070.40	1,560,000.00	5,318,345.38	1,364,861.58	571,079.07	2,555,155.64	22,358,113.44
Home of Utah	48,763.53		57,000.00	37,773.32	8,349.25	5,441.84	61,787.85	219,115.79
Imperial	219,316.32		20,000.00	112,921.91	31,990.43	16,057.89	64,188.62	464,475.17
Insurance Company of North America	3,908,587.95	5,385,375.23	690,000.00	3,488,888.15	858,063.31	293,403.84	1,446,849.73	16,071,168.21
International	2,457,743.75			1,379,534.63	17,808.78	7,138.07	66,851.39	3,929,076.62
Inter-State	194,008.76		10,000.00	111,835.06	30,267.65	2,388.32	19,497.35	367,997.14
Massachusetts Fire and Marine	312,635.07	327,880.18	30,000.00	389,118.15	55,398.54	17,698.97	67,093.76	1,199,824.67
Marquette National	63,610.79			81,749.88	34,911.89	5,986.50	122,039.71	308,298.77
Mechanics	271,444.55		25,000.00	135,017.19	53,726.20	10,494.16	77,622.00	573,304.10
Mechanics and Traders	364,621.47			130,023.21	89,834.84	17,480.24	129,060.76	731,020.52

*Life and Miscellaneous.

TABLE No. II—DISBURSEMENTS.

SHOWING THE DISBURSEMENTS OF FIRE, MARINE AND INLAND COMPANIES (LICENSED TO DO BUSINESS IN THIS STATE) FOR YEAR ENDING DE EMBER 31, 1917.

COMPANIES OF OTHER STATES (STOCK)—CONTINUED.

Name of Company	Fire Losses	Marine and Inland Losses	Interest or Dividends	Commissions or Brokerage	Salaries of Officers and Other Employees	Insurance Department Fees and Taxes	All Other Disbursements	Total Disbursements
Mercantile Insurance Company of America	$ 544,197.17	$ 217,256.90	$ 100,000.00	$ 367,580.90	$ 128,356.26	$ 24,396.96	$ 82,495.68	$1,464,283.87
Milwaukee Mechanics	1,049,748.95	14,260.95	130,000.00	656,870.80	223,963.57	62,491.16	249,188.55	2,386,523.98
National	5,269,562.75	99,133.50	400,000.00	1,884,480.13	1,338,597.61	227,508.21	950,924.94	10,170,207.14
National Union	1,583,773.33	14,623.98	100,000.00	648,475.83	286,315.44	91,398.70	261,854.09	2,986,441.37
Newark	639,936.95	140,934.32	24,973.30	340,970.94	121,622.26	33,718.20	132,364.43	1,434,520.40
New Hampshire	1,612,203.40	6,499.82	202,485.00	798,535.58	251,860.90	71,912.53	272,713.22	3,216,210.45
Niagara	1,962,845.66	255,644.33	250,000.00	1,084,046.90	446,545.84	105,054.92	380,087.83	4,484,225.48
North River	1,300,678.60	67,145.15	59,977.50	724,999.01	275,214.64	53,476.95	227,020.29	2,708,512.14
Northwestern National	1,529,211.69	133,805.85	215,000.00	867,543.35	431,643.42	88,845.76	234,252.52	3,500,302.59
Northwestern Fire and Marine	62,160.72		40,000.00	372,004.37	75,165.02	29,460.23	89,032.45	667,822.79
Old Colony	330,256.99	288,974.64	28,000.00	288,118.26	26,022.80	17,299.66	162,671.45	1,141,343.80
Orient	781,321.26	160,183.29	100,000.00	390,354.99	179,257.04	50,204.75	224,754.73	1,886,076.06
Palmetto	28,433.47		4,000.00	46,192.19	11,961.46	450.48	7,595.89	162,678.21
Pennsylvania	2,335,719.11	64,042.72	525,000.00	903,264.27	400,408.38	98,671.69	331,247.42	4,594,310.87
Petersburg Savings	54,064.26		60,000.00	29,244.90	14,731.48	3,404.59	134,348.55	295,793.78
Phoenix of Hartford	2,736,441.09	444,955.64	711,559.00	1,443,975.47	698,350.58	143,694.28	714,338.90	6,893,315.00
Providence-Washington	1,598,611.20	1,357,971.38	120,000.00	1,082,877.27	360,654.19	122,099.08	339,879.24	4,982,092.36
Queen of America	2,384,057.97	784,743.60	1,425,000.00	1,288,161.78	631,954.62	126,051.98	520,388.28	7,160,358.23
Rhode Island	531,859.36		40,000.00	375,315.11	29,027.79	49,125.35		1,025,327.61
St. Paul Fire and Mar.	3,410,756.00	2,436,247.61	200,000.00	2,216,847.94	442,442.37	245,154.21	421,327.26	9,372,775.39
Security	1,412,522.81		80,000.00	619,144.33	246,522.25	56,285.99	373,449.53	2,787,924.91
Springfield Fire and Marine	3,431,340.55	14,501.50	250,000.00	1,409,294.70	779,313.18	176,797.19	535,979.38	6,687,226.50
Standard	372,925.47		30,000.00	147,269.58	80,567.71	22,115.78	94,475.13	747,353.67
Sterling	258,731.04	4,298.39		202,024.92	10,656.98	19.00	28,371.00	504,101.33
United States	1,900,264.75	322,101.07	140,000.00	1,616,742.66	53,742.28	87,285.62	415,213.73	4,535,350.11
Virginia Fire and Marine	438,535.20		30,000.00	229,881.05	54,004.19	22,253.90	62,388.39	837,062.73
Wn.	2,552,883.19	260,607.09	200,000.00	1,269,884.86	485,114.63	116,986.48	396,757.97	5,282,234.22
Totals	118,890,773.87	31,266,563.12	16,786,693.32	67,761,722.86	21,806,074.86	5,778,135.99	35,764,611.19	298,054,575.21

COMPANIES OF OTHER STATES (MUTUAL).

Arkwright Mutual	287,394.46	1,618,902.95			67,393.61	9,684.49	68,897.55	2,052,273.06
Baltimore Mutual	4,912.13		60,188.65		6,974.00	838.74	34,501.60	107,415.12
Blackstone Mutual	230,679.89		825,790.13		32,631.68	7,887.36	52,134.27	1,149,123.33
Consolidated Underwriters	824,272.44			123,614.52	312,348.02	3,689.75	152,233.03	1,416,157.76
Cotton and Woolen Manufacturers	28,799.03		450,036.57		15,245.14	1,604.85	1,309,984.78	1,805,670.37
Druggists Indemnity Exchange	44,144.26		49,514.43		38,487.57	1,836.72	4,281.44	138,284.42
Firemen's Mutual	276,354.32		1,214,512.50		44,537.65	11,165.44	69,950.41	1,616,520.32
Fitchburg Mutual	102,510.97		51,516.98		16,062.70	4,320.06	46,373.07	220,783.78
Hope Mutual	83,175.97		431,137.78		15,153.28	5,190.63	74,291.90	608,949.56
Indiana Lumbermen's Mutual	179,130.74		204,390.19		38,774.53	8,811.12	43,240.18	474,346.76
Individual Underwriters	144,585.24		268,368.22		42,527.04	2,367.12	17,770.81	475,618.43
Industrial Mutual	18,303.58		286,594.57		9,956.19	1,145.84	11,551.95	327,552.14
Keystone Mutual	61,789.67		310,396.76		18,948.60	1,294.19	12,286.61	404,715.83
Lumber Underwriters	102,540.22				21,092.57	422.91	9,204.64	133,260.34
Lumber Manufacturers Interinsurance	307,340.80				64,183.86	3,424.46	14,209.83	389,158.95
Lumber Mutual	179,078.06		262,638.76	37,091.21	49,313.78	7,531.42	31,022.22	566,675.45
Lumbermen's Mutual	372,141.33		212,617.88	112,286.04	51,426.81	10,760.71	65,052.17	824,284.94
Lumbermen's Underwriters Alliance	478,669.49		142,183.45		193,661.92		13,519.77	828,034.63
Manton Mutual	21,361.84		315,690.32		18,361.93	1,207.28	11,448.76	368,070.13
Manufacturing Lumbermen's Underwriters	527,350.27		192,847.02		198,301.66	691.06	21,611.82	940,801.83
Manufacturing Woodworkers Underwriters	137,192.50		8,865.40		54,211.36	350.84	10,829.83	211,449.93
Merchants Mutual	148,061.05		432,680.93		18,150.52	4,399.19	26,867.56	630,159.25
Mercantile Mutual	19,029.84		228,477.83		13,435.40	3,236.54	16,601.83	280,781.44
Middlesex Mutual	68,916.56		86,393.96		15,141.76	4,964.97	48,962.78	224,380.03
Michigan Millers Mutual	636,647.90		134,631.85		96,720.54	9,809.01	291,907.87	1,169,717.17
Millers Mutual	104,164.14		54,662.12		20,843.79	631.60	7,535.24	187,836.89
Millers Indemnity Underwriters	48,612.73		8,663.94		58,899.47	681.96	28,099.64	144,977.74
Narragansett Mutual	8,334.62		85,861.91		8,487.80	1,439.19	9,539.97	113,663.58
National Mutual	7,047.73		108,754.49		7,758.66	578.77	4,360.53	128,500.18
National Lumber Manufacturers	1,761.37		2,095.89		19,177.91	903.01	141,310.41	165,248.59
Penn Lumbermen's Mutual	175,453.58		218,826.87		41,500.00	7,793.40	134,913.71	578,497.56
Philadelphia Manufacturers Mutual	90,656.85		422,911.80		33,406.09	2,089.48	25,506.95	574,571.17
Reciprocal Exchange	386,204.25		153,306.38		150,067.32	4,274.61	25,007.41	718,949.97
Rubber Manufacturers Mutual	27,075.98		431,326.03		14,541.22	1,544.09	17,113.05	491,600.37
Southern Lumber Underwriters	58,160.73				22,407.95	181.02	847.54	81,597.24
Utilities Indemnity Exchange	86,528.62		30,874.61		56,079.55	1,858.86	40,656.30	215,997.94
Western Reciprocal Underwriters	28,217.66				65,420.59	1,551.48	121,891.72	217,081.45
What Cheer Mutual	93,146.19		444,515.03		15,153.28	5,329.21	68,048.20	626,191.91
Warners Interinsurers (Grocers' Department)	7,618.29		15,657.29		25,405.54	1,596.70	41,175.12	91,452.94
Totals	6,407,455.30	1,618,902.95	9,765,583.49	272,991.77	1,992,191.38	137,088.08	3,124,742.48	21,700,332.50

TABLE No. II—DISBURSEMENTS.

SHOWING THE DISBURSEMENTS OF FIRE, MARINE AND INLAND LINES (COMPANIES LICENSED TO DO BUSINESS IN THIS STATE) FOR YEAR ENDING DECEMBER 31, 1917.

COMPANIES OF FOREIGN COUNTRIES.

Name of Company	Fire Losses	Marine and Inland Losses	*Interest or Dividends	Commissions or Brokerage	Salaries of Officers and Other Employees	Insurance Department Fees and Taxes	All Other Disbursements	Total Disbursements
Atlas	$ 156,578.79	$ -------	$ 29,374.37	$ 89,299.21	$ 99.68	$ 6,252.77	$ 9,605.13	$ 291,209.95
Balkan National	1,170,042.43	16,838.05	94,883.72	427,215.37	247,721.99	35,715.21	229,322.29	2,221,739.06
British	1,554,258.59	-------	3,466.51	465,312.76	64,479.03	4,000.99	32,356.26	2,123,874.14
Caledonian	597,758.07	30,960.50	98,500.00	335,796.97	110,600.00	25,987.50	80,583.96	1,280,187.00
	796,398.23	8,388.27	238.21	363,811.66	138,929.09	32,055.97	174,860.25	1,514,681.68
Century	126,582.51	4,110.63	29,252.50	104,428.58	12,014.04	3,415.31	13,038.24	292,841.81
...al Union Assurance	3,633,358.23	699,059.70	948,072.29	1,723,768.72	513,004.70	174,557.53	610,063.01	8,301,884.18
Fire Reassurance	1,204,388.80	-------	15,013.86	669,071.94	11,358.63	2,434.82	40,499.93	1,942,767.98
First Russian	978,574.51	-------	-------	580,973.38	500.00	26,321.67	16,462.85	1,602,832.41
Hamburg-Bremen	624,902.95	-------	123.65	151,382.42	139,157.28	35,519.31	110,632.22	1,061,717.83
Jakor	2,461,855.08	-------	-------	1,359,568.33	53,450.55	7,035.81	54,505.01	3,936,414.78
Liverpool and London and Globe	4,845,757.58	559,627.37	6,098.24	1,856,319.34	770,546.30	144,392.39	2,129,486.80	10,212,228.02
London Assurance	1,055,448.07	943,703.50	323,515.41	894,959.16	275,621.55	92,108.16	291,962.88	3,877,618.73
London and Lancashire	1,091,828.18	232,698.45	276,841.81	473,477.12	349,974.19	78,513.50	417,038.50	2,920,371.75
...ow	1,409,164.58	-------	630.00	829,397.94	500.00	40,782.87	22,723.11	2,303,198.50
National (Denmark)	42,925.25	3,753.27	52,238.65	196,403.10	1,559.89	1,580.68	4,114.01	302,574.85
Nationale (Paris)	234,868.22	-------	288.08	133,948.85	149.51	9,378.90	14,339.98	392,973.54
Netherlands Fire and Life	238,454.09	-------	3,115.31	115,482.12	46,808.20	15,337.17	89,877.68	509,074.57
Nord-Deutsche	386,796.09	-------	57,203.95	576,793.99	92,003.36	69,983.16	91,393.34	2,454,427.53
...ke Lloyd	739,064.76	1,180,253.64	17,925.78	577,309.68	75,044.02	4,187.04	5,116.98	1,418,648.26
North British and	2,848,369.47	295,676.47	350,051.94	1,258,799.59	501,715.69	113,758.87	401,301.19	5,769,673.22
Northern Assurance	2,007,479.02	18,452.66	712,938.06	811,130.53	356,464.70	66,392.13	308,854.53	4,281,711.63
...an (Moscow)	454,297.14	-------	-------	471,061.01	500.00	5,350.44	36,886.45	968,075.04
Norwegian Assurance	87,764.34	-------	-------	117,117.91	9,160.06	2,535.24	232.43	216,809.98
Norwich Union	1,100,845.36	135,970.59	157,971.54	488,299.27	260,362.13	65,481.40	211,457.58	2,420,387.87
Paternelle	517,356.01	-------	447.71	395,578.39	2,140.90	1,964.90	14,582.00	932,069.91
Phenix Fire	234,868.23	-------	337.55	133,943.85	149.51	9,378.90	24,004.61	402,687.65
Palatine (London)	1,124,909.30	-------	1,886.61	501,236.68	157,814.00	48,555.93	163,711.15	1,998,113.67
Phenix (London)	1,275,129.41	126,064.65	307,580.35	582,606.56	371,049.79	84,466.30	420,918.06	3,167,815.12
Rossia	4,054,027.46	2,648,877.72	240,592.62	3,201,850.90	85,161.43	6,640.01	186,041.47	10,423,191.61
Royal	4,043,785.35	1,156,835.90	1,205,336.79	1,854,530.43	983,273.68	231,857.21	1,215,648.25	10,691,267.51

*Credited to Home Office.

(xii)

RECAPITULATION.

North Carolina companies	460,476.44		124,873.00	147,712.09	111,859.32	10,846.40	305,729.40	1,161,496.65
Companies of other States (stock)	118,890,773.87	31,266,563.12	16,786,693.32	67,761,722.86	21,806,074.86	5,778,135.99	35,764,611.19	298,054,575.21
Companies of other States (Mutual)	6,407,455.30		9,765,853.49	272,991.77	1,992,191.38	137,088.08	3,124,752.48	21,700,332.50
Companies of foreign	56,119,132.94	9,729,759.16	5,889,397.28	30,614,009.88	6,785,277.55	1,853,007.42	8,766,241.27	119,756,825.50
Totals	181,877,838.55	40,996,322.28	32,566,817.09	98,796,436.60	30,695,403.11	7,779,077.89	47,961,334.34	440,673,229.86

TABLE No. III—ASSETS.

SHOWING ASSETS OF FIRE, MARINE AND INLAND INSURANCE COMPANIES (LICENSED TO DO BUSINESS IN THIS STATE) FOR YEAR ENDING DECEMBER 31, 1917.

NORTH CAROLINA COMPANIES.

Name of Company	Value of Real Estate	Mortgage Loans on Real Estate	Loans on Collaterals	Bonds and Stocks	Cash in Office and Banks	Agents' Balances and Unpaid Premiums	Miscellaneous	Total Admitted Assets
Atlantic	$	$ 110,550.00	$ 7,000.00	$ 89,450.00	$ 71,740.75	$ 38,913.79	$ 671.67	$ 318,326.21
___ Mal					3,450.87			3,450.87
___	5,000.00	86,300.00		36,500.00	4,848.60	9,938.31	294.57	142,881.48
Dixie ___ Mut	195,039.98	253,171.30	1,432.80	388,950.00	42,755.47	107,492.56	11,786.72	1,000,628.83
___ Mat					42,700.25			42,700.25
___ Mal (Edgecombe Co.)					467.80			467.80
County ___ Mutual				15,160.00	2,736.36	1,859.95	177.50	19,933.81
___					4,494.24			4,494.24
Hardware ___ Mfg ___ M					2,177.27			2,177.27
Nh ___ fire		214,013.83		442,220.00	36,587.96	48,483.21	9,828.81	537,119.98
___ Bint ___	75,000.00	214,013.83	158,785.00	30,000.00	25,667.66	33,469.48	205.36	537,141.33
an ___ Mal					320.66			320.66
Southern ___ fire					3,967.90		581.10	4,548.00
Southern Stock		105,733.47	48,710.00	215,385.00	71,854.22	29,861.54	2,682.43	474,226.66
Southern ___		152,900.64	24,444.97	140,145.50	60,124.37	36,218.00	3,627.82	417,461.30
State Mal					1,762.84			1,762.84
___ (City Mut)		102,753.50		19,000.00	6,252.72	8,566.68	3,427.10	140,000.00
___ of ___ Mal		79,515.50	12,939.69	97,710.00	52,849.16	16,410.82	1,784.48	261,209.65
Min County ___ Mal					142.47			142.47
	275,039.98	1,104,938.24	253,312.46	1,474,520.50	434,901.57	331,214.34	35,066.56	3,908,993.65

COMPANIES OF OTHER STATES (STOCK).

Name of Company	Value of Real Estate	Mortgage Loans on Real Estate	Loans on Collaterals	Bonds and Stocks	Cash in Office and Banks	Agents' Balances and Unpaid Premiums	Miscellaneous	Total Admitted Assets
Ætna	410,000.00		20,615.00	22,170,140.58	3,221,766.39	3,771,106.34	258,557.51	29,852,185.82
___	30,174.00	518,152.00	124,973.85	4,046,707.00	388,539.74	403,036.41	62,425.60	5,574,008.60
___				2,816,908.70	244,115.25	261,626.62	42,374.06	3,365,024.63
American Alliance				2,472,042.00	100,413.66	121,012.23	22,677.00	2,716,144.89
American ___ (Newark)	497,900.00	1,825,731.00		7,382,452.81	941,761.75	982,906.60	471,586.51	12,102,338.67

Company							
American Central (St. Louis)		25,000.00	79,500.00	2,972,368.60	504,111.53	576,471.54	107,347.44	4,264,809.11
ᴀn. ᴹe.				2,155,299.00	156,274.10	387,293.26	23,300.38	2,722,166.74
Automobile		426,100.00	683,175.00	3,258,636.21	1,636,318.07	1,101,960.01	160,349.52	7,266,538.81
Boston	492,300.00	353,625.00	12,744.73	6,611,945.66	580,186.80	1,325,988.01	224,250.93	9,601,041.13
ᴵ Gin	105,554.50	679,148.00	16,400.00	2,807,581.00	243,043.39	523,721.90	45,900.03	4,481,348.82
Citizens of ᴹri		61,100.00		405,035.00	385,110.89	238,428.83	7,149.31	1,096,824.03
ᴳ ᴹ				1,089,524.24	30,255.85	123,182.88	32,976.11	1,275,939.08
ᴵ ...al in New ᴹ	60,678.60	259,215.10		87,623.33	49,673.53	65,456.87	6,357.67	529,005.10
Commonwealth				1,001,195.25	206,148.02	190,282.46	41,246.85	1,438,872.58
...	68,242.02	212,750.00		2,267,733.90	164,288.65	286,914.34	32,492.19	3,032,421.10
ᴳt.	1,000,000.00	1,033,300.00		1,456,582.99	237,881.89	348,962.08	38,777.68	3,115,504.64
ᴳt.		509,600.00	20,000.00	5,637,788.23	1,390,291.97	688,887.31	168,306.52	8,414,874.03
Gty.		2,700.00	200,000.00	24,873,109.07	4,089,083.25	1,970,818.68	454,943.08	32,590,654.08
ᴹe.	53,724.31	37,900.00		666,463.93	75,263.22	66,888.83	132,013.38	1,032,253.67
...e Fire ᴺd Marine		142,650.00		459,056.00	35,047.37	57,531.79	38,357.58	732,642.74
...e Fire ᴺd Marine	81,680.00	100,450.00	48,175.00	1,084,919.94	159,495.04	58,439.06	63,061.56	1,548,045.60
Equitable (ᴺh Carolina)	15,582.95	70,465.00		285,730.00	70,882.15	36,602.29	9,435.73	536,873.12
Fidelity-Phenix	535,000.00	15,500.00		13,865,599.27	2,404,538.52	1,446,596.77	713,080.74	18,980,315.30
First			54,300.00	1,430,730.00	270,500.31	130,612.29	305,060.15	2,136,902.75
Fire Association of Philadelphia	675,000.00	2,854,048.66		6,678,897.47	677,033.41	1,099,585.53	177,766.52	12,216,631.59
Firemen's ᴴ	404,000.00	1,905,585.76	180,125.00	7,754,705.50	3,646,267.98	2,548,977.93	280,180.45	16,719,842.62
Firemen's (ᴺ...k)	1,074,129.63	2,301,450.00		1,642,197.09	227,728.55	585,998.54	1,970,713.23	7,802,217.04
Franklin	142,476.05	22,400.00		2,165,338.60	211,183.80	407,836.93	26,275.88	2,953,110.66
...ia Home	60,000.00		10,616.15	410,245.50	21,057.45	91,752.77	4,927.74	620,999.61
Germania	688,500.00	768,600.00		5,159,019.93	478,692.97	995,951.45	72,817.47	8,163,581.82
Girard Fire and ᴹe	227,356.55	98,500.00	17,000.00	2,083,666.62	176,930.80	155,660.44	24,587.57	2,556,345.43
ᴳ...ns Falls	78,975.00	1,644,686.23	222,241.00	3,192,385.00	1,102,287.52	713,521.64	47,744.47	7,150,222.41
ᴳ...be and ...	18,200.00	280,900.00		17,036,342.60	1,075,492.40	3,343,326.07	207,191.12	22,022,227.19
...ᴹe Site		35,600.00		1,108,933.17	104,176.08	166,839.71	21,158.20	1,454,907.16
Great	1,750,000.00	26,150.00	9,510.00	17,440,935.00	1,930,580.59	2,098,281.23	199,532.40	23,454,989.22
...ᴴ	907,956.06	418,500.00	2,352.00	3,308,757.54	687,390.57	613,505.57	123,614.00	5,643,575.74
Hartford	721,000.00	5,500.00	7,500.00	23,962,062.18	3,554,518.62	5,311,352.15	679,168.42	34,654,101.37
Home of New York	109,000.00	304,971.75		35,569,125.51	3,639,056.92	4,124,508.15	710,461.00	44,048,651.58
ᴹe of Utah				671,906.60	28,157.37	9,327.41	171,509.40	1,294,872.53
ᴵ ᴹ				878,789.00	57,876.68	122,727.56	12,264.10	1,071,657.34
ᴵ...ᴺy of N ᴼth America	281,077.20	150,855.00		21,436,651.84	2,816,085.66	3,461,587.71	376,768.48	28,523,025.89
...ᴵ...al	502,646.39			4,085,300.00	531,869.77	86,788.28	69,531.04	4,773,489.09
Inter-State			9,000.00	12,128.00	23,513.90	25,479.83	10,731.30	583,499.42
...ts Fire and ᴹe	335,322.83			1,373,662.00	203,142.31	244,050.78	12,374.13	1,833,229.22
ᴹe N ...ᴺal	99,750.00		5,000.00	308,119.57	137,893.92	63,289.12	7,493.25	857,118.69
Mechanics	83,193.77			1,214,258.50	57,534.04	103,305.21	45,729.31	1,603,770.83
...ᴹcs ᴺd Traders	22,000.00			1,316,170.04	183,465.74	207,486.81	25,495.11	1,754,617.70

TABLE No. III—ASSETS.

SHOWING ASSETS OF FIRE, MARINE AND INLAND INSURANCE COMPANIES (LICENSED TO DO BUSINESS IN THIS STATE) FOR YEAR ENDING D☐☐BER 31, 1917.

COMPANIES OF OTHER STATES (STOCK)—Continued.

Name of Company	Value of Real Estate	Mortgage Loans on Real Estate	Loans on Collaterals	Bonds and Stocks	Cash in Office and Banks	Agents' Balances and Unpaid Premiums	Miscellaneous	Total Admitted Assets
☐le Insurance Company of America	$ ——	$ ——	$ ——	$ 2,478,615.00	$ 229,297.22	$ 217,571.59	$ 35,071.20	$2,960,555.01
Milwaukee ☐ ☐rs.	15,300.00	1,550,717.00	——	3,206,424.91	342,556.75	404,474.43	52,868.93	5,572,342.02
☐	577,296.23	1,381,125.00	——	12,453,151.46	2,347,596.19	2,072,029.20	398,335.43	19,229,533.51
National Union	2,172.14	348,800.00	——	3,184,476.33	800,805.49	719,511.75	186,825.50	5,332,591.21
Newark	188,469.96	415,534.35	——	1,258,685.00	196,314.40	288,212.96	23,108.03	2,370,324.70
N☐ ☐re	300,000.00	6,307.50	——	6,021,477.00	411,123.28	574,040.74	70,945.16	7,383,893.68
Niagara	——	233,000.00	——	7,190,184.61	826,161.51	1,005,432.91	20,298.72	9,275,077.75
☐rth River	8,871.18	205,400.00	——	3,051,360.00	422,068.50	545,911.52	31,028.23	4,264,639.43
N☐☐n National	218,000.00	1,704,212.10	——	4,801,441.84	479,673.67	383,679.21	74,252.20	7,661,259.02
N☐☐n Fire and ☐re	——	637,200.00	——	92,647.20	437,772.51	88,037.31	84,279.99	1,339,937.01
Old Colony	178,307.88	16,000.00	——	1,856,982.54	229,159.54	183,523.06	23,885.14	2,309,550.28
Orient	——	——	——	2,877,147.88	643,459.07	483,919.86	76,160.48	4,258,995.17
☐nto	——	——	——	17,141.00	27,303.18	36,408.75	4,597.22	223,215.15
Pennsylvania	125,000.00	137,765.00	——	6,317,315.00	644,853.12	740,330.01	128,022.42	8,084,933.64
Petersburg Savings	60,992.05	126,500.00	2,913.09	491,638.65	699,926.01	20,060.67	4,288,498.98	5,561,116.36
Phœnix (Hartford)	615,166.38	111,000.00	200,000.00	11,939,933.45	1,548,836.49	1,693,184.88	1,932,728.89	18,010,850.09
Providence-Washington	100,000.00	65,000.00	——	3,645,640.83	998,239.21	1,099,026.06	903,984.40	6,811,890.50
☐n of America	——	62,000.00	——	10,999,112.26	1,001,475.72	1,144,907.48	215,367.05	13,422,863.51
Rhode ☐	227,730.46	——	——	1,603,079.00	112,917.82	349,026.70	41,726.70	2,106,750.22
St. Paul Fire ☐re	265,000.00	1,469,978.34	102,970.00	8,834,406.53	964,018.42	1,718,565.67	259,951.38	13,577,620.80
Security	——	459,390.00	——	3,429,882.76	172,949.29	460,114.25	119,692.17	4,906,928.47
Springfield Fire and ☐	300,000.00	2,455,373.88	——	7,673,993.52	1,060,104.41	1,511,738.66	222,822.87	13,224,033.34
Standard	——	——	——	1,258,306.99	77,033.75	121,695.84	17,236.93	1,474,273.51
☐	3,519.47	1,556,349.57	——	131,025.93	63,960.55	21,982.20	33,509.79	1,810,347.51
Sterling ☐	71,375.00	639,900.00	3,000.00	5,230,432.82	726,235.22	695,934.51	158,631.21	7,525,508.76
☐ted ☐	115,000.00	105,996.67	——	1,626,679.00	94,252.68	192,297.67	25,998.82	2,160,194.84
Virginia Fire and Marine	7,252.00	105,010.00	——	6,030,872.17	1,123,427.94	682,062.84	29,747.74	7,978,373.69
☐ls	13,973,153.39	31,821,382.13	2,032,110.82	387,876,823.05	55,928,350.33	59,199,549.95	18,199,647.70	569,031,017.37

(xvi)

COMPANIES OF OTHER STATES (MUTUAL).

Company								
Baltimore	3,025,744.12	35,854.18	115,512.56	269,127.38	205,250.00			
Blackstone Mutual	117,628.49	1,498.85	6,056.66	10,892.98	51,180.00		8,000.00	
	1,746,383.15	7,785.61	83,139.87	226,015.67	1,429,442.00			
	1,204,838.42		273,381.44	2 56,98	9,000.00			
	792,61.37	9,420.79	48,841.19	79,269.39	655,370.00			
Firemen's Exchange	110,606.11	760.04	11,048.90	78,377.17	20,42 0 0		57,000.00	
	2,698,57.92	59,046.38	131,680.37	305,329.87	2,112,461.30			
Hope Mutual	227,832.05	1,622.65	30,731.69	18,158.64	120,39.07		355,350.00	
Indiana	859,539.12	15,899.93	53,909.05	243,096.99	546,633.15			36,500.00
	847,558.70	11,559.59	24,923.11	27,126.00	392,100.00			
	854,582.29	2,145.83	5,784.63	360,531.83	486,120.00			
	537,428.59	7,166.01	25,592.95	47,649.63	457,020.00			
	486,376.82	5,403.88	33,189.82	69,793.12	377,990.00			
Underwriters	99,647.45	25,207.80	14,725.45	50,244.20	9,470.00			
	292,60.54	86,321.24	4,814.28	59,875.02	141,950.00			
Underwriting Alliance	1,210,462.95	14,561.77	26,633.25	126,401.11	1,042,866.82		213,425.28	30,000.00
	1,091,860.06	13,796.95	101,029.08	139,551.25	594,057.50			
	1,200,269.91	2,652.91	114,761.14	704,407.8	378,8.68			
Manufacturing Woodworkers U	454,070.91	5,545.76	30,515.21	56,589.14	361,420.00			
	1,172,788.18	9,919.08	80,326.40	363,523.62	9,019.08			
	207,021.38	1,358.31	17,019.88	88,271.9	100,371.20			
Mutual	957,217.54	3,998.86	47,306.49	5,403.19	790,509.0	1,767.50		
	348,572.23	1,867.18	17,569.86	47,082.23	280,285.46	10,000.00		25,909.35
Millers	657,121.88	21,808.73	17,956.90	11,398.90	552,923.0	39,000.00	17,125.00	17,410.92
Millers Mutual	1,873,597.50	24,193.38	123,325.79	153,980.41	417,363.25		1,098,323.75	
Millers Underwriters	548,160.20		3,345.58	62,580.87	389,245.00		85,700.00	
	176,817.15	1,247.74	49,900.92	59,668.49	10,000.00		56,000.00	
Narragansett Mutual	138,828.26	3,190.82	8,251.37	7,290.02	120,096.05			
National Lumber Manufacturers	186,808.36	2,467.07	11,856.66	21,989.63	150,495.00			
	130,479.83	4,685.68	12,775.25	25,499.40	87,519.50		122,500.0	
	1,025,276.22	59,948.09	32,334.62	91,977.71	718,515.80			
Reciprocal	793,421.25	8,573.73	55,793.01	107,923.51	621,131.00		15,000.00	
	660,608.18	6,997.25	71,746.51	166,679.74	400,184.68			
	781,746.36	9,736.22	46,240.20	73,989.94	651,780.00			
Southern Lumber Underwriters	60,004.73	14,581.37	18,140.79	15,982.57	4,800.00		6,500.00	
Exchange	157,711.22	1,115.27	56,945.38	59,150.57	10,500.57		30,000.00	
Western Reciprocal Underwriters	108,801.99	3,830.22	18,479.21	55,246.16	29,896.40			
Warners	898,341.12	2,003.91	56,982.81	263,855.40	575,499.00		1,350.00	
Warners (Grocers' Dept.)	158,466.29	217.46	13,295.16	94,953.67	50,000.00			
Totals	28,900,998.84	495,279.29	1,895,863.44	5,771,342.37	18,511,651.94	50,767.50	2,009,274.03	166,820.27

TABLE No. III—ASSETS.

SHOWING ASSETS OF FIRE, MARINE AND INLAND INSURANCE COMPANIES (LICENSED TO DO BUSINESS IN THIS STATE) FOR YEAR ENDING DE EMBER 31, 1917.

COMPANIES OF   IN COUNTRIES.

Name of Co'y	Value of Real Estate	Mortgage Loans on Real Estate	Loans on Collaterals	Bonds and Stocks	Cash in Office and Banks	Agents' Balances and Unpaid Premiums	Miscellaneous	Total Admitted Assets
...ble	$ ---	$ ---	$ ---	$ 528,200.00	$ 91,152.35	$ 102,848.52	$ 6,414.15	$ 728,615.02
Atlas	35,000.00	---	---	2,579,399.81	277,216.83	495,862.20	46,360.46	3,433,839.30
Balkan National	---	---	---	1,905,989.33	189,311.76	95,653.43	19,587.16	2,210,541.68
3h America	---	---	---	1,578,770.39	308,468.01	279,638.17	25,296.57	2,192,173.14
Caledonian	410,000.00	---	---	1,579,643.81	197,814.77	355,549.51	22,778.29	2,565,786.38
Century ...	---	---	---	550,303.00	89,169.75	53,258.20	10,573.56	703,304.51
Fire ...	637,000.00	36,000.00	8,625.50	5,861,175.00	3,257,835.99	1,232,593.08	613,913.85	11,647,743.42
...	---	---	---	1,626,900.00	554,676.58	153,600.16	22,254.18	2,357,430.92
...	---	---	---	1,823,070.00	244,761.46	141,313.19	14,497.50	2,223,642.15
...en	---	---	---	1,342,185.00	70,992.99	84,258.65	19,273.82	1,516,710.46
Jakor ...	1,326,682.10	---	---	3,471,592.75	10,784.53	245,515.06	377,223.48	4,105,115.82
...nd ...n nd Globe	---	---	---	8,164,301.41	2,178,899.65	3,043,465.64	467,595.27	16,153,068.57
London Assurance	300,000.00	968,150.00	3,974.50	3,712,208.28	1,410,589.74	651,840.99	88,857.11	5,863,496.12
...n nd	---	---	---	3,153,223.94	1,008,870.58	814,707.17	565,672.12	5,842,473.81
M sow	---	---	---	2,394,635.00	299,762.08	178,623.50	20,166.64	2,893,187.22
...l (Denmark)	---	---	---	736,500.00	135,430.56	241,773.94	163,694.54	1,277,399.04
...e (ds)	---	---	---	741,393.06	83,897.18	154,272.63	22,487.28	1,002,150.15
Netherlands Fire nd Life	---	---	---	969,232.45	117,644.69	126,244.40	12,299.05	1,225,420.59
Nord-Deutsche	---	---	---	2,532,852.70	643,231.71	50,056.70	89,978.87	3,316,119.98
...e Hi	---	---	---	1,709,050.00	98,782.38	228,766.16	17,933.33	2,054,531.87
...n British nd Mercantile	---	---	---	7,075,830.50	694,843.11	1,365,839.68	105,232.94	9,241,746.23
...n Assurance	---	135,000.00	---	5,039,086.45	463,422.69	880,020.16	111,788.20	6,629,317.50
...n (Moscow)	---	---	---	1,064,270.00	357,945.28	207,980.52	19,929.69	1,650,125.49
N ...n ...e	---	---	---	622,150.87	52,103.46	10,543.75	12,592.83	697,390.91
...h ...n	---	---	---	2,759,404.80	522,714.97	504,623.96	39,475.84	3,826,219.57
Paternelle	---	---	---	1,097,403.02	269,400.77	54,019.50	12,620.42	1,433,443.71
...x ...e of	---	---	---	641,586.49	66,603.61	154,272.61	16,145.95	878,608.66
...ne ...	---	---	---	2,078,313.19	1,008,035.17	470,668.15	29,791.00	3,586,807.51
...ix (London)	---	---	---	3,545,476.00	423,015.41	879,824.30	84,820.76	4,933,136.47
...	285,000.00	---	---	5,480,520.00	3,215,020.09	592,965.78	82,007.40	9,656,113.27
...l	4,044,421.81	185,600.00	---	8,121,719.60	1,738,093.30	2,061,862.63	324,228.13	16,475,925.47

Royal Exchange Assurance	3,828,456.15	78,587.76	469,892.99	307,810.85	2,972,164.55	---	---	---
Russian Reinsurance	2,428,427.37	15,657.50	113,328.10	362,601.77	1,936,840.00	---	120,000.00	---
Salamandra	4,078,103.73	50,169.23	168,298.35	312,528.55	3,427,107.60	---	116,200.00	---
Scottish Union and National	7,536,675.65	93,122.48	830,569.25	524,220.56	5,757,535.00	---	---	215,028.36
Second Russian	1,656,183.74	15,873.56	45,220.16	183,810.02	1,411,280.00	---	- -	---
Skandia	1,864,518.12	15,215.30	93,693.60	305,092.22	1,450,517.00	---	---	---
Skandinavia	2,038,707.58	412,143.61	206,075.09	186,538.88	1,233,950.00	---	---	---
Sun Insurance	5,306,790.26	62,932.77	613,364.88	659,402.24	3,799,165.33	---	---	171,925.04
Svea Fire and Life	2,218,018.95	93,456.57	307,071.51	506,325.87	1,311,165.00	---	---	---
Swiss N	2,670,744.98	27,602.50	204,591.88	414,110.60	2,024,440.00	---	---	---
Swiss Reinsurance	1,745,006.02	25,675.84	32,744.03	67,866.15	1,618,720.00	---	---	---
Union	1,944,886.20	12,750.00	197,152.00	456,061.82	1,278,922.38	---	---	---
Union (Paris)	1,241,018.77	16,823.44	212,056.05	86,397.68	925,741.60	---	---	---
Union and Phenix Espagnol	2,064,625.00	20,537.45	117,040.72	511,116.83	1,415,930.00	---	---	---
Warsaw Fire	1,030,077.68	11,318.32	75,186.23	303,083.13	640,490.00	---	---	---
Western Assurance	4,194,579.34	33,336.65	810,718.56	1,065,287.13	2,285,237.00	---	---	---
Yorkshire	1,540,538.48	13,291.07	306,628.87	365,946.74	854,671.80	---	---	---
Totals	179,708,942.96	4,463,984.44	20,716,194.61	26,699,292.49	118,830,264.11	12,600.00	1,561,550.00	7,425,057.31

RECAPITULATION.

North Carolina Companies	3,908,993.65	35,066.56	331,214.34	434,901.57	1,474,520.50	253,312.46	1,104,938.24	275,039.98
Companies of other States (stock)	569,031,017.37	18,199,647.70	59,199,549.95	55,928,350.33	387,876,823.05	2,032,110.82	31,821,382.13	13,973,153.39
Companies of other States (mutual)	28,900,998.84	495,279.29	1,895,863.44	5,771,342.37	18,511,651.94	50,767.50	2,009,274.03	166,820.27
Companies of foreign countries	179,708,942.96	4,463,984.44	20,716,194.61	26,699,292.49	118,830,264.11	12,600.00	1,561,550.00	7,425,057.31
Totals	781,549,952.82	23,193,977.99	82,142,822.34	88,833,886.76	526,693,259.60	2,348,790.78	36,497,144.40	21,840,070.95

TABLE No. IV—LIABILITIES.

SHOWING LIABILITIES OF FIRE, MARINE AND INLAND COMPANIES (LICENSED TO DO BUSINESS IN THIS STATE) FOR YEAR ENDING DECEMBER 31, 1917.

NORTH CAROLINA COMPANIES.

Name of Company	Net Unpaid Losses and Claims	Unearned Premiums, Fire	Unearned Premiums, Marine and Inland	Due for Commissions, Brokerage, Return and Reinsurance Premiums	Other Liabilities	Total	Cash Capital	Net Surplus	Total Liabilities
....	$ 6,780.49	$ 91,053.15	$	$	$ 225.00	$ 98,058.64	$ 150,000.00	$ 70,267.57	$ 318,326.21
Cabarrus Mutual	270.00				270.00	270.00		3,180.87	3,450.87
Carolina	3,319.00	32,675.20			802.70	36,796.90	50,000.00	56,084.58	142,881.48
Dixie	33,734.48	242,777.94		20,126.14	7,867.00	304,505.56	500,000.00	196,123.27	1,000,628.83
Farmers Mutual (Raleigh)					42,700.25	42,700.25			42,700.25
Farmers Mutual (Edgecombe Co.)					467.80	467.80			467.80
Gaston County Farmers Mutual					4,494.24	4,494.24			4,494.24
Hardware Mutual	100.00	6,372.01			595.43	7,067.44		12,866.37	19,933.81
Mecklenburg Farmers Mutual					2,177.27	2,177.27			2,177.27
North Carolina Home	15,291.34	130,594.29			5,000.00	150,885.63	200,000.00	186,234.35	537,119.98
Piedmont	7,664.63	133,700.95				141,365.58	100,000.00	295,775.75	537,141.33
Rowan Mutual					320.66	320.66			320.66
Southern Furniture	214.14	2,423.01				2,637.15		1,910.85	4,548.00
Southern Stock	989.00	110,147.77			8,400.00	119,536.77	220,000.00	134,689.89	474,226.66
Southern Underwriters	1,453.00	131,326.54			12,000.00	144,779.54	200,000.00	72,681.76	417,461.30
State Mutual					1,762.84	1,762.84			1,762.84
Underwriters (Rocky Mount)	45.17	30,458.12			10,550.09	41,053.38	51,500.00	47,446.62	140,000.00
Underwriters of Greensboro	1,528.00	78,379.62			6,000.00	85,907.62	100,000.00	75,302.03	261,209.65
Union Farmers Mutual					142.47	142.47			142.47
Totals	71,389.25	989,908.60		20,126.14	103,507.75	1,184,929.74	1,571,500.00	1,152,563.91	3,908,993.65

COMPANIES OF OTHER STATES (STOCK).

Name of Company	Net Unpaid Losses and Claims	Unearned Premiums, Fire	Unearned Premiums, Marine and Inland	Due for Commissions, Brokerage, Return and Reinsurance Premiums	Other Liabilities	Total	Cash Capital	Net Surplus	Total Liabilities
Ætna	2,033,317.01	12,442,346.22	845,088.11	10,000.00	959,466.79	16,290,218.13	5,000,000.00	8,561,967.69	29,852,185.82
Agricultural	338,610.18	2,336,103.85	117,811.48	20,000.00	360,500.00	3,173,025.51	500,000.00	1,900,983.09	5,574,008.60
Alliance	447,785.00	853,533.46	178,246.25	10,000.00	375,459.92	1,865,024.63	750,000.00	700.0	3,365,024.63
American Alliance	108,816.00	627,318.30	2,698.43		35,000.00	773,832.73	1,000,000.00	942,312.16	2,716,144.89
American (Newark)	489,507.30	6,020,269.28	225,894.83	32,043.59	498,620.00	7,266,335.00	2,000,000.00	2,836,003.67	12,102,338.67

Company									
...al (St. Louis)	270,757.05	1,757,6973	84,554.25	4,020.75	54,802.85	2,167,8088	1,000,000.00	1,097,002.23	1,264,809.11
American Eagle	41,527.18	1,434,362.39	30,421.27	176,610.57	394,000.00	904,131.59	2,000,000.00	818,035.15	2,722,166.74
Automobile	777,672.73	1,142,381.43	772,276.09	58,000.00	217,4063	386,345.45	2,000,000.00	2,180,936	7,266,538.81
Boston	1,500,927.45	2,553,720.52	1,042,199.06	10,000.00	345,0000	5,499,847.03	800,000.00	3,101,194.10	9,601,041.13
Camden	400,577.00	2,076,867.15	91,934.10		61,769.55	2,641,147.71		1,040,201.11	4,481,348.82
...ins of ...iri	40,499.14	159,142.82	1,481.79	412,338.48	3,500.00	616,962.23	90,000.00	279,861.80	1,096,824.03
...ia	44,095.77		190,978.17	7,500.00	13,000.00	255,573.94	400,000.00	620,365.14	1,275,939.08
Columbian	21,570.61	154,378.43	4,9722		4,256.89	184,476.15	215,096.00	129,432.95	529,005.10
...on (New York)	81,606.00		767,233.17	4,500.00	31,235.00	884,574.17	200,000.00		1,438,872.58
Commonwealth	279,452.09	1,222,166.63	248,651.46	5,427.31	40,500.00	1,796,197.49	500,000.00	736,223.61	3,032,421.10
Concordia	176,462.48	1,401,142.53	1,664,365.49	9373	49,999.50	2,009,6330	750,000.00	356,374.34	3,115,504.64
Connecticut	537,439.55	11,124,765.81	233,590.42	12,475.00	257,525.09	5,442,172.50	1,000,000.00	1,972,701.53	8,414,874.03
...ial	964,706.97	203,513.47	503,198.76	107,789.70	1,115,472.32	13,815,933.56	10,000,000.00	8,774,720.52	32,590,654.08
...City	34,906.11	311,502.85		00500	178,3635	417,462.93	400,000.00	214,790.74	1,032,253.67
Eagle	46,666.22			1,000.00	1,500.00	360,669.07	250,000.00	121,973.67	732,642.74
Equitable Fire and Marine	107,820.79	361,368.11	71,591.25	6,121.80	26,373.70	567,153.85	500,000.00	480,891.75	1,548,045.60
...le (86th Carolina)	13,037.31	156,343.89		38,286.52	5,577.17	181,080.12	200,000.00	155,793.00	536,873.12
Fidelity-Phenix	814,509.48	9,465,992.46	395,408.95	144,568.27	583,600.00	11,297,797.41	2,500,000.00	5,182,517.89	18,980,315.30
First Reinsurance	184,750.00	355,364.02		12,730.35	646,441.91	1,331,124.20	500,000.00	305,778.55	2,136,902.75
Fire ...on of Philadelphia	755,173.42	5,449,496.15			1,541,6427	7,759,045.19	000,000.00	3,457,586.40	12,216,631.59
Firemen's Fund	2,727,125.97	5,501,492.51	2,163,799.40	200,000.00	795,500.00	1,387,917.88	1,500,000.00	3,831,924.74	16,719,842.62
...ns (Newark)	517,663.21	3,537,640.94	50,3665	7,500.00	54,076.04	4,67,245.84	1,250,000.00	2,384,971.20	7,802,217.04
Franklin	169,841.00	594,761.00	114,5200	484,141.52	577,6425	1,940,966.77	500,000.00	512,143.89	2,953,110.66
...ia Home	31,9433	186,330.09		28,881.59	84,130.63	330,991.64	200,000.00	00,007.97	620,999.61
Germania	627,3675	4,138,388.96	364,874.64	9,631.36	83,000.00	5,223,031.71	1,000,000.00	1,940,550.1	8,163,581.82
Girard Fire and ...ine	94,304.09	957,153.32	398,987.00	1,500.00	550,976.79	1,603,934.20	500,000.00	452,4.23	2,556,345.43
...ens Falls	631,9300	2,776,929.27	1,820,557.57	78,034.43	275,0000	4,160,884.70	500,000.00	2,489,337.71	7,150,222.41
Globe and Rutgers	2,852,721.27	6,809,668.38		178,609.99	2,565,000.00	13,896,112.93	700,000.00	7,426,4.26	22,022,227.19
Granite State	76,5620	10,885,840.43	198,467.83	50,000.00	32,631.75	921,865.33		1,454,697.16	1,454,997.16
Great American	1,361,81.00				431,840.65	12,927,269.91	2,000,000.00	8,527,719.31	23,454,989.22
Hanover	567,368.98	3,130,299.20	226,947.42	30,000.00	79,556.10	4,034,171.70	1,000,000.00	609,404.04	5,643,575.74
Hartford	2,905,726.28	19,245,916.50	569,9323	100,000.00	1,725,000.00	24,546,5701	2,000,000.00	8,101,526.36	34,654,101.37
Home of New York	2,692,504.50	19,350,525.00	939,826.00	864,545.50	1,200,000.00	25,047,401.00	6,000,000.00	13,001,250.58	4,048,651.58
Home of Utah	13,700.31	124,637.01		4,000.00	10,000.00	148,337.32	300,000.00	846,535.21	1,294,872.53
Imperial	47,562.00	462,368.70		150,000.00	18,500.00	532,430.70	200,000.00	339,226.64	1,071,657.34
Insurance ...pany of North America	4,419,000.00	8,421,674.44	1,485,854.06		5,046,497.39	19,523,025.89	4,000,000.00	5,000,000.00	28,523,025.89
International	835,589.97	3,273,715.86		7,500.00	52,500.00	4,169,3083	200,000.00	404,3.26	4,773,489.09
Inter-State	30,9425	248,713.00			1,386.23	281,045.48	259,150.00	43,303.94	583,499.42
Massachusetts Fire and Marine	295,9865	484,713.16	347,485.63		27,065.02	1,154,9846	500,000.00	178,243.76	1,833,229.22
Marquette ...ial	26,649.86	201,262.29			5,000.00	232,912.15	300,000.00	324,206.54	857,118.69
Mechanics ...nd Traders	69,482.45	596,937.40	1,322.00	1,322.00	327,328.67	995,070.52	250,000.00	358,700.31	1,603,770.83
	99,9387	661,642.40	3,000.00	3,000.00	29,000.00	793,577.27	300,000.00	661,040.43	1,754,617.70

TABLE No. IV—LIABILITIES.

SHOWING LIABILITIES OF FIRE, MARINE AND INLAND COMPANIES (LICENSED TO DO BUSINESS IN THIS STATE) FOR YEAR ENDING DECEMBER 31, 1917.

COMPANIES OF OTHER STATES (STOCK)—Continued.

Name of Company	Net Unpaid Losses and Claims	Unearned Premiums, Fire	Unearned Premiums, Marine and Inland	Due for Commissions, Brokerage, Return and Reinsurance Premiums	Other Liabilities	Total	Cash Capital	Net Surplus	Total Liabilities
Mercantile Insurance Co. of ...	$ 168,455.32	$ 946,567.34	$222,563.03	$ 4,545.02	$ 35,201.52	$1,377,332.23	$1,000,000.00	$ 583,222.78	$2,960,555.01
Milwaukee	290,858.54	2,792,737.08	29,391.77	34,075.11	117,500.00	3,264,562.50	1,250,000.00	1,057,779.52	5,572,342.02
National	1,380,909.72	10,856,965.81	122,617.80	115,594.11	634,002.81	13,110,090.25	2,000,000.00	4,119,443.26	19,229,533.51
National Union	683,155.19	2,703,760.75	97,467.71	20,000.00	155,000.00	3,659,383.65	1,000,000.00	673,207.56	5,332,591.21
———	194,181.95	1,168,566.35	81,101.24	1,000.00	28,089.80	1,472,939.34	500,000.00	397,385.36	2,370,324.70
New Hampshire	378,332.32	3,145,630.86	11,555.68	86,170.29	150,015.00	3,771,704.15	1,500,000.00	2,112,189.53	7,383,893.68
Niagara	681,836.43	4,184,181.23	296,143.29	10,000.00	179,244.00	5,351,404.95	1,000,000.00	2,923,672.80	9,275,077.75
North River	380,595.90	2,224,006.74	2,542.64		50,223.75	2,657,369.03	600,000.00	1,007,270.40	4,264,639.43
Northwestern N... and...	684,502.65	3,599,218.00	236,754.54	30,932.88	673,951.64	5,225,359.71	1,000,000.00	1,435,899.31	7,661,259.02
Northwestern Fire and Marine	60,466.13	251,990.46		412,928.47	31,622.65	757,007.71	400,000.00	182,929.30	1,339,937.01
Old ...	267,562.14	608,733.35	132,187.51	2,845.35	15,961.20	1,027,289.55	600,000.00	682,260.73	2,309,550.28
Orient	219,812.69	1,744,561.81	193,653.89	2,600.00	45,684.77	2,206,313.16	1,000,000.00	1,052,682.01	4,258,995.17
Palmetto	7,170.51	78,696.33	4,867.65		2,000.00	92,734.49	100,000.00	30,480.66	223,215.15
Pennsylvania	588,799.70	3,986,865.73		10,000.00	1,148,992.91	5,734,658.34	750,000.00	1,600,275.30	8,084,933.64
Petersburg Savings and In...	13,305.19	135,544.36			4,356,058.50	4,504,908.05	200,000.00	856,208.31	5,561,116.36
Phoenix (Hartford)	887,759.52	6,361,517.61	420,616.47	25,000.00	486,915.70	8,181,809.30	3,000,000.00	6,859,040.79	18,040,850.09
Providence-Washington	1,012,721.66	2,425,995.98	366,119.27	25,000.00	205,000.00	4,034,836.91	2,000,000.00	1,777,053.59	6,811,890.50
Queen of America	961,455.18	4,976,281.74	512,847.29	33,375.80	706,833.63	7,190,793.64	2,000,000.00	4,232,068.87	13,422,862.51
Rhode Island	111,944.36	954,521.07		115,178.81	22,500.00	1,204,144.24	500,000.00	402,605.98	2,106,750.22
St. Paul Fire and M...	1,509,984.68	5,703,379.89	923,810.48	30,768.22	412,542.04	8,580,485.31	1,000,000.00	3,997,135.49	13,577,620.80
Security	310,324.24	2,704,786.54		192.48	54,152.21	3,069,455.47	1,000,000.00	837,473.00	4,906,928.47
Springfield Fire and Marine	817,123.31	7,151,796.48	74,393.67	25,000.00	130,000.00	8,198,313.46	2,500,000.00	2,525,719.88	13,224,033.34
———	84,308.97	602,448.75			16,393.43	703,151.15	500,000.00	271,122.36	1,474,273.51
Sterling	101,994.97	395,425.39	8,926.00	600.00	24,400.00	531,346.36	850,000.00	429,001.15	1,810,347.51
United States	617,955.00	3,640,607.92	95,575.00		83,005.14	4,437,143.06	1,400,000.00	1,688,365.70	7,525,508.76
Virginia Fire and Marine	87,885.94	870,753.08		7,500.00	42,000.00	1,008,189.02	250,000.00	902,055.82	2,160,194.84
Westchester	708,356.62	4,400,371.59	170,431.78	15,000.00	145,000.00	5,439,159.99	1,000,000.00	1,539,213.70	7,978,373.69
Totals	44,817,969.51	234,295,750.70	20,157,132.60	4,402,188.00	31,724,921.22	335,397,962.03	85,224,246.00	148,408,809.34	569,031,017.37

Arkwright Mutual	66,399.31	1,552,887.46	---	---	17,726.03	1,637,012.80	---	1,388,731.32	3,025,744.12
Baltimore Ml	4,874.42	51,634.87	---	---	1,218.00	57,727.29	---	59,901.20	117,628.49
Blackstone Mal	73,688.81	1,004,603.22	---	---	20,016.92	1,098,308.95	---	648,074.20	1,746,383.15
Gi eld Underwriters Wn	401,125.40	211,283.71	---	---	49,366.94	751,776.05	---	453,062.37	1,204,838.42
en ad Wn	40,044.41	386, 9429	---	---	7,429.40	434,417.10	---	358,484.27	792,901.37
Druggists Indemnity Exchange	8,665.82	58,253.84	---	---	501.27	67,420.93	---	43,185.18	110,606.11
Firemen's Mutual	116,507.50	1,362,281.04	---	---	20,39.15	1,499,327.69	---	1,199,.0923	2,698,517.92
Fitchburg Mutual	22,481.34	149,731.55	---	---	6,399.99	178,612.88	---	49,219.17	227,832.05
Hope Mutual	41,52.60	488,909.48	---	---	9,078.43	539,540.51	---	319,998.61	859,539.12
Indiana Lumbermen's Mutual	20,574.00	282,960.06	---	---	17,845.37	321,379.43	---	526,179.27	847,558.70
Idl Underwriters	93.85	196,905.36	---	---	529,561.10	726,860.31	---	127,721.98	854,582.29
Industrial	26,400.56	234,361.44	---	---	4,841.06	265,603.06	---	271,825.53	537,428.59
Keystone Mal	25,356.78	257,849.32	---	---	2,516.91	285,723.01	---	200,653.81	486,376.82
Lumber U	18,255.30	43,332.02	---	---	500.00	62,087.32	---	37,560.13	99,647.45
Lumber ths Interinsurance	109,230.00	133,239.40	---	---	3,200.00	245,669.40	---	47,291.14	292,960.54
Lumber Mutual M	25,327.93	311,212.71	---	---	213,360.80	549,901.44	---	660,561.51	1,210,462.95
Lumbermen's r ths Alliance	97,965.00	464,136.23	---	---	35,008.14	597,109.37	---	494,.0569	1,091,860.06
Lumbermen's Mn Mal	56,452.44	384,505.71	---	---	26,483.41	467,441.56	---	755,836.41	1,223,277.97
Mn Mg Lumbermen's Unders	19,383.81	240,160.56	---	---	2,280.15	261,824.52	---	192,246.39	454,070.91
Mg ths Unders	23,200.00	389,058.92	---	---	18,671.72	430,930.64	---	741,857.54	1,172,788.18
	47,050.56	81,431.56	---	---	130.02	128,612.14	---	78,409.24	207,021.38
ths M	41,181.67	551,689.39	---	---	11,066.72	603,937.78	---	353,279.76	957,217.54
Me Mr Mutual	9,636.55	191,653.70	---	---	4,150.00	205,440.25	---	143,131.98	348,572.23
Mn Millers M	14,820.69	319,757.34	---	---	96,862.19	431,440.22	---	225,681.66	657,121.88
Millers M	137,943.09	653,865.81	---	---	544,645.40	1,336,454.30	---	537,143.20	1,873,597.50
Millers h My Underwriters	1,550.00	167,241.94	---	---	4,000.00	172,791.94	---	375,368.26	548,160.20
	56,124.99	22,793.15	---	---	6,335.78	85,253.92	---	91,563.23	176,817.15
tht Mutual	2,600.00	72,332.71	---	---	1,950.00	76,882.71	---	61,945.55	138,828.26
Mal Mal	6,569.87	82,700.36	---	---	887.78	90,158.01	---	96,650.35	186,808.36
Ml Lumber Manufacturers	12,500.00	55,319.81	---	---	55,000.00	122,819.81	---	7,660.02	130,479.83
Penn Lumbermen's M	22,122.34	295,364.60	---	---	10,343.79	327,830.73	---	697,45.49	1,025,276.22
Philadelphia ths Mutual	25,277.34	444,824.99	---	---	4,563.64	474,665.97	---	318,755.28	793,421.25
Reciprocal Exchange	16,513.56	206,238.80	---	---	33,654.33	256,406.69	---	404,201.49	660,608.18
Rubber ths M	38,632.52	366,146.52	---	---	7,221.57	412,000.61	---	369,45.75	781,746.36
Southern Lumber Underwriters	---	37,874.32	---	---	6,378.30	44,252.62	---	15,752.11	60,004.73
Ms My the	45,632.35	22,486.47	---	---	32,598.07	100,716.89	---	56,994.33	157,711.22
Western Reciprocal Underwriters	2,900.00	64,642.70	---	---	302.58	67,845.28	---	40,956.71	108,801.99
Mat Cheer M	41,842.40	504,200.10	---	---	9,346.68	555,389.18	---	342,91.94	898,341.12
Warners Interinsurers (Grocers' Dept.)	10,000.00	50,050.83	---	---	844.76	60,895.59	---	97,570.70	158,466.29
l	1,820,777.21	12,394,865.29			1,816,826.40	16,032,468.90		12,891,538.00	28,924,006.90

TABLE No. IV—LIABILITIES.

SHOWING LIABILITIES OF FIRE, MARINE AND INLAND COMPANIES (LICENSED TO DO BUSINESS IN THIS STATE) FOR YEAR ENDING DECEMBER 31, 1917.

COMPANIES OF IN US.

Name of	Net Unpaid Losses and Claims	Unearned Premiums, Fire	Unearned Premiums, Marine and Inland	Due for Commissions, Brokerage, Return and Reinsurance Premiums	Other Liabilities	Total	Cash Capital	Net Surplus	Total Liabilities
Abeille	$ 42,378.91	$ 243, 96.42	$ 24, 54.07	$ 30,854.53	$ 6,000.00	$ 322,731.86	$	$ 405,883.16	$ 728,615.02
Atlas	240,838.92	2,016, 30.15		17,309.98	62,468.22	2,361,411.34		1,072,427.96	3,433,839.30
Balkan	408,765.00	1, 35,342.94	19, 83.72	3,000.00	2,000.00	1,749,107.94	*200,000.00	261,433.74	2,210,541.68
Caledonian	227,114.68	1, 54, 94.59	52,061.64		25,442.53	1,419,245.79	*200,000.00	572,927.35	2,192,173.14
					37,000.00	1,870,370.91		695,415.47	2,565,786.38
Fire Assurance	62,914.04	216, 47.94	9, 78.88	14,000.00	303,110.86		200, 93.65	703,304.51
First Russian	1,454,432.47	6, 57,972.30	223, 64.01	24,110.00	446,163.87	8,705,842.65	*200,000.00	2, 91,900.77	11, 97,743.42
Hamburg-Bremen	308,206.00	1, 47,291.94			20,250.00	1,775,747.94	*200,000.00	81,682.98	2, 37,430.92
	300,904.00	1, 43,297.17		4,258.42	37,402.58	1,690,862.17	*200,000.00	332, 79.98	2,223,642.15
	123,994.00	844,269.82			37,500.00	1,005,763.82	*200,000.00	310, 96.64	1, 56,710.46
Jakor	715,914.23	2, 86,281.11	47, 30.58	5,000.00	10,000.00	3,567,195.34	*200,000.00	37,920.48	4,105,115.82
London Assurance	1,530,763.47	8,640, 64.02	27, 07.04	96,288.27	633,953.68	11,359,090.02		4, 93, 98.55	16, 43,068.57
and Lancashire	1,154,588.30	2, 19,265.55	261, 86.38	36,999.32	338,737.81	4,013,610.45		1, 89, 83.67	5, 83,496.12
	381,994.00	1,880, 59.73		6,500.00	71,636.99	3,414,190.30	*200,000.00	2,428,283.51	5,842,473.81
				2,907.90	56,835.76	2,322,257.39		2, 83,187.22	
N (Denmark)	98,726.07	47, 822.79	58,704.99		28, 76.12	623,429.97	*4 0,000.00	253,969.07	1,277,399.04
(Paris)	63,568.37	365,247.64		46,281.80	9,000.00	44,097.81		518,052.34	1,002,150.15
Fire and Life	74,343.91	98, 83.45	15,491.12	104, 00.00	35, 36.81	46, 44.17	*200,000.00	378,956.42	1,225,420.59
Norsk	921,023.15	47,214.91		4,785.85	389,217.75	1, 86, 96.93	*90,000.00	1,039,173.05	3, 36,119.98
	39,095.17	1,234,128.26			2, 49.26	1, 60, 38.54	*200,000.00	264,373.33	2,054,531.87
North British and Mer	906,093.40	5,314,350.03	290,669.39	18, 80.00	192,410.15	6,722,322.97		2,519,423.26	9,241,746.23
Northern Assurance	93,223.14	3, 96,925.72	51,100.22	6, 98.88	148, 83.48	4, 99,101.44	*200,000.00	2,030,216.06	6,629,317.50
Northern (Moscow)	258,939.84	1,069, 98.08		5, 00.00	20,000.00	1, 33, 37.92	*200,000.00	296,787.57	1,650,125.49
Union	18,651.82	220,011.92	175,049.34		7, 81.72	246, 45.46	*200,000.00	250,945.45	67,390.91
	39,760.95	1, 93, 79.19		8, 00.00	96,296.65	2,552,286.13		1,273,933.44	3,826,219.57
Paternelle	73,403.05	862,527.74		3,800.00	11, 83.47	1,051, 04.26		382,349.45	1, 83,443.71
eHx Fire	63,568.37	365,247.64		46,281.80	9,000.00	84,097.81		394,510.85	88,608.66
de (H)	301,201.00	2,109, 88.00		10, 35.00	76, 98.00	98,552.00		1,088,255.51	86,807.51
P dix (London)	380,186.63	2,510,900.47	141, 86.77	10,000.00	106,227.27	2, 49, 81.14	*200,000.00	1,783,955.33	93,136.47
Rossia	2,287,379.00	4, 43, 08.02	518,691.61		114,500.00	7, 34, 38.63		2,081,594.64	9, 66,113.27

Royal	1,540,104.65	8,782,346.17	691,348.59	55,343.36	1,017,823.76	12,086,966.53	*662,000.00	3,726,958.94	16,475,925.47
Royal Exchange Assurance	471,332.89	1,683,076.92	241,414.93	3,573.07	82,773.50	2,482,171.31	*400,000.00	946,284.84	3,828,456.15
Russian Reinsurance	302,247.00	1,449,753.63		1,734.38	37,401.18	1,791,136.19	*200,000.00	437,291.18	2,428,427.37
Salamandra	714,392.13	2,836,281.06		10,000.00	50,944.18	3,611,617.37		466,486.36	4,078,103.73
Scottish Union and National	370,775.00	2,906,506.79	82,412.13	10,000.00	234,478.88	3,604,172.80	*200,000.00	3,732,502.85	7,536,675.65
Second Russian	258,381.67	1,031,374.96		2,500.00	7,912.69	1,300,169.32		356,014.42	1,656,183.74
Skandia	217,530.31	861,395.39		1,500.00	22,757.07	1,103,182.77	*330,000.00	431,335.35	1,864,518.12
Skandinavia	241,910.69	824,711.45	27,502.42	1,000.00	15,723.72	1,110,848.28	*400,000.00	527,859.30	2,038,707.58
Sun Insurance	399,193.74	3,077,924.71		14,000.00	105,838.02	3,596,956.47	*1,000,000.00	709,833.79	5,306,790.26
Svea Fire and Life	140,158.94	1,142,298.96		3,500.00	27,500.00	1,313,457.90	*200,000.00	704,561.05	2,218,018.95
Swiss National	492,071.00	1,749,550.71		5,000.00	16,337.28	2,262,958.99	*200,000.00	207,785.99	2,670,744.98
Swiss Reinsurance	161,020.73	886,027.41		12,000.00	25,200.00	1,084,248.14		660,757.88	1,745,006.02
Union	99,112.00	773,656.05		4,045.00	31,905.00	908,718.05		1,036,168.15	1,944,886.20
Union (Paris)	90,806.44	530,970.44		69,978.50	14,000.00	705,755.38		535,263.39	1,241,018.77
Union and Phenix Espagnol	284,173.27	1,333,764.73		5,000.00	36,000.00	1,658,938.00		405,687.00	2,064,625.00
New Fire	126,025.62	532,866.39		5,000.00	20,000.00	683,892.01		346,185.67	1,030,077.68
Western	755,831.64	1,449,714.03	253,176.96	2,363.13	65,801.89	2,526,887.65	*400,000.00	1,267,691.69	4,194,579.34
Yorkshire	158,609.68	664,144.38	17,159.60		12,000.00	851,913.66	*200,000.00	488,624.82	1,540,538.48
Totals	21,167,732.11	93,942,889.80	3,936,324.39	712,489.19	4,857,129.29	124,616,564.78	6,592,000.00	48,500,378.18	179,708,942.96

*Statutory deposit.

RECAPITULATION.

North Carolina companies	71,389.25	989,908.60		20,126.14	103,507.75	1,184,929.74	1,571,500.00	1,152,563.91	3,908,993.65
Companies of other States (stock)	44,817,969.51	234,295,750.70	20,157,132.60	4,402,188.00	31,724,921.22	335,397,962.03	85,224,246.00	148,408,809.34	569,031,017.37
Companies of other States (mutual)	1,820,777.21	12,394,865.29			1,816,826.40	16,032,468.90		12,891,538.00	28,924,006.90
Companies of foreign countries	21,167,732.11	93,942,889.80	3,936,324.39	712,489.19	4,857,129.29	124,616,564.78	6,592,000.00	48,500,378.18	179,708,942.96
Totals	67,877,868.08	341,623,414.39	24,093,456.99	5,134,803.33	38,502,384.66	477,231,925.45	93,387,746.00	210,953,289.43	781,572,960.88

TABLE No. V—RISKS AND PREMIUMS, FIRE, 1917.

SHOWING RISKS IN FORCE AT BEGINNING OF YEAR, WRITTEN DURING YEAR, AND GROSS PREMIUMS RECEIVED, RISKS TERMINATED DURING YEAR, RISKS IN FORCE AT END OF YEAR, AND PREMIUMS THEREON, AMOUNT REINSURED AND LOSSES INCURRED DURING THE YEAR 1917.

NORTH CAROLINA COMPANIES.

Name of Company	Risks in Force at Beginning of Year	Risks Written During Year	Gross Premiums on Risks Written	Risks Terminated During Year	Risks in Force at End of Year	Gross Premiums Thereon	Premiums on Amt Reinsured	*Losses Paid
Atlantic	$11,060,880.00	$10,259,430.00	$206,933.66	$8,372,185.00	$12,948,125.00	$253,243.35	$78,667.15	$40,125.08
Cabarrus Mutual	1,329,952.00	42,810.00	2,287.41	143,886.00	1,228,876.00	2,287.41		2,534.25
Carolina	3,152,285.28	3,619,905.00	53,387.71	1,917,423.00	4,854,767.00	81,257.36	21,674.66	5,869.51
Dixie	42,093.1	46,924,749.00	471,935.57	41,510,148.00	47,507,712.00	561,706.71	114,091.87	107,980.47
Farmers Mutual (Raleigh)	19,346,101.00	2,456,559.00	71,814.88	960,350.00	20,842,310.00	71,814.88		44,601.10
Farmers Mutual (Edgecombe Co.)	1,012,326.00	96,750.00	483.75		1,038,548.00	483.75		707.50
Gaston ... Farmers Mutual		66,486.00	2,952.91	40,264.00		2,952.91		3,053.59
Hardware Mutual	683,550.00	746,250.00	12,756.21	683,550.00	746,250.00	12,756.21	44.75	3,417.90
... Farmers Mutual			405.71					466.67
North Carolina Home	24,082,179.00	21,868,420.00	280,728.10	18,086,801.0	27,863,798.00	405,886.34	151,133.57	63,497.39
Piedmont	16,281,464.00	14,447,574.00	235,222.54	12,958,998.0	17,970,040.00	322,640.08	68,241.53	59,380.79
Rowan Mutual	1,733,700.00	167,360.00	2,851.59		1,901,060.00			3,173.50
Southern Mutual Furniture	233,800.00	275,600.00	4,733.68	229,750.0	279,750.00			2,024.35
Southern Stock	16,648,724.00	13,646,301.00	205,185.65	12,172,145.00	18,122,880.00	285,501.70	72,060.09	34,998.92
Southern Underwriters	22,406,979.00	16,326,570.00	232,294.59	14,844,771.00	23,888,778.00	360,087.14	108,990.13	44,909.62
State Mutual	4,435,751.00	336,777.00	5,108.79	2,994,262.00	4,802,265.00	85,837.44	26,901.23	1,791.75
Underwriters (Rocky Mount)	11,551,478.00	9,254,011.00	55,964.75	8,665,655.0	12,139,834.0	187,307.89	37,865.36	13,125.96
Underwriters of ...boro	681,215.00	84,216.00	133,380.26	23,406.00	742,025.00			30,964.81
Union County Farmers Mutual			1,502.00			1,502.00		1,502.00
Totals	176,733,495.28	140,619,768.00	1,979,929.76	123,603,594.00	196,877,018.00	2,635,265.17	679,670.34	464,125.16

COMPANIES OF OTHER STATES (STOCK).

Name of Company	Risks in Force at Beginning of Year	Risks Written During Year	Gross Premiums on Risks Written	Risks Terminated During Year	Risks in Force at End of Year	Gross Premiums Thereon	Premiums on Amt Reinsured	*Losses Paid
Ætna	2,154,347,303.00	1,784,959,308.00	17,764,364.86	1,387,948,908.00	2,551,357,703.00	25,921,470.30	2,222,340.04	6,099,984.34
Agricultural	545,715,500.00	415,101,800.00	3,755,778.10	340,941,000.00	619,876,300.00	5,662,928.00	1,190,037.00	1,046,833.69
Alliance	156,252,741.00	202,075,276.00	1,827,274.86	134,494,252.00	223,833,765.00	2,125,267.76	532,473.43	430,302.14
American Alliance	528,357,575.00	522,222,011.00	4,272,960.38	406,837,883.00	643,741,703.00	5,425,177.58	4,290,791.76	406,585.96
...in (...ark)	1,182,421,231.00	779,121,799.00	7,436,237.81	612,794,849.00	1,348,748,181.00	13,053,118.59	1,672,016.65	2,234,646.97

Company								*Losses paid
American Central (St. Louis)	807,500,626.00	611,926,376.00	5,817,304.76	563,427,504.00	855,999,498.00	8,267,414.94	4,864,070.80	982,355.12
American Eagle	262,687,807.00	372,169,888.00	3,315,728.34	196,608,202.00	438,249,493.00	3,904,442.56	3,176,101.01	168,600.22
Automobile	85,757,453.00	431,232,101.00	3,493,807.72	168,305,549.00	348,684,305.00	3,060,483.04	991,340.16	499,888.92
Boston	605,813,630.00	510,108,003.00	4,545,388.70	392,043,996.00	723,877,637.00	6,580,920.04	1,719,744.47	1,223,428.33
Camden	412,649,510.00	394,725,506.00	3,803,836.14	307,985,766.00	500,085,766.00	4,810,277.01	828,023.39	1,136,267.98
Citizens of Missouri	174,206,540.00	251,056,215.00	2,559,775.41	207,771,667.00	217,491,088.00	2,151,538.83	1,847,857.06	115,155.31
Columbian	19,549,208.00	31,333,669.00	315,639.42	14,780,414.00	36,102,463.00	366,952.28	85,146.97	77,550.83
Commercial Union (New York)	163,527,101.00	155,238,107.00	1,463,580.64	118,938,000.00	199,827,208.00	1,914,579.22	470,417.02	390,178.01
Commonwealth	315,049,796.00	352,917,900.00	2,662,138.42	268,517,240.00	399,450,456.00	3,248,102.29	987,405.85	747,490.86
Concordia	318,939,741.00	225,997,153.00	2,320,107.95	187,047,441.00	357,889,453.00	3,574,408.55	433,427.20	704,633.66
Connecticut	942,582,778.00	682,335,020.00	6,774,591.81	601,079,200.00	1,023,838,598.00	9,834,196.09	1,749,801.46	1,850,962.77
Continental	2,252,575,316.00	1,574,436,895.00	14,584,515.56	1,315,374,428.00	2,511,637,783.00	24,194,124.96	2,798,382.00	4,561,050.75
County	100,902,885.00	85,125,630.00	823,645.82	63,365,182.00	122,663,333.00	1,127,294.15	743,820.52	137,270.80
Eagle	50,794,758.00	156,641,818.00	1,446,168.72	96,714,094.00	110,722,513.00	1,128,785.19	555,971.92	265,008.08
Equitable Fire and Marine	254,978,822.00	257,973,314.00	2,433,972.22	199,380,920.00	313,571,216.00	3,047,609.31	2,346,755.25	220,935.28
Equitable (South Carolina)	28,179,903.00	24,689,589.00	373,458.27	25,852,508.00	27,016,984.00	439,700.41	146,834.22	70,112.65
Fidelity-Phenix	1,761,789,496.00	1,349,651,748.00	12,332,309.57	1,044,136,233.00	2,067,305,011.00	20,365,064.24	2,604,739.63	3,916,574.61
First Reinsurance	158,909,346.00	178,849,223.00	2,050,699.29	279,306,378.00	58,452,191.00	650,722.14	5,914.59	872,729.24
Fire Association of Philadelphia	1,025,484,734.00	901,998,223.00	9,128,705.22	716,702,339.00	1,210,780,618.00	11,712,460.20	1,426,488.00	2,853,662.68
Firemen's Fund	963,449,120.00	809,607,000.00	8,408,717.41	641,820,883.00	1,131,235,237.00	12,418,454.59	2,003,705.03	2,436,310.68
Firemen's (Newark)	915,293,103.00	577,511,462.00	5,735,119.48	566,621,116.00	926,181,449.00	9,006,041.27	1,822,487.82	1,833,081.82
Franklin	357,781,707.00	323,135,393.00	3,683,265.45	199,949,781.00	480,967,319.00	4,405,658.00	3,357,687.00	257,326.83
Georgia Home	45,756,133.00	41,239,510.00	466,876.36	41,390,563.00	45,605,080.00	619,957.84	260,737.71	124,149.87
Germania	901,083,942.00	583,430,921.00	5,554,148.42	483,484,811.00	1,001,030,052.00	9,290,823.09	1,255,445.25	1,842,974.41
Girard Fire and Marine	250,771,944.00	179,079,751.00	1,650,772.75	132,321,934.00	297,529,761.00	2,589,350.65	1,117,417.13	337,847.79
Glens Falls	689,831,095.00	509,288,100.00	4,287,391.95	420,347,013.00	778,772,182.00	6,591,673.70	1,236,317.95	1,373,623.02
Globe and Rutgers	813,147,174.00	1,538,152,915.00	16,172,290.88	978,082,432.00	1,373,217,657.00	15,753,210.31	3,068,177.79	3,502,205.40
Granite State	153,860,594.00	126,703,067.00	1,432,730.95	99,665,9 3.00	180,897,748.00	2,075,176.02	531,633.55	414,935.77
Great American	2,665,643,785.00	2,188,636,555.00	19,351,823.16	1,897,867,002.00	2,956,413,338.00	25,977,124.67	5,004,935.10	5,556,172.64
Hanover	651,400,223.00	466,026,666.00	4,469,687.71	385,877,389.00	731,549,500.00	6,943,223.77	861,497.11	1,361,328.76
Hartford	3,767,914,129.00	3,333,675,197.00	33,438,747.09	2,648,400,853.00	4,453,188,473.00	42,306,143.62	5,127,728.37	10,632,229.18
Home of New York	3,971,400,346.00	3,519,543,452.00	33,480,407.92	2,816,010,134.00	4,674,933,664.00	44,175,965.00	6,641,950.00	10,252,601.37
Home of Utah	30,353,680.00	19,835,054.00	287,2 2.80	17,198,530.00	32,990,204.00	418,405.63	175,703.21	48,763.53
Imperial	129,666,191.00	152,900,783.00	1,125,994.75	114,675,169.00	167,891,805.00	1,299,893.82	418,050.60	219,316.32
Insurance Co. of North America	1,585,179,982.00	1,507,084,626.00	13,862,649.08	1,067,936,141.00	2,024,328,467.00	19,611,252.07	3,416,809.05	3,908,587.95
International	37,836,574.00	1,650,970,176.00	12,231,522.50	348,594,210.00	840,212,540.00	8,207,103.24	1,816,947.32	2,457,743.75
Interstate	36,423,914.00	60,243,981.00	2,589,522.50	34,623,529.00	62,044,366.00	602,529.28	147,775.30	194,008.76
Massachusetts Fire and Marine	101,874,640.00	87,824,109.00	808,415.34	70,913,104.00	118,785,645.00	1,139,861.42	200,209.26	312,635.07
Marquette National	16,003,825.00	43,763,247.00	439,690.83	10,971,787.00	48,795,285.00	469,710.63	138,280.76	63,610.79
Mechanics	115,080,911.00	99,557,072.00	962,410.43	71,801,294.00	142,836,689.00	1,366,280.67	275,801.87	271,444.55
Mechanics and Traders	194,580,698.00	178,883,490.00	1,664,061.77	143,822,357.00	219,641,831.00	2,084,392.18	816,288.03	364,521.47

*Losses paid.

TABLE No. V—RISKS AND PREMIUMS, FIRE, 1917.

SHOWING RISKS IN FORCE AT BEGINNING OF YEAR, WRITTEN DURING YEAR, AND GROSS PREMIUMS RECEIVED, RISKS TERMINATED DURING YEAR, RISKS IN FORCE AT END OF YEAR, AND PREMIUMS THEREON, AMOUNT REINSURED AND LOSSES INCURRED DURING THE YEAR 1917.

COMPANIES OF OTHER STATES (STOCK)—CONTINUED.

Name of Company	Risks in Force at Beginning of Year	Risks Written During Year	Gross Premiums on Risks Written	Risks Terminated During Year	Risks in Force at End of Year	Gross Premiums Thereon	Premiums on Amount Reinsured	*Losses Paid
Mercantile Insurance of America	$231,503,062.00	$276,650,414.00	$2,083,013.43	$180,972,845.00	$327,180,631.00	$2,359,859.10	$ 667,079.53	$ 544,197.17
Mechanics	546,185,180.00	322,121,440.00	3,290,352.67	288,645,361.00	579,661,259.00	5,767,725.33	332,177.28	1,049,748.95
National	2,514,931,032.00	2,035,498,890.00	18,949,211.09	1,649,948,007.00	2,900,482,815.00	27,601,854.26	6,851,639.94	5,269,562.75
National Union	638,736,910.00	587,008,001.00	6,724,728.31	469,091,239.00	756,653,672.00	7,976,395.88	2,837,984.78	1,583,773.33
Newark	255,835,025.00	232,401,882.00	2,288,964.35	207,126,737.00	281,110,170.00	2,725,845.19	547,563.19	639,936.95
New Hampshire	675,236,115.00	499,560,032.00	4,975,231.69	409,913,066.00	764,883,081.00	7,223,682.83	1,136,001.60	1,612,203.40
Niagara	895,166,296.00	811,389,872.00	7,700,489.44	630,312,599.00	1,076,243,569.00	10,013,618.88	2,172,203.41	1,962,845.66
North River	535,638,588.00	550,488,636.00	5,364,301.83	494,499,083.00	591,628,141.00	5,899,934.77	1,631,498.70	1,300,678.60
Northwestern National	857,535,304.00	435,476,923.00	4,432,608.32	376,167,275.00	916,844,952.00	7,953,182.94	974,388.95	1,529,211.69
Northwestern Fire and Marine	108,329,848.00	150,854,807.00	1,902,320.21	110,419,551.00	148,765,104.00	1,748,896.56	1,291,817.12	62,160.72
Old Colony	146,498,478.00	134,872,376.00	1,204,159.33	105,029,783.00	176,341,071.00	1,640,540.47	505,593.35	330,256.99
Gent	435,391,309.00	353,057,350.00	3,081,171.75	289,382,260.00	499,066,399.00	4,509,577.08	1,198,448.26	781,301.26
Palmetto	7,873,218.00	16,664,397.00	254,979.29	9,728,016.00	14,809,599.00	232,242.01	91,369.08	28,435.47
Pennsylvania	886,578,741.00	684,908,090.00	6,421,201.87	596,649,043.00	974,837,788.00	9,181,150.81	1,380,677.89	2,335,719.11
Petersburg Savings	17,087,925.00	11,662,225.00	172,238.97	10,803,594.00	17,946,556.00	286,101.82	22,833.75	54,064.26
Phoenix (Hartford)	1,428,424,336.00	1,146,709,392.00	10,624,423.55	845,213,656.00	1,729,920,072.00	16,152,041.11	3,873,646.11	2,736,441.09
Providence-Washington	632,062,448.00	572,288,656.00	5,237,113.00	504,152,229.00	700,198,875.00	6,745,617.55	1,960,852.11	1,598,611.20
On of America	1,019,228,932.00	869,925,221.00	8,119,802.20	703,674,159.00	1,185,479,994.00	11,365,954.16	1,744,791.75	2,384,464.97
Rhode Island	252,283,521.00	310,582,156.00	2,657,347.67	222,607,075.00	340,258,602.00	3,013,184.74	1,233,787.99	531,859.36
St. Paul Fire and Marine	1,024,153,357.00	804,389,129.00	9,341,745.76	661,829,273.00	1,166,713,213.00	12,462,772.90	1,307,536.87	3,410,756.00
Security	592,094,895.00	469,225,339.00	4,846,971.86	372,181,862.00	689,138,372.00	6,643,922.23	1,474,364.61	1,412,522.81
Springfield Fire and Marine	1,402,087,638.00	1,121,187,096.00	10,022,358.02	960,964,664.00	1,562,310,070.00	15,304,233.61	1,629,982.42	3,431,340.55
Standard	162,488,165.00	131,795,997.00	1,182,068.68	107,107,941.00	187,176,221.00	1,628,953.30	454,413.82	372,925.47
Sterling	169,102,813.00	148,929,574.00	1,357,569.57	78,825,112.00	239,207,275.00	2,342,029.16	1,604,828.99	258,731.04
United States	830,068,177.00	691,662,020.00	6,919,373.07	632,187,899.00	889,542,298.00	8,984,767.57	2,046,877.90	1,900,264.75
Virginia Fire and Marine	130,521,341.00	113,318,203.00	1,477,996.67	91,846,708.00	151,992,836.00	2,074,311.13	374,669.64	438,535.20
Weste	1,003,887,262.00	912,069,374.00	9,056,763.54	734,170,578.00	1,181,786,058.00	11,119,384.55	2,766,151.26	2,552,883.19
	50,092,238,357.00	44,643,676,891.00	425,974,455.46	35,085,482,997.00	63,789,241,722.00	572,777,049.09	119,497,684.91	118,890,773.87

Arkwright Mutual	374,625,183.00	358,463,207.00	2,537,224.06	302,569,152.00	430,519,238.00	3,004,348.81		287,394.46
Baltimore Mutual	10,479,449.00	12,012,513.00	100,391.40	10,595,168.00	11,896,794.00	98,274.55		4,912.13
Blackstone Mutual	209,087,960.00	195,909,780.00	1,419,402.54	158,207,377.00	246,790,363.00	1,765,618.91		230,679.89
Consolidated Underwriters			1,588,420.85			1,483,066.77	1,600.44	824,272.44
Cotton and Woolen Manufacturers	73,232,541.00	85,695,618.00	688,524.52	65,695,547.00	93,232,612.00	740,178.06	251,078.53	28,799.03
Druggists Indemnity Exchange	9,706,259.79	11,720,320.79	178,399.58	11,157,619.79	10,268,960.79	155,343.58	38,835.89	44,144.26
Firemen's Mutual	287,840,960.00	277,295,010.00	2,026,633.38	219,744,409.00	345,391,561.00	2,484,448.47		276,354.32
Fitchburg M	30,057,669.00	25,886,276.00	327,260.61	22,465,318.00	33,478,627.00	418,310.54	135,294.49	102,510.97
Hope Mutual	88,044,469.00	94,367,217.00	751,112.76	71,344,905.00	111,066,781.00	878,296.44		83,175.97
Indiana Lumbermen's Mutual	25,144,240.00	32,732,251.00	248,134.78	28,716,627.00	29,159,864.00	569,300.11	3,379.98	179,130.74
Individual Underwriters	49,821,579.00	62,347,992.00	425,270.33	51,951,247.00	60,218,324.00	393,810.72		144,585.24
Industrial Mutual	45,252,503.00	52,101,364.00	424,305.30	41,289,629.00	56,064,238.00	449,990.94		18,303.58
Keystone Mutual	50,036,108.00	57,044,483.00	493,270.96	48,658,353.00	58,422,238.00	493,753.59		61,789.67
Lumber Underwriters	18,298,545.00	12,369,875.00	214,975.77	22,851,820.00	7,816,600.00	140,539.34	53,875.31	102,540.22
Lumber Mfrs. Interinsurance	19,558,554.00	28,351,111.00	515,237.67	24,627,444.00	23,185,221.00	420,086.96	87,573.05	307,340.80
Lumber Mutual	26,089,715.00	33,948,603.00	717,635.43	30,355,485.00	29,682,833.00	622,450.41	25.00	179,078.06
Lumbermen's Mutual	46,015,022.00	65,375,506.00	1,119,948.53	54,153,045.00	57,637,483.00	907,273.03	13,533.09	372,141.33
Lumbermen's Underwriters Alliance	40,278,921.00	60,428,548.00	1,185,535.27	51,415,112.00	49,292,357.00	961,264.27		478,669.49
Manton Mutual	47,246,227.00	53,852,097.00	468,307.09	46,874,063.00	54,224,261.00	462,193.48		21,361.84
Mfg. Lumbermen's Underwriters	43,152,646.00	60,193,099.00	1,911,845.28	54,459,974.16	48,885,770.84	972,647.30		527,350.27
Mfg. Woodworkers Underwriters	11,461,309.00	15,166,298.00	276,231.66	14,272,473.00	12,355,134.00	224,321.22	61,458.09	137,192.50
Merchants Mutual	112,984,535.00	104,459,521.00	759,556.06	82,829,760.00	134,614,296.00	964,903.22		148,061.05
Mercantile Mutual	27,327,964.00	40,915,963.00	340,840.19	34,509,752.00	43,734,175.00	358,114.06		19,029.84
Middlesex Mutual	54,299,610.00	20,565,026.00	300,105.21	18,740,038.00	56,124,598.00	811,207.25	161,123.74	68,916.56
Michigan Millers Mutual	114,529,419.00	150,351,917.00	1,330,677.85	111,378,558.00	153,502,778.00	1,660,454.30	5,347.07	636,647.90
Millers Mutual	9,736,300.00	4,069,300.00	714,105.67	3,010,750.00	10,794,850.00	2,088,463.60		104,164.14
Millers Indemnity Underwriters								48,612.73
Narragansett Mutual	13,876,495.00	15,587,842.00	131,325.02	13,383,998.00	16,080,339.00	133,772.71		8,334.62
National Mutual	15,648,788.00	19,304,569.00	171,468.42	16,463,117.00	18,490,170.00	160,848.21		7,047.73
National Lumber	6,683,087.00	10,480,505.45	171,061.54	8,049,455.22	9,114,137.23	148,555.70	3,109.94	127,583.19
Penn Lumbermen's Mutual	25,352,961.00	31,105,392.00	653,940.43	28,031,146.00	28,427,207.00	591,050.26	321.06	175,453.58
Philadelphia Manufacturers Mutual	80,311,977.00	95,548,307.00	744,198.42	72,620,570.00	103,239,714.00	792,702.69		90,656.85
Reciprocal Exchange	50,619,181.00	64,439,391.00	767,437.67	61,501,343.00	53,577,229.00	659,293.43	245,520.86	336,294.25
Rubber Manufacturers Mutual	69,488,150.00	81,353,986.00	655,274.99	62,854,787.00	87,987,349.00	699,757.66	15,137.64	27,075.98
Southern Lumber Underwriters	6,109,481.28		122,441.75	1,844,308.85	4,265,172.43	91,707.68		58,160.73
Utilities Indemnity Exchange		16,254,210.00	281,921.72			219,597.26	70,814.15	86,528.62
Wern Reciprocal Underwriters	5,200,290.00	97,610,435.00	263,724.15	8,451,050.00	13,003,450.00	200,099.55		28,217.66
What Cheer Mutual	91,717,748.00	12,342,775.00	774,885.14	73,996,045.00	115,332,138.00	897,950.87		93,146.19
Warners Interins. (Grocers' Dept.)	4,793,320.68		139,130.53	5,982,120.68	11,153,975.00	125,127.06	25,025.41	7,618.29
Totals	2,187,999,615.47	2,365,682,789.52	25,940,162.53	1,935,051,566.70	2,629,030,838.29	28,249,123.01	1,173,053.74	6,533,277.12

TABLE No. V—RISKS AND PREMIUMS, FIRE, 1917.

SHOWING RISKS IN FORCE AT BEGINNING OF YEAR, WRITTEN DURING YEAR, AND GROSS PREMIUMS RECEIVED, RISKS TERMINATED DURING YEAR, RISKS IN FORCE AT END OF YEAR, AND PREMIUMS THEREON, AMOUNT REINSURED AND LOSSES INCURRED DURING THE YEAR 1917.

COMPANIES OF FOREIGN COUNTRIES.

Name of Company	Risks in Force at Beginning of Year	Risks Written During Year	Gross Premiums on Risks Written	Risks Terminated During Year	Risks in Force at End of Year	Gross Premiums Thereon	Premiums on Amount Reinsured	*Losses Paid
Abeille	$ 38,090,362.00	$ 48,144,815.00	$ 434,373.04	$ 37,350,188.00	$ 48,884,989.00	$ 458,360.02	$	$ 156,578.79
Atlas	467,680,400.00	420,317,010.00	3,891,272.72	335,874,526.00	552,122,884.00	5,157,915.35	1,256,918.50	1,170,042.43
Balkan National	293,978,933.00	360,348,470.00	3,176,232.19	337,588,726.00	316,738,677.00	2,896,520.63	412,515.06	1,554,258.59
British America	253,669,034.00	289,777,556.00	2,363,564.03	223,146,855.00	320,299,735.00	3,019,419.95	798,030.33	597,758.07
Caledonian	358,210,397.00	277,149,087.00	2,812,555.58	245,360,164.00	389,999,320.00	3,933,901.81	915,719.87	796,398.23
Century	70,471,763.00	96,870,652.00	677,861.96	79,850,444.00	87,491,971.00	681,318.35	257,360.04	126,582.51
Commercial Union Assurance	429,854,440.00	1,187,286,648.00	10,741,039.21	1,022,469,457.00	1,594,671,631.00	14,976,829.78	2,328,500.88	3,633,358.23
Fire Reassurance	204,888,587.00	333,637,046.00	3,367,017.87	233,781,073.00	304,714,560.00	3,179,935.07	453,547.56	1,204,388.80
First Russian	213,613,512.00	315,805,675.00	2,609,639.51	217,592,909.00	311,826,278.00	2,580,444.26		978,574.51
Hamburg-Bremen	283,814,093.00	132,904,263.00	1,429,566.08	194,326,368.00	222,392,008.00	2,410,843.39	651,226.53	624,902.95
Jakor	865,412,350.00	1,188,860,137.00	10,802,073.10	995,500,536.00	1,058,771,951.00	10,493,371.80	5,007,544.82	2,461,855.08
Liverpool and London and Globe	2,369,461,843.00	2,048,090,056.00	18,532,065.91	1,739,594,046.00	2,677,957,853.00	24,595,332.03	7,944,665.51	4,845,757.58
London Assurance	508,983,884.00	378,147,336.00	3,849,275.67	344,027,431.00	543,103,789.00	5,634,658.05	1,304,263.71	1,085,448.07
London and Lancashire	806,682,154.00	615,142,463.00	5,107,172.47	552,539,174.00	869,285,443.00	7,484,791.29	2,124,832.65	1,091,828.18
Moscow	296,209,372.00	439,568,025.00	3,670,795.03	297,015,665.00	438,761,732.00	3,588,916.00		1,409,164.58
National (Denmark)		70,180,252.00	706,162.53	10,046,528.00	60,133,724.00	614,944.45		42,925.25
Nationale (Paris)	123,518,344.00	147,738,262.00	1,329,526.22	117,010,305.00	154,246,301.00	1,446,673.69	759,133.68	234,868.22
Netherlands Fire and Life	129,359,321.00	150,425,254.00	1,418,496.21	109,818,041.00	169,966,534.00	1,886,010.00	666,206.25	238,454.09
Nord-Deutsche	136,170,993.00	95,530,040.00	958,517.17	115,808,649.00	115,892,384.00	1,207,412.70	312,065.00	336,796.09
Norsk Lloyd	53,230,796.00	296,190,793.00	2,665,781.15	110,047,391.00	239,524,198.00	3,588,916.00		739,064.76
North British and Mercantile	1,383,610,093.00	1,353,193,875.00	10,101,369.87	1,124,393,693.00	1,612,410,275.00	12,975,578.40	2,837,674.17	2,848,369.47
Northern Assurance	778,515,757.00	701,996,976.00	6,725,685.57	612,373,038.00	868,139,695.00	9,012,213.51	2,139,217.12	2,007,479.02
Northern (Moscow)	96,240,708.00	198,908,782.00	1,828,435.38	112,413,913.00	182,735,577.00	1,789,773.09		454,297.14
Norwegian Assurance		47,143,730.00	472,302.08	7,945,020.00	39,198,710.00	407,192.75		87,764.34
Norwich Union	494,190,270.00	421,415,226.00	4,041,494.25	347,475,463.00	568,130,033.00	5,265,593.66	1,528,313.50	1,100,845.36
Paternelle	122,058,627.00	160,750,640.00	1,550,084.80	129,959,748.00	152,849,519.00	1,579,456.42	703,548.74	517,356.01
Phenix Fire	112,234,570.00	140,556,074.00	1,290,579.43	105,127,848.00	147,662,796.00	1,391,088.75		234,868.23
Palatine (London)	441,887,956.00	400,987,143.00	3,960,170.98	318,322,655.00	524,522,444.00	5,230,318.98	1,141,190.58	1,124,909.30
Phenix (London)	781,443,203.00	806,847,071.00	6,268,346.90	631,780,615.00	956,509,659.00	7,629,422.84	2,885,806.07	1,275,129.41
Russia	736,956,399.00	1,123,232,514.00	11,227,331.30	826,395,417.00	1,033,793,496.00	10,633,696.07	2,268,150.06	4,054,027.46
Royal	2,062,724,627.00	1,556,124,643.00	14,435,719.76	1,317,627,680.00	2,301,221,590.00	21,854,534.69	4,681,769.24	4,043,785.35

Company							
Royal Exchange Assurance	454,684,747.00	370,818,539.00	3,131,636.86	319,631,025.00	505,872,261.00	4,340,794.72	1,088,935.66	901,916.79
Russian Reinsurance	231,286,501.00	334,985,693.00	2,846,376.29	238,910,572.00	327,361,622.00	2,777,928.25		1,143,102.88
Salamandra	1,189,580,08.00	1,516,625,282.00	13,310,927.62	1,296,778,972.00	1,409,426,418.00	13,404,241.21	7,918,414.25	2,474,915.96
Scottish Union and National	862,821,667.00	756,272,290.00	6,113,520.09	586,433,195.00	1,032,660,762.00	8,365,243.50	2,710,895.96	1,485,257.88
Second Russian	207,845,497.00	302,435,399.00	2,738,972.86	241,912,400.00	268,368,496.00	2,625,011.23	630,105.05	897,936.13
Skandia	128,605,059.00	166,780,920.00	1,535,478.42	141,215,492.00	154,170,487.00	1,625,048.69		558,180.81
Skandinavia	8,575,231.00	212,846,844.00	1,739,697.64	68,436,425.00	152,985,650.00	1,524,351.43		291,141.70
Sun Insurance Office	686,048,132.00	529,141,208.00	5,281,215.64	458,794,113.00	756,395,227.00	7,483,549.67	1,542,698.68	1,373,039.89
Svea Fire and Life	193,923,116.00	202,605,470.00	2,271,354.78	161,368,233.00	235,160,353.00	2,758,622.49	598,038.73	587,424.54
Swiss National	298,696,226.00	446,869,005.00	4,125,736.95	392,797,905.00	352,767,326.00	3,509,189.85	239,597.89	1,608,049.85
Swiss Reinsurance	153,361,687.00	192,103,484.00	1,612,016.21	158,522,865.00	186,942,306.00	1,710,913.21		659,358.02
Union Assurance	136,347,561.00	178,349,033.00	1,605,094.11	122,925,859.00	191,770,735.00	1,811,052.78	390,680.39	347,383.47
Union (Paris)	109,681,259.00	126,565,314.00	1,179,093.43	98,518,539.00	137,728,034.00	1,331,287.94	334,286.81	366,494.23
Union and Phenix Espagnol	173,641,106.00	265,237,105.00	2,411,260.18	178,628,162.00	260,250,049.00	2,519,545.40		889,384.68
Warsaw Fire	50,857,159.00	104,614,910.00	1,045,529.88	64,243,656.00	91,228,413.00	973,951.29		344,714.69
Western Assurance	344,869,125.00	449,747,318.00	3,592,768.00	316,441,577.00	478,174,886.00	4,326,953.82	1,567,777.84	725,547.46
Yorkshire	147,672,744.00	212,503,632.00	2,092,953.77	151,686,154.00	208,490,222.00	2,150,364.54	869,475.87	367,447.86
Totals	21,291,779,713.00	22,171,741,980.00	199,078,140.76	17,849,808,710.00	25,613,712,983.00	239,316,265.18	61,239,197.00	56,119,132.94

RECAPITULATION.

North Carolina Companies	176,733,495.28	140,619,768.00	1,979,929.76	123,603,594.00	196,877,018.00	2,635,265.17	679,670.34	464,125.16
Companies of other States (stock)	50,092,238,357.00	44,643,676,891.00	425,974,455.46	35,085,482,997.00	63,789,241,722.00	572,777,049.09	119,497,684.91	118,890,773.87
Companies of other States (mutual)	2,187,999,615.47	2,365,662,789.52	25,940,162.53	1,935,051,566.70	2,629,030,838.29	28,249,123.01	1,173,053.74	6,533,277.12
Companies of foreign countries	2,291,779,713.00	22,171,741,980.00	199,078,140.76	17,849,808,710.00	25,613,712,983.00	239,316,265.18	61,239,197.00	56,119,132.94
Totals	73,748,751,180.75	69,321,721,428.52	652,972,688.51	54,993,946,867.70	92,228,862,561.29	842,977,702.45	182,589,605.99	182,007,309.09

*Losses paid.

TABLE No. VI—RISKS AND PREMIUMS, MARINE AND INLAND, 1917.

SHOWING RISKS IN FORCE AT BEGINNING OF YEAR, WRITTEN DURING YEAR, AND GROSS PREMIUMS RECEIVED, RISKS TERMINATED DURING YEAR, RISKS IN FORCE AT END OF YEAR, AND PREMIUMS THEREON, AMOUNT REINSURED AND LOSSES PAID DURING THE YEAR 1917.

COMPANIES OF OTHER STATES.

Name of Company	Risks in Force at Beginning of Year	Risks Written During Year	Premiums on Risks Written in 1917	Risks Terminated During Year	Risks in Force at End of Year	Gross Premiums Thereon	Premiums on Amount Reinsured	*Losses Paid
Ætna	$100,629,654.00	$1,297,557,008.00	$10,771,866.62	$1,278,177,165.00	$120,009,497.00	$2,524,181.58	$ 959,406.83	$2,215,430.36
Agricultural	1,296,957.00	151,456,654.00	755,609.52	134,540,573.00	16,916,081.00	284,002.18	65,710.47	96,908.72
American Alliance	2,997,044.00	4,010,343.00	86,028.69	2,513,295.00	2,794,005.00	64,817.26	59,420.40	654.18
American Eagle		7,702,101.00	185,609.35	3,864,961.00	6,834,184.00	160,323.29	115,532.77	11,338.40
American (Newark)	14,212,998.00	35,077,746.00	686,703.66	28,119,137.00	21,171,607.00	457,450.90	5,661.25	170,447.76
American Central	13,107,173.00	22,210,167.00	438,693.42	15,876,841.00	19,440,499.00	369,475.46	200,366.95	125,428.56
Alliance	20,765,114.00	98,108,623.00	871,297.12	99,703,921.00	19,169,816.00	380,768.64	41,505.17	494,820.32
Baltic	55,130,448.00	746,284,837.00	7,999,437.21	655,858,889.00	145,556,396.00	2,344,448.79	1,064,042.17	996,532.39
Boston	56,077,534.00	471,409,727.00	7,241,690.00	455,965,096.00	71,522,165.00	1,986,395.41	285,200.78	2,154,703.46
Camden	2,136,388.00	39,813,425.00	569,184.30	34,617,093.00	7,332,720.00	115,285.58	5,786.46	118,074.54
Citizens of Missouri	1,781,511.00	3,793,447.00	73,445.20	2,545,062.00	3,029,896.00	59,678.36	56,714.78	229.96
Columbia	34,215,347.00	103,980,658.00	665,122.59	106,725,627.00	31,470,378.00	457,614.38	77,514.91	321,923.47
Columbian		2,174,043.00	67,073.32	1,586,025.00	588,018.00	13,082.25	4,541.82	1,001.06
Commonwealth	12,919,196.00	43,755,396.00	761,246.20	30,242,890.00	26,431,702.00	571,695.47	115,534.59	211,115.66
Concordia	13,000.00	584,550.00	5,599.00	133,450.00	464,100.00	4,311.46	376.43	47.50
Connecticut	1,731,932.00	56,608,753.00	825,609.61	38,771,847.00	19,568,833.00	428,473.49	2,713.52	211,120.07
Continental	18,097,601.00	112,046,288.00	1,530,629.96	78,961,341.00	51,182,548.00	962,299.59	284,069.67	164,644.94
Equitable Fire and Marine	2,449,220.00	28,001,473.00	424,067.29	21,503,087.00	8,947,606.00	210,215.67	87,743.61	101,142.35
Fidelity-Phenix	14,666,973.00	84,915,318.00	1,257,348.53	59,479,200.00	40,103,091.00	784,503.10	125,639.25	159,827.03
Firemen's Fund	207,809,883.00	2,943,221,750.00	20,412,546.77	2,852,612,305.00	298,419,328.00	6,160,124.99	2,120,009.74	3,847,911.41
Firemen's		6,023,548.00	179,998.10	2,933,734.00	3,089,814.00	99,144.60	846.54	6.93
Franklin	5,674,953.00	9,284,566.00	429,250.01	2,933,166.00	12,635,353.00	344,429.00	133,457.00	103,245.33
Great American	1,960,128.00	26,822,658.00	652,858.17	21,366,260.00	17,416,583.00	439,080.57	42,144.91	295,059.30
Glens Falls	22,306,040.00	211,663,995.00	2,182,381.89	192,143,914.00	41,826,121.00	1,043,284.18	245,310.18	450,433.82
Globe and Rutgers	32,688,618.00	612,996,032.00	11,050,656.96	571,467,425.00	74,217,225.00	1,955,793.51		4,037,970.35
Hanover	8,960,727.00	98,566,985.00	1,058,725.71	73,895,721.00	33,631,991.00	551,066.97	98,568.87	261,796.48
Hartford	111,970,843.00	291,053,607.00	3,324,415.57	346,512,060.00	56,512,390.00	1,178,889.15	72,220.18	826,634.28
Home of New York	57,138,664.00	1,208,170,584.00	3,024,899.26	1,191,533,370.00	73,775,878.00	2,075,793.00	392,884.00	736,070.40
Insurance Co. of North America	130,786,746.00	1,705,005,371.00	14,017,613.05	1,635,726,509.00	200,065,608.00	2,742,810.88	158,330.98	5,385,376.23
Massachusetts Fire and Marine	24,612,644.00	157,119,017.00	1,335,644.47	139,969,269.00	41,762,372.00	696,302.31	34,448.59	327,880.18
Milwaukee Mechanics	1,567,111.00	3,493,466.00	70,041.67	2,144,784.00	2,915,793.00	56,235.05	655.70	14,260.95
Mercantile of America	24,147,045.00	79,829,445.00	871,899.58	75,415,802.00	28,560,688.00	701,983.87	267,063.32	217,256.90
National	5,214,951.00	1,937,954.00	967,105.16	104,631,669.00	12,521,236.00	325,871.61	81,843.52	99,133.50

COMPANIES OF FOREIGN COUNTRIES.

Ætna	2,148,518.00•	9,713,084.00	63,220.46	584,259.00	9,128,825.00	51,674.29	2,566.16	16,838.05
British America		15,328,070.00	76,089.63	14,811,285.00	2,665,303.00	52,587.86	12,880.43	30,960.60
Caledonian		4,065,549.00	135,661.11	570,666.00	2,494,883.00	106,649.52	2,526.23	8,388.27
Century	1,429,750.00	1,475,187.00	10,271.05	1,444,850.00	1,460,087.00	10,199.56	420.68	4,110.63
Commercial Union	32,242,881.00	2,261,561,618.00	2,626,297.74	2,259,488,947.00	34,315,552.00	298,929.61	6,230.25	699,059.70
Liverpool and London and Globe	59,696,250.00	305,876,023.00	2,405,053.27	309,023,056.00	56,549,217.00	1,205,621.78	295,136.20	559,627.37
London Assurance	44,837,325.00	633,703,969.00	4,365,981.46	607,669,308.00	70,871,986.00	516,556.46	84,567.88	943,703.50
London and Lancashire	17,476,005.00	94,931,656.00	882,447.30	76,527,282.00	35,880,379.00	634,732.11	110,959.34	232,698.45
North British and Mercantile	16,031,572.00	73,911,458.00	1,078,245.19	54,214,510.00	35,728,520.00	722,562.56	205,531.33	295,676.47
Northern Assurance -		9,525,210.00	122,831.50	1,430,939.00	8,094,271.00	103,599.13	1,398.69	18,452.66
Norwich Union	5,807,413.00	66,727,219.00	575,731.83	50,421,967.00	22,112,665.00	328,274.32	18,113.40	135,970.59
Nord Deutsche	30,474,830.00	524,755,786.00	4,757,058.53	553,207,371.00	2,023,245.00	50,122.08	19,139.83	1,180,253.64
National of Denmark		22,067,562.00	176,262.66	15,492,887.00	6,574,695.00	58,704.99		3,753.27
Phœnix of London	22,509,012.00	106,837,916.00	590,184.08	1,752,005.00	17,594,923.00	347,389.28	65,210.27	126,064.65
Royal	98,461,541.00	702,970,429.00	4,697,156.21	696,748,853.00	104,683,117.00	1,314,128.80	36,651.05	1,156,835.80
Royal Exchange	31,607,422.00	445,781,684.00	2,006,743.14	430,977,376.00	46,411,730.00	727,823.73	281,283.61	577,734.83
Rossia	26,885,212.00	544,797,860.00	5,221,692.33	528,549,097.00	43,133,975.00	1,031,284.57	9,232.50	2,648,877.72
Scottish Union and National	3,865,433.00	15,934,411.00	211,671.08	8,314,817.00	11,485,027.00	167,836.93	3,012.68	63,694.40
Skandinavia	5,853.00	38,535,364.00	263,415.69	36,959,452.00	1,581,765.00	35,082.91	7,580.49	114,802.32
Wärn Assur nœ	36,585,667.00	403,209,263.00	3,408,475.97	394,119,576.00	45,674,754.00	717,907.50	201,513.72	910,792.86
Yorkshire		1,354,761.00	41,245.81	127,208.00	1,227,553.00	37,091.56	2,772.37	1,463.48
Totals	430,064,084.00	6,283,064,079.00	33,685,736.04	6,152,435,691.00	559,692,472.00	8,518,759.55	1,366,727.11	9,729,759.16

*Losses paid.

TABLE No. VII—NORTH CAROLINA BUSINESS, 1917.

SHOWING RISKS WRITTEN, PREMIUMS RECEIVED, LOSSES PAID, LOSSES INCURRED IN NORTH CAROLINA FOR THE YEAR ENDING DECEMBER 31, 1917, BY FIRE, MARINE AND INLAND INSURANCE COMPANIES.

NORTH CAROLINA COMPANIES.

Name of Company	Fire Business					
	Gross Risks Written	Gross Premiums Received	Net Risks Written	Net Premiums Received	Net Losses Paid	Net Losses Incurred
Atlantic	$10,259,430.00	$206,933.66	$4,464,220.00	$100,270.63	$33,544.59	$40,125.08
Cabarrus			35,300.00	2,264.25	2,264.25	2,534.25
Carolina	3,619,905.00	53,387.71	1,564,309.00	26,610.00	5,869.51	6,869.51
Dixie	12,069,339.00	184,481.01	7,544,577.00	120,455.24	33,564.92	40,214.30
Farmers Mutual (Raleigh)	2,456,559.00	71,814.88		71,814.88	44,601.10	50,402.12
Farmers Mutual (Edgecombe County)	96,750.00	483.75	96,750.00	483.75	707.50	707.50
Gaston County Farmers Mutual	66,486.00	332.43	66,486.00	332.43	3,053.59	3,053.59
Hardware Mutual	817,650.00	7,226.15	431,300.00	5,940.55	417.90	417.90
Mecklenburg Farmers Mutual		405.71		405.71	466.67	466.67
North Carolina Home	12,930,004.00	199,739.95	4,317,451.00	93,761.69	39,924.82	39,997.11
Piedmont	12,382,558.00	201,942.58	4,875,021.00	108,882.20	43,859.17	50,173.80
Rowan Mutual	1,901,060.00	2,851.59	1,901,060.00	2,851.59	3,173.50	3,173.50
Southern Mutual Furniture	74,700.00	1,457.17	71,000.00	1,336.74	24.35	24.35
Southern Stock	6,478,816.00	104,276.08	3,853,422.00	65,117.07	19,293.65	16,393.40
Southern Underwriters	6,343,563.00	96,519.28	3,683,487.00	60,174.65	22,741.03	22,017.82
State	409,336.00	5,108.79	409,336.00	5,108.79	1,791.75	1,791.75
Underwriters (Rocky Mount)	3,360,777.00	55,964.75	1,840,439.00	31,020.79	13,125.96	9,639.96
Underwriters of Greensboro	4,240,837.00	67,354.75	2,780,323.00	46,270.41	15,838.72	14,567.09
Union County Farmers Mutual	84,216.00	5,703.74	84,216.00	5,703.74	1,502.00	1,502.00
Totals	77,591,986.00	1,265,983.98	38,018,697.00	748,805.11	285,764.98	304,071.70

COMPANIES OF OTHER STATES (STOCK).

(xxxiv)

American Central (St. Louis)	2,277,789.00	17,408.11	7 5,584.00	5,165.94	3,065.29	2,946.87
American Eagle	6,727,826.00	54,983.36	672,872.00	6,997.83	1,432.43	1,242.36
Automobile	5,706,122.00	28,827.18	4,668,672.00	20,189.43	2,206.08	10,654.66
Boston	4,428,525.00	22,625.53	2,725,716.00	15,524.39	4,832.73	3,779.62
Camden	6,146,101.00	28,312.17	3,932,457.00	19,439.97	7,425.28	6,009.91
Citizens of Missouri	1,899,164.00	21,097.30	1,256,913.00	16,077.74	3,719.41	2,017.63
Columbia	86,732.00	503.07	77,625.00	458.54	1.92	26.64
Columbian	670,335.00	3,393.73	470,869.00	2,121.53	1,428.06	1,203.06
Commercial Union (New York)	1,352,226.00	14,837.76	691,659.00	9,362.46	2,977.45	2,546.85
Commonwealth						
Concordia	1,695,852.00	24,691.22	1,008,823.00	15,330.67	7,137.33	7,422.16
Connecticut	4,216,617.00	36,774.86	2,369,182.00	23,659.91	6,648.26	4,885.44
Continental	16,991,415.00	130,227.75	9,059,001.00	82,776.66	15,678.69	15,407.32
County	429,138.00	5,277.84	382,988.00	4,572.91	1,055.54	825.02
Eagle	1,527,516.00	10,210.61	774,501.00	4,911.92	349.02	1,458.02
Equitable Fire and Marine	2,389,088.00	27,391.48	480,714.00	5,290.69	2,793.13	2,811.19
Eagle (South Carolina)	1,395,515.00	23,529.35	957,279.18	16,257.72	2,479.74	2,513.49
Fidelity-Phenix	11,078,547.00	106,358.58	6,528,649.00	74,240.68	23,373.41	23,373.41
First Reinsurance						
Fire Association of Philadelphia	12,091,789.00	101,063.97	7,932,900.00	67,794.85	25,228.62	26,120.18
Firemen's Fund	10,677,125.00	71,201.62	5,907,018.00	48,336.09	16,807.79	26,433.08
Firemen's (Newark)	3,731,567.00	46,472.47	2,705,166.00	35,771.06	12,970.65	9,088.00
Franklin	2,362,009.00	30,344.91	1,911,366.00	24,856.51	9,326.78	9,178.12
Georgia Home	1,521,207.00	20,187.87	886,015.00	12,421.41	5,215.54	5,559.95
Germania	5,033,815.00	72,715.87	3,068,033.00	47,201.53	17,059.07	20,960.04
Girard Fire and Marine	648,680.00	7,668.66	362,951.00	4,548.85	1.90	36.90
Glens Falls	3,088,063.00	42,552.06	1,448,160.00	25,872.09	3,986.12	3,069.18
Globe and Rutgers	4,713,027.00	84,846.95	2,610,888.00	53,934.24	33,527.78	27,051.92
Granite State	2,031,610.00	28,030.89	1,274,368.00	17,728.48	8,792.97	5,488.65
Great American	25,304,886.00	256,599.50	15,707,123.00	178,170.14	89,119.23	89,640.23
Hanover	3,082,996.00	42,522.65	2,131,653.00	32,809.24	14,792.32	12,271.21
Hartford	36,018,469.00	380,117.88	27,921,195.00	321,687.78	125,924.39	160,971.97
Home of New York	29,876,003.00	310,019.53	26,125,772.00	269,022.51	87,002.97	115,250.73
...e of Utah	789,765.00	2,790.01	620,901.00	559.70	883.50	286.50
Imperial						
Insurance Company of North America	14,339,559.00	129,742.95	8,250,067.00	75,697.91	34,944.44	30,767.84
International	9,144,536.00	65,259.13	4,929,295.00	35,570.38	22,168.62	23,207.19
Interstate	265,303.00	1,971.19	159,275.00	1,029.27	548.1	962.14
Massachusetts Fire and Marine	1,480,933.00	19,466.13	955,522.00	12,336.33	11,218.38	5,479.55
Marquette National	468,025.00	6,279.99	293,357.00	4,066.98	452.31	452.31
Mechanics	2,890,7 0.00	29,539.78	1,609,719.00	15,295.92	6,557.03	12,741.90
Mechanics and Traders						
...lle Insurance of America						
Milwaukee Mechanics	1,992,984.00	29,336.33	1,551,544.00	23,963.69	2,876.76	2,051.05
National	23,476,333.00	176,300.05	8,500,031.00	99,353.68	44,679.00	42,613.46

TABLE No. VII—NORTH CAROLINA BUSINESS, 1917.

...NG RISKS WRITTEN, PREMIUMS RECEIVED, LOSSES PAID, LOSSES INCURRED IN NORTH CAROLINA FOR THE YEAR ENDING DECEMBER 31, 1917, BY FIRE, MARINE AND INLAND INSURANCE COMPANIES.

COMPANIES OF OTHER STATES (STOCK)—CONTINUED.

Name of Company	Fire Business					
	Gross Risks Written	Gross Premiums Received	Net Risks Written	Net Premiums Received	Net Losses Paid	Net Losses Incurred
National Union	$ 2,881,713.00	$ 32,015.13	$ 1,558,871.00	$ 14,113.83	$ 3,864.86	$ 5,878.86
Newark	3,203,523.00	41,018.64	1,494,431.00	21,431.29	8,927.84	12,220.84
New Hampshire	18,737,463.00	86,322.16	16,353,312.00	64,609.42	29,531.74	32,122.82
Niagara	4,546,909.00	43,576.06	3,077,739.00	30,534.64	11,238.18	14,721.64
North River	4,014,069.00	46,290.12	2,381,352.00	29,007.62	23,037.08	1,129.08
Northwestern National	1,519,985.00	23,016.74	1,007,177.00	15,059.05	7,791.34	7,726.35
Northwestern Fire and						
Old Colony	1,106,109.00	9,322.75	798,441.00	6,391.59	1,809.39	1,179.85
Orient	2,691,138.00	26,036.54	1,483,266.00	16,820.74	4,928.06	5,930.39
Palmetto	419,534.00	5,705.18	372,684.00	5,020.89	28.91	28.91
Pennsylvania	2,271,601.00	40,876.23	1,478,158.00	27,905.43	14,969.45	17,742.56
Petersburg Savings	3,190,155.00	57,836.52	2,175,353.05	41,241.97	16,043.60	14,155.38
Phenix (Hartford)	20,235,614.00	115,757.19	12,155,594.00	69,077.69	15,031.13	26,265.62
Providence-Washington	8,685,049.00	53,218.17	3,889,963.00	35,927.56	13,754.19	16,255.66
...n of America	6,285,600.00	57,129.00	3,608,351.00	36,800.04	14,675.96	20,136.96
Rhode Island	4,772,657.20	54,775.25	2,899,152.46	34,955.18	9,624.95	12,417.35
St. Paul Fire and Marine	8,688,929.00	46,216.03	7,810,847.00	33,044.80	13,968.89	12,477.88
Security	5,976,167.00	23,199.42	2,823,156.00	14,573.06	6,236.49	5,600.78
Springfield Fire and Marine	8,093,718.00	89,948.92	4,114,325.00	56,643.32	34,394.58	31,368.08
Standard	4,981,814.00	27,269.09	2,366,778.00	16,403.85	3,635.73	3,487.61
Sterling	2,105,288.00	18,458.85	585,100.00	7,805.56	2,973.44	3,983.44
United States	4,736,658.00	84,121.28	3,331,501.00	62,512.58	14,734.71	14,141.45
Virginia Fire and Marine	8,085,128.00	58,385.46	4,915,982.00	36,230.45	18,704.15	19,656.94
Totals	438,615,235.20	4,070,552.91	275,280,167.69	2,779,003.78	1,064,952.38	1,873,487.80

COMPANIES OF OTHER STATES (MUTUAL).

Name						
...ht Mal	1,292,762.00	10,671.89	1,236,142.00	2,706.75	185.37	67.48
Baltimore Mal	445,744.00	3,795.79	367,014.00	899.36	50.98	50.98
Blackstone Mal	770,685.00	6,307.36	739,655.00	3,444.10	172.41	86.14
Consolidated Underwriters				55,675.37	22,772.12	22,772.12
...an and Win M	2,100,752.00	20,225.35	1,804,902.00	1,884.74	144.66	144.66
Druggists Indemnity	163,296.00	2,675.51	143,646.00	1,225.79	4,600.00	5,650.00
Firemen's M	1,735,443.00	13,947.90	1,584,048.00	13,199.69	273.15	273.15
...ng M	308,050.00	5,742.33	152,175.00	5,144.77	50.46	50.46
...he Mutual	1,687,722.00	15,967.98	1,472,062.00	14,948.92	49.06	49.06
Indiana Lumbermen's Mal	665,210.00	22,430.38	598,910.00	14,031.58	5,382.80	5,382.80
Individual Underwriters Mal	301,175.00	2,722.43	301,175.00	1,592.75		
Industrial Mal	1,453,948.00	13,981.00	1,254,458.00	1,326.38	93.34	93.34
...he Mal M	1,473,901.00	18,382.59	1,120,151.00	2,793.39	73.26	73.26
Lumber U (M	553,968.00	9,969.15	264,855.00	6,015.88	3,744.29	3,744.29
Lumber Manufacturers Interinsurance	635,547.00	13,359.65	436,896.00	7,389.25	5,798.83	5,672.20
Lumber Mutual M	1,114,646.23	37,739.89	938,752.77	33,701.38	8,241.06	8,104.83
Lumbermen's M	781,232.00	24,205.39	691,595.00	22,151.30	3,560.20	3,560.20
Lumbermen's Underwriters Alliance	722,450.00	16,578.30	619,850.00	12,093.29	5,722.11	5,722.11
...Mn Mutual	1,766,726.00	17,628.83	1,464,676.00	2,093.69	76.57	76.57
...ng M Underwriters	2,139,154.00	51,539.91	1,521,618.00	31,398.02	17,466.08	17,466.08
Manufacturing Mrs Underwriters	572,150.00	12,685.68	352,000.00	8,067.71	12,038.00	12,038.00
...de Mal	458,377.00	3,746.38	436,489.00	998.79	102.51	48.97
...de Mal	1,378,045.00	12,654.15	1,168,685.00	2,396.18	127.23	127.23
...M Mutual	204,275.00	2,779.78	186,575.00	2,465.65	38.10	38.10
...lan Millers Mutual	741,076.00	5,611.82	499,060.00	4,706.43	1,661.13	1,951.93
Millers Mal	149,150.00	32,192.00	145,150.00	31,742.00	2,179.00	2,179.00
...Mrs Indemnity Underwriters		7,610.36		5,327.1	448.67	1,911.15
Narragansett Mutual	845,870.00	6,959.34	720,200.00	1,028.24	107.81	107.81
N mal M	523,556.00	6,653.30	409,346.00	878.68	7.26	17.76
...Mal Lumber	317,500.00	6,490.95	278,500.00	5,599.35	4,909.93	
Penn Lumbermen's Mal	1,069,385.00	34,736.36	990,535.00	31,873.20	6,617.41	6,617.41
Philadelphia Mrs Mal	1,740,106.00	15,271.34	1,513,146.00	3,299.69	114.01	114.01
Reciprocal Exchange Mrs M	538,475.00	7,547.12	488,475.00	4,483.61	925.00	75.00
Rubber Mrs M	2,091,452.00	20,116.94	1,801,002.00	1,877.54	136.82	136.82
Southern Lumber Underwriters	335,250.00	6,801.85	229,750.00	4,883.31	34.48	34.48
Utilities Indemnity M		417.98		353.67	150.00	166.60
...Mn Reciprocal Underwriters	77,250.00	844.00	61,810.00	844.00		
...Mat Cheer M	1,701,075.00	16,021.76	1,482,915.00	14,989.23	177.91	177.91
...Mrs Interinsurers (Grocers' Dept.)	326,200.00	4,615.15	296,200.00	3,129.66	10,000.00	10,000.00
Totals	33,181,603.23	567,303.26	27,772,418.77	362,660.45	118,242.52	114,781.91

TABLE No. VII—NORTH CAROLINA BUSINESS, 1917.

SHOWING RISKS WRITTEN, PREMIUMS RECEIVED, LOSSES PAID, LOSSES INCURRED IN NORTH CAROLINA FOR THE YEAR ENDING DECEMBER 31, 1917, BY FIRE, MARINE AND INLAND INSURANCE COMPANIES.

COMPANIES OF FOREIGN COUNTRIES.

Name of Company	Gross Risks Written	Gross Premiums Received	Net Risks Written	Net Premiums Received	Net Losses Paid	Net Losses Incurred
	Fire Business					
??e	$ 1,034,818.00	$ 11,331.07	$ 733,489.00	$ 8,639.91	$ 2,723.12	$ 3,079.62
Atlas	7,617,552.00	44,881.66	3,981,694.00	29,831.22	15,828.84	15,009.84
?n	66,910,264.00	514,597.14	35,076,177.00	299,494.77	231,293.21	313,809.21
Brtish	1,938,663.00	27,823.51	1,483,841.00	22,420.47	6,493.03	9,239.16
?n	1,183,190.00	14,501.87	584,836.00	8,267.42	4,690.92	5,528.87
?al Union	793,722.00	10,233.91	639,670.00	8,710.61	7,085.06	7,320.44
Fire Reassurance	6,514,920.00	56,182.74	3,984,162.00	35,035.22	17,684.01	19,733.85
Fit ?n	3,300,838.00	27,567.20	2,384,808.00	20,305.95	10,108.06	9,613.06
?n	3,533,902.00	27,467.48	2,488,336.00	20,597.83	9,554.98	10,657.98
Hamburg-Bremen	1,543,557.00	25,444.96	872,523.00	15,493.23	10,133.72	5,503.72
Jakor	12,039,582.00	80,350.74	4,307,447.00	31,304.59	15,483.63	18,029.77
?ol nd London and Gl be	25,856,998.00	288,650.13	21,517,633.00	234,546.46	104,636.34	120,667.34
?n nd Lancashire	4,048,110.00	61,855.01	2,958,175.00	48,094.10	15,196.79	12,761.79
?n	8,425,947.00	50,011.75	4,495,183.00	29,525.01	11,036.02	13,526.22
Mw	4,023,902.00	34,922.61	3,219,121.00	27,456.85	10,491.94	10,354.94
Nal	995,600.00	5,638.30	855,761.00	4,791.66	45.38	1,213.88
Nnle (Paris)	3,677,655.00	38,658.88	1,100,234.00	12,959.87	4,084.71	4,619.44
Ms Fire and Life	438,637.00	6,142.05	294,477.00	4,182.41	1,360.13	1,474.65
Nord-Deutsche	1,339,291.00	17,398.88	544,319.00	9,253.53	6,495.86	2,885.99
Norsk Lloyd	2,163,659.00	18,842.89	1,804,383.00	16,360.75	9,771.00	12,593.35
?th British and ??	11,136,994.00	67,218.09	5,951,843.00	41,193.86	22,750.65	23,606.66
?n A ?e	9,817,553.00	61,338.85	4,893,601.00	37,707.04	19,313.65	26,186.91
?n (Moscow)	1,426,515.00	12,853.81	1,192,104.00	10,486.66	2,604.17	2,604.17
?n ?e	1,036,974.00	5,322.95	812,319.00	4,023.92	185.69	910.81
N ?h ?n	7,516,453.00	36,449.84	3,568,820.00	21,250.44	7,319.66	8,788.32
Paternelle	2,447,529.00	27,882.90	1,100,234.00	12,959.87	4,084.68	4,619.44
Phenix Fre (?n)	2,134,133.00	18,282.74	1,192,849.00	11,888.63	4,841.79	4,076.79
Palatine (?on)	10,143,919.00	48,327.14	5,291,150.00	24,445.85	10,576.98	11,310.98
Phoenix	12,981,835.00	123,153.77	7,343,392.00	41,920.85	49,059.39	47,476.39
Rossia						

RECAPITULATION.

North Carolina Companies	77,591,986.00	1,265,983.98	38,018,697.00	748,805.11	285,764.98	304,071.70
Companies of other States (stock)	438,615,235.20	4,070,552.91	275,280,167.69	2,779,003.78	1,064,952.38	1,873,487.80
Companies of other States (mutual)	33,181,603.23	567,303.26	27,772,418.77	362,660.45	118,242.52	114,781.91
Companies of foreign countries	301,987,720.00	2,426,383.01	172,706,067.00	1,504,288.22	795,850.22	919,861.26
Totals	851,376,544.43	8,330,223.22	513,777,350.46	5,394,757.56	2,264,810.10	3,212,202.67

xxix)

STATISTICAL TABLES

RELATING TO LIFE INSURANCE COMPANIES

Name of Company	Premiums
Ætna Life	$ 17,377,586.14
Atlantic Life	1,195,435.95
American Central	1,264,186.48
American National	2,309,404.59
Business Men's Mutual	
Columbian National	2,513,989.56
Connecticut Mutual	8,626,128.73
Durham Life	350,150.42
Equitable Life	64,004,005.69
Fidelity Mutual	5,212,288.12
Gate City Life and Health	167,670.70
George Washington	339,189.45
Guardian Life	6,656,204.01
Home Life of New York	4,872,966.32
Home Security	82,817.20
Imperial Mutual Life and Health	182,865.47
Jefferson Standard	2,150,497.15
LaFayette Mutual	34,072.91
Life Insurance Company of Virginia	4,404,121.90
Manhattan Life	1,707,988.06
Life and Casualty	1,368,976.11
Maryland Life	451,024.28
Maryland Assurance	
Massachusetts Mutual	14,619,930.66
Merchants Life	1,031,633.78
Metropolitan	138,455,648.75
Michigan Mutual	1,700,646.75
Missouri State	5,087,382.16
Morris Plan Life	1,093.60
Mutual Benefit Life	32,071,307.70
Mutual Life	64,751,710.72
National Life of America	3,019,442.26
National Life of Vermont	8,197,856.92
New England Mutual	12,340,506.56
New York Life	103,444,086.59
North Carolina Mutual and Provident	606,697.86
Northwestern Mutual Life	55,157,828.41
Ohio National	352,550.49
Pacific Mutual	6,697,634.34
Pan-American	1,582,842.86
Penn Mutual	27,687,561.31
Philadelphia Life	1,125,213.42
Phœnix Mutual Life	7,517,764.55
Provident Life and Trust	14,010,446.55
Prudential of America	111,336,383.43
Reliance Life	2,698,388.62
Reserve Loan Life	1,677,161.87
Security Mutual Life	1,854,087.31
Southern Life and Trust	713,062.12
State Life	2,943,765.59
State Mutual of Massachusetts	7,602,067.08
Travelers Life	16,618,937.99
Union Central Life	17,911,478.20
Union Mutual Life and Health	1,059.47
United Life and Accident	267,834.93
Volunteer State Life	796,985.02
Totals	789,152,567.11

NCOME.

O BUSINESS IN THIS STATE) FOR THE YEAR ENDING DECEMBER 31, 1917.

Interest and Rents	All Other Sources	Total Income	Income Over Disbursements	Disbursements Over Income
5,617,069.11	$ 582,192.10	$ 23,576,847.35	$ 5,314,576.49	$............
231,565.92	25,411.30	1,452,413.17	664,387.23	....
326,692.74	11,811.64	1,602,690.86	479,424.70	....
285,878.79	505,551.24	3,100,834.62	884,038.41	....
644,797.49	407,854.71	3,566,641.76	1,343,490.06	....
3,734,813.61	474,583.25	12,835,525.59	2,755,366.50	....
4,921.78	840.48	355,912.68	40,007.14	....
25,845,988.19	3,431,223.45	93,281,217.33	14,409,668.12	....
1,769,618.35	98,960.09	7,080,866.56	2,279,426.77	....
2,630.43	167.32	170,468.45	26,227.38	....
96,331.30	5,054.49	440,575.24	174,625.04	....
2,642,769.04	153,053.22	9,452,026.27	1,229,641.25	....
1,620,295.65	131,664.09	6,624,926.06	1,862,189.80	....
2,876.09	....	85,693.29	....	7,418.67
1,282.91	127.00	184,275.38	14,196.58	....
448,629.18	16,820.19	2,615,946.52	1,141,420.68	....
1,959.91	4,062.92	40,095.74	21,377.37	....
839,945.29	47,506.65	5,291,573.84	1,872,840.28	....
1,047,686.07	32,210.04	2,787,884.17	....	296,107.08
30,631.01	5,922.60	1,405,529.72	98,610.74	....
183,516.65	7,907.46	642,448.39	85,616.05	....
....	445,000.00	445,000.00	289,661.15	....
4,606,074.03	1,009,258.14	20,235,262.83	7,407,863.84	....
97,587.89	560,681.68	1,689,903.35	743,664.14	....
31,021,179.83	24,215,087.02	193,691,915.60	94,106,582.62	....
655,388.09	18,492.05	2,374,526.89	355,028.44	....
971,260.13	73,735.20	6,132,377.49	2,754,821.10	....
....	103,976.28	105,069.88	90,537.84	....
10,130,857.61	1,180,170.55	43,382,335.86	16,094,671.11	....
29,676,089.56	2,033,269.42	96,461,069.70	12,033,294.96	....
728,891.59	51,060.50	3,799,394.35	946,963.35	....
3,227,548.50	142,176.86	11,567,582.28	2,685,489.26	....
3,648,552.22	207,122.24	16,196,181.02	5,547,477.52	....
39,957,421.84	3,166,755.03	146,568,263.46	36,606,682.93	....
14,834.54	3,261.91	624,794.31	100,878.61	....
18,529,621.32	1,806,255.78	75,493,705.51	22,544,317.08	....
73,435.94	39,229.87	465,216.30	177,322.95	....
2,129,604.47	128,753.98	8,955,992.79	5,758,119.19	....
323,969.46	334,622.44	2,241,434.76	632,340.77	....
8,567,903.56	899,711.68	37,155,176.55	11,533,049.78	....
296,613.88	59,501.68	1,481,328.98	576,100.04	....
2,237,751.78	472,525.71	10,228,042.04	3,472,458.54	....
4,381,167.75	342,418.76	18,734,033.06	4,146,482.41	....
21,197,478.97	1,219,083.36	133,755,945.76	47,009,190.87	....
331,593.91	145,888.30	3,175,870.83	1,101,675.43	....
215,192.59	43,266.28	1,935,620.74	28,081.98	....
389,141.10	26,550.46	2,269,778.87	647,183.43	....
105,258.05	1,964.85	820,285.02	341,505.35	....
1,023,067.52	33,047.16	3,999,880.27	1,410,066.53	....
2,480,185.65	295,569.46	10,377,822.19	3,553,217.22	....
4,475,726.97	1,897,259.82	22,991,924.78	9,244,754.41	....
7,190,045.75	879,399.10	25,980,923.05	6,495,144.51	....
189.68	....	1,249.15	100.22	....
63,486.33	7,951.83	339,273.09	73,217.78	....
154,816.27	29,620.05	981,421.34	458,576.56	....
244,281,836.29	47,818,591.69	1,081,252,995.09	333,663,652.51	....

Name of Company	Death and Endowment Claims	Annuities, Surrender Values, Dividends, etc., Paid to Policyholders	Total Paid to Policyholders
Ætna Life	$ 8,978,042.44	$ 4,161,407.11	$ 13,139,449.55
Atlantic Life	170,735.79	183,537.34	354,273.13
American Central	251,859.40	386,338.89	638,198.29
American National	641,745.36	110,022.31	751,767.67
Business Men's Mutual			
Columbian National	537,533.29	369,384.79	906,918.08
Connecticut Mutual	4,620,899.61	2,633,507.15	7,254,406.76
Durham Life	136,909.25	7,755.96	144,665.21
Equitable Life	33,997,181.93	28,833,990.45	62,831,172.38
Fidelity Mutual	1,631,690.01	1,816,390.57	3,448,080.58
Gate City Life and Health	59,534.26		59,534.26
George Washington	59,845.57	59,586.73	119,432.30
Guardian Life	3,523,486.19	2,403,811.30	5,927,297.49
Home Life of New York	1,905,989.85	1,561,833.59	3,467,823.44
Home Security	30,183.00		30,183.00
Imperial Mutual Life and Health	63,171.24		63,171.24
Jefferson Standard	404,093.92	272,982.74	677,076.66
LaFayette Mutual	3,749.00	958.34	4,707.34
Life Insurance Company of Virginia	1,326,254.20	167,189.38	1,493,443.58
Life and Casualty	486,944.49	2,498.86	489,443.35
Manhattan Life	1,287,869.46	1,030,761.57	2,318,631.03
Maryland Life	208,222.54	172,947.32	381,169.86
Maryland Assurance			
Massachusetts Mutual	4,507,627.31	4,663,353.97	9,170,981.28
Merchants Life	463,021.94	18,903.07	481,925.01
Metropolitan	44,157,100.79	14,635,839.27	58,792,940.06
Michigan Mutual	992,345.56	433,704.45	1,426,050.01
Missouri State	895,520.63	538,464.14	1,433,984.77
Morris Plan Life			
Mutual Benefit Life	10,335,652.97	10,358,786.65	20,694,439.62
Mutual Life	33,424,955.63	36,604,208.87	70,029,164.50
National Life of America	1,029,543.83	642,784.25	1,672,328.08
National Life of Vermont	3,536,753.99	3,476,331.84	7,013,085.83
New England Mutual	4,412,960.63	3,398,977.99	7,811,938.62
New York Life	44,216,465.54	42,722,172.38	86,938,637.92
North Carolina Mutual and Provident	231,283.83	6,580.17	237,864.00
Northwestern Mutual Life	20,975,456.88	20,845,051.99	41,820,508.87
Ohio National	87,925.61	18,107.65	106,033.26
Pacific Mutual	1,821,332.00	1,777,497.82	3,598,829.82
Pan-American	240,230.01	329,582.01	569,812.02
Penn Mutual	10,570,652.84	8,706,362.03	19,277,014.57
Philadelphia Life	274,762.87	176,695.78	451,458.65
Phœnix Mutual	2,753,779.38	2,046,554.14	4,800,333.52
Provident Life and Trust	5,933,624.19	3,920,624.24	9,854,248.43
Prudential of America	33,668,672.46	16,801,570.77	50,470,243.23
Reliance Life	463,094.07	291,933.97	755,028.04
Reserve Loan Life	233,542.45	1,209,057.55	1,442,600.00
Security Mutual Life	609,561.55	366,035.06	975,596.61
Southern Life and Trust	89,293.84	89,512.16	178,806.00
State Life	870,489.15	788,407.79	1,658,896.94
State Mutual of Massachusetts	2,620,811.83	2,421,637.80	5,042,449.63
Travelers Life	5,793,044.72	1,429,164.96	7,222,209.68
Union Central Life	7,948,654.07	6,142,713.09	14,091,367.16
Union Mutual Life and Health	474.10		474.10
United Life and Accident	83,232.75	14,391.75	97,624.50
Volunteer State Life	145,105.24	92,500.46	237,605.70
Totals	303,712,913.46	229,142,412.47	532,855,325.93

DISBURSEMENTS.

DO BUSINESS IN THIS STATE) FOR THE YEAR ENDING DECEMBER 31, 1917.

Supplementary Contracts, Dividends to Stockholders, etc.	Commissions, Agency Expenses, Medical Examiners' Fees, etc.	Salaries, Rents, Advertising, Printing, etc.	Department License, Fees and Taxes	Miscellaneous Items	Total Disbursements
$ 580,597.08	$ 2,154,936.48	$ 958,850.04	$ 204,480.64	$ 1,223,957.07	$ 18,262,270.86
800.00	287,612.40	77,988.89	23,779.77	43,571.75	788,025.94
12,727.48	235,090.48	128,555.69	18,370.59	90,323.63	1,123,266.16
26,518.24	546,623.09	169,676.60	27,111.31	695,099.30	2,216,796.21
77,664.89	311,718.09	204,122.74	39,660.17	683,067.73	2,223,151.70
60,688.97	982,892.16	446,600.84	103,486.56	1,232,083.80	10,080,159.09
----	10,209.23	25,644.31	785.70	134,601.09	315,905.54
1,535,150.34	6,958,774.13	2,665,813.09	698,767.47	4,181,871.80	78,871,549.21
40,246.63	594,321.93	337,569.55	83,817.00	297,404.10	4,801,439.79
2,000.00	59,480.55	16,799.21	562.84	5,864.21	144,241.07
10,382.78	64,019.23	45,629.93	3,811.81	22,674.15	265,950.20
104,893.47	770,055.87	397,318.49	64,514.75	892,996.63	8,157,076.70
26,227.50	647,973.95	322,726.98	68,911.98	229,072.41	4,762,736.26
----	53,215.58	7,652.68	219.39	1,841.31	93,111.96
----	7,386.35	20,857.93	408.40	78,254.88	170,078.80
73,381.84	500,088.82	125,108.88	17,333.58	81,536.06	1,474,525.84
----	11,689.34	2,005.90	179.70	136.09	18,718.37
177,687.00	878,490.47	368,400.49	70,819.31	429,892.71	3,418,733.56
46,000.00	497,974.06	72,789.20	12,333.72	188,378.65	1,306,918.98
21,741.89	161,426.97	203,432.93	29,801.69	348,956.74	3,083,991.25
7,000.00	75,981.88	38,906.69	7,548.41	46,225.50	556,832.34
----	----	----	----	155,338.85	155,338.85
116,141.52	2,254,039.41	685,659.50	169,511.53	431,065.75	12,827,398.99
250.00	130,081.74	77,037.27	20,002.31	236,942.88	946,239.21
332,830.77	7,422,298.85	7,568,048.57	1,668,651.01	23,800,563.72	99,585,332.98
45,258.41	299,461.16	136,895.78	27,144.11	84,688.98	2,019,498.45
65,682.32	1,269,449.39	308,606.65	73,037.47	226,795.79	3,377,556.39
----	2,427.30	6,072.08	202.00	5,830.66	14,532.04
635,756.13	3,715,540.74	793,362.66	367,611.75	1,080,953.85	27,287,664.75
534,687.06	6,505,266.02	2,819,109.49	757,203.27	3,782,344.40	84,427,774.74
63,679.20	597,828.10	236,181.19	44,395.10	238,019.33	2,852,431.00
35,938.73	980,997.31	364,716.86	117,934.11	369,420.18	8,882,093.02
91,301.69	1,571,907.30	461,046.11	184,012.12	528,497.66	10,648,903.50
788,260.99	9,730,955.24	3,372,986.04	1,070,579.37	8,060,160.97	109,961,580.53
----	214,904.95	40,623.20	6,570.61	23,952.94	523,915.70
704,381.48	6,077,610.32	1,511,538.13	555,035.34	2,280,314.29	52,949,388.43
----	92,835.84	29,516.08	1,126.52	58,381.65	287,893.35
114,053.96	1,028,676.12	517,934.53	102,597.41	396,027.35	5,758,119.19
81,542.50	452,785.01	137,878.69	25,098.38	341,977.39	1,609,093.99
429,437.37	347,715.16	1,028,145.64	390,995.65	4,148,818.08	25,622,126.77
33,869.20	217,890.05	122,997.99	13,110.31	65,902.74	905,228.94
43,356.90	840,130.28	373,227.88	86,640.74	611,894.18	6,755,583.50
87,349.96	1,596,293.93	839,934.51	176,047.08	2,033,676.74	14,587,550.65
1,020,593.27	18,204,510.32	5,735,264.31	1,509,931.35	9,806,212.41	86,746,754.89
83,350.00	731,893.02	136,723.04	43,218.60	323,982.70	2,074,195.40
10,029.20	304,199.00	100,088.13	17,007.96	33,614.47	1,907,538.76
4,193.01	246,581.52	155,336.23	29,991.66	210,896.41	1,622,595.44
8,592.82	180,552.11	76,895.93	4,047.95	29,884.86	478,779.67
9,670.57	521,484.47	200,483.92	46,580.18	152,697.66	2,589,813.74
42,907.21	924,600.74	303,831.52	74,587.43	436,228.44	6,824,604.97
1,115,345.09	2,433,874.80	943,263.87	204,617.64	1,827,859.29	13,747,170.37
355,874.93	2,288,549.68	905,113.58	45,727.17	1,799,146.02	19,485,778.54
----	47.02	160.20	69.84	397.77	1,148.93
----	78,083.53	49,123.91	6,021.27	35,202.10	266,055.31
18,123.94	159,698.76	64,068.93	10,514.97	32,832.48	522,844.78
9,676,166.34	87,233,130.25	36,738,323.48	9,326,527.00	74,558,332.60	750,387,805.60

SHOWING THE ASSETS OF LIFE INSURANCE COMPANIES (LICENSED TO DO

Name of Company	Value of Real Estate	Mortgage Loans	Collateral Loans	Premium Notes and Policy Loans
Ætna Life	$ 1,112,981.92	$ 58,665,748.56	$12,717,353.51	$ 74,742.90
Atlantic Life	14,015.08	3,074,395.41	675,367.55	40,985.29
American Central	504,361.65	3,781,570.25	1,221,187.75	
American National	856,877.30	2,653,228.75	496,009.39	
Business Men's Mutual				
Columbian National	1,029,892.81	2,005,971.64	2,009,117.84	130,627.40
Connecticut Mutual	2,370,847.72	38,127,242.53	8,736,178.66	109,999.01
Durham Life	19,303.98	52,235.00		128.58
Equitable Life	19,895,565.26	112,870,908.73	92,584,104.96	
Fidelity Mutual	1,580,686.40	14,967,087.69	6,909,854.50	421,945.34
Gate City Life and Health		61,280.00		
George Washington	26,076.04	877,279.49	308,449.68	36,832.55
Guardian Life	5,412,224.76	25,559,979.10	7,450,617.66	
Home Life of New York	1,500,000.00	7,021,650.00	5,326,703.02	751,465.14
Home Security		50,000.00		
Imperial Mutual Life and Health				
Jefferson Standard	276,481.06	5,017,298.63	1,536,481.95	327,399.49
LaFayette Mutual		31,550.00	5,041.52	
Life Insurance Company of Virginia	467,607.57	13,286,905.46	636,451.57	1,432.31
Manhattan Life	4,892,733.54	5,661,861.30	3,972,715.78	150,598.90
Life and Casualty	97,300.00	316,300.22	7,000.00	
Maryland Life	232,500.00	205,756.36	500,030.44	16,590.73
Maryland Assurance				
Massachusetts Mutual	1,107,375.15	37,587,200.57	14,507,578.41	1,391,844.54
Merchants Life		2,191,913.92	69,047.99	4,362.86
Metropolitan	25,518,094.11	266,535,469.96	47,901,070.02	6,922,837.41
Michigan Mutual	86,747.75	10,389,464.91	1,820,383.71	57,268.81
Missouri State	335,998.56	11,599,380.80	2,543,971.22	117,922.85
Morris Plan Life				
Mutual Benefit Life	2,859,938.81	106,345,221.05	42,442,904.30	
Mutual Life	18,866,170.76	109,834,056.64	88,170,554.98	
National Life of America	69,500.92	6,098,651.43	2,757,305.53	200,213.10
National Life of Vermont	248,000.00	31,966,646.98	8,493,775.89	2,067,772.48
New England Mutual	1,808,017.00	16,493,008.03	12,928,737.35	1,022,555.14
New York Life	15,888,000.00	166,687,476.31	156,049,998.27	4,481,373.01
N. C. Mutual and Provident	56,656.50	35,844.98	7,618.26	
Northwestern Mutual Life	4,082,905.94	207,139,244.87	57,309,037.42	1,733,908.33
Ohio National		1,218,960.00	44,559.33	2,533.15
Pacific Mutual	1,813,100.73	21,413,088.41	8,505,864.76	974,405.67
Pan-American	122,534.09	3,170,240.98	955,802.94	41,238.21
Penn Mutual	3,130,693.43	73,719,672.56	26,388,103.11	6,414,695.60
Philadelphia Life	589,510.83	2,270,600.00	1,070,122.28	26,416.64
Phœnix Mutual Life	737,053.39	26,961,978.34	6,217,242.52	33,041.98
Provident Life and Trust	859,790.85	27,100,890.53	14,628,267.04	200.98
Prudential of America	19,496,490.73	129,635,655.47	41,502,332.38	
Reliance Life	163,596.40	960,692.86	779,407.74	433,736.36
Reserve Loan Life	97,250.00	2,511,904.85	1,227,504.28	12,290.60
Security Mutual Life	738,644.85	2,712,650.00	1,551,147.69	47,766.83
Southern Life and Trust		1,295,099.80	422,648.64	
State Life	1,059,427.27	10,540,569.33	4,541,156.12	57,050.56
State Mutual of Massachusetts	1,738,000.00	17,927,662.06	8,165,460.56	13,973.00
Travelers Life	3,233,492.93	39,326,381.43	13,378,779.03	
Union Central Life	2,712,109.21	90,550,720.12	18,431,742.65	2,077,921.96
Union Mutual Life and Health		21,562.83		
United Life and Accident	17,150.94	659,652.57	107,718.34	1,915.05
Volunteer State Life	402,730.91	1,267,644.76	702,010.07	11,114.96
Totals	148,128,437.15	1,720,457,456.47	728,714,518.61	30,211,107.72

*Minus.

ASSETS.

Value of Bonds and Stocks	Cash in Office, Banks, and Deposited with Trust Companies	Accrued Interest and Dividends	Unpaid and Deferred Premiums	Other Assets Less Deductions	Total Admitted Assets
$ 43,322,762.84	$ 3,657,878.36	$ 2,610,772.87	$ 1,554,190.32	$ 10,767.47	$ 123,727,198.75
151,585.61	148,303.44	48,910.09	59,737.35	2,537.50	4,215,837.32
154,300.00	99,711.27	102,101.10	103,791.38	*908.55	5,966,114.85
487,431.00	400,431.10	180,343.92	83,981.89	48,450.78	5,206,754.13
----------	1,882.03	----------	----------	----------	1,882.03
7,836,040.01	393,822.33	209,656.46	222,630 76	70,936.78	13,908,696 03
25,855,864.00	1,579,417.06	1,610,634.75	934,163.75	405,702.40	79,730,049.88
31,600.00	21,495.27	2,384.42	1,999.95	----------	129,147.20
328,566,748.73	9,288,449.43	7,188,711.92	6,317,016.33	125,838.27	576,837,343.63
9,085,146 99	595,469.67	448,461.84	455,859.46	*14,208.66	34,450,303.23
----------	16,395.04	1,079.04	27.06	3,078.08	81,859.22
173,875 00	61,051.31	18,446.50	26,503.46	*915.40	1,527,598.63
12,430,856 95	1,036,894.46	775,396 07	1,570,016 49	513,832.03	54,749,817.52
18,600,573.50	507,834.30	299,642.09	534,586.12	*150.09	34,542,304.08
----------	1,851.69	377.73	1,140.72	1,148.21	54,518.35
36,500.00	5,795.42	805.00	----------	1,090.60	44,191.02
418,475.00	621,934.07	119,882.10	153,625.11	*7,172.31	8,464,405.10
1,500.00	3,073.77	822.40	2,334.20	17,655.85	61,977.74
1,084,083.15	645,589.57	231,737.15	147,612.69	59,019.57	16,560,439.04
3,850,350.00	327,877.53	411,125.83	141,748.77	10,431.45	19,419,443.10
18,976.88	55,322.23	4,112.08	----------	1,968.60	500,980.01
2,577,783.25	106,066.14	38,100.76	36,084.06	*1,756.39	3,711,155.35
676,642.68	113,018.47	9,585.41	----------	----------	799,246 56
41,787,678 81	865,820.43	1,638,048.71	1,875,458.21	7,575.00	100,768,579.83
110,815.00	190,872.03	69,778.96	86,087.29	*651.39	2,722,226.66
322,292,663.04	6,641,925.15	10,377,519.00	13,499,710.17	4,336,226.45	704,025,515.31
105,000.00	401,843.20	177,170.53	137,777.58	19,005.01	13,194,661.50
318,777.85	1,187,002.33	461,263.04	433,957.63	26,793.43	17,025,067.71
101,729.11	88,408.73	2,250.00	176.25	----------	192,564.09
56,392,891.95	4,238,727.23	4,033,147.56	3,071,209.55	*5,305.99	219,378,734.46
400,820,386.14	1,814,088.16	8,404,972 05	4,964,690.77	1,124,649.87	633,999,569.37
4,900,592.62	595,109.63	164,365.83	291,551.71	182,939.02	15,260,229.79
22,567,598.48	732,425.60	1,603,465.85	912,159.46	*1,136.52	68,590,708 22
49,123,627.00	948,009 93	1,111,988.30	773,742 40	339,602.00	84,549,287.15
550,273,280.89	15,566,342.97	13,402,035.66	12,275,741.18	305,133.23	934,929,381.52
196,800.00	9,484.83	2,442.08	32,317.32	17,200 00	358,363.97
110,408,459.06	1,736,706.66	6,278,902.22	4,695,341.65	149,417.45	393,533,922.60
27,151.34	84,164.03	13,231.48	45,616 33	----------	1,436,215.66
4,205,627.94	1,438,397.88	634,409 50	665,021 34	*3,007.26	39,646,908 97
1,391,066.12	207,035.56	105,989.11	103,413.58	12,571.46	6,109,892.05
64,015,536.70	3,142,693.84	2,557,218.96	3,710,808.56	11,077.54	183,090,500.30
1,161,319.34	345,350.10	83,627.19	72,020.00	37,391.23	5,656,357.61
9,476,939.10	1,051,895 37	823,125.47	580,940.49	59,379.25	45,941,595.91
49,660,031.48	371,975.42	1,274,985.46	1,756,510.36	1,906,347.65	97,558,999.77
256,094,054.79	13,624,746.31	6,208,366.34	8,379,177.06	431,091.19	475,371,914.27
3,990,057.81	734,087.63	82,927.05	355,447.51	50,549 01	7,550,502.37
72,495.60	152,265.71	53,859.53	61,165.60	*320.19	4,188,415 98
2,920,217.00	307,056.90	149,452.39	211,461.15	123,355.15	8,761,751.96
58,387.50	225,151.96	32,309.30	68,296.12	593,321 81	2,695,215.13
1,764,430.00	413,726.99	217,027.03	178,520.96	148,759.65	18,920,667.91
24,778,535.08	782,303.10	774,975.77	1,057,388.41	2,534.00	55,240,831.98
36,106,083.20	3,376,437.81	1,461,108.89	2,255,443.28	678,151.30	99,815,877 87
1,320,546.00	1,452,996.94	4,090,204.27	755,085.17	8,121.19	121,399,447.51
1,800.00	2,072.90	280.00	----------	----------	25,715 73
417,031.44	32,745.22	25,647.72	23,909.92	1,582.44	1,287,353.64
414,989.50	192,017.51	47,616.33	69,671.99	*1,082.10	3,106,713.93
2,472,637,695.48	82,643,452.02	80,676,801.11	75,746,868.87	11,808,617.07	5,351,024,954 50

(xlvii)

Name of Company	Net Reserve	Value Supplementary Contracts and Liability on Canceled Policies	Unpaid Policy Claims	Premiums, Interest and Rents Paid. in Advance
Ætna Life	$ 101,544,616.00	$ 898,828.98	$ 708,479.49	$ 360,717.54
Atlantic Life	3,223,327.22	8,386.40	11,691.00	24,695.10
American Central	5,222,513.91	18,138.87	36,841.00	40,277.61
American National	3,689,258.52	12,890.67	28,720.01	14,597.68
Business Men's Mutual				
Columbian National	11,530,412.00	102,078.65	80,805.30	49,896.89
Connecticut Mutual	70,655,163.34	469,310.82	402,098.62	219,890.97
Durham Life	59,815.00		251.50	12,433.17
Equitable Life	467,522,041.00	4,052,473.04	4,554,513.37	2,478,420.79
Fidelity Mutual	29,246,199.00	404,916.29	180,385.08	221,672.01
Gate City Life and Health	26,542.00		110.00	2,568.20
George Washington	1,183,370.34	2,978.47	13,000.00	11,040.00
Guardian Life	47,056,417.00	173,922.67	581,487.88	143,100.03
Home Life of New York	31,819,110.00	236,846.80	132,940.20	196,892.11
Home Security	3,101.00			1,232.45
Imperial Mutual Life and Health	20,478.00		208.00	1,361.70
Jefferson Standard	6,519,243.00	52,893.56	60,108.67	53,570.44
LaFayette Mutual	55,570.00		2,000.00	507.10
Life Insurance Company of Virginia	13,730,513.00	45,602.00	61,191.79	89,979.55
Life and Casualty	176,057.53		2,902.90	27,884.76
Manhattan Life	18,366,459.00	122,032.00	142,625.53	99,980.15
Maryland Life	3,143,779.13	787.96	17,950.79	2,374.46
Maryland Assurance				
Massachusetts Mutual	87,915,767.00	1,238,041.27	268,906.49	123,259.81
Merchants Life	1,400,952 00	5,319.00	37,500.00	19,714.20
Metropolitan	644,603,968.00	1,033,656 54	2,085,230.10	2,169,614.84
Michigan Mutual	11,806,253.45	42,535.71	89,818.35	32,103 17
Missouri State	13,296,791.85	42,721.54	143,532.07	89,880.96
Morris Plan Life	163.57			856.25
Mutual Benefit Life	196,091,555.00	4,724,372.00	799,740.07	459,852.46
Mutual Life	521,060,090.00	4,718,024.33	7,313,330.01	1,240,107.23
National Life of America	13,190,524.88	115,592.84	81,331.66	86,251.37
National Life of Vermont	57,505,259.00	402,896.18	208,777.84	10,054.82
New England Mutual	74,370,877.73	826,513.71	346,646.16	146,763.69
New York Life	728,484,785.00	5,930,683.97	10,350,318.67	4,230,294.35
N. C. Mutual and Provident	258,918.00		1,678.70	1,270.93
Northwestern Mutual Life	348,110,148.00	6,845,553.68	1,279,207.60	31,066.36
Ohio National	685,882.00	4,838 00	5,500.00	6,182.99
Pacific Mutual	34,108,961.00	142,810 00	245,126.22	223,906.33
Pan-American	4,062,767.76	14,447.44	86,327.25	13,939.60
Penn Mutual	151,637,443.00	4,133,799.89	712,553.58	609,290.49
Philadelphia Life	4,522,730.00	26,338 33	64,532.00	31,608.06
Phœnix Mutual	40,593,987.00	319,713.53	104,301 86	162,029.78
Provident Life and Trust	86,046,958.00	1,029,166.23	413,689 30	543,562.01
Prudential of America	413,058,936.00	1,946,832.46	- 2,630,202.66	2,803,626.84
Reliance Life	5,990,264.00	39,274.89	19,089.23	20,016.20
Reserve Loan Life	3,584,911.78	13,021.16	33,829.05	27,878.34
Security Mutual Life	8,005,638.00	58,418.58	53,132.84	29,182.32
Southern Life and Trust	1,773,846.42			1,931.51
State Life	15,162,216.44	99,047.91	93,988.48	125,437.40
State Mutual of Massachusetts	48,227,392 00	565,234.48	85,029.86	82,862.85
Travelers Life	86,027,307.00	5,056,339.50	452,263.16	396,328.89
Union Central Life	98,809,148.00	1,312,039.00	388,518.61	111,919.42
Union Mutual Life and Health	299.06			
United Life and Accident	493,047.00	252.78	10,046.00	3,186.67
Volunteer State Life	2,618,039.59	21,881.08	24,000.00	21,556.99
Totals	4,518,499,813.52	47,311,453.21	35,446,543.95	17,908,629.84

*Minus.

Commissions, Salaries, Cost of Collections, Rents and Unpaid Dividends to Stockholders	Dividends Due and Apportioned to Policy-holders (Including Provisional Assignment for Deferred Dividends)	All Other Liabilities	Capital Stock	Surplus	Total Liabilities
$ 97,336.32	$ 1,658,875.84	$16,786,418.68	$ 5,000,000.00	$13,529,172.06	$ 140,584,444.91
1,000.00	123,178.64	297,332.61	300,000.00	226,226.35	4,215,837.32
1,730.26	3,590.22	131,804.59	137,000.00	374,218.39	5,966,114.85
7,568.86	8,701.26	321,376.48	250,000.00	873,640.65	5,206,754.13
7,938.83	3,732.35	612,453.15	1,000,000.00	521,378.86	13,908,696.03
12,986.99	160,974.66	4,143,492.94		3,666,131.54	79,730,049.88
264,171.22	17,313,053.60	2,093.25	25,000.00	29,554.28	129,147.20
34,164.43	658,537.13	68,907,412.31	100,000.00	11,645,258.30	576,837,343.63
		2,186,138.58		1,518,290.71	34,450,303.23
325.43		1,639.10	25,000.00	25,674.49	81,859.22
81.74	3,310.42	13,817.66	250,000.00	50,000.00	1,527,598.63
8,549.11	877,605.94	3,944,263.39	200,000.00	1,764,471.50	54,749,817.52
6,486.36	373,221.28	264,359.40		1,512,447.93	34,542,304.08
		69.80	50,000.00	*115.10	54,518.35
		344.59		21,798.73	44,191.02
11,804.50	152,316.36	914,468.57	350,000.00	350,000.00	8,464,405.10
196.73	200.00	242.00		3,261.91	61,977.74
42,929.07	23,576.75	349,834.12	800,000.00	1,416,812.76	16,560,439.04
13,598.92		13,984.78	200,000.00	66,551.12	500,980.01
20,194.18	37,856.97	222,331.70	100,000.00	307,963.57	19,419,443.10
2,629.62	26,036.05	193,851.16	100,000.00	223,746.18	3,711,155.35
1,000.00			500,000.00	298,246.56	799,246.56
9,042.49	1,554,830.87	2,953,846.84		6,704,885.06	100,768,579.83
1,624.74	3,081.00	774,977.11	400,000.00	79,058.61	2,722,226.66
943,008.37	12,315,261.60	9,347,317.36		31,527,458.50	704,025,515.31
9,535.20	56,335.93	257,923.82	250,000.00	650,155.87	13,194,661.50
15,238.30	282,788.81	786,568.66	1,000,000.00	1,367,545.52	17,025,067.71
642.87			100,000.00	90,901.40	192,564.09
152,647.97	7,605,488.98	9,545,077.98			219,378,734.46
43,302.07	21,393,724.31	78,230,991.42			633,999,569.37
12,942.23	104,829.92	850,160.03	500,000.00	318,596.86	15,260,229.79
44,401.22	1,789,183.48	4,862,554.77		3,767,580.91	68,590,708.22
65,787.66	2,616,224.10	756,467.36		5,420,006.74	84,549,287.15
211,148.42	28,302,286.29	157,419,864.82			934,929,381.52
1,933.88		7,000.00		87,562.46	358,363.97
101,456.66	14,088,148.65	3,388,910.09		19,689,432.56	393,533,923.60
2,425.00		20,304.70	447,210.00	263,872.97	1,436,215.66
28,622.41	762,464.69	4,438,550.95	1,000,000.00	1,118,341.68	42,068,783.28
4,486.54	40,393.37	443,722.69	1,000,000.00	443,812.40	6,109,892.05
77,820.72	7,337,933.26	18,581,659.36			183,090,500.30
4,919.14	62,035.00	119,996.21	560,320.00	263,878.87	5,656,357.61
15,290.13	1,329,268.88	3,417,004.73			45,941,595.91
25,534.44	2,510,530.56	4,514,771.05	2,000,000.00	474,788.18	97,558,999.77
754,514.01	15,097,113.05	21,683,804.44	2,000,000.00	15,405,794.81	475,371,914.27
3,205.50	57,212.15	239,491.85	1,000,000.00	181,948.55	7,550,502.37
2,043.72	25,056.67	241,194.00	100,000.00	160,481.26	4,188,415.98
25,549.95	39,339.05	389,469.32		161,021.90	8,761,751.96
5,266.45	113,120.66	336,850.64	400,000.00	64,199.45	2,695,215.13
37,776.86	317,284.92	470,795.13		2,614,120.77	18,920,667.91
4,778.15	1,685,923.40	1,213,758.11		3,375,853.13	55,240,831.98
54,242.90	72,975.14	23,188,709.97	6,000,000.00	8,062,943.09	129,311,109 65
319,683.15	5,029,686.56	8,541,815.39	2,000,000.00	4,886,637.38	121,399,447.51
			25,000.00	416.67	25,715.73
200.00	750.00	27,758.13	500,000.00	252,113.06	1,287,353 64
3,915.26	16,443.06	95,756.33	200,000.00	105,121.62	3,106,713.93
3,508,678.98	146,034,481.83	456,454,802.12	28,869,530.00	145,963,491.27	5,399,797,424.72

EXHIBIT OF POLICIES OF LIFE INSURANCE COMPANIES (LICENSED TO DO

Name of Company	Policies in Force at Beginning of Year		Policies Issued, Revived, and Increased During Year	
	Number	Amount	Number	Amount
Ætna Life	202,971	$ 467,545,656.81	34,678	$185,707,587.68
Atlantic Life	17,758	32,317,215.00	3,985	566,484.00
American Central	19,347	40,456,046.00	4,859	12,485,070.00
American National (Ordinary)	17,221	25,644,237.00	6,170	8,736,643.00
American National (Industrial)	275,181	38,574,460.00	132,160	16,280,143.00
Business Men's Mutual	3,227	127,847.00	2,694	126,462.00
Columbian National Life	29,864	74,169,850.50	5,765	15,818,754.25
Connecticut Mutual	107,776	254,612,404.12	14,184	35,029,934.13
Durham Life	63,901	3,824,000.00	57,872	3,087,843.00
Equitable Life	635,576	1,607,089,581.00	72,551	255,018,688.00
Fidelity Mutual Life	65,486	135,643,006.00	6,822	18,412,379.00
Gate City Life and Health	30,079	1,306,533.00	27,145	1,017,072.00
George Washington	4,748	9,274,152.84	1,403	2,457,707.00
Guardian Life	82,780	158,622,130.00	10,831	25,071,969.00
Home Life of New York	64,876	133,493,328.00	9,215	22,692,684.00
Home Security	12,141	661,543.50	28,950	1,486,371.00
Imperial Mutual Life and Health				
Jefferson Standard	31,257	50,726,743.00	10,054	18,565,456.00
LaFayette Mutual	996	529,274.00	182	212,445.00
Life and Casualty	167,343	7,015,731.00	281,097	12,289,764.00
Life Insurance Co. of Virginia (Ordinary)	24,545	26,557,350.00	5,400	7,900,262.00
Life Insurance Co. of Virginia (Industrial)	700,574	91,791,862.00	164,010	23,736,203.00
Manhattan Life	32,484	60,058,189.00	1,854	4,267,168.00
Maryland Life	8,162	13,221,912.00	1,402	2,084,579.00
Maryland Assurance				
Massachusetts Mutual	180,358	410,166,920.00	23,811	63,212,576.00
Merchants Life	24,981	50,104,102.00	8,626	12,739,448.63
Metropolitan Life (Ordinary)	1,527,836	1,450,061,328.00	387,261	436,803,832.00
Metropolitan Life (Industrial)	15,424,933	2,032,370,668.00	2,495,946	354,255,170.00
Michigan Mutual	37,606	57,219,150.56	4,600	9,147,885.04
Missouri State	72,332	129,199,279.46	24,450	47,152,745.04
Morris Plan Life			1,432	170,950.00
Mutual Benefit Life	339,608	830,768,806.00	41,574	121,878,433.00
Mutual Life	756,623	1,687,797,276.00	75,502	209,054,920.00
National Life of America	52,853	88,105,276.94	9,748	19,820,004.58
National Life of Vermont	106,027	212,037,400.00	11,498	27,463,965.00
New England Mutual	139,200	337,404,704.00	20,489	54,783,039.00
New York Life	1,228,601	2,511,607,274.00	150,971	332,064,081.00
N. C. Mutual and Provident (Ordinary)	3,130	1,424,123.00	2,811	1,837,689.00
N. C. Mutual and Provident (Industrial)	100,533	6,835,426.00	67,850	4,979,648.00
Northwestern Mutual Life	576,197	1,505,464,984.00	53,846	165,816,275.00
Ohio National	5,928	8,907,784.00	2,715	4,156,280.00
Pacific Mutual	89,293	171,913,618.00	12,387	27,568,513.00
Pan-American	19,337	40,446,446.00	5,547	12,652,276.00
Penn Mutual	253,793	699,026,546.00	33,669	108,032,740.00
Philadelphia Life	10,916	27,664,642.00	4,500	957,948.00
Phœnix Mutual	92,808	179,815,823.00	11,739	28,919,066.00
Provident Life and Trust	137,525	353,127,209.00	23,099	63,695,084.00
Prudential of America	1,057,562	1,241,132,909.00	197,481	273,459,049.00
Reliance Life	38,823	71,542,913.00	13,352	26,363,586.00
Reserve Loan Life	15,672	27,355,078.00	5,020	9,507,624.00
Security Mutual Life	33,864	51,786,159.00	7,621	11,181,315.00
Southern Life and Trust	9,663	17,182,650.00	3,595	6,648,931.00
State Life	38,432	81,946,127.00	6,320	10,800,732.00
State Mutual of Massachusetts	81,754	203,684,314.00	10,736	29,678,701.00
Travelers Life	170,597	476,315,842.00	45,948	161,824,923.00
Union Central Life	212,250	472,603,217.00	27,772	82,978,095.00
Union Mutual Life and Health			16	8,000.00
United Life and Accident	4,141	5,667,821.00	2,286	3,422,263.00
Volunteer State Life	13,551	26,143,689.00	3,002	6,100,118.00
Totals	25,455,020	18,700,092,556.73	4,680,503	3,402,187,573.35

No. XII.

BUSINESS IN THIS STATE) FOR THE YEAR 1917—PAID-FOR BUSINESS.

Policies Terminated During Year		Policies in Force at End of Year		Increase		Decrease	
Number	Amount	Number	Amount	Number	Amount	Number	Amount
22,835	$80,336,962.04	214,814	$ 572,916,282.45	11,843	$105,370,625.64	.....	$.....
1,776	3,369,972.00	19,967	36,513,647.00	2,209	4,196,432.00		
2,571	6,085,298.00	21,635	46,855,818.00	2,288	6,399,772.00		
4,058	7,917,872.00	19,333	26,462,988.00	2,112	818,751.00		
121,097	15,552,552.00	286,244	39,302,051.00	11,063	727,591.00		
		5,921	254,309.00				
3,115	7,928,753.50	32,514	82,059,851.25	2,650	7,890,000.75		
7,593	18,073,567.88	114,367	271,568,770.37	6,591	16,956,366.25		
42,450	2,127,808.00	79,303	4,784,035.00	15,402	960,035.00		
42,713	153,649,446.00	665,414	1,754,868,908.00	29,838	147,779,327.00		
5,291	12,032,816.00	67,017	142,022,569.00	1,531	6,379,563.00		
26,983	1,177,277.00	30,241	1,146,328.00	162			160,205.00
758	1,360,676.00	5,399	10,356,491.73	651	1,082,338.89		
7,232	14,584,549.00	86,379	169,109,550.00	3,599	10,487,420.00		
4,565	10,135,867.00	69,526	146,050,145.00	4,650	12,556,817.00		
22,782	1,134,135.50	18,309	1,013,779.00	6,168	352,235.50		
		34,281	1,675,565.00				
3,962	6,877,977.00	37,349	62,414,222.00	6,092	11,687,479.00		
		1,178	241,719.00	182	212,445.00		
244,441	10,315,521.00	203,999	8,989,974.00	36,656	3,299,790.00		
1,995	2,286,548.00	27,950	32,171,064.00	3,405	5,613,714.00		
125,825	15,908,567.00	738,759	99,619,498.00	38,185	7,827,636.00		
2,928	6,858,237.00	31,410	57,467,120.00			1,074	2,591,069.00
884	1,471,760.00	8,680	13,834,731.00	518	612,819.00		
8,490	23,167,315.00	195,679	450,212,181.00	15,321	40,045,261.00		
3,326	6,322,318.50	30,281	56,521,232.13	5,300	6,417,130.13		
132,874	113,657,349.00	1,782,223	1,773,207,811.00	254,387	323,146,483.00		
1,440,169	223,652,751.00	16,480,710	2,162,974,087.00	1,055,777	130,603,419.00		
3,546	6,237,661.56	38,660	60,129,374.04	1,054	2,910,223.48		
10,020	19,403,482.39	86,762	156,948,542.11	14,430	27,749,262.65		
4	3,150.00	1,428	167,800.00				
15,933	37,349,817.00	365,249	915,297,422.00	25,641	84,528,616.00		
48,226	123,440,670.00	783,899	1,773,411,526.00	27,276	85,614,250.00		
5,611	10,745,384.15	56,990	97,179,897.37	4,137	9,074,620.43		
7,078	15,907,499.00	110,447	223,593,866.00	4,420	11,556,466 00		
6,151	16,693,085.00	153,538	375,494,658.00	14,338	38,089,954.00		
77,603	170,337,019.00	1,301,969	2,673,334,336.00	73,368	161,727,062.00		
669	370,700.00	5,272	2,891,112.00	2,142	1,466,989 00		
57,340	3,549,214.00	111,043	8,265,860.00	10,510	1,430,426.00		
25,463	66,854,935.00	604,580	1,604,426,324.00	28,383	98,961,340.00		
1,032	1,681,438.00	7,611	11,384,532.00	1,683	2,476,748.00		
6,488	13,523,672.00	95,192	185,958,459.00	5,899	14,044,841.00		
3,429	7,295,608.00	21,455	45,803,114.00	2,118	5,356,668.00		
17,450	51,326,772.00	270,012	757,732,514.00	16,219	58,705,968 00		
1,237	3,505,388.00	14,182	35,117,202.00	3,266	7,452,559.00		
5,770	11,637,380.00	98,777	197,097,509.00	5,969	17,281,686.00		
9,213	27,748,744.00	151,411	389,073,549.00	13,886	35,494,340.00		
81,003	95,921,520.00	1,174,040	1,418,670,438.00	116,478	177,537,529.00		
5,890	11,342,782.00	46,285	86,563,717.00	7,462	15,020,804.00		
3,786	7,233,122.00	16,906	29,629,580.00	1,234	2,274,502.00		
5,253	8,351,256.00	36,232	54,616,218.00	2,368	2,830,059 00		
920	1,804,018.00	12,338	22,195,563.00	2,675	5,012,913.00		
3,271	6,571,666.00	41,481	86,536,246.00	3,049	4,590,119.00		
4,136	10,854,742.00	88,354	222,508,273.00	6,600	18,823,959.00		
13,789	45,920,557.00	202,756	617,239,004.00	32,159	140,923,162.00		
14,936	33,240,885.00	225,086	522,340,427.00	12,836	49,737,210.00		
		16	8,000.00				
932	1,327,683.00	5,495	7,762,401.00	1,354	2,094,580.00		
1,746	3,430,913.00	14,807	28,812,894.00	1,256	2,669,205.00		
2,718,638	1,559,596,658.52	27,451,155	20,634,805,084.45	1,958,790	1,937,311,512.72	1,074	2,751,274.00

Name of Company	By Death	
	Number	Amount
Ætna Life	2,659	$ 6,179,177.68
Atlantic Life	109	185,948.00
American Central	115	251,447.00
American National (Ordinary)	142	159,319.00
American National (Industrial)	3,210	442,655.00
Business Men's Mutual		
Columbian National Life	194	505,509.50
Connecticut Mutual	1,636	4,130,972.45
Durham Life	944	45,710.00
Equitable Life	7,451	23,488,970.00
Fidelity Mutual Life	693	1,538,346.00
Gate City Life and Health		59,534.26
George Washington	31	88,691.00
Guardian Life	974	1,975,672.00
Home Life of New York	636	1,217,301.00
Home Security	353	979,797.50
Imperial Mutual Life and Health		
Jefferson Standard	233	410,160.00
LaFayette Mutual		
Life Insurance Company of Virginia (Ordinary)	211	188,916.00
Life Insurance Company of Virginia (Industrial)	9,932	1,110,424.00
Life and Casualty	2,421	95,914.00
Manhattan Life	520	1,169,577.00
Maryland Life	81	147,489.00
Maryland Assurance		
Massachusetts Mutual	1,580	4,221,919.00
Merchants Life	244	469,293.00
Metropolitan Life (Ordinary)	13,213	12,213,601.00
Metropolitan Life (Industrial)	196,383	25,516,238.00
Michigan Mutual	462	706,743.65
Missouri State	446	852,544.18
Morris Plan Life		
Mutual Benefit Life	3,147	8,444,261.00
Mutual Life	9,011	25,657,490.80
National Life of America	550	927,825.00
National Life of Vermont	943	2,317,961.00
New England Mutual	1,235	3,630,672.00
New York Life	12,901	31,043,287.00
N. C. Mutual and Provident (Ordinary)	47	17,750.00
N. C. Mutual and Provident (Industrial)	1,678	118,628.00
Northwestern Mutual Life	4,979	14,280,507.00
Ohio National	54	89,250.00
Pacific Mutual	763	1,480,034.00
Pan-American	115	289,424.00
Penn Mutual	2,500	8,005,744.00
Philadelphia Life	120	333,631.00
Phœnix Mutual	927	1,751,951.00
Provident Life and Trust	858	2,615,631.00
Prudential of America	8,440	10,211,975.00
Reliance Life	216	493,430.00
Reserve Loan Life	117	239,092.00
Security Mutual Life	334	580,174.00
Southern Life and Trust	48	83,625.00
State Life	345	824,860.00
State Mutual of Massachusetts	661	1,793,011.00
Travelers Life	1,490	4,711,337.00
Union Central Life	1,741	4,272,247.00
Union Mutual Life and Health		
United Life and Accident	54	74,730.00
Volunteer State Life	70	159,197.00
Totals	298,217	212,799,593.22

No. XIII.

TERMINATED DURING THE YEAR 1917—MODE OF TERMINATION.

By Maturity		By Disability		By Expiry	
Number	Amount	Number	Amount	Number	Amount
1,774	$ 2,714,498.00	-----	$ -----	8,879	$ 3,887,585.00
3	3,016.00	-----	-----	63	110,877.00
-----	-----	-----	-----	203	462,290.00
-----	-----	-----	-----	52	57,436.00
-----	-----	-----	-----	47	659.00
4	14,731.00	-----	-----	33	88,108.00
234	462,818.50	-----	-----	111	210,770.50
4,195	11,760,005.00	-----	-----	3,821	16,314,909.00
88	171,584.00	-----	-----	412	1,176,979.00
1	5,000.00	-----	-----	14	15,000 00
1,287	1,776,083.00	-----	-----	395	1,073,318.00
234	686,612.00	-----	-----	202	500,668.00
8	13,000.00	7	7,000.00	12	20,000.00
1	1,000.00	-----	-----	166	132,454.00
381	16,685.00	-----	-----	33	636.00
88	133,128.00	-----	-----	216	569,574.00
28	71,975.00	-----	-----	37	53,826.00
147	319,704.00	-----	-----	335	929,771.00
				5	8,000.00
6,416	5,130,483.00	-----	-----	2,969	2,686,642.00
11,018	1,050,371.00	-----	-----	27,560	4,408,886.00
205	389,470.57	-----	-----	51	102,000.47
29	35,773.00	-----	-----	345	715,609.85
823	1,991,777.00	-----	-----	4,863	9,398,341.00
3,845	8,313,741.00	-----	-----	4,460	14,123,388.00
112	127,843.00	-----	-----	3,129	5,443,247.00
714	1,183,850.00	-----	-----	775	1,383,601.00
368	835,418.00	-----	-----	369	871,374.00
8,229	14,324,505.00	-----	23,200.00	10,587	27,502,092.00
2,734	6,552,505.00	-----	-----	3,232	8,414,269.00
				20	38,000.00
444	402,278.00	12	35,893.00	1,584	3,059,738.00
3	3,000.00	-----	-----	136	228,884.00
1,154	2,525,912.00	-----	-----	2,574	6,819,178.00
1	1,000.00	-----	-----	34	40,500.00
502	928,097.00	1	5,000.00	1,119	1,930,096.00
1,280	3,409,320.00	-----	-----	3	13,010.00
2,220	2,383,535.00	170	310,697.00	33,980	35,228,682.00
6	5,050.00	-----	-----	362	876,230.00
				238	403,786.00
30	37,400.00	-----	-----	192	304,257.00
4	5,500.00	-----	-----	8	22,768.00
12	20,000.00	-----	-----	258	437,731.00
322	752,786.00	-----	-----	107	349,388.00
555	1,393,991.00	5	11,798.00	1,379	2,916,110.00
1,564	2,450,870.00	-----	-----	1,918	3,596,884.00
-----	-----	-----	-----	2	2,000.00
1	1,000.00	-----	-----	75	115,225.00
51,064	72,405,315.07	194	393,588.00	117,365	157,044,777.82

(liii)

SHOWING POLICIES OF LIFE INSURANCE COMPANIES

Name of Company	By Surrender	
	Number	Amount
Ætna Life	4,518	$ 10,907,709.96
Atlantic Life	310	689,095.00
American Central	401	837,630.00
American National (Ordinary)	360	491,372.00
American National (Industrial)	1,409	234,230.00
Business Men's Mutual		
Columbian National Life	550	1,368,892.75
Connecticut Mutual	1,849	4,547,825.43
Durham Life		
Equitable Life	11,425	30,909,789.00
Fidelity Mutual Life	1,527	3,183,901.00
Gate City Life and Health		
George Washington	213	423,508.00
Guardian Life	2,050	4,032,472.00
Home Life of New York	1,580	3,341,675.00
Home Security		
Imperial Mutual Life and Health		
Jefferson Standard	575	1,011,362.00
LaFayette Mutual		
Life Insurance Company of Virginia (Ordinary)	486	472,984.00
Life Insurance Company of Virginia (Industrial)	1,777	234,461.00
Life and Casualty		
Manhattan Life	1,233	2,788,164.00
Maryland Life	105	146,782.00
Maryland Assurance		
Massachusetts Mutual	3,382	9,257,582.00
Merchants Life	90	122,061.00
Metropolitan Life (Ordinary)	21,079	17,831,538.00
Metropolitan Life (Industrial)	80,212	13,023,787.00
Michigan Mutual	760	1,206,506.79
Missouri State	1,143	2,167,709.39
Morris Plan Life		
Mutual Benefit Life	3,555	9,220,542.00
Mutual Life	16,743	47,060,502.00
National Life of America	588	999,492.00
National Life of Vermont	1,532	3,791,522.00
New England Mutual	1,562	3,330,324.00
New York Life	19,038	42,176,988.00
N. C. Mutual and Provident (Ordinary)	18	6,050.00
N. C. Mutual and Provident (Industrial)		
Northwestern Mutual Life	7,198	17,565,562.00
Ohio National	69	112,175.00
Pacific Mutual	1,792	3,994,181.00
Pan-American	588	1,285,062.00
Penn Mutual	3,483	11,123,414.00
Philadelphia Life	187	451,883.00
Phœnix Mutual	1,225	2,787,461.00
Provident Life and Trust	3,079	9,580,703.00
Prudential of America	8,613	9,850,956.00
Reliance Life	207	378,790.00
Reserve Loan Life	1,117	2,704,434.00
Security Mutual Life	317	572,247.00
Southern Life and Trust	159	278,773.00
State Life	536	1,339,187.00
State Mutual of Massachusetts	1,354	2,508,604.00
Travelers Life	2,356	5,796,189.00
Union Central Life	5,167	11,690,916.00
Union Mutual Life and Health		
United Life and Accident	117	131,923.00
Volunteer State Life	305	516,020.00
Totals	217,939	298,484,937.32

TERMINATED DURING THE YEAR 1917—MODE OF TERMINATION.

By Lapse		By Decrease		Total Terminated	
Number	Amount	Number	Amount	Number	Amount
5,005	$ 17,624,392.00		$ 39,023,603.40	22,835	$ 80,336,962.04
1,285	2,314,015.00	6	67,021.00	1,776	3,369,972.00
1,846	4,080,389.00	6	453,542.00	2,571	6,085,298.00
3,504	7,163,155.00		46,590.00	4,058	7,917,872.00
116,431	14,875,008.00			121,097	15,552,552.00
2,334	5,154,451.50		797,060.75	3,115	7,928,753.50
2,465	4,756,179.00		546,378.00	6,295	14,654,943.88
41,506	2,082,097.90			42,450	2,127,808.00
15,821	31,994,370.00		39,181,403.00	42,713	153,649,446.00
2,549	5,526,522.00	22	435,484.00	5,291	12,032,816.00
				26,983	1,177,277.00
498	820,477.00	1	8,000.00	758	1,360,676.00
2,526	4,992,694.00		734,310.00	7,232	14,584,549.00
1,913	4,001,795.00		387,816.00	4,565	10,135,867.00
22,429	1,124,338.00			22,782	1,134,135.50
				17,501	44,965.35
3,127	5,191,384.00		225,071.00	3,962	6,877,977.00
				1,178	741,719.00
1,131	1,421,790.00		89,404.00	1,995	2,286,548.00
113,702	14,253,566.00		292,795.00	125,825	15,908,567.00
242,020	10,219,607.00			244,441	10,315,521.00
871	1,914,296.00		283,498.00	2,928	6,858,237.00
633	1,018,262.00		33,426.00	884	1,471,760.00
3,046	6,347,969.00		2,090,370.00	8,490	23,167,315.00
2,976	5,605,368.00	11	117,595.00	3,326	6,322,318.00
75,795	64,236,318.00	13,402	11,558,767.00	132,874	113,657,349.00
1,124,996	162,547,528.00		17,084,469.00	1,440,169	223,652,751.00
2,068	3,733,915.95		99,024.13	3,546	6,237,661.56
8,057	15,291,184.48		340,661.49	10,020	19,403,482.39
4	3,150.00			4	3,150.00
3,530	7,261,712.00	15	1,033,184.00	15,933	37,349,817.00
14,008	27,177,426.00	159	1,108,123.00	48,226	123,440,670.00
1,232	2,735,803.00		511,172.00	5,611	10,745,384.00
1,833	3,418,085.00	1,281	3,812,480.00	7,078	15,907,499.00
2,617	5,964,771.00		2,060,526.00	6,151	16,693,085.00
26,848	48,454,350.00		6,812,597.00	77,603	170,337,019.00
604	346,900.00			669	370,700.00
55,662	3,430,586.00			57,340	3,549,214.00
7,301	17,822,740.00	19	2,219,352.00	25,463	66,854,935.00
577	872,023.00	27	32,982.00	1,032	1,681,438.00
1,893	3,907,778.00			6,488	13,523,672.00
2,587	5,313,653.00		175,585.00	3,429	7,295,608.00
5,923	14,234,969.00	1,816	8,617,555.00	17,450	51,326,772.00
895	2,429,850.00		248,524.00	1,237	3,505,388.00
1,996	3,927,604.00		307,171.00	5,770	11,637,380.00
3,993	9,993,599.00		2,136,481.00	9,213	27,748,744.00
27,580	36,275,506.00		1,660,169.00	81,003	95,921,520.00
5,093	9,246,371.00	6	342,911.00	5,890	11,342,782.00
2,310	3,776,845.00	4	108,965.00	3,786	7,233,122.00
4,380	6,718,540.00		138,638.00	5,253	8,351,256.00
680	1,320,369.00	21	92,983.00	920	1,804,018.00
2,119	3,719,237.00	1	230,651.00	3,271	6,571,666.00
1,597	3,213,351.00	95	2,237,602.00	4,136	10,854,742.00
8,004	15,804,037.00		15,287,095.00	13,789	45,920,557.00
4,546	10,066,808.00		1,163,160.00	14,936	33,240,885.00
				16	8,000.00
759	1,119,030.00			932	1,327,683.00
1,160	2,327,093.00	135	312,378.00	1,746	3,430,913.00
1,988,265	649,173,257.83	17,026	164,546,572.77	2,736,035	1,556,972,718.22

Name of Company	Whole Life Policies	
	Number	Amount
Ætna Life	35,303	$ 116,597,412.00
Atlantic Life	17,547	32,292,916.00
American Central	16,653	32,423,560.00
American National (Ordinary)	17,999	25,083,956.00
American National (Industrial)	235,389	33,873,242.00
Business Men's Mutual		
Columbian National Life	24,472	58,898,770.00
Connecticut Mutual	61,017	153,376,229.32
Durham Life (Industrial)	27,351	3,093,752.00
Equitable Life	476,303	1,213,857,859.00
Fidelity Mutual Life	34,629	72,587,413.00
Gate City Life and Health	4,771	349,846.00
George Washington	4,392	8,323,800.00
Guardian Life	45,675	93,920,196.00
Home Life of New York	52,638	105,041,970.00
Home Security	4,611	487,908.00
Imperial Mutual Life and Health	5,972	680,068.00
Jefferson Standard	34,948	57,507,207.00
LaFayette Mutual	718	469,142.00
Life Insurance Company of Virginia (Ordinary)	25,010	28,617,267.00
Life Insurance Company of Virginia (Industrial)	581,444	81,287,432.00
Life and Casualty	197,277	8,427,652.00
Manhattan Life	26,567	48,410,467.00
Maryland Life	6,401	10,216,782.00
Massachusetts Mutual	166,558	388,233,213.00
Merchants Life	11,088	18,377,688.00
Metropolitan Life (Ordinary)	861,179	989,539,950.00
Metropolitan Life (Industrial)	9,124,432	1,263,535,395.00
Michigan Mutual	26,174	37,549,155.25
Missouri State	70,320	126,721,244.27
Morris Plan Life		
Mutual Benefit Life	320,178	807,485,106.00
Mutual Life	646,107	1,451,923,845.00
National Life of America	31,178	47,753,195.87
National Life of Vermont	69,370	145,999,107.00
New England Mutual	114,721	275,247,180.00
New York Life	867,849	1,880,266,686.00
N. C. Mutual and Provident (Ordinary)	5,272	2,891,112.00
N. C. Mutual and Provident (Industrial)	111,043	8,265,860.00
Northwestern Mutual Life	466,715	1,234,653,678.00
Ohio National	5,231	7,485,215.00
Pacific Mutual	64,356	122,798,288.00
Pan-American	17,996	35,586,585.00
Penn Mutual	201,194	573,301,652.00
Philadelphia Life	9,418	21,449,662.00
Phœnix Mutual	10,915	21,309,645.00
Provident Life and Trust	22,155	73,353,764.00
Prudential of America	828,181	1,003,936,768.00
Reliance Life	38,243	68,240,193.00
Reserve Loan Life	15,988	27,408,226.00
Security Mutual Life	24,337	34,829,462.00
Southern Life and Trust	10,748	18,823,106.00
State Life	32,435	67,441,184.00
State Mutual of Massachusetts	64,429	165,620,237.00
Travelers Life	141,302	375,094,093.00
Union Central Life	184,851	436,041,123.00
Union Mutual Life and Health	16	8,000.00
United Life and Accident	5,051	6,747,763.00
Volunteer State Life	13,341	25,139,667.00
Totals	16,519,458	13,948,881,894.71

Endowment Policies		Term and Other Policies, Including Return Premium Additions		Additions to Policies by Dividends	Total Numbers and Amounts	
Number	Amount	Number	Amount	Amount	Number	Amount
144,758	$ 272,654,862.00	34,753	$ 183,504,836.00	$ 159,172.45	214,814	$ 572,916,282.45
2,017	3,268,557.00	403	952,174.00	----	19,967	36,513,647.00
2,385	4,433,696.00	2,597	9,907,790.00	90,772.00	21,635	46,855,818.00
957	1,045,110.00	377	254,927.00	78,995.00	19,333	26,462,988.00
50,209	5,374,990.00	646	53,819.00	----	286,244	39,302,051.00
4,983	9,682,655.00	3,059	13,333,847.75	144,578.50	32,514	82,059,851.25
49,987	108,792,199.40	2,931	7,973,396.00	101,402.65	113,935	270,243,227.37
815	65,697.00	51,137	1,624,586.00	----	79,303	4,784,035.00
148,540	289,909,202.00	40,571	236,932,550.00	14,169,297.00	665,414	1,754,868,908.00
24,660	50,013,911.00	7,728	19,103,760.00	317,485.00	67,017	142,022,569.00
346	16,126.00	25,124	780,356.00	----	30,241	1,146,328.00
809	1,261,400.00	198	705,744.00	65,546.00	5,399	10,356,491.00
39,045	67,743,014.00	1,659	6,681,948.00	764,392.00	86,379	169,109,550.00
11,536	18,991,041.00	5,352	18,310,336.00	3,706,798.00	69,526	146,050,145.00
13,698	525,871.00				18,309	1,013,779.00
1,497	73,040.00	26,812	912,457.00	----	34,281	1,665,565.00
1,165	2,154,642.00	1,236	2,743,018.00	9,355.00	37,349	62,414,222.00
460	272,577.00	32	43,500.00	----	1,178	741,719.00
2,048	1,984,097.00	892	1,564,662.00	5,038.00	27,950	32,171,064.00
151,443	18,183,802.00	5,872	148,264.00	----	738,759	99,619,498.00
6,722	562,322.00				203,999	8,989,974.00
3,565	5,123,336.00	1,278	3,858,765.00	74,552.31	31,410	57,467,120.00
1,971	2,929,255.00	308	662,550.00	26,144.00	8,680	13,834,731.00
21,445	35,238,904.00	7,676	24,555,147.00	2,184,917.00	195,679	450,212,181.00
1,293	1,803,706.00	17,900	36,310,237.00	29,601.00	30,281	56,521,232.00
889,588	699,125,945.00	31,456	82,284,815.00	2,257,101.00	1,782,223	1,773,207,811.00
6,914,227	857,475,648.00	442,051	41,961,528.00	1,516.00	16,480,710	2,162,974,087.00
8,795	13,146,439.23	3,691	9,292,976.57	140,802.99	38,660	60,129,374.04
10,874	14,366,856.00	5,568	15,833,980.95	26,460.89	86,762	156,948,542.11
		1,428	167,800.00		1,428	167,800.00
31,279	65,787,282.00	13,792	31,463,929.00	10,561,105.00	365,249	915,297,422.00
107,905	187,382,611.00	29,887	101,979,536.00	32,125,534.00	783,899	1,773,411,526.00
11,943	20,132,793.85	13,869	29,280,286.65	13,621.00	56,990	97,179,897.37
26,904	43,695,303.00	14,173	33,116,359.00	783,097.00	110,447	223,593,866.00
28,774	57,463,471.00	10,043	38,809,918.00	3,974,089.00	153,538	375,494,658.00
393,179	668,798,885.00	40,941	110,612,353.00	13,656,412.00	1,301,969	2,673,334,336.00
					5,272	2,891,112.00
					111,043	8,265,860.00
87,934	177,743,212.00	49,931	166,470,836.00	25,558,598.00	604,580	1,604,426,324.00
1,582	1,940,205.00	798	1,959,012.00	----	7,611	11,384,532.00
19,761	33,880,894.00	11,075	25,712,469.00	3,566,808.00	95,192	185,958,459.00
2,440	7,002,067.00	1,019	3,214,462.00	----	21,455	45,803,114.00
37,130	72,507,290.00	31,688	108,950,982.00	2,972,590.00	270,012	757,732,514.00
2,272	3,907,731.00	2,492	9,687,828.00	71,981.00	14,182	35,117,202.00
77,934	146,529,893.00	9,928	27,527,789.00	1,730,182.00	98,777	197,097,509.00
114,369	251,031,759.00	14,887	60,606,475.00	4,081,551.00	151,411	389,073,549.00
270,889	243,595,746.00	74,970	169,427,764.00	1,710,160.00	1,174,040	1,418,670,438.00
6,107	9,510,455.00	1,935	8,638,314.00	174,755.00	46,285	86,563,717.00
142	253,771.00	776	1,964,635.00	2,947.00	16,906	29,629,580.00
5,754	7,615,278.00	6,141	12,097,750.00	73,728.00	36,232	54,616,218.00
1,021	1,577,719.00	569	1,784,266.00	10,472.00	12,338	22,195,563.00
4,678	6,799,267.00	4,368	12,261,697.00	34,098.00	41,481	86,536,246.00
19,266	40,953,662.00	4,659	13,417,008.00	2,517,366.00	88,354	222,508,273.00
41,326	73,083,656.00	20,128	168,730,295.00	330,960.00	202,756	617,239,004.00
29,573	50,091,177.00	10,662	30,668,265.00	5,539,862.00	225,086	522,340,427.00
					16	8,000.00
358	433,970.00	86	563,750.00	16,918.00	5,495	7,762,401.00
509	803,302.00	957	2,858,844.00	11,081.00	14,807	28,812,894.00
9,832,867	4,658,740,300.48	1,092,509	1,892,264,592.92	133,871,841.79	27,444,802	20,633,715,231.59

EXHIBIT OF POLICIES, LOSSES INCURRED, LOSSES PAID AND PREMIUMS RECEIVED

Name of Company	Policies in Force December 31, 1916		Policies Issued During 1917	
	Number	Amount	Number	Amount
Ætna Life	4,041	$ 6,523,133.56	819	$4,730,318.82
Atlantic Life	3,314	5,582,641.00	779	1,410,926.00
American Central	227	371,947.00	232	332,469.00
American National (Ordinary)	654	665,508.00	1,236	608,114.00
American National (Industrial)	14,696	1,601,416.00	6,644	589,594.00
Business Men's Mutual	3,227	127,847.00	2,694	126,462.00
Columbian National Life	1,218	2,111,026.00	302	491,529.00
Connecticut Mutual	1,253	2,769,829.00	268	519,784.00
Durham Life (Ordinary)	389	123,550.00	175	55,650.00
Durham Life (Industrial)	63,901	3,824,000.00	57,852	3,087,843.00
Equitable Life	7,693	14,179,692.00	1,158	2,175,581.00
Fidelity Mutual Life	1,519	2,875,332.00	218	473,168.00
Gate City Life and Health	30,079	1,306,533.00	27,145	1,017,072.00
George Washington			38	43,268.00
Guardian Life	937	1,908,576.00	390	916,540.00
Home Life of New York	740	1,025,853.00	154	345,458.87
Home Security	12,141	661,543.50	28,950	1,486,371.00
Imperial Mutual Life and Health (Ordinary)				
Imperial Mutual Life and Health (Industrial)				
Jefferson Standard	18,034	27,619,849.00	4,104	6,701,335.00
LaFayette Mutual	996	529,274.00	182	212,445.00
Life Insurance Company of Virginia (Ordinary)	4,920	4,771,926.00	1,226	1,589,672.00
Life Insurance Company of Virginia (Industrial)	146,256	19,163,093.00	36,794	5,326,925.00
Life and Casualty				
Manhattan Life	613	744,295.00	113	157,362.00
Maryland Life	1,234	1,752,383.00	351	527,394.00
Massachusetts Mutual	1,545	3,271,874.00	179	400,710.00
Merchants Life	130	240,000 00		
Metropolitan Life (Ordinary)	10,815	12,575,065.00	4,086	4,954,182.00
Metropolitan Life (Industrial)	135,092	17,290,740.00	35,717	4,483,451.00
Michigan Mutual	1,369	2,057,617.53	387	561,255.17
Missouri State	1,034	1,525,995.33	659	940,441.66
Morris Plan Life				
Mutual Benefit Life	11,287	19,104,244.00	1,482	2,950,536.00
Mutual Life	10,960	18,978,700.00	1,540	2,933,685.80
National Life of America	60	95,124.20	274	453,049.20
National Life of Vermont	3,479	5,722,581.39	614	1,194,497.88
New England Mutual	1,554	2,909,150.00	605	1,135,543.00
New York Life	9,458	17,223,587.00	1,602	3,195,696.00
N. C. Mutual and Provident (Ordinary)	1,240	540,575.00	912	614,950.00
N. C. Mutual and Provident (Industrial)	45,014	2,233,297.00	22,000	1,228,427.00
Northwestern Mutual Life	4,069	7,965,991.00	221	467,900.00
Ohio National	38	67,450.00	17	19,000.00
Pacific Mutual	960	1,249,683.00	278	459,049.00
Pan-American	467	714,588.00	322	492,000.00
Penn Mutual	5,875	11,264,536.00	407	875,082.00
Philadelphia Life	1,184	1,996,472.00	510	873,912.00
Phœnix Mutual	2,212	3,203,020.05	296	482,428.10
Provident Life and Trust	735	1,496,751.00	246	570,178.00
Prudential of America	5,029	10,041,820.00	477	1,069,728.00
Reliance Life	677	956,485.00	369	561,070.00
Reserve Loan Life	164	205,500.00	100	130,000.00
Security Mutual Life	900	1,340,283.51	204	279,699.50
Southern Life and Trust	6,824	11,546,563.00	1,983	3,501,300.00
State Life	699	1,574,199.00	177	238,585.00
State Mutual of Massachusetts	1,574	2,914,022.00	236	514,960.00
Travelers Life	1,317	3,570,099.00	385	1,029,883.00
Union Central Life	6,620	10,235,140.00	657	1,117,989.00
Union Mutual Life and Health (Ordinary)			16	8,000.00
Union Mutual Life and Health (Industrial)			4	684.00
United Life and Accident	144	230,500.00	157	197,000.00
Volunteer State Life	545	1,428,930.00	279	678,472.00
Totals	591,152	276,009,830.07	249,122	71,538,626.00

*Including policies reinsured from the North State Life Insurance Co.

IN NORTH CAROLINA.

OF LIFE INSURANCE COMPANIES FOR THE YEAR ENDING DECEMBER 31, 1917.

Policies Ceased During 1917		Policies in Force December 31, 1917		Losses Unpaid December 31, 1916	Losses Incurred During 1917	Losses Paid During 1917	Premiums Received
Number	Amount	Number	Amount				
421	$1,987,278.00	4,439	$ 9,266,174.38	$ 1,783.00	$ 106,685.00	$ 107,557.00	$ 231,214.09
345	641,650.00	3,748	6,351,917.00	3,050.00	31,574.54	34,624.54	246,281.63
77	116,655.00	382	587,761.00	----------	3,011.00	3,011.00	18,038.97
182	140,683.00	1,708	1,132,939.00	----------	7,374.00	6,117.70	36,383.23
6,127	650,439.00	15,213	1,540,571.00	----------	24,704.69	24,704.69	72,910.97
		5,921	254,309.00	----------	----------	10,218.03	37,233.01
209	336,744.00	1,311	2,265,811.00	----------	15,000.00	12,000.00	67,245.41
192	381,736.00	1,329	2,907,877.00	----------	74,801.00	64,440.00	102,207.27
147	46,800.00	417	132,400.00	250.00	3,098.77	3,348.77	4,370.68
42,450	2,127,808.00	79,303	4,784,035.00	----------	45,961.60	45,710.10	345,779.74
617	1,176,168.00	8,234	15,179,105.00	2,315.00	213,105.83	196,934.93	504,974.71
120	298,778.00	1,617	3,049,722.00	1,595.00	26,710.00	26,305.00	100,338.81
26,983	1,177,277.00	30,241	1,146,328.00	105.00	59,539.26	59,534.26	167,670.70
1	2,000.00	37	41,268.00	----------	----------	----------	1,316.28
103	287,576.00	1,224	2,537,540.00	----------	5,000.00	5,000.00	90,450.28
78	124,628.87	816	1,246,683.00	----------	24,445.87	20,445.87	37,142.37
22,782	1,134,135.50	18,309	1,013,779.00	----------	10,162.75	10,162.75	82,817.20
----------	----------	33	16,250.00	----------	----------	----------	----------
----------	----------	34,281	1,675,565.00	285.00	44,488.35	44,965.35	182,865.47
1,545	2,474,610.00	20,593	31,846,574.00	----------	227,985.36	213,940.36	1,140,889.12
----------	----------	1,178	741,719.00	----------	----------	3,749.00	34,072.91
511	513,345.00	5,635	5,848,253.00	500.00	42,813.30	42,157.30	163,498.54
26,898	3,433,377.00	156,152	21,056,641.00	1,626.40	220,310.99	219,195.99	699,494.49
90	125,097.00	636	776,560.00	----------	10,200.00	10,200.00	29,271.84
267	408,636.00	1,318	1,871,141.00	----------	11,954.00	10,954.00	64,967.79
122	257,957.00	1,602	3,414,627.00	----------	43,097.00	43,097.00	107,559.87
27	57,500.00	103	182,500.00	----------	4,000.00	4,000.00	4,652.42
1,247	1,309,902.00	13,654	16,219,345.00	1,000.00	216,460.85	203,460.85	466,339.59
19,977	2,616,242.00	150,832	19,157,949.00	1,590.00	193,443.89	192,226.89	671,942.99
201	286,335.01	1,555	2,332,537.69	----------	8,593.07	8,593.07	68,165.47
195	259,200.00	1,498	2,207,236.99	14.00	5,048.00	5,048.00	65,475.58
563	1,064,493.00	12,206	20,990,287.00	10,000.00	225,972.00	220,972.00	689,446.44
663	1,297,763.80	11,837	20,614,622.00	2,024.00	328,554.20	329,672.20	702,891.50
10	27,519.00	324	520,654.40	----------	----------	----------	16,341.00
229	426,203.58	3,864	6,490,875.69	----------	51,500.00	41,500.00	213,882.03
109	204,299.00	2,050	3,840,394.00	----------	22,764.00	21,764.00	124,443.36
642	1,299,598.00	10,418	19,119,685.00	1,006.00	226,334.29	214,746.29	681,683.12
275	155,350.00	1,877	1,000,175.00	----------	4,450.00	4,450.00	30,625.00
20,360	451,510.00	46,654	3,010,214.00	----------	105,411.36	104,919.36	225,386.69
127	71,943.00	4,163	8,361,948.00	8,000.00	102,946.00	100,616.00	220,399.78
10	16,300.00	45	70,150.00	----------	----------	----------	1,915.65
56	86,037.00	1,182	1,622,695.00	8,000.00	12,604.00	15,604.00	52,407.49
148	223,250.00	641	983,338.00	1,500.00	----------	1,500.00	25,782.87
270	662,498.00	6,012	11,477,120.00	9,616.91	166,263.00	162,853.91	389,628.85
148	221,332.00	1,546	2,649,052.00	----------	15,974.57	5,974.57	88,621.32
138	211,802.00	2,370	3,473,646.15	15,000.00	31,995.63	45,995.63	107,108.00
80	199,878.00	901	1,867,051.00	5,000.00	15,000.00	20,000.00	51,892.46
235	534,828.00	5,271	10,576,720.00	12,925.00	125,158.00	128,083.00	299,174.40
82	106,283.00	964	1,411,272.00	----------	13,000.00	13,000.00	48,614.02
35	57,500.00	229	278,000.00	----------	5,000.00	5,000.00	9,763.99
124	195,043.00	980	1,388,940.01	----------	11,000.00	10,000.00	45,723.74
547	1,012,767.00	8,260	14,035,096.00	----------	53,125.00	53,125.00	456,978.10
45	108,902.00	731	1,703,882.00	1,000.00	13,500.00	13,500.00	37,786.89
82	169,315.00	1,728	3,259,667.00	4.00	10,426.67	10,426.67	102,826.65
84	143,137.00	1,618	4,456,845.00	----------	11,636.00	11,636.00	113,048.63
507	835,949.00	6,770	10,517,180.00	5,140.00	157,871.84	160,871.84	338,566.58
----------	----------	16	8,000.00	----------	----------	----------	163.32
----------	----------	58	4,064.00	----------	----------	----------	17.00
49	71,500.00	*1,741	*2,041,860.00	----------	19,976.00	15,976.00	70,866.42
94	285,826.00	730	1,821,576.00	4,000.00	9,000.00	13,000.00	54,173.69
177,626	32,513,383.76	698,505	318,380,127.31	97,329.31	3,419,031.68	3,356,888.82	11,045,730.42

STATISTICAL TABLES

RELATING TO MUTUAL LIFE ASSESSMENT ASSOCIATIONS

SHOWING INCOME AND DISBURSEMENTS, 1917, AND ASSETS AND

Name of Association	Income		
	From Members	All Other Sources	Total
Afro-American Mutual	$ 6,690.30	$ 2,556.50	$ 9,246.80
Catawba Benevolent	2,112.23		2,112.23
Citizens' Mutual	6,749.65	7,023.25	13,772.90
Cumulative Coffin Club	549.65	227.18	776.83
Cumberland Mutual Life and Health	5,840.35	3,817.00	9,657.35
Eastern Relief	4,831.59	57.00	4,888.59
International Mutual	21,525.94	175.00	21,700.94
Mutual Christian Burial Aid	381.00		381.00
Toilers Mutual	3,445.90	80.00	3,525.90
Winston Mutual Life			
Totals	52,126.61	13,935.93	66,062.54

MENT LIFE ASSOCIATIONS.
LIABILITIES FOR THE YEAR ENDING DECEMBER 31, 1917.

Disbursements			Total Admitted Assets	Total Liabilities	Balance on Hand to Protect Contracts
To Members	All Other Payments	Total			
$ 2,440.81	$ 5,218.23	$ 7,659.04	$ 10,200.11	$ 1,854.60	$ 8,345.51
2,020.00	357.68	2,377.68	333.18	560.00	----------------
1,297.28	11,856.01	13,153.29	619.61	15.13	603.48
249.15	292.63	541.78	239.05	216.00	23.05
956.55	7,462.88	8,419.43	1,574.17	2,757.00	----------------
3,716.48	1,616.37	5,332.85	5,231.32	84.00	5,147.32
10,816.08	9,835.41	20,651.49	7,040.22	500.00	6,540.22
201.00	36.50	237.50	143.50	14.00	129.50
1,407.18	1,366.20	2,773.38	3,105.05	----------------	3,105.05
23,104.53	38,041.91	61,146.44	28,486.21	6,000.73	23,894.08

Name of Association	Certificates in Force December 31, 1916		Certificates Written During 1917	
	Number	Amount	Number	Amount
Afro-American Mutual	8,755	$ 450,458.05	390	$ 11,446.00
Catawba Benevolent	300		5	
Citizen's Mutual			7,560	
Cumulative Coffin Club			5,938	105,855.00
Cumberland Mutual Life and Health				
Eastern Relief	1,392	51,340.00	1,703	72,460.00
nternational Mutual	9,844		5,300	
Mutual Christian Burial Aid	68		39	
Toilers Mutual	919	26,630.00	253	6,750.00
Winston Mutual Life				
Totals	21,278	528,428.05	21,188	196,511.00

USINESS IN NORTH CAROLINA DURING 1917.

Certificates Terminated During 1917		Certificates in Force December 31, 1917		Premiums or Assessments Received	Losses Incurred	Losses Paid	Losses Unpaid
Number	Amount	Number	Amount				
436	$ 12,292.00	9,709	$ 449,612.05	$ 6,690.30	$ 2,440.81	$ 2,440.81	$ _____
30	------------	275	------------	2,112.23	2,020.00	2,020.00	560.00
64	------------	3,536	------------	6,749.65	1,297.28	1,297.28	-----------
--------	------------	--------	------------	549.65	249.15	249.15	65.00
11	200.00	5,949	106,055.00	5,840.35	956.55	956.55	-----------
2,071	72,130.00	1,024	51,670.00	4,831.59	3,716.48	3,716.48	81.00
6,872	------------	8,272	------------	21,525.94	10,816.08	10,816.08	-----------
--------	------------	107	------------	381.00	201.00	201.00	-----------
465	13,970.00	707	19,410.00	3,445.90	1,407.18	1,407.18	-----------
--------	------------	--------	------------	----------	----------	----------	----------
9,945	98,592.00	29,579	626,747.05	52,126.61	23,104.53	23,104.53	706.00

STATISTICAL TABLES

RELATING TO ACCIDENT, CASUALTY, FIDELITY, SURETY AND LIVE-STOCK COMPANIES

SHOWING INCOME OF FIDELITY AND CASUALTY COMPANIES (LICENSED T

Name of Company	Accident	Health	Liability
			Premiu
Ætna Casualty and Surety	$ 15,963.38	$ 2,241.86	$ 1,080,634.
Ætna Life (Accident)	2,512,937.38	836,808.45	5,114,226.
American Automobile			
American Credit Indemnity			
American National Life (Accident)	186,938.11	130,341.00	
American Surety			
Columbian National Life (Accident)	187,134.67	150,129.08	
Continental Casualty	2,612,365.61	1,023,385.33	255,249.
Employers Liability	340,556.32	109,631.41	4,456,341.
Fidelity and Casualty	1,730,461.00	1,241,872.25	2,481,165.
Fidelity and Deposit	466,469.81	320,225.75	1,149,609.
General Accident	656,290.83	451,933.40	1,527,947.
Georgia Casualty	11,626.82	9,986.74	1,259,748.
Hartford Accident and Indemnity	194,815.90	78,091.13	1,519,923.
Hartford Steam Boiler			
Lloyd's Plate Glass			
London Guarantee and Accident	181,090.27	80,857.44	2,160,893.
Maryland Casualty	768,747.22	465,895.22	3,794,979.
Massachusetts Bonding	*1,901,449.79		799,918.
Metropolitan Casualty	134,185.66	49,220.56	
Metropolitan Life (Accident)	*319,296.38		
National Surety			
National Casualty	*741,720.11		
National Life of America (Accident)	*1,235,303.81		
New Amsterdam Casualty	254,673.06	79,900.70	675,086.
New York Plate Glass			
North American Accident	1,504,627.76		
Ocean Accident and Guarantee	379,432.98	120,278.08	2,643,157.
Pacific Mutual Life (Accident)	1,507,628.84	574,402.96	
Provident Life and Accident	758,270.28		
Preferred Accident	963,694.44	292,851.68	916,600.
Reliance Life (Accident)	69,616.95	42,092.43	
Royal Indemnity	222,266.91	73,617.63	1,606,937.
Standard Accident	1,599,815.86	399,865.98	1,387,739.
Travelers (Accident)	4,691,664.80	1,229,219.77	6,714,687.
Travelers Indemnity	105,795.90	88,632.83	71,690.
United States Casualty	480,371.15	270,696.19	1,213,211.
U. S. Fidelity and Guaranty	260,943.84	109,031.95	3,325,054.
Western Live Stock			
Totals	26,996,155.84	8,231,209.82	

*Accident and Health.

INCOME.

Received

Workmen's Compensation	Fidelity	Surety	Plate-glass	Steam-boiler	Burglary and Theft	Credit
$ 316,072.08 7,746,643.30	$ 298,387.12	$ 1,360,635.91	$ 252,966.89	$	$ 459,197.79	$
						802,954.36
	1,871,391.25	2,370,983.92				
440,873.46 7,410,598.68 3,318,005.59	88,777.19 398,557.60	9,326.39 562,115.60	107,250.57 463,587.00	62,092.64 516,261.03	297,412.54 675,645.67	
110,529.38 910,416.75 338,154.42 1,932,206.04	1,318,461.18 211,071.87	2,460,391.00 25.00 397,199.34	274,948.65 41,298.36 144,350.44		292,756.99 54,079.52 13,208.09 238,042.83	
				1,892,260.70		
			655,946.89			
4,413,758.07 4,398,998.73 397,745.14	232,129.33 322,873.49	930,189.09 616,593.18	332,213.06 205,499.95 605,225.30	43,422.96 379,611.77	168,611.75 422,862.01 252,197.65 46,951.25	427,591.97
	1,767,441.89	3,062,443.85			564,445.71	
823,003.33	241,611.27	480,273.68	139,298.76		164,096.46	
			729,745.76			
4,270,724.40	79,418.04		132,726.52	152,185.93	281,346.30	435,369.02
2,889.01	49,419.02	72,689.33			149,314.34	
1,715,197.73 1,750,183.80 12,991,880.01	241,686.44	240,250.83	141,936.40	85,958.01	277,161.09	
311,842.28 1,108,217.03 4,237,456.19	1,712,956.86	3,481,040.44	201,248.37 85,381.62 209,773.75	383,876.61 32.73	376,578.99 110,556.86 501,399.83	
58,945,395.33	8,834,182.55	16,044,157.56	4,723,398.29	3,515,702.38	5,345,865.67	1,665,915.35

SHOWING INCOME OF FIDELITY AND CASUALTY COMPANIES (LICENSED TO

Name of Company	Premiums		
	Sprinkler	Physicians' Deferse	Fly-wheel
Ætna Casualty and Surety	$ 142,841.95	$	$ 12,496.73
Ætna Life (Accident)			
American Automobile			
American Credit Indemnity			
American National Life (Accident)			
American Surety			
Columbian National Life (Accident)			
Continental Casualty			
Employers Liability			30,222.06
Fidelity and Casualty			93,073.97
Fidelity and Deposit			
General Accident			
Georgia Casualty			
Hartford Accident and Indemnity			
Hartford Steam Boiler			142,365.57
Lloyd's Plate Glass			
London Guarantee and Accident			
Maryland Casualty	214,613.55	27,097.21	46,432.75
Massachusetts Bonding			
Metropolitan Casualty			
Metropolitan Life (Accident)			
National Surety			
National Casualty			
National Life of America (Accident)			
New Amsterdam Casualty			
New York Plate Glass			
North American Accident			
Ocean Accident and Guarantee			16,842.11
Pacific Mutual Life (Accident)			
Provident Life and Accident			
Preferred Accident			
Reliance Life (Accident)			
Royal Indemnity			30,556.52
Standard Accident			
Travelers (Accident)			
Travelers Indemnity			12,441.49
United States Casualty			
U. S. Fidelity and Guaranty			
Western Live Stock			
Totals	357,455.50	27,097.21	384,431.20

INCOME—Continued.

DO BUSINESS IN THIS STATE) FOR THE YEAR ENDING DECEMBER 31, 1917.

Received			Total Premiums	Interest, Dividends and Rents	All Other Items	Total Income
Automobile and Team Property Damage	Workmen's Collective	Live Stock				
$3,662,342.81	$	$	$ 7,603,780.95	$ 290,228.46	$	$7,894,009.41
	20,993.36		16,231,609.24	432,166.24	323,625.00	16,987,400.48
2,089,716.08			2,089,716.08	40,715.88	543.16	2,130,975.12
			802,954.36	73,905.00	1,545.98	878,405.34
			317,279.11		6,868,496.34	7,185,775.45
			4,242,375.17	601,725.30	119,645.82	4,963,746.29
			337,263.75			337,263.75
69,204.60	1,159.32		4,402,238.00	68,717.66	259,226.30	4,730,181.96
704,722.69	16,956.16		13,633,888.42	397,906.18	33,806.27	14,065,600.87
388,623.60	733.76		11,870,102.79	655,075.83	470,831.04	12,996,009.66
266,522.78			6,659,915.04	518,208.51	109,958.60	7,288,082.15
355,062.62	954.99		3,956,685.62	93,213.05	657,707.12	4,707,605.79
263,856.28	3,971.64		1,941,876.26	70,008.65		2,011,884.91
236,542.98		280,864.53	5,233,108.53	141,955.96		5,375,064.49
			2,034,626.27	306,781.59	74,799.65	2,416,207.51
			655,946.89	48,504.03	2,220.13	706,671.05
333,402.34	22,933.67		7,832,561.69	254,874.18	234,874.29	8,322,310.16
467,504.76	37,109.40		12,518,383.98	455,949.42	147,701.57	13,122,034.97
111,065.64			4,607,342.98	152,840.34	201,427.66	4,961,610.98
			835,582.77	40,595.49	34.12	876,212.38
			319,296.38			319,296.38
			5,394,331.45	528,521.84	862,550.56	6,785,403.85
			741,720.11	16,163.73	29,867.32	787,751.16
			1,235,303.81		44,694.00	1,279,997.81
134,755.30	45,246.63		3,037,945.63	127,904.62	64,264.87	3,230,115.12
			729,745.76	32,145.71	12,810.51	774,701.98
			1,504,627.76	39,536.71	158,847.00	1,703,011.47
405,086.09	2,781.36		8,919,348.42	293,778.11	22,064.82	9,235,191.35
			2,082,031.80	119,715.65	35,109.58	2,236,857.03
			758,270.28	15,878.68	105,443.46	879,592.42
320,575.73			2,768,034.34	147,900.37		2,915,934.71
			111,709.38		3,064,161.45	3,175,870.83
359,359.26	829.52		4,995,758.22	195,391.97	1,420.42	5,192,570.61
291,796.82	3,981.32		5,433,382.89	278,982.51	44,311.00	5,756,676.40
	18,448.66		25,645,901.20	942,558.98	108,267.68	26,696,727.86
1,385,685.46			2,937,792.55	154,110.78	12,324.52	3,104,227.85
153,083.32	2,677.73		3,424,227.68	156,677.17	1,331.46	3,582,236.31
463,816.27	88,685.03		14,390,158.36	543,748.77	41,260.40	14,975,167.43
		288,355.28	288,355.28	20,338.63		308,693.91
12,462,725.43	267,462.55	569,219.81	192,525,179.20	8,256,726.00	14,115,172.10	214,897,077.30

SHOWING DISBURSEMENTS OF FIDELITY AND CASUALTY COMPANIES (LICENSED

Name of Company	Losses			
	Accident	Health	Liability	Workmen's Compensation
Ætna Casualty and Surety	$ 7,377.75	$	$ 349,743.91	$ 89,668.01
Ætna Life (Accident)	1,158,045.22	355,456.75	1,876,631.15	3,337,306.18
American Automobile				
American Credit Indemnity				
American National Life (Accident)	66,145.23	63,613.34		
American Surety				
Columbian National Life (Accident)	94,623.39	54,012.92		
Continental Casualty	978,108.59	484,868.95	41,351.62	219,580.87
Employers Liability	157,582.75	54,692.51	1,306,407.62	3,219,103.61
Fidelity and Casualty	801,087.34	693,835.98	849,222.95	1,423,343.71
Fidelity and Deposit	174,433.66	173,963.79	525,999.00	277,722.97
General Accident	351,309.17	187,555.42	911,490.61	532,859.95
Georgia Casualty	10,692.12	11,424.49	499,708.61	197,358.87
Hartford Accident and Indemnity	92,687.27	31,479.64	494,965.03	866,786.10
Hartford Steam Boiler				
Lloyd's Plate Glass				
London Guarantee and Accident	119,849.37	55,889.13	726,206.36	1,699,956.94
Maryland Casualty	348,189.11	206,957.45	1,466,838.15	1,894,959.99
Massachusetts Bonding	*826,214.19		395,314.75	452,759.28
Metropolitan Casualty	67,935.57	21,327.47		
Metropolitan Life (Accident)	*268,078.26			
National Surety				
National Casualty	*321,713.25			
National Life of America (Accident)	*402,531.23			
New Amsterdam Casualty	82,632.47	48,452.75	243,369.98	380,423.33
New York Plate Glass				
North American Accident	658,788.52			
Ocean Accident and Guarantee	153,445.15	60,268.23	1,106,941.24	1,610,150.36
Pacific Mutual Life (Accident)	669,486.06	259,291.14		
Provident Life and Accident	*369,275.16			
Preferred Accident	353,660.38	138,198.58	285,214.83	
Reliance Life (Accident)	20,828.95	13,873.09		
Royal Indemnity	151,162.16	51,928.77	663,193.50	920,451.37
Standard Accident	759,214.16	203,791.89	375,187.32	760,698.93
Travelers (Accident)	2,013,282.25	576,520.21	2,648,173.13	5,506,571.52
Travelers Indemnity	25,723.72	29,964.49	21,109.07	80,047.95
United States Casualty	232,350.63	163,627.41	549,031.51	442,179.20
U. S. Fidelity and Guaranty	96,114.09	40,171.57	1,250,665.89	2,139,680.42
Western Live Stock				
Totals	11,832,567.17	4,011,170.97	16,586,766.23	26,051,609.56

*Accident and Health.

DISBURSEMENTS.

TO DO BUSINESS IN THIS STATE) FOR THE YEAR ENDING DECEMBER 31, 1917.

Paid

Fidelity	Surety	Plate-glass	Steam-boiler	Burglary and Theft	Credit	Sprinkler
$ 64,902.81	$ 261,201.48	$ 119,128.31	$............	$ 165,575.21	$............	$ 54,496.00
					40,182.81	
374,408.59	409,104.06					
18,116.58		75,644.51	7,003.11	102,724.01		
29,293.09	180,190.79	194,133.15	41,397.81	245,164.22		
321,625.04	506,220.12	149,420.49		125,798.77		
				24,956.44		
		25,365.97		6,277.28		
43,344.09	128,538.35	58,812.37		138,818.75		
			163,995.37			
		269,235.28				
			2,598.99	76,340.58	19,667.79	
56,213.74	318,688.93	158,188.75	33,810.44	151,536.22		66,979.24
56,526.36	137,019.60	120,327.57		120,465.30		
		273,241.40		11,157.54		
467,179.52	367,655.78			261,348.29		
19,134.69	150,678.04	70,844.63		66,981.75		
		356,489.92				
25,114.04		64,667.12	7,716.55	100,214.11	9,280.59	
5,215.37	8,407.53	69.36		64,665.38		
57,454.26	133,825.80	76,925.21	5,386.92	97,208.92		
		67,262.71	25,843.93	67,491.08		
		41,357.36	4,500.00	51,084.54		982.45
382,855.27	1,106,234.53	92,329.23		158,021.00		
1,921,383.45	3,707,765.01	2,213,443.34	292,253.12	2,035,829.39	69,131.19	122,457.69

SHOWING DISBURSEMENTS OF FIDELITY AND CASUALTY COMPANIES (LICENSED

Name of Company		Losses	
	Fly-wheel	Automobile and Team Property Damage	Workmen's Collective
Ætna Casualty and Surety	$ 615.01	$ 1,046,838.29	$
Ætna Life (Accident)			6,236.03
American Automobile		851,976.87	
American Credit Indemnity			
American National Life (Accident)			
American Surety			
Columbian National Life (Accident)			
Continental Casualty		22,749.22	476.76
Employers Liability	211.34	246,903.05	12,625.22
Fidelity and Casualty	24,303.70	167,537.24	100.41
Fidelity and Deposit		131,789.08	
General Accident		176,858.92	1,164.06
Georgia Casualty		141,391.89	1,583.69
Hartford Accident and Indemnity		107,852.94	
Hartford Steam Boiler	16,667.67		
Lloyd's Plate Glass			
London Guarantee and Accident		129,067.05	14,522.49
Maryland Casualty	2,502.26	205,219.95	16,191.61
Massachusetts Bonding		44,662.19	
Metropolitan Casualty			
Metropolitan Life (Accident)			
National Surety			
National Casualty			
National Life of America (Accident)			
New Amsterdam Casualty		54,170.07	18,082.25
New York Plate Glass			
North American Accident			
Ocean Accident and Guarantee	336.53	164,712.56	218.39
Pacific Mutual Life (Accident)			
Provident Life and Accident			
Preferred Accident		107,830.16	
Reliance Life (Accident)			
Royal Indemnity	1,472.88	149,281.55	
Standard Accident		121,526.32	1,684.10
Travelers (Accident)			9,513.13
Travelers Indemnity		569,235.39	
United States Casualty		82,344.07	814.57
U. S. Fidelity and Guaranty		198,877.01	56,025.79
Western Live Stock			
Totals	46,109.39	4,720,823.82	139,238.50

*Physician's Defense.

DISBURSEMENTS—Continued.

TO DO BUSINESS IN THIS STATE) FOR THE YEAR ENDING DECEMBER 31, 1917.

Paid Live Stock	Total Losses Paid	Commissions	Dividends	Salaries of Officers and Agents	All Other Expenditures	Total Disbursements
$-----------	$ 2,159,546.78	$1,392,257.03	$ 125,000.00	$ 579,604.97	$1,790,752.98	$ 6,047,161.76
-----------	6,733,675.33	3,022,857.60	250,000.00	1,073,143.75	2,595,512.84	13,675,189.52
-----------	851,976.87	419,014.46	37,500.00	173,293.48	219,616.59	1,701,401.40
-----------	40,182.81	192,712.83	56,000.00	80,349.56	135,214.46	504,459.66
-----------	129,763.57	99,361.33	-----------	15,038.10	1,972,633.21	2,216,796.21
-----------	783,512.65	787,107.73	400,000.00	1,311,054.86	866,980.68	4,148,655.92
-----------	178,636.31	99,298.74	-----------	35,983.82	37,652.86	351,571.73
-----------	1,747,136.01	1,174,849.53	60,000.00	573,575.76	660,261.32	4,215,822.62
-----------	5,201,014.31	2,796,921.33	-----------	514,394.44	2,757,529.27	11,269,859.35
-----------	4,649,610.39	2,671,948.46	250,000.00	1,134,595.00	2,343,374.47	11,049,528.32
-----------	2,386,972.92	1,668,596.55	480,000.00	1,084,137.10	1,757,015.78	7,376,722.35
-----------	2,186,194.57	964,726.21	-----------	275,146.81	1,062,982.29	4,489,049.88
-----------	893,802.92	481,423.24	21,037.80	70,582.08	364,149.35	1,830,995.39
123,579.50	2,086,864.04	1,041,901.09	-----------	467,045.69	751,087.49	4,346,898.31
-----------	180,663.04	324,529.59	200,000.00	398,938.67	898,193.84	2,002,325.14
-----------	269,235.28	202,944.80	51,000.00	78,769.63	102,559.42	704,509.13
-----------	2,844,098.70	1,526,832.73	-----------	541,198.96	1,089,649.20	6,001,779.59
*15,487.90	4,941,763.74	2,559,873.18	300,000.00	630,749.86	2,034,859.51	10,467,246.29
-----------	2,153,289.24	1,157,054.72	-----------	630,881.04	769,588.47	4,710,813.47
-----------	373,661.98	263,761.85	36,000.00	120,853.37	65,232.12	859,509.32
-----------	268,078.26	-----------	-----------	27,914.47	15,557.21	311,549.94
-----------	1,096,183.59	1,280,297.25	490,000.00	909,630.19	1,324,724.92	5,100,835.95
-----------	321,713.25	270,299.48	16,000.00	70,493.14	95,605.16	774,111.03
-----------	402,531.23	451,616.45	-----------	293,357.09	2,983,095.32	4,130,600.09
-----------	1,134,769.96	702,710.39	120,000.00	236,919.71	436,710.75	2,631,110.81
-----------	356,489.92	255,366.31	38,000.00	69,397.17	38,828.44	758,081.84
-----------	658,788.52	537,182.98	30,000.00	198,477.48	295,022.18	1,719,471.16
-----------	3,303,064.87	1,696,687.45	-----------	501,228.74	1,304,026.57	6,805,007.63
-----------	928,777.20	688,497.85	130,000.00	204,334.51	250,555.17	2,202,164.73
-----------	369,275.16	192,398.08	44,000.00	68,337.91	119,582.83	793,593.98
-----------	963,261.59	697,282.41	168,000.00	252,367.23	249,512.48	2,330,423.71
-----------	34,702.04	10,238.59	-----------	36,415.48	1,992,839.29	2,074,195.40
-----------	2,308,335.21	1,066,264.76	-----------	403,396.49	675,159.61	4,453,156.07
-----------	2,222,102.72	1,285,522.00	100,000.00	443,232.84	628,538.53	4,679,396.09
-----------	10,754,060.24	4,303,211.00	480,000.00	1,957,485.70	4,076,956.65	21,571,713.59
-----------	895,678.34	600,557.05	80,000.00	276,324.59	497,418.33	2,349,978.31
-----------	1,568,271.74	754,002.09	49,960.00	217,888.53	256,024.45	3,046,147.41
-----------	5,520,974.80	2,593,063.59	360,000.00	1,774,647.99	1,592,616.84	11,841,303.22
99,778.21	99,778.21	1,135.68	11,250.00	21,497.39	92,549.12	226,210.40
238,845.61	73,998,438.31	40,234,307.01	4,383,747.80	17,752,683.60	39,400,170.00	175,769,346.72

SHOWING ASSETS OF FIDELITY AND CASUALTY COMPANIES (LICENSED TO

Name of Company	Real Estate	Loans on Mortgages	Loans on Collaterals
Ætna Casualty and Surety	$	$ 1,544,100.00	$ 586,815.05
Ætna Life (Accident)	9,618.93	3,324,390.00	282,380.00
American Automobile			
American Credit Indemnity		25,000.00	
American National Life (Accident)			
American Surety	3,166,047.91		763,088.04
Columbian National Life (Accident)*			
Continental Casualty	75,000.00	668,255.00	
Employer's Liability			
Fidelity and Casualty	1,268,833.45		33,174.89
Fidelity and Deposit	2,618,236.14	128,244.00	
General Accident	180,000.00	11,000.00	
Georgia Casualty	375,000.00	358,766.18	
Hartford Accident and Indemnity		190,000.00	
Hartford Steam Boiler	90,000.00	1,544,400.00	
Lloyd's Plate Glass	275,000.00	52,750.00	
London Guarantee and Accident		4,000.00	
Maryland Casualty	1,540,899.15	54,401.33	25,397.00
Massachusetts Bonding	14,813.36		
Metropolitan Casualty			
Metropolitan Life (Accident)			
National Surety	114,827.92	89,632.37	51,500.00
National Casualty		26,500.00	5,000.00
National Life of America (Accident)			
New Amsterdam Casualty	142,300.96	92,000.00	
New York Plate Glass		41,000.00	
North American Accident		300,225.00	30,000.00
Ocean Accident and Guarantee		105,000.00	
Pacific Mutual Life (Accident)		1,567,561.27	131,500.00
Provident Life and Accident		171,265.00	20,000.00
Preferred Accident		82,000.00	
Reliance Life (Accident)			
Royal Indemnity			
Standard Accident		190,050.00	59,276.59
Travelers (Accident)			955,388.75
Travelers Indemnity		440,553.00	28,100.00
United States Casualty	250.00	173,900.00	9,030.24
United States Fidelity and Guaranty	740,445.48	24,800.00	87,286.64
Western Live Stock		213,050.00	20,000.00
Totals	10,611,273.30	11,422,843.15	3,087,937.20

*See Life Statement.   †Minus.

ASSETS.

Bonds and Stocks	Cash in Office and Banks	Interest and Rents Due and Accrued	Outstanding Premiums	All Other Assets	Total Assets
$ 4,709,225.84	$ 1,817,380.65	$ 97,162.92	$ 1,552,698.68	$ 387,665.39	$ 10,695,048.53
6,326,768.42	3,115,577.49	160,737.22	2,653,259.04	984,515.06	16,857,246.16
1,134,001.31	199,883.17	18,178.17	447,739.39	82,123.93	1,881,925.97
1,518,782.72	110,656.71	16,311.65		44,795.14	1,715,546.22
			20,706.98	5,186,047.15	5,206,754.13
4,464,907.74	688,175.23	45,718.15	484,048.60	458,285.11	10,070,270.78
1,044,662.32	121,024.27	24,883.57	924,615.74	154,595.82	3,013,036.72
10,107,485.90	586,947.02	129,696.61	3,421,693.95	530,747.10	14,776,570.58
10,910,860.67	445,538.69	108,188.94	1,902,810.38	407,923.60	15,077,330.62
6,293,588.51	1,352,160.71	687.06	1,106,061.62	535,713.76	12,034,691.80
2,352,437.00	149,516.97	24,113.74	675,844.06		3,392,911.77
387,240.80	217,318.80	11,653.80	517,786.96	6,466.43	1,874,232.97
2,899,140.00	818,620.67	43,601.70	1,223,155.11	120,651.07	5,295,168.55
4,569,226.63	387,950.61	104,020.74	414,095.11	16,391.15	7,126,084.24
473,434.98	28,812.63	5,510.89	116,748.35		952,256.85
6,111,116.60	495,210.22	102,149.87	1,698,113.15	157,579.20	8,568,169.04
8,028,935.43	862,239.99	58,877.00	2,038,824.88	92,831.17	12,702,405.95
3,540,638.85	529,822.69	43,293.60	702,635.84	174,049.71	5,005,254.05
697,187.34	58,742.56	6,830.84	178,732.08	1,159.10	942,651.92
11,365,436.08	1,011,022.38	137,461.67	1,039,086.01	290,898.11	14,099,864.54
298,980.80	33,963.77	5,658.84	5,250.00	5,151.80	380,505.21
	200.00		6,497.96	15,253,531.83	15,260,229.79
2,101,100.91	469,560.41	15,443.47	661,722.46	85,387.09	3,567,515.30
697,929.63	48,959.80	2,991.30	170,976.02		961,856.75
391,430.91	89,899.86	8,482.86	53,170.33	†4,781.50	873,208.96
7,204,842.00	399,336.86	102,441.86	1,358,127.39	194,120.32	9,363,868.43
190,011.18	120,381.65	35,619.54	381,582.17		2,421,874.31
145,795.00	39,978.90	4,623.27	77,336.10	12,224.96	471,223.23
3,728,088.00	212,665.56	48,998.87	585,337.91	582.08	4,657,672.42
			24,761.32	7,525,741.05	7,550,502.37
4,450,453.83	541,694.77	65,335.09	1,116,857.72	133,574.13	6,307,915.54
5,996,315.32	235,874.80	114,970.54	677,360.32	92,833.12	7,366,680.69
20,537,839.00	3,482,726.85	227,391.13	4,290,680.05	1,206.00	29,495,231.78
3,112,353.97	59,309.83	51,680.46	475,778.16		4,167,775.42
3,006,670.00	167,854.48	26,708.16	472,702.37		3,919,435.87
10,266,421.12	2,101,463.12	135,791.00	2,263,368.87	62,320.62	16,041,264.06
144,548.00	42,461.57	6,419.64	46,971.92	421,687.83	473,451.13
149,207,856.81	21,042,933.69	1,991,634.17	33,787,137.00	33,416,017.33	264,567,632.65

SHOWING LIABILITIES OF FIDELITY AND CASUALTY COMPANIES (LICENSED

Name of Company	Unpaid Claims and Expense of Settlement	Unearned Premiums
Ætna Casualty and Surety	$ 2,016,792.21	$ 3,146,106.22
Ætna Life (Accident)	6,268,351.78	5,206,803.28
American Automobile	384,186.87	880,945.41
American Credit Indemnity	467,051.49	405,043.94
American National Life (Accident)	10,518.93	41,761.51
American Surety	1,071,147.69	2,662,043.23
Columbian National Life (Accident)	59,605.74	139,583.57
Continental Casualty	524,858.48	1,297,491.56
Employer's Liability	5,517,839.00	5,112,015.22
Fidelity and Casualty	3,919,858.46	6,062,098.16
Fidelity and Deposit	2,435,377.18	3,652,453.00
General Accident	1,163,539.69	1,372,155.86
Georgia Casualty	457,776.99	749,125.30
Hartford Accident and Indemnity	1,470,636.76	2,085,222.42
Hartford Steam Boiler	122,761.60	3,013,990.80
Lloyd's Plate Glass	71,825.54	339,022.61
London Guarantee and Accident	3,645,388.95	2,479,077.76
Maryland Casualty	3,290,421.79	5,210,104.53
Massachusetts Bonding	1,388,306.90	1,444,607.65
Metropolitan Casualty	63,494.35	415,062.94
Metropolitan Life (Accident)	5,000.00	13,545.59
National Surety	1,465,189.63	3,239,280.34
National Casualty	28,078.00	19,125.00
National Life of America (Accident)	40,532.39	46,100.71
New Amsterdam Casualty	831,685.25	1,219,300.65
New York Plate Glass	42,009.93	374,488.93
North American Accident	146,954.20	270,099.03
Ocean Accident and Guarantee	2,910,681.65	3,103,162.93
Pacific Mutual Life (Accident)	251,735.77	859,580.09
Provident Life and Accident	34,800.00	57,129.41
Preferred Accident	741,262.12	1,365,474.96
Reliance Life (Accident)	3,340.00	53,775.94
Royal Indemnity	1,701,258.25	2,114,187.69
Standard Accident	2,648,032.11	2,035,348.66
Travelers (Accident)	8,563,138.43	8,778,899.07
Travelers Indemnity	650,371.36	1,699,156.77
United States Casualty	851,323.00	1,447,140.28
United States Fidelity and Guaranty	4,227,115.00	6,101,802.79
Western Live Stock	19,828.26	126,275.05
Totals	59,512,075.75	78,638,588.86

LIABILITIES.

Other Liabilities	Total Liabilities, Except Capital and Surplus	Cash Capital	Surplus	Surplus to Policyholders	Total Liabilities, Including Capital and Surplus
$ 676,267.08	$ 5,839,165.51	$ 2,000,000.00	$ 2,855,883.02	$ 4,855,883.02	$ 10,695,048.53
110,580,117.79	122,055,272.85	5,000,000.00	13,529,172.06	18,529,172.06	140,584,444.91
156,706.61	1,421,838.89	300,000.00	160,087.08	460,087.08	1,881,925.97
93,450.79	965,546.22	350,000.00	400,000.00	750,000.00	1,715,546.22
4,030,833.04	4,083,113.48	250,000.00	873,640.65	1,123,640.65	5,206,754.13
629,741.12	4,362,932.04	5,000,000.00	707,338.74	5,707,338.74	10,070,270.78
37,198.64	236,387.95	---------	---------	---------	236,387.95
590,686.68	2,413,036.72	300,000.00	300,000.00	600,000.00	3,013,036.72
1,656,464.33	12,286,318.55	200,000.00	2,290,252.03	2,490,252.03	14,776,570.58
1,553,386.91	11,535,343.53	1,000,000.00	2,541,987.09	3,541,987.09	15,077,330.62
1,134,538.83	7,222,369.01	3,000,000.00	1,812,322.79	4,812,322.79	12,034,691.80
250,166.43	2,785,861.98	250,000.00	357,049.79	607,049.79	3,392,911.77
185,726.10	1,392,628.39	300,540.00	181,064.58	481,604.58	1,874,232.97
507,262.22	4,063,121.40	800,000.00	432,047.15	1,232,047.15	5,295,168.55
334,036.98	3,470,789.38	2,000,000.00	1,655,294.86	3,655,294.86	7,126,084.24
77,489.59	488,337.74	250,000.00	213,919.11	463,919.11	952,256.85
1,388,092.42	7,512,559.13	250,000.00	805,609.91	1,055,609.91	8,568,169.04
1,160,315.52	9,660,841.84	1,500,000.00	1,541,564.11	3,041,564.11	12,702,405.95
301,231.01	3,134,145.56	1,500,000.00	371,108.49	1,871,108.49	5,005,254.05
72,213.89	550,771.18	200,000.00	191,880.74	391,880.74	942,651.92
5,659.46	24,205.05	---------	---------	---------	24,205.05
966,309.42	5,670,779.39	4,000,000.00	4,429,085.15	8,429,085.15	14,099,864.54
14,000.00	61,203.00	200,000.00	119,302.21	319,302.21	380,505.21
14,354,999.83	14,441,632.93	500,000.00	318,596.86	818,596.86	15,260,229.79
265,933.45	2,316,919.35	1,000,000.00	250,595.95	1,250,595.95	3,567,515.30
71,227.50	487,726.36	200,000.00	274,130.39	474,130.39	961,856.75
47,408.34	464,461.57	200,000.00	208,747.39	408,747.39	873,208.96
2,006,416.11	8,020,260.69	250,000.00	1,093,607.74	1,343,607.74	9,363,868.43
38,839,125.74	39,950,441.60	1,000,000.00	1,118,341.68	2,118,341.68	42,068,783.28
94,977.37	186,906.78	200,000.00	84,316.45	284,316.45	471,223.23
850,935.34	2,957,672.42	700,000.00	1,000,000.00	1,700,000.00	4,657,672.42
6,187,504.54	6,244,620.48	1,000,000.00	305,881.89	1,305,881.89	7,550,502.37
922,377.00	4,737,822.94	1,000,000.00	570,092.60	1,570,092.60	6,307,915.54
353,711.79	5,037,092.56	1,000,000.00	1,329,588.13	2,329,588.13	7,366,680.69
97,906,129.06	115,248,166.56	6,000,000.00	8,062,943.09	14,062,943.09	129,311,109.65
202,473.96	2,552,002.09	1,000,000.00	615,773.33	1,615,773.33	4,167,775.42
370,972.59	2,669,435.87	500,000.00	750,000.00	1,250,000.00	3,919,435.87
878,624.73	11,207,542.52	3,000,000.00	1,833,721.54	4,833,721.54	16,041,264.06
16,641.57	162,744.88	225,000.00	85,706.25	310,706.25	473,451.13
289,771,353.78	427,922,018.39	46,425,540.00	53,670,652.85	100,096,192.85	528,018,211.24

SHOWING PREMIUMS IN FORCE OF FIDELITY AND CASUALTY COMPANIES (LICENSED

Name of Company	Accident	Health
Ætna Casualty and Surety	$ 15,324.39	$ 2,129.70
Ætna Life (Accident)	2,297,632.84	750,554.26
American Automobile		
American Credit Indemnity		
American National Life (Accident)	74,456.67	
American Surety		
Columbian National Life (Accident)	154,348.88	124,455.77
Continental Casualty	1,642,180.24	422,849.59
Employer's Liability	317,233.38	96,575.62
Fidelity and Casualty	1,784,569.09	1,363,896.92
Fidelity and Deposit	449,499.23	302,368.66
General Accident	294,949.71	114,332.66
Georgia Casualty	8,552.09	6,738.06
Hartford Accident and Indemnity	176,981.55	69,954.03
Hartford Steam Boiler		
Lloyd's Plate Glass		
London Guarantee and Accident	159,591.25	67,009.07
Maryland Casualty	686,147.70	416,133.69
Massachusetts Bonding	*465,488.27	
Metropolitan Casualty	123,905.34	40,780.61
Metropolitan Life (Accident)		27,091.17
National Surety		
National Casualty	*35,050.00	
National Life of America (Accident)	*75,862.46	
New Amsterdam Casualty	223,086.65	72,035 52
New York Plate Glass		
North American Accident	499,373.33	
Ocean Accident and Guarantee	346,463.72	100,680.96
Pacific Mutual Life (Accident)	1,204,369.15	508,560.88
Provident Life and Accident	*104,754.75	
Preferred Accident	881,075.33	284,142.21
Reliance Life (Accident)	68,189.52	39,362.35
Royal Indemnity	210,074.77	65,464.53
Standard Accident	1,116,364.89	351,192.96
Travelers (Accident)	4,022,297.78	1,023,225.30
Travelers Indemnity	108,043.02	86,647.65
United States Casualty	455,104.54	237,639.59
United States Fidelity and Guaranty	249,240.47	100,833.90
Western Live Stock		
Totals	18,250,211.01	6,674,655.66

*Accident and Health.

Liability	Workmen's Compensation	Fidelity	Surety	Plate-glass	Steam-boiler
1,091,258.27	$ 109,786.26	$ 294,333.09	$ 1,352,958.83	$ 261,110.10	$
3,863,839.83	3,908,723.08				
		1,197,476.85	3,108,911.39		
219,286.82	221,495.88				
4,005,983.17	4,294,588.98	89,676.96	9,581.56	108,218.72	178,297.89
2,156,108.12	2,279,439.88	410,368.47	595,350.87	470,950.86	1,365,002.63
1,075,121.72	9,692.01	764,050.04	3,466,945.44	333,439.84	
1,416,717.25	525,482.83				
976,160.08	187,073.43		25.00	43,617.10	
1,315,224.23	895,211.65	210,548.04	465,421.69	143,486.64	
					5,313,761.50
				670,427.64	
1,635,326.12	2,100,782.24				200,656.01
2,607,978.82	2,395,411.88	226,163.09	1,027,710.08	333,962.57	946,334.52
774,612.26	49,136.70	335,773.46	543,766.74	210,153.43	
				610,497.80	
		1,914,915.60	3,534,111.14		
580,935.76	431,667.16	232,124.85	409,321.82	140,801.52	
				756,181.55	
1,912,087.28	1,997,571.91	85,140.87		132,120.81	422,349.48
890,878.36	2,972.09	35,835.18	94,607.54		
1,443,459.56	755,307.90	248,048.41	249,425.38	145,786.32	252,153.89
1,265,511.64	1,030,437.14				
5,566,432.00	6,967,436.63				
67,894.40	103,350.51			202,419.93	891,846.66
1,027,562.00	771,575.37			89,044.94	
2,705,474.31	1,783,833.02	1,650,534.78	4,063,299.51	209,400.19	
36,597,852.00	30,820,976.55	7,694,989.69	18,921,436.99	4,861,619.96	9,570,402.58

SHOWING PREMIUMS IN FORCE OF FIDELITY AND CASUALTY COMPANIES (LICENSED

Name of Company	Burglary and Theft	Credit
•Ætna Casualty and Surety	$ 600,485.87	$
Ætna Life (Accident)		
American Automobile		
American Credit Indemnity		776,875.17
American National Life (Accident)		
American Surety		
Columbian National Life (Accident)		
Continental Casualty		
Employer's Liability	367,660.70	
Fidelity and Casualty	887,948.99	
Fidelity and Deposit	358,173.00	
General Accident	61,568.74	
Georgia Casualty	14,676.32	
Hartford Accident and Indemnity	288'174.55	
Hartford Steam Boiler		
Lloyd's Plate Glass		
London Guarantee and Accident	200,656.01	355,200.54
Maryland Casualty	580,575.25	
Massachusetts Bonding	320,360.96	
Metropolitan Casualty	48,753.16	
Metropolitan Life (Accident)		
National Surety	742,267.89	
National Casualty		
National Life of America (Accident)		
New Amsterdam Casualty	185,460.37	
New York Plate Glass		
North American Accident		
Ocean Accident and Guarantee	365,977.02	375,769.0
Pacific Mutual Life (Accident)		
Provident Life and Accident		
Preferred Accident	203,487.65	
Reliance Life (Accident)		
Royal Indemnity	332,350.75	
Standard Accident		
Travelers (Accident)		
Travelers Indemnity	426,302.78	
United States Casualty	141,095.85	
United States Fidelityyand Guaranty	626,640.15	
Western Live Stock		
Totals	6,752,616.01	

OF PREMIUMS—Continued.

TO DO BUSINESS IN THIS STATE) FOR THE YEAR ENDING DECEMBER 31, 1917.

Sprinkler	Fly-wheel	Automobile and Team Property Damage	Workmen's Collective	Live Stock	Physicians' Defense
$ 232,180.40	$ 23,451.88	$ 2,076,713.14	$	$	$
		1,761,890.82	8,214.16		
		65,675.54			
	65,485.54	682,654.43	6,637.11		
	270,320.90	367,025.64	329.72		
		252,626.73			
		335,958.17			
		256,029.89	1,468.10		
		267,683.44		290,052.88	
	353,876.33				
353,701.80	101,609.12	317,434.88	9,789.92		
		438,234.48	16,020.06		28,134.27
		101,639.78			
		129,349.43	2,310.75		
	41,410.64	366,301.34	1,078.21		
		311,981.81			
	98,261.70	329,265.39	270.00		
		278,070.84	1,474.38		
			5,478.55		
	36,258.34	1,282,960.33			
		141,613.29	2,189.80		
		452,145.70	9,405.14		
				252,550.11	
585,882.20	990,674.45	10,215,255.07	64,665.90	542,602.99	28,134.27

SHOWING PREMIUMS COLLECTED AND LOSSES PAID OF FIDELITY AND CASUALTY COMPANIES

Name of Company	Accident	Losses Paid	Health	Losses Paid	Liability
Ætna Casualty and Surety	$	$	$	$	$ 2,572.79
Ætna Life (Accident)	7,984.63	7,869.97	12,005.68	6,909.69	102,847.60
American Automobile					
American Credit Indemnity					
American National Life (Accident)	1,507.39	148.20	1,507.39	359.40	
American Surety					
Columbian National Life (Accident)	150.52	61.42	285.91	37.14	
Continental Casualty	67,031.23	22,956.51	23,672.23	13,545.56	
Employers Liability	2,759.51	243.78	1,891.49	566.95	56,345.25
Fidelity and Casualty	7,688.81	6,741.63	8,058.55	2,243.24	45,061.99
Fidelity and Deposit	21,220.72	4,692.18	20,699.89	13,648.31	10,257.32
General Accident	9,967.24	11,935.50	10,364.26	4,797.04	46,241.68
Georgia Casualty	659.61	116.66	886.75	911.86	37,584.38
Hartford Accident and Indemnity	1,008.02	95.71	704.25	96.78	26,485.54
Hartford Steam Boiler					
Lloyd's Plate Glass					
London Guarantee and Accident					
Maryland Casualty	19,292.00	3,842.10	20,938.93	11,367.26	199,171.27
Massachusetts Bonding	*13,984.96	5,618.94			3,388.64
Metropolitan Casualty					
Metropolitan Life (Accident)	*2,488.48	1,874.16			
National Surety					
National Casualty	*8,534.09	3,196.34			
National Life of America (Accident)	*11,168.33	2,766.47			
New Amsterdam Casualty	5,887.97	1,217.18	3,746.36	2,009.00	8,839.37
New York Plate Glass					
North American Accident	2,310.82	877.67			
Ocean Accident and Guarantee	2,489.94	642.52	2,483.78	1,674.99	20,410.27
Pacific Mutual Life (Accident)	9,695.27	8,938.85	3,662.72	2,208.86	
Provident Life and Accident	*46,660.28	23,483.77			
Preferred Accident	2,584.24	520.34	1,515.50	117.85	
Reliance Life (Accident)	1,382.15	90.64	1,711.16	362.74	
Royal Indemnity	4,906.23	2,100.73	4,574.78	3,775.79	11,624.88
Standard Accident	27,869.20	11,068.80	11,203.83	6,564.18	107.50
Travelers (Accident)	14,721.74	8,973.90	7,561.55	3,837.08	47,994.73
Travelers Indemnity	263.13	200.00	17.50		
United States Casualty	3,891.24	694.81	5,899.63	3,484.01	56,673.44
United States Fidelity and Guaranty	1,924.23	7,160.15	1,786.35	185.24	23,604.68
Western Live Stock					
Totals	300,031.98	138'128.93	145,178.49	78,702.97	699,211.33

*Accident and Health.

LICENSED TO DO BUSINESS IN THIS STATE) FOR THE YEAR ENDING DECEMBER 31, 1917.

Losses Paid	Fidelity	Losses Paid	Surety	Losses Paid	Plate-glass	Losses Paid	Steam-boiler	Losses Paid
$ 143.70	$ 2,345.48	$........	$ 3,253.97	$ 66.92	$ 1,477.03	$........	$........	$........
11,437.49	----------	----------	----------	----------	----------	----------	----------	----------
----------	----------	----------	----------	----------	----------	----------	----------	----------
----------	----------	----------	----------	----------	----------	----------	----------	----------
----------	15,019.98	4,087.76	14,675.91	2,338.17	----------	----------	----------	----------
----------								
24,476.96	88.31	----------	----------	----------	576.12	232.73	----------	----------
15,329.17	1,559.90	650.00	310.45	----------	4,151.12	1,808.88	4,253.13	3,478.05
2,274.03	23,095.34	21,529.00	23,235.64	4,634.35	1,815.44	1,095.87	----------	----------
37,277.14								
12,112.98					217.16	45.00		
6,461.32	1,300.99	----------	2,709.82	----------	1,490.70	927.71		
							30,112.10	28.17
----------					2,817.14	1,456.68		
80,270.99	3,487.13	86.45	11,152.43	13,092.13	3,871.32	2,343.95	11,235.59	50.00
2,496.40	1,814.37	1,987.29	7,004.86	----------	899.94	993.36	----------	----------
----------					2,017.77	1,023.72		
----------	18,006.31	2,726.61	12,823.56	361.50	----------	----------	----------	----------
----------								
613.38	1,939.46	41.23	5,644.60	----------	124.06			
----------					4,342.92	2,171.17		
9,617.08	390.83	----------	----------	----------	1,112.17	485.85	538.19	----------
----------								

2,787.00	2,446.41	----------	664.35	----------	1,469.99	882.08	771.45	----------
140.06								
19,409.95								
----------	----------	----------	----------	----------	424.73	87.51	277.11	128.73
20,081.06					282.99	220.16	----------	----------
8,690.46	19,314.82	7,682.37	29,171.10	74,603.63	1,454.59	638.25		

253,619.71	90,809.33	38,790.71	110,646.69	95,096.70	28,545.19	14,412.92	47,187.57	3,684.95

SHOWING PREMIUMS COLLECTED AND LOSSES PAID OF FIDELITY AND CASUALTY COMPANIES

Name of Company	Burglary and Theft·	Losses Paid	Credit	Losses Paid	Sprinkler	Losses Paid
Ætna Casualty and Surety	$ 702.17	$ 780.05	$	$	$ 427.47	$116.9(
Ætna Life (Accident)						
American Automobile						
American Credit Indemnity			16,881.11	3,318.99		
American National Life (Accident)						
American Surety						
Columbian National Life (Accident)						
Continental Casualty						
Employers Liability	1,060.88	254.10				
Fidelity and Casualty	2,086.88	203.53				
Fidelity and Deposit			5,398.21	545.45		
General Accident	46.67					
Georgia Casualty	106.48					
Hartford Accident and Indemnity	1,234.69	101.35				
Hartford Steam Boiler						
Lloyd's Plate Glass						
London Guarantee and Accident			19,885.37	465.35		
Maryland Casualty	5,944.63	151.50			658.39	
Massachusetts Bonding	250.36	108.75				
Metropolitan Casualty						
Metropolitan Life (Accident)						
National Surety	1,089.26	85.00				
National Casualty						
National Life of America (Accident)						
New Amsterdam Casualty	125.22					
New York Plate Glass						
North American Accident						
Ocean Accident and Guarantee	905.58		1,580.00	72.00		
Pacific Mutual Life (Accident)						
Provident Life and Accident						
Preferred Accident						
Reliance Life (Accident)						
Royal Indemnity	887.79	360.29				
Standard Accident						
Travelers (Accident)						
Travelers Indemnity	248.68					
United States Casualty	368.16					
United States Fidelity and Guaranty	3,309.58	274.00				
Western Live Stock						
Totals	18,367.03	2,318.57	43,744.69	4,401.79	1,085.86	

*Policy Fees.

.ICENSED TO DO BUSINESS IN THIS STATE) FOR THE YEAR ENDING DECEMBER 31, 1917.

Fly-wheel	Losses Paid	Auto and Team Property Damage	Losses Paid	Work-men's Col-lective	Losses Paid	Live Stock	Losses Paid	Phy-sicians' Defense	Losses Paid
$_____	$_____	$ 21.85	$_____	$3,867.45	$1,004.34	$_____	$_____	$_____	$_____
		2,414.67	278.81	2,454.09					
1,544.01		1,695.00	145.40						
		1,290.33	254.70						
		10,430.03	397.95						
		1,857.52	276.07						
		3,132.44	558.15			296.70			
2,362.08									
1,586.27		4,265.53	806.51					673.94	250.00
		450.51	17.25						
		534.74	26.00						
490.76		523.25	167.13	944.82					
		1,381.82	88.00						
		8.95				*14.80			
		1,153.11	592.25						
		406.05	146.23						
		1,046.36	304.89						
						11,388.91	8,315.00		
5,983.12		30,612.16	4,068.34	7,266.36	1,004.34	11,700.41	8,315.00	673.94	250.00

STATISTICAL TABLES

RELATING TO FRATERNAL ORDERS

Name of Order	Income	
	Paid by Members	All Other Sources
Atlantic Coast Line Relief Department	$ 195,406.56	$ 54,105.58
Ben Hur, Supreme Tribe	1,549,387.71	83,098.62
Benefit Association of all Railway Employees	412,382.61	4,576.51
Brothers and Sisters Aid Society	260.30	25.28
Brothers and Sisters Union of America	2,187.40	438.35
District Household of Ruth, No. 10	16,195.89	1,280.77
Eastern Star	19,077.16	10.00
Funeral Benefit Association	465,970.35	6,649.95
Fraternal Mystic Circle	420,398.18	27,970.41
Grand Court of Calanthe	3,538.40	980.75
Grand United Order of Abraham		
Grand United Order of Brothers and Sisters of Love and Charity	9,578.25	160.00
Grand United Order of Odd Fellows (colored)	50,881.59	1,191.97
Household of David	317.78	
Independent Order of Good Samaritans (Raleigh)	717.81	
Independent Order of Good Samaritans (Kinston)	1,622.50	733.00
Independent Order of True Reformers		
Independent Order of Good Samaritans and Daughters of Samaria	1,306.19	
Independent Order of St. Luke	110,956.50	19,974.35
Independent Order of J. R. Giddings and Jollifee Union	15,597.25	4,012.50
Independent Order of Brith Sholom	280,672.76	88,863.70
Junior Order United American Mechanics	753,536.78	32,921.91
Knights of Gideon Mutual Society	40,442.25	3,241.11
Knights of Columbus	2,030,915.31	340,575.64
Knights of the Guiding Star of the East	948.15	
Knights of Pythias Supreme Lodge	2,401,400.45	465,449.02
Knights of Pythias (colored)		
Lincoln Benefit Society	4,593.83	20.00
Loyal Order of Moose	683,550.07	216,905.64
Masons Annuity	200,699.43	58,854.05
Masonic Benefit Fund (colored)	66,097.09	572.42
Masonic Mutual Life	509,323.53	51,113.67
Modern Brotherhood of America	1,452,727.57	169,580.94
Modern Woodmen of America	16,434,427.80	678,156.18
Mutual Life and Indemnity	1,074.31	
Oasis and Omar Temples	40,340.30	37.13
Order of the Golden Seal	304,781.56	52,004.27
Order United Commercial Travelers	977,410.35	49,782.59
North Carolina Camp, Patriotic Order Sons of America		
Norfolk and Western Relief Department	118,605.05	60,719.70
Patriotic Order Sons of America	22,438.00	25,789.61
Pink Hill Fraternal		
Peoples Independent Order True Reformers	757.32	280.00
Raleigh Union Society	5,775.47	2,000.00
Red Men's Benefit	15,545.56	647.74
Royal Arcanum	8,026,906.90	144,741.22
Royal Fraternal Association	6,634.63	60.00
Royal Knights of King David	35,381.45	1,946.67
Sons and Daughters of Peace	859.25	30.00
The Maccabees	6,141,306.83	941,667.67
Travelers Protective Association	554,064.41	14,399.43
United Order of J. R. Giddings and Jollifee Union	18,298.70	5,061.80
Woodmen of the World Sovereign Camp	13,167,699.34	1,760,104.10
Woodmen Circle Supreme Forest	2,196,022.11	283,477.17
Wise Men of North Carolina		
Woman's Association of the Maccabees	2,314,420.14	506,441.22
Woman's Union Burial Association	9,015.84	
Totals	62,092,454.97	6,160,652.64

INSURANCE ORDERS.

AND LIABILITIES FOR YEAR ENDING DECEMBER 31, 1917.

| Total Income | Disbursements | | | Total Assets | Total Liabilities |
	Paid for Claims	All Other Disbursements	Total Disbursements		
$ 249,512.14	$ 193,041.68	$ 48,834.70	$ 241,876.38	$ 39,592.52	$
1,632,486.33	1,099,846.44	434,411.26	1,534,257.70	1,727,579.69	201,597.53
416,959.12	203,195.15	191,012.44	394,207.59	114,553.72	24,148.69
285.58	75.00	158.30	233.30	210.97	210.97
2,625.75	2,243.00	346.10	2,589.10	210.41	250.00
17,476.66	14,983.66	2,063.30	17,046.96	6,929.45	975.00
19,087.16	15,140.00	909.37	16,049.37	3,037.79	1,312.50
472,620.30	423,125.00	16,801.50	439,926.50	223,738.03	
448,368.59	378,272.99	92,807.72	471,080.71	540,086.38	398,738.37
4,519.15	3,075.00	1,736.73	4,811.73	2,574.42	650.00
9,738.25	7,127.25	745.26	7,872.51	9,386.88	
52,073.56	42,415.19	3,868.46	46,283.65	41,598.03	3,483.33
317.78	250.00	70.70	320.70	231.19	
717.81	600.00	126.00	726.00	4,665.54	
2,355.50	211.00	523.28	734.28	1,651.22	840.00
1,306.19	875.00	511.78	1,386.78	2,619.49	500.00
30,930.85	66,864.16	61,003.35	127,867.51	112,955.19	5,920.00
19,609.75	7,247.75	15,256.14	22,503.89	7,910.84	625.00
369,536.46	210,719.67	104,186.78	314,906.45	312,760.62	68,950.00
786,458.69	671,475.85	36,960.67	708,436.52	666,699.43	62,827.89
43,683.36	27,000.00	9,813 13	36,813.13	24,560.74	1,375.00
2,371,490.95	987,925.62	363,856.28	1,351,781.90	8,190,124.27	6,188,790.23
948.15	700.00	230.50	930.50	125.16	150.00
2,866,849.47	1,583,180.81	385,102.74	1,968,283.55	9,701,148.27	8,463,653.42
4,613.83	3,359.25	1,066.44	4,425.69	1,000.00	675.00
900,455.71		696,118.33	696,118.33	1,750,934.91	540,765.35
259,553.48	178,566.45	53,122.80	231,689.25	993,351.54	969,325.77
66,669.51	54,900.00	4,499.95	59,399.95	24,718.77	3,000.00
560,437.20	103,614.20	175,688.91	279,303.11	1,359,858.73	1,291,292.66
1,622,308.51	995,831.59	173,590.60	1,169,422.19	3,637,697.89	156,293.06
17,112,583.98	14,968,437.35	1,791,509.22	16,759,946.57	16,114,502.38	2,489,516.06
1,074.31	900.00	144.05	1,044.05	139.61	
40,377.43	31,500.00	3,667.30	35,167.30	7,778.13	
356,785.83	145,085.96	151,818.99	296,904.95	702,649.38	589,829.70
1,027,192.94	674,941.70	197,393.71	868,335.41	886,496.85	278,838.67
179,324.75	41,928.76	59,571.95	101,500.71	77,824.04	1,500.00
48,227.61	24,000.00	680.01	24,680.01	22,791.60	2,000.00
1,037.32	420.50	553.08	973.58	63.77	420.50
7,775.47	5,175.00	2,382.18	7,557.18	1,098.85	2,530.00
16,193.30	7,850.00	2,918.68	10,768.68	26,377.02	2,300.00
8,171,648.12	6,892,330.56	2,303,613.17	9,195,943.73	5,297,006.59	783,233.62
6,694.63	3,449.74	2,500.71	5,950.45	9,716.35	476.00
37,328.12	13,130.00	12,715.47	25,845.47	26,162.17	2,000.00
889.25	400.00	249.50	649.50	1,739.75	800.00
7,082,974.50	5,970,191.08	997,347.52	6,970,538.60	7,960,378.66	1,910,282.25
568,463.84	440,616.45	95,007.64	535,624.09	313,211.25	88,931.90
23,360.50	17,975.00	4,480.54	22,455.54	38,779.33	750.00
14,927,803.44	8,847,939.92	2,086,208.01	10,934,147.93	35,236,695.19	3,010,755.63
2,479,499.28	1,088,372.18	565,470.33	1,653,842.51	6,773,443.23	285,048.40
2,820,861.36	1,329,175.57	448,792.35	1,777,967.92	11,507,040.34	201,763.57
9,015.84	8,177.93	623.74	8,801.67	574.14	479.79
68,253,107.61	47,787,859.41	11,603,071.67	59,390,931.08	114,506,980.72	28,037,805.86

Name of Order	Certificates in Force December 31, 1916		Certificates Issued During 1917	
	Number	Amount	Number	Amount
Atlantic Coast Line Relief Department	11,765	$		$
Ben Hur, Supreme Tribe	86,349	85,251,745.00	16,856	15,556,450.00
Benefit Association of all Railway Employees	27,665	531,500.00	18,665	531,500.00
Brothers and Sisters Aid Society	150		12	600.00
Brothers and Sisters Union of America	1,075		194	
District Household of Ruth, No. 10	7,030	448,819.00	502	25,100.00
Eastern Star			533	26,650.00
Funeral Benefit Association				
Fraternal Mystic Circle	17,590	14,560,195.00	4,560	1,598,448.00
Grand Court of Calanthe	1,353			
Grand United Order of Abraham				
Grand United Order of Brothers and Sisters of Love and Charity	3,033	303,300.00	740	
Grand United Order of Odd Fellows (colored)				
Household of David				
Independent Order of Good Samaritans (Raleigh)	240	2,400.00	49	4,900.00
Independent Order of Good Samaritans (Kinston)			645	31,475.00
Independent Order of True Reformers				
Independent Order of Good Samaritans and Daughters of Samaria (New Bern)	892		180	
Independent Order of St Luke	31,892	3,438,828.20	6,807	676,000.00
Independent Order of J. R. Giddings and Jollifee Union (Wilmington)	5,879	587,900.00	1,987	99,350.00
Independent Order of Brith Sholom	52,457	25,699,200.00	6,373	3,126,500.00
Junior Order United American Mechanics	216,286	91,573,000.00	39,540	17,546,000.00
Knights of Gideon Mutual Society	23,400		2,178	
Knights of Columbus	117,968	124,941,334.33	11,971	13,042,000.00
Knights of the Guiding Star of the East	361	36,100.00	20	2,000.00
Knights of Pythias Supreme Lodge	71,682	96,398,817.00	4,957	6,089,000.00
Knights of Pythias (colored)				
Lincoln Benefit Society	3,749	656,800.00	810	81,000.00
Loyal Order of Moose				
Masons Annuity	4,735	1,668,500.00	665	173,400.00
Masonic Benefit Fund (colored)				
Masonic Mutual Life	10,437	15,081,011.00	3,755	6,325,250.00
Modern Brotherhood of America	65,360	78,120,000.00	3,005	2,959,250.00
Modern Woodmen of America	1,008,410	1,588,098,500.00	85,576	107,916,000.00
Mutual Life and Indemnity				
N. C. Camp, Patriotic Order Sons of America				
Norfolk and Western Relief Department				
Oasis and Omar Temples	1,284	2,568.00	390	780.00
Order of the Golden Seal	9,502	12,530,658.45	4,877	7,508,550.00
Order United Commercial Travelers	75,051	375,255,000.00	7,073	35,365,000.00
Patriotic Order Sons of America	919	944,600.00	8	7,000.00
Pink Hill Fraternal				
Peoples Independent Order True Reformers				
Raleigh Union Society	1,500	225,000.00	222	25,530.00
Red Men's Benefit				
Royal Arcanum	177,235	305,665,528.00	1,092	1,185,000.00
Royal Fraternal Association	698	114,975.00	280	28,290.00
Royal Knights of King David	12,641	914,900.00	4,685	321,380.00
Sons and Daughters of Peace	204		115	
The Maccabees	302,531	364,332,477.49	19,182	19,040,000.00
Travelers Protective Association	59,329	296,645,000.00	14,383	71,915,000.00
United Order of J. R. Giddings and Jollifee Union				
Woodmen of the World Soverign Camp	804,291	1,073,968,500.00	111,277	139,973,900.00
Woodmen Circle Supreme Forest	170,631	169,336,100.00	25,361	25,670,100.00
Wise Men of North Carolina				
Woman's Association of the Maccabees	175,252	132,026,049.18	17,405	12,367,950.00
Woman's Union Burial Association				
Totals	3,560,826	4,859,359,305.65	416,930	489,219,353.90

Certificates Terminated During 1917		Certificates in Force December 31, 1917		Increase		Decrease	
Number	Amount	Number	Amount	Number	Amount	Number	Amount
	$	11,168	$		$	597	$
18,357	17,842,765.00	85,224	83,431,065.00			1,125	1,820,680.00
12,386	27,500.00	33,676	504,000.00	6,011			27,500.00
13		149				1	
330		946				129	
		7,582	476,419.00	552	27,600.00		
321	31,615.00	8,429	810,825.00				
5,505	2,780,938.00	16,652	13,377,705.00			938	1,182,490.00
24		1,329				24	
73	7,300.00	3,720	372,000.00	687	68,700.00		
		272	47,175.00				
		289	28,900.00	49	4,900.00		
46		599				46	
245		853				39	
5,326	523,860.35	34,058	3,659,167.85	2,166	220,339.65		
150	11,647.75	8,013	690,452.25	4,134	102,552.25		
6,685	2,928,400.00	52,596	25,788,650.00	139	89,450.00		
27,657	12,001,000.00	228,169	97,529,750.00	11,883	5,956,750.00		
		25,704		2,304			
5,960	6,303,934.00	123,979	131,679,400.33	6,011	6,738,066.00		
		383	38,400.00	23	2,300.00		
5,104	7,097,922.00	72,461	96,506,135.00	779	107,318.00		
		4,579	739,800.00	830	83,000.00		
460	120,200.00	4,940	1,721,700.00	205	53,200.00		
		9,000	2,700,000.00				
946	1,596,749.00	13,246	19,809,512.00	2,809	4,728,501.00		
10,825	12,946,500.00	58,428	69,209,750.00	6,932	8,910,250.00		
46,975	60,493,500.00	1,047,011	1,638,899,500.00	38,601	508,010.00		
		10,467	9,636,500.00				
496	992.00	1,552	3,104.00	268	536.00		
4,833	7,287,782.88	9,546	12,751,425.57	44	220,767.12		
8,289	41,445,000.00	76,619	383,095,000.00	1,558	7,840,000.00		
38	27,000.00	896	931,600.00			23	13,000.00
		180					45,100.00
142	16,340.00	1,580	179,900.00	80			
36,987	74,587,366.12	145,568	246,382,161.88			31,667	59,283,366.12
289	30,509.00	689	112,756.00			9	2,219.00
		14,686	1,030,000.00	2,045	115,100.00		
58		272					
21,652	23,547,789.67	300,061	359,824,687.82			2,470	4,507,787.67
9,306	46,530,000.00	65,201	326,005,000.00	5,872	29,360,000.00		
85,136	106,896,400.00	842,546	1,122,930,200.00	38,255	48,961,700.00		
13,312	12,534,500.00	183,424	183,307,900.00	12,793	13,971,800.00		
14,429	9,954,033.72	178,228	134,439,965.46	2,976	2,413,916.28		
342,355	447,571,544.49	3,684,970	4,968,650,507.06	148,006	130,484,756.30	37,068	66,882,144.79

Name of Order	Certificates in Force December 31, 1916		Certificates Issued Durin 1917	
	Number	Amount	Number	Amount
Atlantic Coast Line Relief Department	11,765	$		$
Ben Hur, Supreme Tribe	39	59,250.00	1	2,(
Benefit Association of all Railway Employees	86		258	
Brothers and Sisters Aid Society	150		12	(
Brothers and Sisters Union of America	1,075		201	
District Household of Ruth, No. 10	7,030	448,819.00	552	27,(
Eastern Star	8,210	815,440.00	540	27,(
Funeral Benefit Association				
Fraternal Mystic Circle	648	865,241.00	3	4,(
Grand Court of Calanthe	1,353			
Grand United Order of Abraham				
Grand United Order of Brothers and Sisters of Love and Charity	3,033	303,300.00	760	
Grand United Order of Odd Fellows (colored)				
Household of David				
Independent Order of Good Samaritans (Raleigh)	240	2,400.00	49	4,!
Independent Order of Good Samaritans (Kinston)			645	
Independent Order of True Reformers				
Independent Order of Good Samaritans and Daughters of Samaria (New Bern)	892		206	
Independent Order of St. Luke	1,383	149,560.00	468	46,!
Independent Order of J. R. Giddings and Jollifee Union	5,879	587,900.00	2,284	114,:
Independent Order of Brith Sholom	131	65,500.00	13	6,!
Junior Order United American Mechanics	37,667	18,131,500.00	4,857	2,345,:
Knights of Gideon Mutual Society	23,400		2,304	
Knights of Columbus	149	168,000.00	8	10,(
Knights of the Guiding Star of the East	361	36,100.00	23	2,:
Knights of Pythias Supreme Lodge	2,767	3,714,057.00	161	186,(
Knights of Pythias (colored)				
Lincoln Benefit Society	3,749	656,800.00	830	8,:
Loyal Order of Moose				
Masons Annuity	11	3,700.00		
Masonic Benefit Fund (colored)				
Masonic Mutual Life	1,335	1,706,700.00	124	159,(
Modern Brotherhood of America				
Modern Woodmen of America	4,682	6,335,500.00	2,161	2,516,(
Mutual Life and Indemnity				
Oasis and Omar Temple	1,284		764	
Order of the Golden Seal	40	29,000.00	18	39,(
Order United Commercial Travelers	771	3,855,000.00	70	350,(
N. C. Camp, Patriotic Order Sons of America				
Norfolk and Western Relief Department				
Patriotic Order Sons of America	2	2,000.00		
Pink Hill Fraternal				
Peoples Independent Order True Reformers				
Raleigh Union Society	1,500	2,250.00	222	25,
Red Men's Benefit	5,037			
Royal Arcanum	2,728	5,408,260.00	74	152,(
Royal Fraternal Association	698	114,975.00	280	28,:
Royal Knights of King David	5,195	373,150.00	3,773	271,(
Sons and Daughters of Peace	204		126	
The Maccabees	757	1,210,000.00	142	145,.
Travelers Protective Association	2,287	11,435,000.00	839	4,195,(
United Order of J. R. Giddings and Jollifee Union			4,616	5,691,
Woodmen of the World Sovereign Camp	26,042	32,752,000.00		
Woodmen Circle Supreme Forest	1,594	1,496,400.00	511	493,
Wise Men of North Carolina				
Woman's Association of the Maccabees	243	198,250.00	65	45,:
Woman's Union Burial Association				
Totals	164,417	90,926,052,00	27,960	16,897,:

Certificates Terminated During 1917		Certificates in Force December 31, 1917		Received from Members During the Year	Claims Incurred During the Year	Claims Paid During the Year	Claims Unpaid December 31, 1917
Number	Amount	Number	Amount				
	$........	11,168	$.........	$195,406.56	$64,000.00	$57,100.00	$19,400.00
20	32,250.00	20	29,000.00	445.35	----	----	----
26	----	318	500.00	2,566.00	1,243.53	1,037.27	234.92
13	----	149	----	260.30	50.00	75.00	----
330	----	946	----	2,187.40	2,600.00	2,243.00	232.00
210	24,576.60	7,372	451,842.40	16,195.89	15,201.60	14,951.60	975.00
321	31,615.00	8,429	810,825.00	19,077.16	16,415.00	15,140.00	1,175.00
				26,453.20	14,187.50		
78	128,500.00	573	740,741.00	18,186.11	6,847.62	6,860.00	4,987.48
24	----	1,329	----	3,538.40	3,075.00	3,075.00	150.00
73	7,300.00	3,720	372,000.00	9,578.25	7,300.00	7,300.00	----
				50,881.59	41,715.19	42,415.19	3,483.33
----	----	272	47,175.00	317.78	250.00	250.00	----
----	----	289	28,900.00	717.81	600.00	600.00	----
46	----	599	----	1,622.50	600.00	210.00	340.00
245	----	853	----	1,306.19	----	875.00	500.00
378	37,800.00	1,473	158,560.00	4,937.25	2,900.00	3,400.00	----
150	11,647.75	8,013	690,452.25	15,597.25	6,672.75	7,247.75	500.00
2	1,000.00	142	71,000.00	757.24			
3,510	1,689,750.00	39,014	18,787,000.00	145,029.39	110,000.00	100,500.00	10,250.00
2,304		23,400		40,442.25		27,000.00	1,375.00
7	7,000.00	150	171,000.00	2,292.60	2,000.00	2,000.00	1,000.00
----	----	384	38,400.00	948.15		700.00	150.00
147	193,349.00	2,781	3,706,708.00	84,063.69	41,500.00	36,000.00	9,000.00
682	68,610.00	3,897	671,190.00	4,593.83	3,685.00	3,210.00	675.00
----	----	11	3,700.00	385.12		300.00	----
				66,097.09		54,900.00	
134	139,000.00	1,325	1,726,700.00	45,342.20	15,500.00	15,500.00	----
779	834,000.00	6,064	8,017,500.00	69,769.26	18,000.00	19,000.00	500.00
				1,074.31		900.00	
496	----	1,552	----	40,340.30	31,500.00	31,500.00	----
20	21,000.00	38	47,000.00	506.16	40.00	40.00	----
107	535,000.00	734	3,670,000.00	9,024.00	12,600.00	6,100.00	6,500.00
----	----	10,467	9,636,000.00	118,605.05	15,000.00	13,500.00	1,500.00
----	----	2	2,000.00				
		180	----	757.32		420.50	
142	16,340.00	1,580	179,900.00	5,775.47	6,440.00	5,175.00	2,530.00
----	----	4,926		15,545.56		7,850.00	
550	1,137,993.00	2,252	4,476,251.00	137,947.70	101,043.00	83,843.50	19,672.00
289	30,509.00	689	112,756.00	----	1,851.75	1,830.25	341.50
----	----	6,206	444,510.00		5,560.00	5,800.00	500.00
58	----	272	----	859.25	500.00	400.00	200.00
220	335,500.00	679	1,020,000.00	12,457.09	1,000.00	1,000.00	----
535	2,675,000.00	2,591	12,955,000.00	25,850.00	10,000.00	5,000.00	5,000.00
3,095	3,753,000.00	27,563	34,689,600.00	416,852.01	187,700.00	159,216.67	53,333.33
218	195,800.00	1,887	1,793,700.00	19,716.41	14,600.00	10,916.65	2,466.66
35	28,500.00	273	215,000.00	3,332.18	1,500.00	500.00	1,000.00
----	----	----		9,015.84		8,177.93	479.79
5,244	11,935,040.35	184,582	105,764,910.65	1,646,654.46	763,677.94	764,060.31	148,451.01

ANNUAL REPORT

OF THE

INSURANCE COMMISSIONER

OF THE

STATE OF NORTH CAROLINA

FOR THE

YEAR ENDING APRIL 1, 1919

———

JAMES R. YOUNG, INSURANCE COMMISSIONER

ANNUAL REPORT

OF THE

INSURANCE COMMISSIONER

OF THE

STATE OF NORTH CAROLINA

FOR THE

YEAR ENDING APRIL 1, 1919

JAMES R. YOUNG
INSURANCE COMMISSIONER

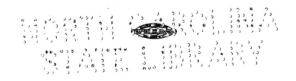

RALEIGH
EDWARDS & BROUGHTON PRINTING CO.
STATE PRINTERS
1919

INSURANCE COMMISSIONER'S REPORT

STATE OF NORTH CAROLINA,
INSURANCE DEPARTMENT,
RALEIGH, April 1, 1919.

To His Excellency, THOS. W. BICKETT,
Governor of North Carolina.

DEAR SIR:—As Insurance Commissioner, it becomes my duty to submit to you, as required by law, a report of the Insurance Department, embodying a statement of the work for the past year, as well as the condition of all companies and associations supervised by the Commissioner as shown by the reports filed with him. The report filed herewith covers the fiscal year ending April 1, 1919.

DEPARTMENT

The Department was formed in 1899, and has fully demonstrated the wisdom of its creation. Its value to the State and her citizens increases each year.

REVENUE

The revenue collected and paid into the State Treasury by this Department has increased each year, until there was collected and paid in for the past fiscal year $543,294.02.

The gradual increase of the revenues collected from insurance companies through this Department and paid into the State Treasury is more clearly shown by a comparison with the amount ($84,879.28) collected for the fiscal year ending April 1, 1899, the year prior to the formation of the Department.

The amount collected by the Department and paid into the State Treasury each year since its formation is as follows:

For the first fiscal year 1899-00...................$ 91,973.49
For the fiscal year 1900-01......................   91,072.92
For the fiscal year 1901-02......................   132,034.03
For the fiscal year 1902-03......................   153,667.12
For the fiscal year 1903-04......................   174,633.60
For the fiscal year 1904-05......................   197,402.23
For the fiscal year 1905-06......................   205,124.07
For the fiscal year 1906-07......................   215,331.56
For the fiscal year 1907-08......................   224,680.58

For	the	fiscal	year	1908-09 ....$	234,469.63
For	the	fiscal	year	1909-10	246,566.89
For	the	fiscal	year	1910-11	270,300.08
For	the	fiscal	year	1911-12	285,040.50
For	the	fiscal	year	1912-13	319,389,67
For	the	fiscal	year	1913-14	344,546.28
For	the	fiscal	year	1914-15	352,047.20
For	the	fiscal	year	1915-16	348,780.90
For	the	fiscal	year	1916-17	372,044.12
For	the	fiscal	year	1917-18	415,468.16
For	the	fiscal	year	1918-19	543,294.02

Total   ....$ 5,217,867.10

Of course, these licenses, fees and taxes collected make a good showing, but the amount saved to the citizens of the State by proper supervision is really greater and of more value in the end than the revenues collected. In the opinion of many the State should not collect from insurance companies more than is necessary to finance the Insurance Department; but the Commissioner has always held, and insists, that the companies should pay their pro rata part of the cost of running the Government—no more, and no less.

SUPERVISION

The collection of the licenses, taxes, and fees from insurance companies above referred to is an important matter, and adds very materially to the State's revenue; but by far the most important work of the Department and that of greatest benefit to the citizens of the State is the proper supervision of insurance companies, associations, and societies, as well as their representatives operating in the State. The great improvement in the practices of the companies and their agents show the work accomplished in this respect. This supervision takes in:

INSURANCE COMMISSIONER

1. *The admission and regulation of all companies doing or proposing to do any kind of insurance in the State.*—There are about four hundred companies, associations, and societies doing the following classes of insurance: Life, health, accident, casualty, fire, marine, credit, burglary, plate-glass, liability, steam-boiler, automobile, etc.

2. *Annual Statements.*—The Commissioner is required to examine and check up financial statements filed with him by the different companies operating in the State; to make an abstract for publication; to collect the fees for the publication of the same and have them published in the newspapers of the State.

3. *Complaints and Violations.*—It is also the duty of the Insurance Commissioner to seek out and prosecute all violations of the insurance law, to look into all complaints made to him by the citizens of the State, and to give them such information as they may desire at his hands in regard to companies and associations under his supervision, and such aid as they may need in any controversy or misunderstanding. The work and correspondence in these matters take practically the time of a first-class man, though much of it must be done by the Commissioner because of its technical character.

4. *Approval of Contracts.*—Under the law the Insurance Commissioner must approve all insurance contracts issued in the State, and every company, association, or society is required to submit to the Insurance Commissioner for his approval all applications for as well as contracts of insurance, with clauses modifying the same, before it is lawful to offer them in the State. While this involves a considerable amount of work, largely technical, it is a very valuable law, and certainly helpful in regard to the character of the contracts of insurance issued in the State.

5. *Rate-making Bureaus and Associations.*—These associations and bureaus of practically every class of insurance are subject to the inspection and examination of the Insurance Commissioner, and it requires much labor of a technical and painstaking character to keep in touch with the various rules, regulations, and rates promulgated. Under the law every company must file with the Insurance Department the schedules and rules on which they base their rates, and fire companies must not only do this, but furnish each owner of property with each rate made (or changed), in detail.

FIRE MARSHAL (EX OFFICIO)

6. *Fire Prevention.*—The Commissioner is also *ex officio* fire marshal, and has charge of the investigation of all suspicious fires, and the prosecution of those supposed to be responsible for them. There have been many of these investigations and prosecutions which have been very beneficial in their results. A number of convictions are obtained each year and the deterrent effect is especially good. The average convictions each year are from 15 to 20. This is a fine record when it is remembered that it is more difficult to convict for burning than perhaps for any other crime. There can be no question but that these convictions obtained, as well as the vigorous prosecutions conducted even where no conviction followed, have had a good effect and are materially reducing fires in the State.

7. *Building and Inspection Laws.*—The Commissioner is charged with the enforcement of the building and inspection laws. This involves not only having inspections made throughout the State by men sent from the Department, but also in seeing that the work is kept up and the laws enforced by the officers of the different cities and towns. The State Building Code and its enforcement in the different cities and towns in the State is not only greatly improving the fire conditions and liability to conflagrations in our cities and towns, but is having a fine effect in the education of our people as to the advantage of better and safer buildings and the protection they afford against the destruction by fire of life and property throughout the State. The Legislature of 1915 provided that the license fees collected from fire insurance companies should be used for this purpose. This gave a sufficient sum and has enabled the Commissioner to start out upon different lines of fire prevention and lay a broader foundation for a great and effective work along this line in the State.

8. *Exits and Fire-escapes.*—Under chapter 637, Public Laws 1909, the Insurance Commissioner is given supervision over and charged with the enforcement of the law in regard to sufficient exits and proper fire-escapes for buildings in the State where people congregate. This is a most important law and one that has called for considerable thought and work from the Insurance Commissioner and his deputies; over 2,000 fire-escapes having been erected under their direction. It is to be greatly regretted that so many of our public buildings, especially theaters, dormitories, and school buildings, should be so erected that it is impossible to arrange for an absolutely safe escape of the inmates in case of fire. Of course, the Commissioner has endeavored to do what he could in the way of having buildings already erected put in proper shape, but some provision should be made so that plans for new buildings of this character must be passed upon by the Insurance Commissioner or some expert in his Department to secure not only the safety of the building itself, but especially of the inmates, from fire. The last legislature made such provision as to school buildings, the plans of which must now be approved by the Insurance Commissioner.

9. *Prevention of Accidents.*—The last General Assembly in their wisdom added to the duties of the Insurance Commissioner that of doing what he could in the prevention of accidents. This work fits in very well with that of fire prevention, both being largely matters of education. It is estimated that the bulk of fires and accidents are caused by ignorance and carelessness and that from two-thirds to three-fourths can be prevented by the exercise of even ordinary care.

10. *Firemen's Relief Fund.*—The Insurance Commissioner is also required to collect from all Fire Insurance Companies doing business in the State taxes for the benefit of our firemen and to distribute these taxes among the firemen of the different cities and towns complying with the requirements for the collection of these taxes. Heretofore under the law a tax of one-half of one percent has been collected on the premiums received in the cities and towns by foreign fire insurance companies, but the last General Assembly removed the provision by which domestic companies were relieved of this tax and they are now required to pay the same tax. The fund so collected on the fire premiums collected in any city and town constitutes the Firemen's Relief Fund of that city or town.

11. *Insurance on State buildings and inspections thereof.*—Under the law the Insurance Commissioner is required to make an annual inspection of all the State institutions and buildings, not only as to their safety from fire but as to the safety of the inmates in case of fire. This is a most important duty as it involves not only the protection of the property of the State but of the lives of the inmates of our State institutions, most of whom are helpless, especially in case of fire. The difficulties attending the discharge of this duty are enhanced by the fact that heretofore little or no attention has been paid to the character of buildings erected from the standpoint of safety from fire or the protection of their inmates in case of fire, and not sufficient attention is being paid even now to this most important and vital matter.

The Insurance Commissioner is also required to prepare schedules and place insurance upon all the different State properties. Heretofore an appropriation of $10,000 annually has been made for this purpose but the last General Assembly very wisely increased the amount to $20,000.

12. *Building and Loan Associations.*—The Commissioner is also charged with the supervision of Building and Loan Associations and the collection of all taxes from them. The great value to the State of these Associations, their success and great increase in numbers, as well as in assets, makes this work of great importance and necessary for the protection of the citizens of the State.

13. *Investment and Promotion Companies.*—The looking after these companies calls for prompt and active work that our citizens may be protected from such companies and their representatives. It is hard to believe that our people can protect themselves from the professional stock sellers. The importance and necessity for intelligent work and discrimination in looking after these companies was greatly increased

by the fact that the last Legislature provided that this law should apply to domestic as well as foreign companies.

14. *Lightning Rods.*—The Insurance Commissioner is also charged with licensing lightning rod manufacturers as well as their representatives who sell and erect the rods. There is no doubt of the real value and protection afforded by a good rod properly installed, so that a proper supervision of the business is most important and necessary. It will also serve to do away with the existing prejudice against the business and cause our citizens to seek this protection for their lives and property.

CLASSES OF WORK

In looking over the foregoing statement it will readily be seen how varied and important are the matters entrusted by law to this Department.' They embrace:

1. *Insurance Department* (proper).—Those things usually handled and supervised by Insurance Departments as admission, licensing and supervising of insurance companies, associations and societies, checking and publication of annual statements, handling complaints and violations, passing on forms of contracts and supervising rating bureaus.

2. *Fire Marshal Department.*—Under this head will be found such work as is usually entrusted to a Fire Marshal as investigations and prosecution of suspicious fires, enforcing building and inspection laws, requiring proper exits and fire escapes and the prevention of accidents.

3. *Miscellaneous Work.*—Under this head may be classed such duties and responsibilities as are not usually lodged in either the Insurance Department or Fire Marshal's office as (*a*) the collection and disbursement of the Firemen's Relief Fund. (*b*) The inspection of State buildings and the insurance of State property. (*c*) The supervision of Building and Loan Associations and collection of taxes from them. (*d*) The licensing and supervision of investment and other companies selling stock. (*e*) The supervision of the lightning rod business in the State.

Of course when the Department was established in 1899 it was small and few of these matters were embraced in its work. They have been gradually added and the work of the department has expanded until now it taxes to the utmost the Commissioner and his assistants. The taxes collected and paid annually into the State Treasury have increased from about $80,000 to over $540,000, while the supervisory work and responsibility has increased to such extent as is hard to be realized much less stated. Every move calls for more work and brings additional responsibility.

COMPANIES ADMITTED

The following companies and associations were admitted to do business in the State during the year:

LIFE

Federal Life

Standard Life

FIRE (STOCK)

American Equitable
Christiana General
Columbian National
Cleveland National
Eagle Star and British Dominion
Federal
Fidelity
Globe National
Home Fire and Marine
Hudson
Independence
Iowa National

Liberty
Merchants National
Norwegian Atlas
North Branch
North Carolina State
Prudentia Co- and Reinsurance
South Carolina
Star of America
Tokio Fire and Marine
Union Hispano Am De Serquiros
Urbane
Western Alliance

MISCELLANEOUS

Belt Auto Indemnity
Liberty Mutual

Lumbermen's Reciprocial

FRATERNAL

Gates Mutual Burial
G. U. O. Tent Sisters of North Carolina
United Order Sons and Daughters of Salem

STOPPED BUSINESS

The following companies or associations either did not renew their license at the close of the year 1918, or ceased to do business in the State during the past year:

LIFE

Ohio National Life

Cumberland Mutual

FIRE

Lumber Underwriters
Merchants National Fire

Swiss National
Wilson County Farmers Mutual

During the year the following companies made changes in names as indicated below.

Petersburg Savings and Insurance Co. to Petersburg Insurance Co.
N. C. Mutual and Provident Association to N. C. Mutual Life Insurance Co.

COMPANIES LICENSED

The following companies were admitted to do business in the under the general insurance laws (where they had not been a admitted) and were licensed for the year ending April 1, 1919.

LIFE COMPANIES

Ætna Life	Morris Plan Life
Atlantic Life	Mutual Benefit
American Central	Mutual Life
American National	National Life of America
Business Mens Mutual	National Life of Vermont
Columbian National Life	New England Mutual Life
Connecticut Mutual Life	New York Life
Durham Life	N. C. Mutual Life
Equitable Life Assurance	Northwestern Mutual Life
Federal Life	Pacific Mutual Life
Fidelity Mutual Life	Pan-American Life
Gate City Life and Health	Penn Mutual Life
Guardian Life of America	Philadelphia Life
George Washington	Phœnix Mutual Life
Home Life of New York	Provident Life and Trust
Home Security Life	Prudential of America
Imperial Mutual Life and Health	Reliance Life
Jefferson Standard Life	Reserve Loan Life
LaFayette Mutual Life	Security Mutual Life
Life Insurance Company of Virginia	Southern Life and Trust
Life and Casualty	State Life
Manhattan Life	Standard Life
Maryland Life	State Mutual of Massachusetts
Maryland Assurance	Travelers Life
Massachusetts Mutual Life	Union Central Life
Metropolitan Life	United Life and Accident
Michigan Mutual Life	Union Mutual Life and Health
Missouri Life	Volunteer State Life

MUTUAL OR ASSESSMENT LIFE COMPANIES

Afro-American Mutual	International Mutual
Catawba Benevolent	Mutual Christian Burial Aid
Citizens Mutual	Toilers Mutual
Cumulative Coffin Company	Winston Mutual Life

FIRE AND FIRE AND MARINE COMPANIES (STOCK)

Ætna	American of Newark
Agricultural	American Central
American Alliance	Alliance
American Eagle	Atlantic

Atlas
Automobile
British America
Boston
Caledonian
Camden
Carolina .
Citizens of Missouri
Columbia
Commercial Union Assurance
Commercial Union
Commonwealth
Concordia
Connecticut Fire
Continental
County
Dixie
Equitable Fire and Marine
Equitable of South Carolina
Fidelity-Phenix
Fidelity
Fire Association of Philadelphia
Fireman's Fund
Firemen's of Newark
Franklin of Pennsylvania
Georgia Home
Great-American
Glens Falls
Girard Fire and Marine
Globe and Rutgers
Granite State
Hanover
Hartford
Home Fire and Marine
Home of New York
Hudson
Insurance Co. of North America
Liberty
Liverpool & London & Globe
London Assurance
London and Lancashire
Massachusetts Fire and Marine
Mechanics
Mechanics and Traders
Merchants National
Milwaukee Mechanics
Nationale of Paris

National
National Liberty
National Union
Netherlands Fire and Life
Newark Fire
New Hampshire
Niagara
North British and Mercantile
North Carolina Home
North Carolina State
Northern Assurance
North River
Northwestern National
Norwich Union
Old Colony
Orient
Palatine
Pennsylvania
Petersburg Insurance
Phenix of Paris
Phœnix of Hartford
Phœnix of London
Piedmont
Providence-Washington
Queen of America
Rhode Island
Royal
Royal Exchange Assurance
St. Paul Fire and Marine
Scottish Union and National
Security Insurance
Southern Stock
Southern Underwriters
Springfield Fire and Marine
Standard
Star of America
Sun Insurance Office
Svea Fire and Life
Underwriters of Rocky Mount
Underwriters of Greensboro
Union Assurance
Union of Paris
United States
Virginia Fire and Marine
Westchester
Western Assurance
Yorkshire

REINSURANCE ONLY

Abeille
American Equitable
Century
Cleveland National
Columbian
Christiana General
Columbian National
Eagle
Eagle Star and British Dominion
Federal
First Reinsurance
Fire Reassurance
First Russia
Globe National
Home of Utah
Imperial
Iowa National
International
Inter-State
Independence
Jakor
Marquette National
Mercantile Insurance of America
Moscow
Norwegian Assurance
Norwegian Atlas
National of Denmark
North Branch
Norske Lloyd
Northern of Moscow
Northwestern Fire and Marine
Palmetto
Peoples National
Paternelle
Prudentia Re- and Co- Insurance
Rossia
Russian
Salamandra
Second Russian
Skandia
Skandinavia
South Carolina
Sterling
Swiss Reinsurance
Tokio Fire and Marine
Union Hispano Americano
Union and Phenix Espagnol
Urbaine
Warsaw
Western Alliance

MUTUALS

Alamance Farmers Mutual
Arkwright Mutual
Baltimore Mutual
Blackstone Mutual
Cabarrus County Mutual
Cotton and Woolen Manufacturers
Davidson County Mutual
Farmers Douglas Mutual
Farmers Mutual of Edgecombe
Farmers Mutual
Firemen's Mutual
Fitchburg Mutual
Gaston County Farmers Mutual
Hardware Mutual
Hope Mutual
Indiana Lumbermen's Mutual
Industrial Mutual
Keystone Mutual
Lumbermen's Mutual
Lumber Mutual
Manton Mutual
Michigan Millers Mutual
Methodist Mutual
Mecklenburg Farmers Mutual
Merchants Mutual
Mercantile Mutual
Millers Mutual
Middlesex Mutual
Narragansett Mutual
National Mutual
Pennsylvania Lumbermen's Mutual
Philadelphia Manufacturer's Mutua
Rowan Mutual
Rubber Manufacturers Mutual
Southern Mutual Furniture
Stanly Mutual
State Mutual
Union County Farmers Mutual
What Cheer Mutual

RECIPROCAL OR INTERINSURANCE EXCHANGES

Consolidated Underwriters
Druggist Indemnity Exchange
Individual Underwriters
Lumber Manufacturers
Lumbermen's Reciprocal
Lumbermen's Underwriters Alliance
Mfrs. Lumbermen's Underwriters
Mfg. Woodworkers Underwriters

Millers Indemnity Underwriters
National Lumber Manufacturers
Reciprocal Exchange
Southern Lumber Underwriters
Utilities Indemnity Exchange
Warners Inter-Ins. (Gro. Dept.)
Western Reciprocal Underwriters

UNDERWRITERS' AGENCIES

Ætna Underwriters
Atlanta Home Underwriters
Colonial Underwriters
Delaware Underwriters
Exchange Underwriters
Fire and Marine Underwriters
Globe Underwriters

Home Underwriters
London Underwriters
New York Underwriters
Philadelphia Underwriters
Rochester Underwriters
Sun Underwriters
Washington Underwriters

MISCELLANEOUS COMPANIES

Ætna Casualty and Surety
Ætna Life (Accident)
American Automobile
American Credit Indemnity
American National Life (Accident)
American Surety
Belt Auto Indemnity
Columbian National Life (Accident)
Continental Casualty
Employers' Liability
Fidelity and Casualty
Fidelity and Deposit
General Accident
Georgia Casualty
Hartford Accident and Indemnity
Hartford Steam-boiler
Liberty Mutual
Lloyds Plate-glass
London Guarantee and Accident
Maryland Casualty

Massachusetts Bonding and Insurance
Metropolitan Casualty
National Surety
National Casualty
National Life of America (Accident)
New Amsterdam Casualty
New York Plate-glass
North American Accident
Ocean Accident and Guarantee
Pacific Mutual Life (Accident)
Provident Life and Accident
Preferred Accident
Reliance Life (Accident)
Royal Indemnity
Standard Accident
Travelers (Accident)
Travelers Indemnity Company
United States Casualty
U. S. Fidelity and Guaranty

LIVE STOCK COMPANIES

Western Live Stock Company, Peoria, Ill.

TRUST AND INVESTMENT COMPANIES

American Trust Company
Asheville Morris Plan Company
Bankers Trust and Title
Branch Banking and Trust Company
Citizens Savings and Loan
Citizens Bank and Trust Company
Community Savings and Loan
Durham Morris Plan Company
High Point Morris Plan Company
New Bern Banking and Trust Co.
Raleigh Savings Bank and Trust
Rocky Mount Savings and Trust
Southern Real Estate and Trust
Wachovia Bank and Trust
Wilson Morris Plan Company

FRATERNAL ORDERS OR SOCIETIES

A. C. L. Relief Department
Benefit Association of All Railway
  Employees
Ben Hur Supreme Tribe
Brothers' and Sisters' Aid Society
Brothers' and Sisters' Union of
  America
District Household of Ruth, No. 10
Eastern Star.
Fraternal Mystic Circle
Funeral Benefit Association of U. S.
Gates Mutual Burial
Grand Court of Calanthe
G. U. O. Tent Sisters of N. C.
Grand United Order Abraham
Grand United Order of Brothers and
  Sisters of Love and Charity
Grand United Order O. F. (col.)
Household of David
Independent Order of Good Samari-
  tans, No. 1
Independent Order of Good Smari-
  tans, No. 10
Independent Order of G. S. and D. S.
Independent Order St. Luke
Independent Order of J. R. Giddings
  and Jollifee Union
Independent Order Brith Sholom
Independent Order of True Reform-
  ers
Jr. O. U. A. M.
Knights of Gideon Mutual Society
Knights of Columbus
Knights of the Guiding Star of the
  East
Knights of Pythias, Supreme Lodge
Knights of Phythias (col.)
Lincoln Benefit Society
Loyal Order of Moose
Masons Annuity
Masonic Benefit Fund (col.)
Masonic Mutual Life
Modern Brotherhood of America
Modern Woodman of America
Mutual Life and Indemnity
N. C. Camp Patriotic Order Sons of
  America
Norfolk and Western Relief Depart-
  ment
Oasis and Omar Temples Widows'
  Fund
Order of the Golden Seal
Order United Commercial Travelers
Patriotic Order Sons of America
Pink Hill Fraternal
Peoples Ind. Order True Reformers
Raleigh Union Society
Red Men's Benefit
Royal Arcanum
Royal Fraternal Association
Royal Knights King David
Sons and Daughters of Peace
The Maccabees
Travelers Protective Association
United Order of J. R. Giddings and
  Jollifee Union
U. O. Sons and Daughters of Salem
Woodmen of the World, Sovereign
  Camp
Woodmen Circle, Supreme Forest
Wise Men of North Carolina
Women's Benefit Association of the
  Maccabees
Woman's Union Burial Association

CHARTERS

Under the law enacted several years ago, all charters for insurance companies and associations are now issued by the Honorable Secretary of State upon the approval of the Insurance Commissioner. This saves considerable time to the Legislature and expense in its work, and subjects all charters to the critical examination of the official who is presuumed to have the technical knowledge of the business, and is responsible for their supervision after they are licensed.

During the year ending April 1, 1919, the Commissioner has examined, approved, and certified to the Honorable Secretary of State articles of incorporation for the following companies and associations:

LIFE

Gate City Life and Health   Royal Mutual
   (*amendment*)

FIRE

Merchants Mutual Fire   Wilson County Farmers Mutual
Rockingham Fire

RECOMMENDATIONS

In accordance with our law (Section 4688) the following recommendations were submitted to our last General Assembly, in January 1919.

1. *Building and Clerical Help.*—Until recently the Department did not have adequate quarters, but now has offices that are commodious and convenient, on the third floor of the State Departments Building.

In order that the Department may not be subjected to frequent changes in its force, and to provide adequate support, it is important that the salaries of the employees, especially those requiring technical knowledge and experience, should be increased, and that provision should be made for the employment of regular examiners for building and loan associations and for insurance companies. It is necessary to check up each home company and building and loan association once a year, and our law requires a full examination and audit once in three years. It will take the full time of a competent man for each class, to say nothing of the examination of foreign insurance companies and societies doing business here, which are important and necessary.

2. *Standard Fire Policy.*—Among the many important changes made in the law affecting the fire insurance business in the State by the last General Assembly was the adoption of what is known as the "North Carolina Standard Fire Policy." The valuable laws enacted upon the

recommendation of the Fire Investigating Committee make unnecessary the placing of much fire insurance legislation upon our books by this General Assembly, but it is necessary to make some minor changes in the Standard Fire Policy, as the policy, with these changes, will be presented to and no doubt adopted by the legislatures of a number of states at their present sessions. The policy is a decided improvement on the old form of standard fire policy, and it is very desirable to have uniformity in all insurance contracts.

3. *Change in Charters and Capital Stock.*—Under the present insurance law in this State no change in a charter of a domestic insurance company or in the amount of the capital stock can be made without the approval of the Insurance Commissioner. The Commissioner recommends that this law be amended to apply not only to domestic companies, but also to foreign insurance companies doing business in the State, with a *proviso* that this requirement may be waived in case of an insurance company where the laws of its domicile give like authority to a supervising insurance official. The necessity of this law is apparent, but has been emphasized by the action of the Union Central Life Insurance Company of Ohio, doing business in this State. This company for years operated with only $100,000 capital, and eight or ten years ago increased their capital stock to $500,000 by a stock dividend of $400,000. The Convention of Insurance Commissioners took up this matter with the company and protested against the action as unfair and unjust to its policy-holders, in view of the fact that through its literature and agents, as well as officers of the company, it had held out to the insuring public that it was practically a mutual company, and that the profits of the company would go to its policy-holders. There was nothing in the law of Ohio, or any authority vested in the Superintendent of Insurance of that State, that would prevent the action objected to.

It was generally believed that the action and expression of the views of the Insurance Commissioners of the different states through their convention, and the general tendency to mutualize life companies and do away entirely with all capital stock, would end the action of this company along this line, but within the last two years the company has again increased their capital stock, now to $2,000,000 using $1,500,000 of surplus as a stock dividend. The officers of the company not only uphold this action, but so far have failed and refused to give any assurance that additional increase of capital stock by the use of surplus will not be made. It does not help the matter for the company to say that the surplus used was obtained from its nonparticipating business. It certainly has not shown this to the satisfaction of a committee of the Insurance Commissioners, and even if they had, it is a question whether the company would not be acting in better faith with its policy-holders to withdraw this surplus in a cash dividend, if they are entitled to it, and not place it in capital stock, where it will continue to be a liability and charge upon the participating policy-holders of the company.

Shall this State allow a foreign company doing business with its citizens to do what would not be allowed to a home company, especially when it is a clear violation of the statements and literature upon which the business was solicited and written?

4. *Workmen's Compensation Law.*—Our laws are very deficient as to employers' liability and kindred matters. The Commissioner has called the attention of the last two General Assemblies to the fact that it would be well to have these laws added to and improved and a workmen's compensation act in force in this State. There can be no question but that the principles of the workmen's compensation laws in force in so many of our states are right. It is the best and most progressive way to deal with these matters, and in the end will prove best for the citizens of our State. The Commissioner believes that this General Assembly should enact such a law as will be up to date, will contain the principles of these acts, and can be administered by the State at the smallest cost. The employers and employees of the State should, and your Commissioner believes do, favor the principles involved in these laws, the only question being as to the details or special provisions of the law. The matter should be taken up discussed, passed upon, not as a law in the interest of employers or in the interest of employees as against the other, but as a law that will prove in the end best for all the employers as well as the employees who come under its provisions. The principles of the workmen's compensation acts are right and the State cannot afford not to be progressive enough in its legislation to have these and in fact all laws for the good not only of the State but of its different classes of citizens. There should also be enacted the uniform bill recently approved and recommended by the National Convention of Insurance Commissioners for computing the reserve on this class of business.

5. *Licensed Electricians.*—That no person be allowed to install electrical apparatus or do electrical wiring in this State unless licensed by the Insurance Commissioner upon showing to the satisfaction of the Commissioner that he is competent to do this work. Of course, it would be well to provide that the Commissioner might waive this requirement where it is shown that the party proposing to do the work

is licensed by a city or town under a provision providing for the licensing of only skilled and competent workmen.

6. *Fire-escapes.*—Under chapter 637' Public Laws of 1909, the Insurance Commissioner is required to see that all public buildings, especially theaters, dormitories, school buildings and buildings of like character where people are accustomed to congregate, shall be provided with sufficient exits, and if necessary, fire-escapes. In view of the fact that there is no supervision in this respect as to the character of school and other public buildings erected in the State and the selection of the plans is entirely with different boards, it seems to the Commissioner to be absolutely necessary for the protection of the people of the State, especially the children, that the plans for these public school buildings should be required to be submitted to the Insurance Commissioner for his approval as to their safety from fire and the safety of the inmates in case of fire.

7. *Reinsurance Companies.*—There are licensed in this State an unusually large number of insurance companies, especially fire. Some are entered to do only a reinsurance business and special provisions should be made as to their license and the fees required of them.

8. *Steam Boiler Inspection.*—It is very important that there should be laws requiring and governing the inspection of steam boilers in the State. It is most important for the protection of life and property, and such laws are found in most of the states.

9. *Capital and Surplus.*—An increase should be made in the minimum capital for marine insurance companies, as $25,000 is entirely too little. Your Commissioner believes that new companies being organized in the State should be required to have a surplus in addition to the amount of capital required by law.

10. *Medical Examinations.*—That the maximum life policy not requiring a medical examination be raised to $300 and the provisions extended to Group Insurance contracts, on which there is no occasion for medical examinations.

STATE INSTITUTIONS

11. *Insurance on State Property.*—Under the law it is made the duty of the Insurance Commissioner to inspect each State institution as to its safety from fire and the protection of its inmates, and to place upon the State property insurance which is provided for under the law. An annual appropriation of $10,000 is made to cover the fire insurance upon the State property. At the time this amount was first agreed upon it was sufficient to carry practically 50 per cent of the value of the property; but now, because of the great increase in the

insurable value of the State property (being practically $7,000,000), the appropriation does not enable the Commissioner to carry more than 30 per cent of the value. This, in the opinion of the Commissioner, is not sufficient, and the appropriation should be increased $5,000 or $10,000. This opinion is shared by the boards having State property in charge, some of whom have taken out as much as $150,000 of insurance, paying for the same out of their appropriation.

The records show that the State has collected for fire losses more than it has paid in fire insurance premiums, besides receiving an annual protection of $2,250,000 against the fire hazard. The Commissioner feels that he cannot emphasize too strongly the protection of State property by better buildings and insurance. The State property, records, etc., as well as the inmates of our institutions should be safeguarded as fully as possible. The character of new buildings required under the work of the State Building Commission and the steps taken to safeguard the old buildings are certainly steps in the right direction.

12. *State Capitol.*—Your Commissioner would again strongly recommend that some steps be taken for the better protection of the State Capitol from destruction by fire. This is a magnificent building, but is far from fireproof, and an inspection of the building, especially under the roof, would disclose to any committee or member of your body the urgent necessity and importance of this recommendation.

13. *Agricultural Building.*—In the opinion of your Commissioner the new part of the Agricultural Building can by the use of automatic sprinklers be made as safe from fire as its contents would admit; but the main or old part of the building, formerly known as the National Hotel, can never be made safe from fire. This part of the building should be taken down and the Department of Agriculture authorized to erect in its place a five or six-story building, not only adapted to the uses of the Department and its varied work, but safe for its records and statistics, which become more valuable each year.

BUILDING AND LOAN ASSOCIATIONS

14. *Building and Loan Associations.*—The Commissioner recommends that a provision for the annual licensing of building and loan associations should be more clearly expressed than in our present statute, and that a nominal fee should be charged for the same; also, that this fee should be used for the expenses of the examination and checking up of building and loan associations in the State, and that an additional deputy or clerk should be allowed to the Commissioner for this purpose. The proper supervision of these associations calls for addi-

tional legislation. Their increased business in this State and their great value in the upbuilding of our State and the teaching of our people thrift, make it most important that they should be encouraged and their conduct properly safeguarded.

NEW LEGISLATION

Comparatively little legislation was enacted by the General Assembly of 1919. This was no doubt well although there are a number of laws important and valuable to the State and her citizens that should be enacted as stated by the Insurance Commissioner in his recommendations to the Legislature. While our State has now a most valuable code of laws governing insurance companies and their operations in this State, others can and no doubt will be added from time to time which will add to its efficiency and value.

The following laws were enacted:

1. Allowing life insurance companies to insure lives up to $300.00 and on the "Group" insurance plan without a medical examination.

2. Allowing fire insurance companies not licensed in the State to form an underwriters agency and be licensed through it to do a reinsurance business only.

3. Requiring all plans for school buildings to be approved by the Insurance Commissioner as to the safety of the proposed buildings from fire, as well as the protection of the inmates in case of fire.

4. Requiring any part of the fund collected for fire prevention unexpended at the end of the fiscal year to be paid into the State Treasury for general purposes.

5. Providing for the payment by domestic companies also of the tax for the Firemen's Relief Fund.

FIRE INSURANCE RATES

While the fire insurance rates in North Carolina are lower than those in any State in this section of the country or similarly situated, yet the matter of rates is in a very unsatisfactory condition so far as the people or policy-holders are concerned. This is no doubt largely due to the fact that the companies have not adopted any system of rate making that they can or are willing to explain and defend to any policy-holder who may be dissatisfied with the rate named on his property.

Under the law the Insurance Commissioner has the supervisory power not only those given to the Commissioner of New York but also given under the Massachusetts laws on this subject. Of course the rates must be made adequate and should be not only uniform but fair and the Commissioner believes that they should be made upon the experience of both the State and country-wide conditions. They not only should not be arbitrary but should be worked out through the best underwriting judgment on statistics obtained in the business. The companies and the Bureaus whom they use to make these rates cannot be said to make them arbitrarily without any regard to conditions, but it does seem that they are not sufficiently willing or anxious to defend them and explain to the people on what they are based, how they are made, and that they are supposed to be fair and just and that any evidence to the contrary will be gladly received and proper corrections made where they should be.

The Commissioner does not believe in rates arbitrarily made, nor does he understand that this is the method or desire of the companies in regard to their rates, nor does he believe that rates should be fixed by a flat increase extending over the whole country regardless of the experience of companies in the different sections or upon the different classes of business. The Companies and their Bureaus who make these rates agree with our view that the rate is, or should be, a measure of the hazard, and that the question is largely one of a distribution of the rate in accordance with the hazard of the different sections of the country and the different classes of insurance risks. Every effort should be made by the companies and their rate-makers as well as by the supervising officials and the people to put aside every unimportant objection or prejudice and work out the best and most satisfactorily method of arriving at and promulgating fire insurance rates. The question of rate making is one of the greatest, most important, and yet most perplexing problems in the business, but we are not prepared to believe that it cannot and will not be, with proper efforts, solved in the interest of and to the satisfaction of all parties concerned.

THE REDUCTION OF FIRE WASTE

Under the law of our State the Insurance Commissioner is *ex officio* Fire Marshal, and what is commonly known as the Fire Marshal Law and Building Code is embraced in three different laws on the statute books of the State.

1. A bill along the line of the regular Fire Marshal bill is chapter 58, Public Laws of 1899. (Revisal 1905, secs. 4815-4823.)

2. A bill known as "Fire Waste Bill" is practically a building code, and is embraced in chapter 506, Public Laws of 1905. (Revisal 1905, secs. 2981-3011.)

3. The bill for proper exists and fire escapes is chapter 637, Pu
Laws of 1909.

The Insurance Commissioner is charged with seeing that the
quirements of these statutes are carried out. He is given large po
and much discretion. The spirit of the law is to protect life and pr
erty. The law requires that each incorporated city and town in
State shall have a chief of fire department, and prescribes cert
duties that he must perform.

The people of the State and fire insurance companies are at l
awaking to the importance, yea, necessity of cutting down the
waste. That there is room for this is shown by the heavy loss ra
in this country as compared with that in European countries. Wi
immensely better equipped fire departments to put out fires wh
once started, our loss is, yet, several times as great. This clear
shows that the fight must be made in preventing rather than in p
ting out fires. The public as well as the companies are certainly bei
aroused to a realization of what can be accomplished by safer buil
ing, better equipment, and the necessary care in looking after t
building and its equipment. Of course there are losses intentional
brought about by the assured for gain or an enemy for revenge or m
ice. These are largely preventable by the companies and their repr
sentatives. The losses through malic constitute a comparatively sma
proportion and are lessened by the retardant effect of strict laws vi
orously enforced. The burning for gain must be reduced or stoppe
by a proper vigilance and thorough efficiency of companies and agen
against over-insurance and the reckless placing of risks. If there :
no over-insurance then there is no profit in burning nor inducemer
for burning from malice. Of course, the Fire Marshal Departmer
can by efficient service greatly aid in reducing incendiary fires. Cor
viction for burning and vigorous prosecutions, even where no verdic
is obtained, greatly reduce this class of fires and prove of great benef
to the people as well as the companies.

SAFETY FIRST

We consider in North Carolina that the reduction of fire wast
covers the loss of life and property and that both can be worked togethe
to great advantage. The "Fire Waste" is an unpardonable faul
There is no excuse for its loss of life and property, amounting in thi
State alone to over three hundred lives and four million dollars c
property values annually. It is from five to ten times as great as lik

losses in European countries. It is largely—certainly two-thirds—due to ignorance and carelessness, and can be easily avoided and should be.

How long will our American people continue to "build to burn" and have their buildings, especially hotels, theaters, school buildings, and even homes, a menace to the lives of our men, women, and children? There is no excuse, as in the end it is cheaper, even in money cost, to erect a better class of buildings, as a protection against fire and for the safety of the inmates. There was never a time in the country when the cost of fire retardant and even fire proof buildings were so close to the first cost of the ordinary frame or brick with inside hollow wall construction. This difference is quickly met by difference in cost of insurance, upkeep, etc., to say nothing of safety to the building and its contents.

The expense of the investigation of fires and the enforcement of the fire-waste or building law is now paid from a special fund made up of the annual licenses collected of fire insurance companies doing business in the State. During the past year there has been collected for this fund $39,713.30, and expended, in accordance with the provisions of the law as follows:

Salaries	$ 19,121.40
Traveling and other expenses.....................	9,182.33
Expenses of courts and attorneys.................	1,050.00
Publicity, furniture, maps, and supplies...........	5,607.55
	$ 34,961.28

VIOLATIONS

The insurance laws are made for the protection of our citizens and do not impose upon them burdens or unnecessarily harass them. They provide that no insurance company, association, or society can do business in this State unless their application is passed upon and they are licensed by the Insurance Commissioner. It is also provided that each and every agent of these companies shall be licensed by the Commissioner so that the State and her citizens know what companies the agents represent and what companies are responsible for their acts. The Insurance Commissioner is also required to look after all violations of the insurance laws.

It is not proposed by the law to curtail the right or liberty of any citizen, but provide for his protection. This is most important, as any company or association that will withhold from the State the legal licenses and taxes will, when an opportunity occurs, not hesitate to defraud her citizens. The violations of the law have lessened, no doubt

brought about largely by the law passed by the General
1915, requiring that any citizen taking out insurance in
company should retain 5 per cent of the premium to be pa
over to the Insurance Commissioner.

Under this head your attention and that of the people o
called to the supervision of investment companies under
and what is commonly known as the "Blue Sky" Law, s
Thousands and thousands of dollars have been saved to o
the restriction of the sale of stock of foreign corporations,
to evade this law by forming domestic corporations ca
General Assembly to make this law applicable to domestic
also.

FIREMEN'S RELIEF FUND

The General Assembly of North Carolina at their ses
created a "Firemen's Relief Fund," as set forth in chapte
Laws 1907. Under this law each foreign fire insurance c
poration, or association doing a fire business in the State
to report to the Insurance Commissioner the premiums ı
in each city and town that met the requirements of the l
to fire equipment and observance of the building laws,
panies were also required to pay to the Insurance Com
half of 1 per cent upon the amount of the premiums in
town, to go to this fund for the relief of the firemen o
town. A board of trustees was created in each city and t
and disburse the funds in accordance with the provisio
In obedience to this law the Commissioner has collected
men's Relief Fund" as follows:

On premiums during 1907..........................
On premiums during 1908..........................
On premiums during 1909..........................
On premiums during 1910..........................
On premiums during 1911..........................
On premiums during 1912..........................
On premiums during 1913..........................
On premiums during 1914..........................
On premiums during 1915..........................
On premiums during 1916..........................
On premiums during 1917..........................
On premiums during 1918..........................

These amounts have been disbursed among the citie
accordance with the premiums collected by fire insur
therein.

This law is a proper recognition of the value of the firemen and their work, and the last General Assembly provided that this tax should be paid by domestic fire companies also.

STATEMENT AND TABLES

No insurance company, association, or order can do business in the State unless licensed by the Insurance Commissioner after he is satisfied as to their methods of business and financial standing. Each of these companies doing business in the State is required to file on or before March 1st of each year an annual statement showing its financial condition as of the preceding December 31st. The Commissioner furnishes the blanks upon which these statements are made out and filed, and they give the condition in such detail that he can readily, as required by law, audit them and prepare abstracts to be published in some newspaper in the State, and to be filed with the clerk of the Superior Court in each county. This is done for the information of the people of the State, and that they may not only see them published in the press, but also find a copy on file in the office of the clerk of the Superior Court of their county, as well as in the publications and records of the Insurance Department. The statements published in this report are those filed for the year ending December 31, 1918, and with the statistical tables will give much information to those desiring to be informed as to the financial condition of companies and societies doing business in this State. In a large number of cases this information is all that is desired, but other and fuller information, not only in regard to the financial condition of the companies, but their general standing and methods, can be obtained on application to the Commissioner.

FINANCIAL

All licenses, taxes, and fees required of insurance companies, associations, and orders doing business in the State are payable to the Insurance Commissioner. During the past year the Commissioner has collected and paid to the Honorable State Treasurer:

For taxes on gross receipts	$457,323.17
For licenses from companies	62,583.72
For fees and licenses for agents	23,387.13
Total paid Treasurer	$543,294.02
For publication annual statements in newspapers	4,015.50
For investigation of fires	39,713.30
Total	$573,306.63

CONCLUSION

The Commissioner desires to bear testimony to and expr
ciation of the aid rendered to him by the solicitors, sheri
fire departments, building inspectors, and other officers th
State, as well as to the efficient help rendered by the
employees in his Department.

Respectfully submitted,

Insurance   om

STATISTICAL TABLES

RELATING TO FIRE, MARINE AND INLAND INSURANCE COMPANIES

(NOTE.—These figures were compiled prior to the
Department's audit of the companies' statements.)

TABLE No. I—INCOME.

SHOWING THE INCOME OF FIRE, MARINE AND INLAND COMPANIES (LICENSED TO DO BUSINESS IN THIS STATE) FOR YEAR ENDING DECEMBER 31, 1918.

NORTH CAROLINA [CO]NIES.

Name of Company	Fire Premiums, Including Perpetuals	Marine and Inland Premiums	Interest, Dividends, and Rents	From Other Sources	Total Income	Income Over Disbursements	Disbursements Over Income
Alamance	$ 2,224.68	$	$	$ 477.93	$ 2,702.61	$	$
Atlantic	118,291.48		12,324.08	122.50	130,738.06		1,949.97
Cabarrus Mutual	2,491.36				2,491.36	1,239.73	
Carolina	31,472.87		5,392.92		36,875.49	4,507.77	
Davidson County Mutual			119.29	9.70	119.29		1,028.72
Dixie	468,950.86	88,680.52	55,251.89	357.98	613,241.25	174,084.85	
Farmers [Mutual] (Raleigh)	60,618.95		509.63	9,680.33	70,808.91	14,262.70	
Farmers Douglas	288.16			67.81	355.97	2.05	
Farmers Mutual (Edgecombe County)	1,824.66			202.73	2,027.39	428.62	
Gaston County Farmers Mutual	2,659.34		148.54	391.07	3,198.95	1,653.92	
Hardware M	16,117.97		956.81	554.24	17,074.78	5,475.78	
[M]rg Farmers Mutual	3,208.00		119.36		3,911.60	663.71	
Methodist Mutual	2,256.08				2,256.08		501.94
[N]th Carolina M	222,694.96		20,947.78	4,339.09	247,981.83	92,875.70	
North Carolina State	7,032.26		1,890.98		8,923.24	4,729.26	
Piedmont M	157,226.39		44,903.74	51,980.60	254,110.73	76,223.80	
Rowan M	8,960.24		185.40		8,960.24	1,078.55	
Southern Mutual Furniture	5,902.55			88.75	6,176.70	3,869.06	
Southern Stock	151,279.52		18,381.72	9,500.00	179,161.24	60,307.48	
Southern Underwriters	158,153.61		17,317.51	1,202.35	176,673.47	30,082.53	
Stanly County M	1,146.74			318.25	1,464.99	152.78	
State Mut	9,196.16		45.00	1,298.17	10,539.33	2,121.16	
Underwriters (Rocky Mount)	38,608.19		6,793.90		45,402.09	19,757.01	
[Farme]rs of Greensboro M	110,168.19		12,068.23	9,000.00	131,236.42	34,440.61	
Union County Farmers M	1,112.38			11.18	1,123.56	505.28	
Total	1,581,885.60	88,680.52	197,356.78	89,632.68	1,957,555.58	528,462.35	3,480.63

(ii)

a.	14, 85, 07.08	3, 82, 48.98	1, 47,772.80	48,495.38	10,514.524.24	2,660. 47.88	
Agricultural	2, 68, 06.59	63, 09.14	280,054.20	11,440.31	3,944. 00.24	559,803.94	
Alliance	1, 57, 30.12	65, 30.34	145,501.14	1,344.46	2,199,606.06	469,028.42	
Ame in Elle.	1, 08, 84.42	5, 32.95	138,334.81	43.43	1,242,885.61	242, 47.94	
	1, 84, 04.61	44, 05.24	14,662.65	3.54	2,235,531.04	1,509,089.98	
An (Newark)	5, 81, 83.03	65, 63.88	523,797.44	450,127.07	7,650.801.42	1,733,729.34	
An Gitral (St. Louis)	1, 61, 96.17	22, 81.85	160,033.14	1,343.66	2,335,554.82	258, 81.43	
An Me	1, 00, 30.48	86, 82.41	145,365.36	1,145,407.64	2,798. 05.89	229,087.97	
An Me	3, 99, 29.28	85, 02.12	250,961.69	61,767.61	8, 46,900.70	1,982,705.82	
30	4, 07, 82.51	37, 88.93	387,583.75	27,941.36	7,980,778.55	1,530,133.24	
Ga	3, 09, 45.95	32, 42.47	04, 60.03	822.88	3, 806, 921.33	17, 422.46	
Gs of Mouri.	3, 00, 87.05		33, 81.28	102.60	04,330.93	95, 452.63	
Gb	89, 06.82	33, 39.90	54, 34.98		627,924.88	215,256.31	
Gi National	76, 98.37	71, 30.35	25, 33.15	285.38	365,865.70	554.63	
		5, 02.59	7, 07.69	86, 423.61	816,222.26		14,841.86
Gl in New York	1, 65, 02.22	14, 81.75	53, 61.31	1,397.55	1, 03, 65.28	193,183.75	
Ga. Fi	1, 39, 32.51	50, 94.78	142,890.02	39,807.43	2, 44, 84.86	199,922.39	
Gai N al	1, 85, 51.92	76, 81.19	132. 14.43	10,010.00	3, 94, 84.97	274,032.79	
Gt.	5, 55, 61.62		69,985.30	4,945.68	65, 36.92		
	5, 67, 01.01	99, 02.45	319,115.01		6, 00, 14.15	1, 76,848.57	
Gi	12, 31, 83.47	1 22, 63.53	1,763,127.52	1,920.001.54	17,536,541.06	3,910. 17.12	
	31, 36.40		43,314.36	796.55	375,267.31		
Eagle Fe and Marine	39, 87.77		40,124.31	158,334.38	528,346.46	12, 87.75	
Fe (th Carolina)	90, 83.53	32, 42.71	71,782.33		844,883.87	09, 97.53	
	22, 30.48	5,	26,075.56	1,498.05	250,324.09	78, 68.59	
tral	10, 34, 79.61	3, 98, 85.64	199, 654.58	7, 921.42	4, 930, 71.25	317, 868.72	
r t td	1, 84, 94.55	1 69, 63.07	982,868.91	882,638.31	14,059,724.84	3,418,890.49	
Fe Me	7, 62, 96.57		89.413.58	38.56	1,691,948.71	285,312.19	
Fs An of Philadelphia	7, 04, 28.20	6 97, 97.95	549,472.57	30,486.49	8,182,615.21	1,464,402.11	
F	6, 90, 66.85	26, 80.72	661, 44.77	2,099.00	14,309,891.34	851,428.25	
Fs of York	4, 02, 44.94	63, 82.85	391,270.70	45,547.77	5,092,386.26	917,682.19	
F	1, 91, 68.38	43, 35.76	120,942.42	277,980.18	2,003,316.74	854,979.34	
Fa Fire al Me	56, 00.60		29,378.77	192,546.28	577,975.65	108,785.43	
Girard Fire a d Me	1, 86, 86.63		09,377.59	49,021.92	1,545,235.14	241,316.31	
Gas Falls	3, 62, 91.02	73, 57.01	322,521.63	46,634.81	4,905,504.47	698,703.49	
Globe National	59, 90.65		19,079.42	1,817,406.15	1,895,886.22	1,431,306.50	
Ge & Fs	12, 63, 27.27	7 34, 64.15	1,095, 672.73	1,621,226.99	23,054,801.14	8,463,459.32	
Granite St s	1, 04, 30.83		51,659.12	9,723.47	1,087,713.42	1,087, 880.11	
Gt An	15, 72, 91.38	1 83, 63.34	1,259,405.27	1,549,225.20	19,805,225.19	3,618, 91.69	
Hartford	3, 74, 41.36	50, 08.35	258,976.40	25,977.14	3,959,421.88	218,715.03	
Fe, Fire and Marine	27, 79, 89.45	03, 04.10	1,253,480.10	5,077.14	32, 31,560.79	5,549,128.05	
	94, 31.38	31, 88.84	38, 81.31		1,084,781.53	543,055.70	

(iii)

TABLE No. I— NE.

SHOWING THE I ME OF FIRE, MARINE AND INLAND COMPANIES (LICENSED TO DO BUSINESS IN THIS STATE) FOR YEAR ENDING DECEMBER 31, 1918.

COMPANIES OF UR STATES (STOCK)—CONTIN D.

Me of Co	Fire Premiums, Including Perpetuals	Marine and Inland Premiums	Interest, Dividends, and Rents	From Other Sources	Total Income	Income Over Disbursements	Disbursements Over Income
He of New York	$28,555,845.63	$3,042,401.77	$1,959,020.99	$144,050.56	$33,701,318.95	$6,284,565.37	$
He of Utah	605,229.50		95,706.15	10,329.03	711,264.68	278,292.27	
	594,049.35		42,251.40	376,521.50	1,012,822.25	505,697.41	
Gy of North a.	11,705,236.27	9,097,856.48	1,174,446.61	60,118.58	22,037,657.94	2,903,913.70	
	160,292.31	652.01	17,318.59		178,262.91	17,630.72	
nal	4,071,402.04		212,202.80	2,077.52	4,285,682.36	129,617.01	
	365,013.85		42,166.03		407,179.88	6,211.34	
va	229,795.42		36,587.19	35,986.31	302,368.92	103,829.32	
Ms E and M	606,198.39	658,229.79	67,708.74	1,167.27	1,33,64.19	15,184.15	
Me Nati d	610,597.53		39,869.50	500.00	650,967.03	175,406.90	
Ms &	840,762.73		69,738.95	25,681.14	936,182.82	8,136.57	
Ms e	927,249.35		75,232.44	528.45	1,03,00.24	82,972.02	
Ms Mi ghany of America	1,399,227.80	370,884.67	130,830.91	346.50	1,901,289.88	251,827.92	
Ms Ms	283,406.15	193,421.53	17,357.61	10,078.65	504,263.94	17,939.66	
	2,791,304.29	164,714.97	250,804.31	824.11	3,207,67.68	544,717.35	
Mi ity	11,802,900.46	1,312,048.08	744,858.21	8,960.58	13,868,767.33	1,0,995.88	
Mi n	4,304,105.13	850,536.25	395,957.72	1,009,404.63	6,650,003.73	1,35,204.45	
Mi i	2,911,817.43	369,600.77	196,301.72	361.11	3,478,081.03	7,524.31	
Mi lge	1,588,794.07	275,982.04	101,874.43	293.31	1,966,48.85	374,514.22	
Vw	3,806,284.53	204,478.69	321,221.51	1,454.26	4,33,48.99	727,562.09	
	5,628,470.58	793,599.40	403,276.75	6,717.18	6,832,063.31	1,092,635.96	
Mi River	3,417,973.93	455,968.55	210,850.66	22,785.64	4,07,578.78	935,741.67	
North Branch	810,576.97	376,433.93	35,600.61	100,181.86	1,322,793.37	325,045.92	
Mi Mial	3,412,554.00	682,932.90	347,919.41	616.02	4,44,022.33	747,351.10	
Mi Fire and Marine	619,684.03		51,298.25	494,432.57	1,65,44.85	74,369.36	
Cl	929,274.09	573,014.41	95,301.24		1,597,589.	298,015.65	
Orient	1,362.76	339,350.48	160,601.34	25,175.00	2,471,314.58	3,093.21	
to in	321,457.98	30,997.05	13,075.53		390,705.56	212,419.40	
Ms in Mi	4,157,947.06	181,108.93	358,252.76	38,220.78	4,735,529.53	147,266.88	
Mi Mi	99,366.47	86,095.79	100,027.60	66,199.84	1,81,689.70	92,320.78	
dx rd)	70,14.67		6,348.49	152,007.17	229,100.33	9,240.06	
	7,976,844.77	1,260,615.44	25.01	489	10,188,352.11	2,776,632.71	

(v)

Arkwright M	2,776,847.50	133,166.21	7,336.62	2,917,350.33	609,715.14
Blackstone	105,645.59	4,716.36		110,361.95	19,068.14
Underwriters	1,37,97.48	83,123.38	88.65	1,461,90.51	280,456.39
Cotton Wn Ma rfacturers	2,206,84.37	28,783.87	236,234.42	2,471,202.66	475,623.27
	759,578.64	34,41.12	1,092.54	795,112.30	152,259.85
Druggists ch age	157,568.19	3,244.60		160,812.79	20,588.92
Firemen's Mutual	1,991,850.34	121,572.46	91.76	2,114,674.56	388,458.33
	341,958.36	13,216.36	862.37	356,037.09	64,047.62
Hope ial	770,464.69	40,055.43	.40	810,520.52	158,362.15
	657,712.28	45,520.93		703,233.21	14,246.27
ll Underwriters	470,755.99	29,242.41	38,000.00	537,998.40	91,397.47
	436,890.83	23,407.72	247.64	460,546.19	62,171.43
Mrs hterins e	459,476.14	18,711.46	1,602.64	479,790.24	48,876.67
	240,906.53	8,126.77	205,684.67	454,717.97	48,84.90
Lumber Mutual	714,980.93	54,953.94	32,981.61	802,916.48	115,68.90
ial	917,545.14	44,189.78	28,475.62	90,210.54	81,305.49
	1,278,216.15	41,527.55	178.91	1,319,922.61	25,45.20
Lumbermen's U Mrs lerwriters	434,085.11	17,450.05	1,383.36	452,918.52	40,820.27
	1,231,675.32	48,579.24		1,280,254.56	16,619.48
Manufacturing	271,237.72	7,738.00	107,144.88	386,120.60	41,89.0
Merchants Mutual	736,266.78	46,043.13		782,309.91	155,751.17
Mercantile	353,928.37	15,179.57	5,273.66	374,381.60	43,670.34
Middlesex ial	271,184.59	28,967.38		300,151.97	30,392.97
Michigan Millers ial	1,202,132.78	83,062.48	460,943.11	1,746,138.37	271,340.53
Millers Mutual	260,120.76	26,77.98	15,023.68	301,862.42	88,157.30
Mrs Underwriters	495,952.80	6,133.93	35,139.64	537,226.37	181,47.38

TABLE No. I—INCOME.

SHOWING THE INCOME OF FIRE, MARINE AND INLAND COMPANIES (LICENSED TO DO BUSINESS IN THIS STATE) FOR YEAR ENDING D███ER 31, 1918.

COMPANIES OF OTHER S███TES (MUTUAL)—CONTINUED.

Name of Company	Fire Premiums, Including Perpetuals	Marine and Inland Premiums	Interest, Dividends, and Rents	From Other Sources	Total Income	Income Over Disbursements	Disbursements Over Income
Narragansett Mutual	$ 152,090.44	$	$ 6,076.04	$ 5,233.81	$ 163,400.29	$ 38,123.64	$
National Mutual	158,127.20		7,181.31	169.46	165,477.97	11,572.07	
███l Lumber Manufacturers	171,223.95		4,958.98		176,182.93	2,███205	
Penn Lumbermen's Mutual	667,043.35		46,723.15	113,987.75	827,754.25	173,804.23	
Philadelphia Manufacturers Mutual	752,076.89		38,405.07	7,531.91	798,013.87	150,617.68	
Reciprocal Exchange	650,664.93		24,678.30	341.38	675,684.61	40,150.22	
Rubber Manufacturers ███l	700,235.50		33,461.26	3,622.71	737,318.47	129,189.41	
Southern Lumber Underwriters	95,984.51		1,437.16	3,139.98	100,561.65	16,███514	
Utilities Indemnity Exchange	285,883.22		2,440.33		288,323.55		10,850.48
Western Reciprocal Underwriters	248,456.83		2,634.78	25,000.00	276,091.61	37,070.31	
███at Cheer Mutual	798,784.99		40,931.31	.40	839,716.70	169,742.89	
Warners Interinsurers (Grocers' Dept.)	263,822.78		5,952.56	145,547.10	415,322.44	137,441.16	
Totals	25,865,357.97		1,222,752.36	1,483,520.68	28,571,630.01	4,805,734.47	27,469.96

Company							
Nationale (Paris)	625,137.57		33,174.22	16,357.80	658,311.79	140,333.41	
Netherlands Fire and Life	677,895.13		43,175.61		737,428.54	130,283.79	
Norske Lloyds	3,268,473.28		87,897.48	347,886.23	3,704,256.99	1,040,910.90	
North British and Mercantile	6,324,326.96	454,132.01	352,750.32	431.01	7,131,640.30	433,740.42	
Northern Assurance	4,612,290.04	205,471.63	248,167.89	19,451.58	5,085,381.14	521,158.53	
Northern (Moscow)	724,769.09		53,582.88		778,351.97	1,048,527.64	212,946.84
Norwegian Assurance	1,636,714.49	925,556.87	29,345.46	400,235.58	2,066,295.53	676,714.99	
Norwich Union	2,635,002.03		132,099.95	375,570.48	4,068,229.33	271,669.84	
Paternelle	1,514,881.26		56,266.12	38.75	1,571,186.13		
Phenix Fire	625,137.57		31,519.78	9,702.82	666,360.17	154,326.28	
Palatine (London)	2,387,270.94	193,405.27	127,736.79	92,082.96	2,800,495.96	402,327.21	
Phenix (Loncon)	3,267,088.56	369,921.75	167,284.88	240,917.35	4,045,212.54	411,515.56	
Prudential Company and Reinsurance	902,230.34		20,833.47	1,056,114.63	1,979,178.44	1,609,746.11	
Rossia	9,084,947.10	4,330,686.95	381,325.82		13,796,959.87	1,841,669.44	
Royal	9,504,994.78	2,636,209.68	766,665.71	576,335.50	13,484,205.67	1,966,627.95	
Royal Exchange Assurance	2,175,873.46	1,043,274.51	144,447.00	43.72	3,363,638.69	352,836.40	
Russian Reinsurance	1,873,204.42		92,645.06		1,965,849.48	58,312.80	
Salamandra	3,503,986.90		176,846.75	3,993.92	3,684,827.57	122,112.99	
Scottish Union and National	3,356,096.63	357,513.96	304,687.36	720.24	4,019,018.19	377,894.36	
Second Russian	1,443,363.01		71,344.46	508.85	1,515,216.32	169,584.18	
Scandia	1,500,078.17		74,856.06		1,574,934.23	332,073.81	
Scandinavia	4,526,542.87	393,670.00	74,744.21	500,638.59	5,495,595.67	1,417,250.02	
Sun Insurance Office	3,246,023.52	757,526.57	212,775.47	282,686.89	4,499,012.45	639,359.23	
Svea Fire and Life	1,543,134.43		66,958.84	7,816.86	1,617,910.13	276,814.90	
Swiss National	2,413,415.72		81,695.39	40,020.07	2,535,131.18	706,134.46	
Tokio Marine and Fire	865,266.91	1,109,010.86	66,282.30		3,548,762.87	1,820,421.54	
Union Assurance	1,036,301.94	73,183.88	70,493.25	1,508,202.80	1,337,446.75	318,360.61	
Union of Paris	862,431.66		46,471.61	157,467.68	908,903.27	189,115.26	
Union and Phenix Espagnol	2,868,273.33		87,584.10	100,930.56	3,056,787.99	747,408.05	
Union Hispanus Americai	319,710.84		11,370.57	50,000.00	381,081.41	153,823.90	
Urbaine	4,055,109.79		75,619.22	572,668.95	4,703,397.96	2,262,262.51	
Warsaw Fire	869,572.17		36,941.21		906,513.38	62,680.59	
Western Assurance	1,871,308.71	1,148,053.44	142,525.08	518,319.21	3,680,206.44	513,805.21	
Yorkshire	1,144,405.09	127,881.22	44,548.63	302,532.19	1,619,367.13	583,376.81	
Totals	134,358,277.07	20,742,379.70	6,819,627.55	10,081,426.90	172,001,711.22	31,488,513.49	309,683.91

RECAPITULATION.

North Carolina Companies	1,581,885.60	88,680.52	197,356.78	89,632.68	1,957,555.58	528,462.35	3,480.63
Companies of other States (stock)	319,985,968.90	76,757,045.30	25,614,656.50	14,018,173.67	436,375,844.37	77,698,164.55	14,841.86
Companies of other States (mutual)	25,865,357.97		1,222,752.36	1,483,520.68	28,571,630.01	4,805,734.47	27,469.96
Companies of foreign countries	134,358,277.07	20,742,379.70	6,819,627.55	10,081,426.90	172,001,711.22	31,488,513.49	309,683.91
Grand totals	481,791,489.54	97,588,105.52	33,854,393.19	25,672,753.93	638,906,741.18	114,520,874.86	355,474.36

(vii)

TABLE No. II—DISBURSEMENTS.

SHOWING THE DISBURSEMENTS OF FIRE, MARINE AND INLAND COMPANIES (LICENSED TO DO BUSINESS IN THIS STATE) FOR YEAR ENDING DECEMBER 31, 1918.

NORTH CAROLINA COMPANIES.

Name of Company	Fire Losses	Marine and Inland Losses	Interest or Dividends	Commissions or Brokerage	Salaries of Officers and Other Employees	Insurance Department Fees and Taxes	All Other Disbursements	Total Disbursements
Alamance	$ 1,685.90	$	$	$ 408.04	$ 237.00	$ 50.82	$ 320.85	$ 2,702.61
At Mal	26,779.02		65,000.00	8,391.52	14,937.03	10,603.85	6,976.61	132,688.03
us Mal	533.05				600.46	43.05	75.07	1,251.63
Davidson uty Mual	11,808.67		5,002.70	2,753.93	5,851.20	3,953.98	2,997.24	32,367.72
	964.00				125.00	51.01	8.00	1,148.01
Dixie	152,164.87	15,219.88	30,318.00	108,970.67	44,058.72	15,249.54	73,174.72	439,156.40
Farmers Mutual (Raleigh)	40,124.64			4,629.77		359.54	11,432.26	56,546.21
Farmers Douglas				40.68		60.00	253.24	353.92
Farmers Mutual (Edgecombe County)	774.67			202.73	400.00	48.97	172.40	1,598.77
Gaston City Farmers Mutual	690.61			367.43	210.75	50.89	225.35	1,545.03
Hardware Mutual	5,350.64		3,120.13		1,903.10	239.57	985.56	11,599.00
g Farmers M al	2,781.97				89.00	48.70	489.99	3,409.66
Methodist Mutual	6.40				496.00	133.00	756.89	1,392.29
North a Home	64,059.40		12,000.00	31,286.13	10,585.24	6,143.94	31,031.42	155,106.13
N rh Carolina State				1,349.68		478.18	2,366.12	4,193.98
Piedmont	46,474.16		15,000.00	21,886.77	11,150.60	489.66	82,885.74	177,886.93
Rowan Mutual	7,005.04				610.50	52.15	214.00	7,881.69
Southern Mutual Furniture	214.14		611.62		909.80	165.53	406.45	2,307.54
Southern Stock	27,451.89		9,682.02		1,764.85	2,499.76	198,070.20	239,468.72
Southern Underwriters	41,331.20		12,000.00		2,280.57	7,960.72	83,018.45	146,590.94
Stanly County Mutual	576.00			573.37		45.67	117.17	1,312.21
State Mual	2,674.50			1,960.81	1,820.00	124.77	1,838.09	8,418.17
Underwriters (Rocky Mt)	4,438.56		4,120.00	6,188.45	500.00	1,063.37	9,334.70	25,645.08
Underwriters of eo	31,752.53		6,000.00		1,796.27	200.45	57,046.56	96,795.81
Union County Farmers Mutual	333.79				101.83	42.59	70.07	548.28
Wilson County Farmers Mutual						54.00		54.00
Totals	469,975.65	15,219.88	162,854.47	189,009.98	100,427.92	50,213.71	564,267.15	1,551,968.76

COMPANIES OF OTHER STATES (STOCK).

Ætna	6,575,059.52	2,232,746.67	1,000,000.00	3,540,342.83	1,255,437.13	807,275.67	1,443,184.54	16,854,046.36
Agricultural	1,269,071.29	366,773.87	200,000.00	853,883.94	209,964.21	82,889.11	401,623.88	3,384,206.30
?de	557,678.67	459,899.71	75,000.00	363,437.79	107,540.37	51,983.02	115,038.08	1,730,577.64
?an	422,636.10	165,165.86	135,000.00	344,322.51	11,896.11	24,284.92	62,432.17	1,000,737.67
?an Equitable	92,212.42	101,611.49		502,755.79		12,393.56	17,467.80	726,441.06
?ark)	2,429,800.67	333,203.96	400,000.00	1,588,279.06	455,783.19	175,664.66	534,340.54	5,917,072.08
American Central (St. ?uis)	1,049,109.68	124,642.81		583,461.70	109,495.30	66,280.39	143,883.51	2,076,873.39
American Eagle	241,029.96	170,642.69	130,000.00	240,717.58	70,814.33	20,124.44	1,515,598.92	2,388,927.92
? ?le	798,304.23	579,291.45	200,000.00	1,377,595.68	614,922.12	137,214.28	2,456,867.12	6,164,194.88
Boston	1,656,736.66	1,896,023.40	240,000.00	1,482,260.14	462,355.52	156,103.48	557,166.11	6,450,645.31
?d	1,314,321.70	275,614.60	95,979.60	944,072.17	150,388.95	70,225.17	238,896.68	3,089,498.87
?ons of Missouri	161,092.46		16,000.00	133,697.25	119.46	1.50	27,967.63	338,878.30
?na		241,511.56		131,187.56	17,186.96	9,402.05	13,380.44	412,668.57
?in	143,766.23	6,989.00	7,687.27	87,121.95	33,251.64	9,603.09	24,823.67	365,311.07
?han National	465,488.59	59,057.22	39,067.00	193,304.66	42,523.38	23,582.98	67,097.51	831,064.12
?al Union (New York)	404,840.92	51,616.61	20,000.00	251,723.77	65,809.71	32,154.14	54,176.38	880,321.53
?h	724,668.22	345,334.55	50.00	450,189.73	180,512.34	57,306.14	137,021.49	1,945,032.47
Concordia	853,009.26		75,000.00	617,313.12	129,274.53	62,963.01	216,003.26	1,960,552.18
Cleveland National	215,231.01			136,139.98	51,731.29	20,190.06	32,263.99	455,556.33
Connecticut	2,170,844.35	456,899.08	275,000.00	1,519,287.19	475,218.73	169,865.62	456,840.61	5,523,895.58
?y	4,871,308.34	865,789.93	1,400,000.00	2,904,464.91	961,463.41	334,709.54	2,288,627.81	13,626,363.94
	157,818.28		20,000.00	70,715.06	10,183.42	17,760.00	30,548.10	307,024.86
Eagle	222,644.44		16,875.00	86,023.21	24,965.88	3,292.15	62,235.03	416,033.71
?tje Fire and Marine	231,101.32	149,362.39	50,000.00	257,561.33	11,652.57	3,506.58	34,802.15	734,936.34
Equitable (South Carolina)	57,270.36		16,000.00	31,744.39	22,635.49	9,973.31	34,031.95	171,655.50
Federal	60,715.12	2,297,926.58	190,000.00	1,540,170.49	4,444.68	101,213.75	418,371.91	4,612,842.53
Fidelity-Phenix	4,135,497.68	815,715.34	550,000.00	2,694,445.04	873,615.06	292,876.18	1,278,676.05	10,640,825.35
Fire Reinsurance	505,471.03			478,921.71	26,215.90	21,679.37	374,348.51	1,406,636.52
Fire ?ion of Philadelphia	3,276,366.98	116,006.31	400,000.00	1,524,950.66	645,730.75	186,687.08	568,471.32	6,718,213.10
Firemen's ?	2,980,243.40	5,249,999.42	300,000.00	2,325,684.98	924,872.86	371,767.40	1,305,895.03	13,458,463.09
Firemen's ?rk)	1,837,501.85	144,406.90		1,071,541.05	286,332.06	127,149.60	407,772.61	4,174,704.07
Franklin	373,445.64	175,351.71	50,000.00	437,412.82	43,282.71	4,500.00	64,344.52	1,148,337.40
Georgia Home	112,913.33			78,150.41	31,739.83	13,075.40	233,311.25	469,190.22
Girard Fire and Marine	453,070.78		60,000.00	337,800.82	111,041.57	46,277.87	295,727.79	1,303,918.83
?s Falls	1,638,563.48	531,404.81	185,000.00	992,686.66	317,820.71	132,650.66	408,674.66	4,206,800.98
?be National	1,000.00			19,058.27	9,966.43	1,819.29	432,735.73	464,579.72
?e ?d Rutgers	4,870,594.00	4,468,729.01	336,000.00	2,969,351.67	484,812.74	170,492.60	1,291,361.80	14,591,341.82
?e ?te	473,378.14		20,000.00	245,488.14	72,990.83	27,456.51	60,519.69	899,833.31
Great	7,952,555.89	513,914.63	600,000.00	3,714,730.86	1,342,522.09	380,304.21	1,742,255.82	16,246,283.50
Hanover	1,644,528.27	344,247.14	100,000.00	848,395.22	274,407.17	116,655.77	411,473.28	3,739,706.85
Hartford	12,880,493.34	1,505,912.38	800,000.00	5,810,770.29	2,186,544.32	939,385.58	2,459,326.83	26,582,432.74
?e Fire and Marine	41,440.79	126,688.41		203,855.86	87,337.43	10,506.25	71,907.09	541,735.83

TABLE No. II—DISBURSEMENTS.

SHOWING THE DISBURSEMENTS OF FIRE, MARINE AND INLAND COMPANIES (LICENSED TO DO BUSINESS IN THIS STATE) FOR YEAR ENDING DECEMBER 31, 1918.

COMPANIES OF OTHER STATES (STOCK)—Continued.

Name of Company	Fire Losses	Marine and Inland Losses	Interest or Dividends	Commissions or Brokerage	Salaries of Officers and Other Employees	Insurance Department Fees and Taxes	All Other Disbursements	Total Disbursements
...ire of New York	$12,687,120.07	$1,505,424.87	$1,500,000.00	$6,657,046.61	$1,717,326.79	$728,883.30	$2,620,951.94	$27,416,753.58
...ce of Utah	119,221.23		60,000.00	201,464.07	8,397.20	6,255.37	37,634.54	432,972.41
	248,297.46		20,000.00	125,272.38	35,277.69	22,049.87	56,227.44	507,124.84
Insurance Company of North America	4,882,751.94	5,746,664.51	640,000.00	3,713,325.66	1,591,507.39	552,243.39	2,007,251.35	19,133,744.24
	85,270.50		10,000.00	53,158.83	310.00	4,001.90	7,890.96	160,632.19
International	2,843,105.64			1,331,342.20	38,698.77	23,212.05	119,706.69	4,156,065.35
Interstate	234,614.48			96,303.04	5,796.40	50,507.15	13,747.47	400,968.54
Iowa	52,640.71			60,677.26	27,050.39	3,224.61	54,946.63	198,539.60
...s Fire and Me	317,997.93	480,340.55		342,607.22	63,172.45	23,249.32	121,120.87	1,348,488.34
...e N	160,684.28		15,000.00	183,872.68	49,314.31	11,662.81	55,026.05	475,560.13
	347,153.31		25,000.00	194,475.45	65,762.18	26,838.85	158,816.46	818,046.25
...d Traders	461,286.25			158,607.14	94,277.21	40,593.25	65,274.37	820,038.22
...Insurance Co...pny of America	559,283.04	265,833.13	100,000.00	423,487.13	157,422.92	46,893.94	96,541.80	1,649,461.96
	126,531.00	153,321.86		116,755.48	33,251.53	3,238.05	53,226.36	486,324.28
	1,195,160.11	76,609.82		716,267.00	217,253.51	98,597.75	379,042.14	2,682,930.33
National	5,712,520.49	545,997.85	400,000.00	2,158,466.28	1,422,433.34	495,957.27	1,192,813.94	11,927,771.45
...l Bury	1,899,157.70	624,356.90	200,000.00	1,224,668.28	369,991.78	149,604.72	847,019.90	5,314,799.28
...l Union	1,758,767.38	225,655.90	100,000.00	658,979.61	298,824.60	153,284.96	275,044.27	3,470,556.72
...t	764,058.67	112,984.17	31.20	380,661.15	29,297.02	53,533.10	251,869.32	1,592,434.63
New ...	1,747,558.15	39,973.80	180,006.00	1,029,900.30	254,753.64	94,147.64	259,537.37	3,605,876.90
N...ga	2,500,648.30	476,233.99	250,000.00	1,235,466.46	555,963.92	151,422.71	569,692.57	5,739,427.95
...th	1,391,487.16	134,544.92	59,977.50	975,533.19	334,737.12	80,250.63	195,286.59	3,171,837.11
...h Branch	460,140.99	67,724.08	32,000.00	312,600.02	52,778.60	13,834.47	58,669.29	997,747.45
...rn N...al	1,350,681.13	354,963.62	185,000.00	1,192,377.27	211,109.12	142,560.04	259,980.05	3,696,671.23
...tern Fire and	289,688.34		40,000.00	498,426.63	83,595.53	38,368.24	140,966.75	1,091,045.49
Old ...ty	410,547.14	269,358.43	42,000.00	367,587.40	44,085.79	29,393.60	136,601.73	1,299,574.09
Orient	826,733.46	183,880.04	100,000.00	423,859.56	197,919.97	112,451.50	230,052.91	2,074,897.44
Palmetto	51,228.90	16,728.53	18,000.00	55,317.60	3,951.43	25,434.03	7,625.67	178,286.16
Pennsylvania	2,298,939.47	93,357.86	375,000.00	911,720.17	403,112.69	140,795.33	364,337.13	4,587,262.65
Peoples National	381,121.52	18,221.50	12,500.00	279,599.60	5,570.85	98,973.73	293,381.72	1,089,368.92
Petersburg	9,009.51			14,823.61	9,641.78	743.34	5,582.03	39,860.27
...ix (...rd)	3,240,297.40	700,759.35	697,589.25	1,883,724.18	787,802.37	297,767.03	793,779.82	8,401,719.40

(x)

Providence-Washington	1,876,615.36	1,762,266.35	120,000.00	1,277,406.64	348,092.55	196,920.00	376,214.56	5,957,515.46
Gn of	2,764,941.28	804,349.41	500,000.00	1,495,890.31	745,255.89	426,376.49	621,922.45	7,358,735.83
Me id Me	627,783.24		50,000.00	509,000.35	211.87	52,984.36	71,252.15	1,311,231.97
S. Paul Fire nd Me	3,560,702.53	2,819,268.60	300,000.00	2,433,362.23	370,596.00	298,312.94	623,729.70	10,405,972.00
Security	1,796,229.37	18,640.64	80,000.00	936,621.27	305,626.75	120,255.58	269,182.48	3,526,556.09
Sh Ga	25,211.83	53,094.73	51,500.00	64,123.77	23,406.20	3,207.33	8,849.17	229,393.03
Sild Fire nd M	3,906,338.16	34,106.66	250,000.00	1,829,633.00	872,590.15	241,295.25	607,356.28	7,741,319.50
Standard nd	340,046.43			168,571.19	81,512.02	25,410.70	68,647.10	684,187.53
Star of A	241,420.80		30,000.00	96,762.66	50,641.70	25,648.75	55,876.87	500,350.78
Sterling	379,728.71	10,371.33	25,500.00	243,716.91	11,808.64	17,754.50	21,804.41	710,684.50
Id States	2,006,994.75	292,660.89	140,031.30	1,853,820.67	48,901.28	116,568.87	326,644.57	4,785,622.33
Es Fire nd Me	438,148.06		35,000.00	280,452.87	61,944.03	35,262.97	78,764.71	929,572.34
Wr	2,920,551.92	395,551.48	250,000.00	1,590,?45.70	376,117.68	175,539.26	526,062.19	6,234,288.23
Bls	140,421,300.50	43,290,725.26	15,246,744.12	84,742,821.56	25,665,896.23	10,755,697.43	38,177,444.03	358,300,629.13

COMPANIES OF OTHER STATES (MUTUAL).

Baltimore t Mtual	163,348.02		1,971,244.08	32.54	70,966.55	413.84	101,630.16	2,307,635.19
Ml Ml	6,937.66		67,999.15	20.00	9,472.16	1,049.11	5,815.73	91,293.81
Pe Ml	172,745.73		897,084.86	32.54	38,620.79	547.06	71,522.14	1,180,553.12
Gn nd Vn	1,192,729.89		165,595.08		448,249.48	933.20	188,071.74	1,995,579.39
M	64,335.74		534,095.71	65.04	16,053.78	410.51	27,891.67	642,852.45
Ds nity E dge	40,592.85		51,247.23		39,754.89	1,946.51	6,682.39	140,223.87
Firemen's Mutual	233,563.76		1,333,003.42	20.00	46,593.95	571.68	112,463.42	1,726,216.23
Fitchburg Mutual	140,593.15		54,836.08	38,275.16	16,007.60	1,928.22	40,349.26	291,989.47
De Mutual	87,262.63		506,909.26		20,918.55	400.24	36,867.69	652,158.37
Indiana m's Mtual	248,410.36		235,352.48	2,057.33	46,243.62	2,524.87	54,398.28	588,986.94
Ial us	166,804.78		204,734.99		59,308.66	451.25	15,301.15	446,600.83
Ial Ml	38,813.99		331,508.46	62.54	10,346.78	410.51	17,232.48	398,374.76
Be Ml	53,389.69		336,378.06		20,211.46	441.80	20,492.56	430,913.57
hr Ms Interinsurance	297,628.17		10,240.60		35,154.78	911.80	61,798.56	405,733.91
hr Mual	282,252.73		262,632.67	44,513.86	43,143.37	1,130.25	53,562.73	687,235.61
In's M	401,971.60		241,393.37	107,532.34	65,019.79	1,388.50	91,599.45	908,905.05
In's us Ance	670,296.78		166,417.35		240,032.98		27,700.30	1,104,447.41
Manton Mutual	44,473.98		327,938.95		19,979.94	446.40	19,258.98	412,098.25
Manufacturing	789,556.08		229,985.40		238,391.72	1,169.97	37,770.87	1,296,874.04
Mg Wo Ms Underwriters	156,185.86		6,000.02		64,781.80	338.00	16,945.53	244,251.21
Ms Mutual	103,570.59		462,624.46	32.54	20,461.19	531.04	39,338.12	626,557.94
Me Mutual	34,597.98		255,889.09	30.00	16,367.70	600.17	23,227.32	330,711.26
Nk M	78,573.31		82,829.40	42,622.42	16,958.67	839.00	48,135.20	269,959.00
Mn Mrs Ml	816,085.13		146,617.00	309,204.77	76,563.13	1,916.04	124,411.72	1,474,797.79
Ms Ml	115,103.72		61,567.74		9,092.01	258.00	27,683.65	213,705.12
Ms Indemnity uiters	127,445.16		36,985.36		124,876.60	1,671.18	65,100.69	356,078.99

TABLE No. II—DISBURSEMENTS.

SHOWING THE DISBURSEMENTS OF FIRE, MARINE AND INLAND COMPANIES (LICENSED TO DO BUSINESS IN THIS STATE) FOR YEAR ENDING DECEMBER 31, 1918.

COMPANIES OF OTHER STATES (MUTUAL)—CONTINUED

Name of Company	Fire Losses	Marine and Inland Losses	Interest or Dividends	Commissions or Brokerage	Salaries of Officers and Other Employees	Insurance Department Fees and Taxes	All Other Disbursements	Total Disbursements
Narragansett Mual	$ 9,494.64	$ ------	$ 98,896.13	$ 30.00	$ 9,123.94	$ 312.20	$ 7,419.74	$ 125,276.65
Mtl Mut	18,234.13	------	120,674.45	------	7,693.82	550.60	6,752.90	153,905.90
fr Mers	85,601.67	------	804.38	------	18,567.33	181.00	68,907.50	174,061.88
Penn Lumbermen's Ml	251,999.44	------	244,430.46	42,957.41	46,217.98	1,466.34	66,878.39	653,950.02
Ha Ms Mutual	59,210.01	------	501,774.66	------	38,398.46	473.34	47,539.72	647,396.19
Reciprocal E ge	272,157.47	------	154,010.55	------	176,704.42	830.10	31,831.85	635,534.39
Rubber Ms M	60,567.77	------	505,334.76	------	15,292.83	410.51	26,460.65	608,129.06
fn Ir Underwriters	56,268.04	------	8,739.88	62.54	5,762.50	372.60	7,904.22	84,526.51
ies Iry Ig	127,064.54	------	41,947.53	5,479.27	94,198.73	2,206.81	33,756.42	299,174.03
Vn l Underwriters	106,280.89	------	33,194.47	------	88,689.16	744.47	10,112.31	239,021.30
Wt fir M	89,113.38	------	522,054.15	------	20,918.57	400.24	37,487.47	669,973.81
Ms Interinsurers (Gs' Departm nt)	103,425.06	------	38,471.69	------	53,392.14	1,066.47	81,525.92	277,881.28
Tls	7,766,686.38	------	11,251,443.38	593,030.30	2,388,531.83	32,243.83	1,761,628.88	23,793,564.60

COMPANIES OF FOREIGN COUNTRIES.

(xii)

Company	(1)	(2)	(3)	(4)	(5)	(6)	(7)	Total
Nationale (Paris)	293,680.98			181,791.13	342.54	16,890.27	25,273.46	517,978.38
... Fire and Life	332,228.00			145,179.82	29,813.97	32,299.05	67,605.91	607,144.75
... Globes	1,618,162.30			888,728.41	93,412.55	7,357.20	55,705.63	2,663,366.09
North British and Mercantile	3,015,726.15	397,277.31		1,440,927.85	610,993.49	217,168.05	1,015,807.03	6,697,899.88
... Assurance	2,195,663.88	92,180.86		929,753.74	417,337.38	132,672.17	796,614.58	4,564,222.61
... (Moscow)	712,875.45			255,862.56	500.00	6,943.62	15,117.18	991,298.81
Norwegian ...	473,776.91			476,795.06	38,856.63	2,835.90	25,503.39	1,017,767.89
... Union	1,257,764.30	317,560.62		615,574.10	281,282.43	102,965.56	1,016,367.33	3,591,514.34
Paternelle	731,560.00			518,624.99	3,291.00	29,933.97	16,106.27	1,299,516.29
... Fire	293,680.98			181,791.13	342.54	16,890.27	19,328.97	512,033.89
Palatine (London)	1,150,817.83	75,319.16		556,940.58	193,798.92	89,444.51	331,847.75	2,398,168.75
Phœnix (London)	1,556,441.68	164,609.95		564,901.25	426,033.22	143,022.56	778,688.32	3,633,696.98
Prudentia Co. and Reinsurance	67,517.51			289,445.34	2,152.29	1,693.30	8,673.89	369,482.33
Rossia	4,744,351.87	2,767,782.50		3,591,431.83	119,661.69	161,384.51	570,678.03	11,955,290.43
Royal Exchange ...	4,446,820.21	1,218,320.51	723,020.20	1,903,382.09	1,271,559.55	436,199.70	1,518,275.46	11,517,577.72
... Assurance	1,109,104.75	577,910.77		697,893.76	196,377.93	102,674.17	327,290.91	3,011,252.29
Russian Reinsurance	1,230,984.95			556,471.19	500.00	35,223.51	84,357.03	1,907,536.68
Salamandra	2,404,660.05			1,022,799.86	24,344.85	48,112.76	62,787.06	3,562,704.58
Scottish Union and National	1,474,828.61	92,448.93		780,376.82	313,162.87	143,873.37	826,433.23	3,631,123.83
Second Russian	849,678.59			464,985.10	3,514.53	21,347.70	6,106.22	1,345,632.14
Scandia	699,877.17			471,616.62	7,288.46	1,378.22	62,699.95	1,242,860.42
Scandinavia	1,290,681.62	240,785.71		1,435,162.97	24,412.82	10,661.60	76,640.93	3,078,345.65
Sun ...	1,571,473.44	264,248.38		855,294.53	277,586.27	121,072.96	769,977.64	3,859,653.22
Svea Fire and Life	695,883.76			395,521.51	95,046.15	54,660.26	99,983.55	1,341,095.23
Swiss National	964,570.53			772,955.99	9,815.42	3,335.67	78,319.11	1,828,996.72
... and Fire	89,582.56	801,627.76		570,129.33	4,333.15	41,959.74	220,708.79	1,728,341.33
Union Assurance	370,283.79	51,616.61		238,767.61	93,240.21	32,399.97	232,777.95	1,019,086.14
Union of Paris	394,598.01			274,951.19	606.87	23,745.50	25,886.44	719,788.01
Union and Phenix Espagnol	1,282,921.41			940,886.75	600.00	13,961.69	71,010.09	2,309,379.94
Union ...	4,740.60			111,898.75		1,526.24	8,891.92	127,157.51
Urbaine	888,850.97			1,412,631.58	27,435.46	15,526.27	96,691.17	2,441,135.45
... Fire	540,937.66			278,476.82	500.00	7,161.62	16,746.69	843,822.79
...	965,195.37	839,533.86		686,851.36	156,402.74	104,590.79	413,827.11	3,166,401.23
Yorkshire	505,703.53	29,728.81		257,385.38	108,178.56	43,764.31	91,229.73	1,035,990.32
Totals	63,021,004.24	11,281,261.85	723,020.20	37,194,309.63	7,635,931.78	3,466,521.11	16,580,232.83	139,902,281.64

RECAPITULATION.

	(1)	(2)	(3)	(4)	(5)	(6)	(7)	Total
...	469,975.65	15,219.88	162,854.47	189,009.98	100,427.92	50,213.71	564,267.15	1,551,968.76
... of ... States (stock)	140,421,300.50	43,290,725.26	15,246,744.12	84,742,821.56	25,665,896.23	10,755,697.43	38,177,444.03	358,300,629.13
... of ... States (Mutual)	7,766,636.38		11,251,443.38	593,030.30	2,388,531.83	32,243.83	1,761,628.88	23,793,564.60
... of foreign ...	63,021,004.24	11,281,261.85	723,020.20	37,194,309.63	7,635,931.78	3,466,521.11	16,580,232.83	139,902,281.64
Grand totals	211,678,966.77	54,587,206.99	27,384,062.17	122,719,171.47	35,790,787.76	14,304,676.08	57,083,572.89	523,548,444.13

(xiii)

TABLE No. III—ASSETS.

SHOWING ASSETS OF FIRE, MARINE AND I ■ INSURANCE COMPANIES (LICENSED TO DO BUSINESS IN THIS STATE) FOR YEAR ENDING DECEMBER 31, 1918.

NORTH CAROLINA COMPANIES.

Name of	Value of Real Estate	Mortgage Loans on Real Estate	Loans on Collaterals	Bonds and Stocks	Cash in Office and Banks	Agents' Balances and Unpaid Premiums	Miscellaneous	Total Admitted Assets
Ae.	$ ----	----	$ ----	$ -----	$ 1,868.23	$ -----	$ -----	$ 1,868.23
a. Mutual	----	105,850.00	7,000.00	146,750.00	50,037.40	56,338.62	2,131.05	368,107.07
Gs Mutual	----	----	----	----	4,690.60	----	----	4,690.60
...	5,000.00	77,750. 0	----	49,584.00	5,135.75	9,818.83	10.00	147,298.58
Davidson C ty Mial	----	----	----	----	3,648.84	----	----	3,648.84
Duie	195,039.98	244,840. 0	1,232.80	536,026.00	64,930.00	120,683.64	14,208.04	1,176,960.46
as M (Raleigh)	----	----	----	15,828.00	41,134.95	----	----	56,962.95
Farmers Douglas	----	----	----	----	146.24	----	----	146.24
Farmers M (Edgecombe Co ty)	----	----	----	----	1,896.42	----	----	1,896.42
Gn s Mtual	----	----	----	----	6,148.16	----	----	6,148.16
Ide Mutual	----	----	----	20,660.00	2,770.89	----	1,975.87	25,406.76
rg Farmers Mutual	----	----	----	----	2,679.21	----	----	2,679.21
Methodist Mutual	----	----	----	----	364.34	----	11,771.54	12,135.88
North Carolina Home	----	----	----	510,326.00	40,916.82	70,911.07	8,740.06	630,893.95
North Carolina State	----	40,950. 0	----	17,500.00	8,210.25	569.01	831.33	68,060.59
Piedmont	75,000.00	234,570.26	142,580.00	80,846.00	27,448.61	52,484.47	435.79	613,365.13
n Mutual	----	----	----	----	1,399.21	----	----	1,399.21
Southern Mutual	----	----	----	2,000.00	5,726.84	504.82	185.40	8,417.06
Southern Stock	----	D9,668.60	66,090.00	133,221.00	19,751.21	41,975.48	----	370,706.29
Southern Underwriters	----	149,272.43	24,184.97	174,520.48	48,023.05	47,259.91	5,330.21	448,591.05
Sy Mutual	----	----	----	----	152.78	----	----	152.78
Sae Mal	----	----	----	2,900.00	312.47	596.67	75.00	3,884.14
Underwriters (Rocky Mt.)	----	100,627.55	----	34,625.00	9,822.44	11,224.31	3,620.06	159,919.36
Underwriters of o.	----	87,260. 0	30,214.69	105,046.00	42,823.37	26,633.36	----	291,977.42
Union nty Farmers Mtual	----	----	----	----	717.75	----	----	717.75
	275,039.98	1,150,788.84	271,302.46	1,829,832.48	390,755.83	439,00.19	49,314.35	4,406,034.13

Company	Capital								Total
Ætna	41,000.00			43,590.0	25,083,706.59	2,984,056.88	3,233,757.63	319,667.05	32,074,778.15
Agricultural	40,000.00	67,92.00		98,85.50	4,544,824.00	545,088.67	359,460.53	72,288.87	6,168,419.57
—			47,00.0		3,260,852.00	248,368.66	290,837.21	31,887.88	3,831,945.75
—le					2,759,91.00	102,805.77	131,234.63	27,226.00	3,021,207.90
—					1,285,391.26	198,845.67	377,621.84	38,969.26	1,947,828.03
— (St. Louis)	472,500.00	1,	61,81.00	4,60.00	9,220,710.57	825,054.33	912,225.73	431,41.94	13,623,743.57
—n Eagle		20,00.00		82,75.00	3,337,392.09	521,005.84	592,000.52	88,029.74	4,562,928.19
the—	68,00.00	62,60.0		15,89.06	2,223,062.50	286,642.71	615,833.31	9,263.84	3,134,802.36
Boston		97,80.00			4,634,404.14	2,054,101.46	1,252,94.28	129,805.85	9,216,200.73
—					8,167,01.25	736,766.93	1,160,109.15	161,420.25	11,047,646.64
Camden	26,00.00	82,88.00		18,00.00	3,874,91.50	179,757.38	469,024.55	60,632.06	5,352,623.49
—s of		41,00.00			518,545.0	440,960.15	77,351.31	8,71.48	1,186,667.94
—Mi		60,63.0		83,45.10	1,222,892.61	59,107.94	135,156.46	41,942.14	1,459,099.15
Columbian		39,25.00		3,60.00	98,290.33	30,896.59	46,925.46	8,942.32	529,198.40
—nio nha				20,00.00	903,158.00	71,093.90	192,362.12	66,113.58	1,765,472.60
—ion (New Yk.)	95,645.12	82,50.0			1,164,761.36	210,405.87	205,000.21	27,41.50	1,607,578.94
—l		91,00.00			2,802,189.35	107,767.58	244,990.68	42,843.06	3,475,985.79
— National		89,60.43			1,823,142.00	156,690.57	331,312.22	51,998.29	1,662,212.57
—Gl		61,00.00			976,700.00	148,685.80	120,946.29	26,240.05	
—					6,992,229.29	1,121,083.19	644,429.75	178,492.78	9,457,835.01
County	725,000.00	2,00.00			30,226,791.75	3,066,378.76	2,153,872.32	283,444.56	36,458,187.39
—	64,800.00	37,00.00			878,819.50	18,753.92	74,704.16	10,025.85	1,085,003.43
—re and M— (South)	19,358.96	35,50.00		39,25.00	575,91.96	51,109.47	21,686.97	7,539.95	811,217.31
—	81,680.00	94,40.00			1,314,658.41	131,003.43	74,166.80	17,831.36	1,625,456.40
—	20,000.00	71,05.00			393,974.0	34,873.95	44,245.12	6,04.21	609,847.28
Federal	42,00.00	26,00.00			3,803,779.64	374,030.84	1,139,680.88	193,943.11	5,537,434.47
F—	63,75.00	15,60.00			17,74,903.25	2,654,184.84	1,548,960.42	498,165.51	22,304,214.02
Fire	25,44.97	86,63.6	73,50.00		1,579,549.90		89,678.17	523,780.43	2,49,766.50
—in of —lelphia		91,20.00	97,45.00		7,136,905.00	1,152,448.59	1,306,367.00	153,271.69	13,481,581.02
—(Wk.)	2,1.	2,89,50.00			9,267,331.12	2,373,030.01	3,020,319.20	664,452.28	17,939,822.58
—L	1,09,57.65	39,60.00	38,06.15		4,131,686.61	220,722.49	763,753.31	145,789.50	8,530,979.56
—a Home	42,26.05	37,90.0	7,00.00		2,725,078.25	267,579.13	601,355.87	35,924.85	3,772,44.15
—e and M— —e	60,00.00	68,60.00			433,575.23	55,806.89	19,773.84	8,987.02	755,099.15
—Falls—		33,94.14	00,02.00		2,391,906.40	150,252.56	220,433.39	43,325.56	2,881,47.91
—	27,26.55	97,80.00	1,		4,136,790.32	91,99.15	726,548.77	91,772.23	7,894,153.16
—					419,700.00	41,902.47	27,185.34	47,312.77	1,453,460.58
—al S—te—	78,975.00	38,60.00	4,23.00		23,954,256.00	2,497,039.66	3,296,255.89	304,535.0	30,389,461.55
—	18,200.00	53,60.00	9,28.50		1,204,424.00	165,289.58	71,342.24	35,558.35	1,648,334.17
—		23,30.00	84,60.00		23,401,497.00	2,090,950.58	2,308,879.96	1,137,696.51	30,716,447.05
Hanover	1,750,000.00				3,866,350.00	254,337.68	628,260.37	102,198.05	5,840,184.60
Hartford	979,300.00	46,00.00			27,308,251.10	4,236,935.68	6,300,052.21	656,249.63	39,723,888.62
Home Fire and Marine	721,000.00				1,265,868.87	553,396.99	183,115.78	26,938.59	2,029,320.23

*Minus.

TABLE No. III—ASSETS.

SHOWING ASSETS OF FIRE, MARINE AND INLAND INSURANCE COMPANIES (LICENSED TO DO BUSINESS IN THIS STATE) FOR YEAR ENDING DECEMBER 31, 1918.

COMPANIES OF OTHER STATES (STOCK)—CONTINUED.

Name of Company	Value of Real Estate	Mortgage Loans on Real Estate	Loans on Collaterals	Bonds and Stocks	Cash in Office and Banks	Agents' Balances and Unpaid Premiums	Miscellaneous	Total Admitted Assets
...fe of New York		$5,500.00	$ ----	$40,993,259.56	$3,661,872.52	$4,790,909.41	$839,464.25	$50,291,005.74
Home of Utah	$109,000.00	322,030.00		1,091,183.00	89,495.67	53,388.43	49.70	1,665,146.80
Imperial				1,370,609.00	44,652.58	154,156.91	16,316.69	1,585,735.18
Insurance Company of North America	272,431.01	121,324.25		24,280,745.19	2,395,335.33	3,176,365.84	617,066.96	30,863,268.58
Independence		27,500.00		320,680.00	32,080.94	22,334.74	7,960.86	410,556.74
...tite				4,663,030.00	143,427.10	5,771.29	71,090.61	4,883,319.00
...a National	152,410.66	352,950.00		16,378.00	30,981.11	46,551.96	6,354.10	605,625.83
Massachusetts ...d Marine		771,985.00	1,845.00	95,693.83	27,648.16	20,732.36	29,025.56	946,929.91
...te				1,446,106.00	150,301.71	193,814.93	53,136.53	1,843,359.17
...		382,850.00	4,900.00	525,718.77	133,834.51	96,843.35	10,700.53	1,154,847.16
...ds	98,000.00	88,750.00		1,373,025.00	68,677.99	124,973.26	17,704.00	1,771,130.25
...cs	23,500.00			1,459,440.00	179,235.14	230,403.75	46,464.54	1,939,043.43
...e Company of America				3,150,080.00	65,871.18	230,610.62	40,141.77	3,486,703.57
...s N	12,653.46	213,650.00		173,710.00	82,364.69	61,940.82	16,098.30	565,317.27
...le	15,300.00	1,414,217.00		3,997,108.30	170,662.20	429,836.06	52,116.35	6,079,239.91
N...	625,200.00	1,387,850.00		13,896,907.37	1,984,781.02	2,537,182.62	831,371.83	21,263,292.84
N...	663,500.00	766,100.00		6,863,000.00	475,603.20	1,094,338.73	142,125.57	10,004,667.50
N...al Union	2,172.14	279,500.00		3,526,938.39	525,538.99	712,129.48	169,394.85	5,215,673.85
N...k	241,226.47	394,950.06		1,478,118.40	293,573.08	317,077.40	19,056.49	2,744,001.90
New Hampshire	299,500.00	6,307.50		6,781,714.00	284,688.04	559,964.98	79,235.30	8,011,409.82
Niagara		232,000.00		7,916,600.33	836,923.10	1,140,022.47	161,038.07	10,286,583.97
North River	8,871.18	203,900.00		3,892,881.00	565,155.99	616,514.76	34,841.86	5,322,164.79
North ...		450,457.70	1,730.00	285,424.84	381,608.59	249,737.77	23,597.54	1,392,556.44
N...rn National	227,960.96	1,671,822.50		5,565,953.05	400,898.26	721,751.77	90,918.67	8,679,305.21
Northwestern Fire and Marine		821,800.00		155,827.59	290,053.93	100,354.56	70,403.58	1,428,439.66
Q...		16,000.00		2,052,713.16	366,325.74	183,172.70	20,190.54	2,638,402.14
Gt...	178,307.88			3,072,871.44	779,386.03	485,447.67	80,101.01	4,596,114.03
...to		228,300.00	3,000.00	60,950.00	98,382.64	139,226.29	6,008.61	535,867.54
Pennsylvania	125,000.00	110,500.00	2,888.76	6,962,734.50	249,835.85	961,409.61	113,703.92	8,526,072.64
...s	198,295.84	469,300.00	7,000.00	1,218,701.00	38,597.85	209,399.33	31,296.11	2,172,590.13
Petersburg				189,078.66	269,850.23	22,745.47	7,565.70	489,240.06
Ph...ix (Hartford)	637,734.42	106,500.00	200,000.00	15,501,847.00	1,366,260.30	1,814,535.66	79,320.47	19,706,197.85

COMPANIES OF OTHER STATES (MUTUAL).

Company							
Arkwright Mutual			3,192,004.17	265,043.09	112,863.74	55,546.89	3,625,457.00
Baltimore ⫶ M⫶	8,000.00		110,600.00	12,814.94	5,702.84	3,471.38	140,589.16
⫶⫶ ⫶ ⫶			1,667,503.00	235,363.76	60,774.67	9,764.21	1,973,395.64
⫶⫶ ⫶al Underwriters⫶			145,550.00	1,156,299.03	364,581.56	1,424.35	1,668,154.94
Cotton and ⫶h Manufacturers⫶			790,770.67	95,874.72	36,560.21	12,549.24	935,754.84
Druggists Indemnity Exchange⫶			39,838.00	82,920.08	7,880.34	807.59	131,446.01
⫶⫶'s ⫶			2,409,295.00	471,297.92	96,731.16	23,128.47	3,000,452.55
⫶g ⫶ ⫶l	56,000.00		174,137.38	21,41.57	41,319.12	2,598.96	295,467.03
⫶⫶ ⫶			753,798.00	199,616.06	37,801.90	3,187.19	994,403.15
Indiana Lumbermen's Mutual⫶	338,150.00	36,500.00	518,791.56	23,429.98	26,465.40	11,039.27	954,376.21
⫶ i ⫶il Underwriters⫶			539,120.00	383,394.50	21,319.53	2,796.87	946,630.90
⫶ ⫶l ⫶il			511,691.34	49,547.28	22,742.58	8,588.63	592,569.83
⫶pe ⫶ ⫶Mil			411,920.00	80,724.38	33,287.59	5,770.33-	531,702.30
Lumber M ⫶l			129,650.00	178,474.67	2,496.55	20,451.00	331,072.22
⫶r ⫶ rs Interinsurance⫶			1,135,260.28	123,400.84	29,301.37	17,829.18	1,305,791.67
Lumbermen's ⫶ ⫶l ⫶Mc	204,500.00	35,000.00	643,970.00	158,383.63	113,255.89	9,826.22	1,164,935.74
Lumbermen's Underwriters⫶			611,037.56	598,716.88	188,887.58	5,497.96	1,404,139.98
Manton Mutual⫶			379,700.00	72,331.55	31,766.02	5,749.22	489,546.79
Manufacturing Lumbermen's Underwriters⫶			788,924.43	237,197.68	109,349.53	10,01.20	1,145,572.84
Manufacturing ⫶ ⫶s Underwriters⫶			14,44.00	132,663.22	45,232.14	46,218.18	338,527.54
⫶s ⫶ ⫶ M⫶			916,679.00	126,832.19	32,306.42	4,998.46	1,080,816.07
⫶⫶ ⫶ M			318,602.61	39,904.97	20,178.38	3,131.78	387,670.24
⫶ ⫶h Mutual⫶	16,925.00	5,852.50	549,446.00	18,11.17	39,027.66	67,950.77	717,184.95
⫶ ⫶h Millers Mutual⫶	1,357,088.92	25,724.35	596,612.35	84,957.69	63,703.58	35,299.52	2,147,662.06
Millers ⫶ ⫶M	83,600.00	10,000.00	474,060.00	66,732.03	12,787.11	637,179.14	
⫶s ⫶ ⫶y Underwriters⫶	75,425.00		38,500.00	123,590.42	116, ⫶2. 3	4,662.34	358,579.94

(xvii)

TABLE No. III—ASSETS.

SHOWING ASSETS OF FIRE, MARINE AND I█ █D INSURANCE COMPANIES (LICENSED TO █O BUSINESS IN THIS STATE) FOR YEAR ENDING D█ █ █ER 31, 1918.

COMPANIES OF OTHER STATES (MUTUAL)—Continued.

█e of █████	Value of Real Estate	Mortgage Loans on Real Estate	Loans on Collaterals	Bonds and Stocks	Cash in Office and Banks	Agents' Balances and Unpaid Premiums	Miscellaneous	Total Admitted Assets
Narragansett █ █l	$ ----	$ ----	$ ----	$ 143,831.00	$ 20,920.33	$ 8,954.16	$ 1,463.52	$ 175,169.01
National Mutual █ █ █				163,170.00	17,965.30	12,484.14	2,619.13	196,238.57
█l █ █ █ar █ █ M				87,519.50	26,092.44	15,460.88	2,104.93	131,177.75
Penn Lumbermen's █Ml		122,500.00		931,999.27	90,000.60	32,532.71	13,690.33	1,190,722.91
Philadelphia █ █s Mial				782,067.50	113,638.31	36,374.14	9,963.30	942,043.25
█al Exchange		15,000.00		411,100.43	217,955.29	75,711.11	3,066.04	722,832.87
Rubber Manufacturers █ █l				766,190.00	89,656.53	35,100.02	11,281.11	902,227.66
Southern █ █s				19,028.23	42,652.53	36,515.42	23,680.83	85,724.48
Utilities █y Exchange		6,500.00		40,800.00	42,652.53	29,550.66	41,277.40	171,280.59
Western █al Underwriters		17,000.00		67,586.00	56,916.32	12,882.33	7,987.39	145,372.04
█t █ █r █ █ars (Grocers' Dept.)				791,040.50	208,796.67	38,900.60	3,301.38	1,042,039.15
Warners				75,000.00	188,316.59	32,102.27	477.86	295,896.72
Totals	163,224.35	2,244,688.92	5,852.50	22,222,479.55	6,130,963.39	2,026,506.38	506,089.54	33,299,804.63

COMPANIES OF █N COUNTRIES.

█████	Value of Real Estate	Mortgage Loans on Real Estate	Loans on Collaterals	Bonds and Stocks	Cash in Office and Banks	Agents' Balances and Unpaid Premiums	Miscellaneous	Total Admitted Assets
█ll e				575,600.00	121,147.53	117,809.08	6,993.29	821,549.90
█A	35, 0 .00			2,819,377.02	353,650.13	694,933.53	54,124.89	3,957,085.57
British America	410, 0 .00			1,784,268.87	370,857.72	279,293.65	27,762.00	2,442,182.24
█G█				1,831,361.78	357,473.82	380,395.13	20,875.22	3, 0 605.95
				576,227.50	96,869.73	41,586.30	11,687.16	726,370.69
█a █al G█ █n				2,085,180.89	223,847.89	1,202,467.71	32,977.90	2, █4,474.39
█ █al █h █a █	960, 0 .00		16,666.50	6,821,960.00	2,699,257.36	1,521,578.90	388,584.39	12, 44,647.65
Eagle Star █al British D █aion		36,600.00		1,272,455.00	52,036.07	165,228.69	16,806.54	1,506,526.30
Fire Reassurance █ █n				1,981,950.00	572,539.52	16,170.20	25,349.55	2,596,009.27
				2,371,667.24	209,654.10	96,228.19	21,328.22	2,698,877.75
█r █ █ █l █l █ █h and Globe	1,194, 0 .00	969,250.00	837.50	3,603,658.25	12,782.82	77,865.12	298,754.75	3,993,060.94
				9,811,470.76	2,091,157.66	2,740,105.86	277,575.60	17,084,397.38
█h				4,817,509.00	457,770.24	595,598.96	222,257.35	6,093,135.55
█h █al Lancashire	300, 0 .00			3,877,708.79	624,231.07	858,637.18	785,134.31	6,445,711.35
█v				2,884,518.00	177,180.20	74,774.54	25,677.06	3,162,149.80
█li (Denmark)				2,099,840.00	340,843.65	330,631.21	21,763.84	2,793,078.70

Company	(A)	(B)	(C)	(D)	(E)			
Nationale (Paris)	1,127,003.04	15,321.32	181,576.33	96,926.89	833,208.50	----	----	----
Netherlands Fire and life	1,336,313.89	13,712.17	195,902.78	117,606.79	1,009,092.15	----	----	----
Norske ...	3,104,641.48	626,381.91	149,102.72	29,136.85	2,300,020.00	----	----	----
North British and Mercantile	10,373,470.13	166,773.22	1,198,636.12	619,163.29	8,388,897.50	135,000.00	----	----
Northern Assurance	7,132,368.38	228,784.60	946,658.48	597,992.70	5,223,932.60	----	----	----
... (Norwegian ...)	1,424,451.44	19,161.38	4,209.19	95,080.87	1,306,000.00	----	----	----
Norwegian ...ance	1,760,144.59	441,994.74	*5,632.73	2,141.57	1,321,641.01	----	----	----
... Union	4,261,173.07	74,204.63	799,594.77	350,402.69	3,036,970.98	----	----	----
...	1,695,395.49	15,525.23	19,208.58	367,286.78	1,293,374.90	----	----	----
Phenix Fire	1,021,590.93	9,607.79	163,120.90	11,775.75	737,086.49	----	----	----
Palatine (London)	3,976,134.46	90,895.95	485,910.08	840,872.11	2,558,456.32	----	----	----
Phœnix (London)	5,359,591.17	99,334.06	1,083,538.93	417,682.18	3,759,036.00	----	----	----
Prudentia Co. and ...	1,676,485.79	66,789.68	191,019.73	279,689.88	1,138,986.50	----	----	----
Rossia	11,468,405.21	110,642.90	198,043.77	2,151,168.54	8,718,550.00	290,000.00	----	----
Royal	18,269,657.00	516,141.09	2,217,272.92	1,252,972.99	11,432,870.00	2,668,500.00	181,900.00	----
Royal Exchange Assurance	4,219,965.53	165,121.44	489,108.47	191,319.67	3,373,360.00	----	----	1,065.00
Russian Reinsurance	2,456,950.28	18,761.66	46,753.30	200,584.17	2,190,851.15	----	----	----
Salamandra	4,179,940.05	58,980.08	122,504.72	137,706.45	3,740,748.80	215,028.36	----	----
Scottish Union and Na...	7,884,295.27	93,665.29	854,706.06	575,301.56	6,052,094.00	120,000.00	----	----
Second Russian	1,816,089.24	19,301.00	30,689.81	152,628.43	1,613,470.00	93,500.00	----	----
Scandia	2,185,943.33	17,947.21	99,638.17	307,197.95	1,761,160.00	----	----	----
Scandinavia	4,492,820.88	388,794.10	499,174.26	240,602.52	3,364,250.00	----	----	----
Sun ... fire	5,862,307.58	79,994.92	793,055.96	550,255.03	4,267,076.63	----	----	----
Svea Fire and life	2,501,403.62	121,835.83	356,786.64	192,718.65	1,830,062.50	171,925.04	----	----
Swiss National	2,462,773.08	37,308.44	143,065.28	65,349.36	2,217,050.00	----	----	----
Tokio Marine and Fire	3,259,003.11	215,166.17	328,511.88	558,460.01	2,156,865.05	----	----	----
Union Assurance	3,257,133.52	19,626.33	239,545.39	444,421.80	1,553,540.00	----	----	----
... and Phenix Espagnol	2,797,814.76	26,569.16	65,534.54	310,031.06	2,395,680.00	----	----	----
Union Hispano Americana	776,805.15	2,381.25	192,326.34	61,597.56	520,500.00	----	----	----
...baine	3,890,188.75	75,435.62	186,451.30	39,304.83	3,588,997.00	----	----	----
Warsaw Fire	1,086,872.25	11,289.29	*9,356.78	46,589.74	1,038,350.00	----	----	----
Western Assurance	4,693,580.53	39,802.95	722,821.43	1,129,319.42	2,801,636.73	----	----	----
Yorkshire	2,144,572.69	25,115.10	267,206.41	693,589.38	1,158,661.80	----	----	----
Totals	205,285,179.17	6,150,019.08	21,450,490.00	21,988,167.98	147,897,229.71	6,244,453.40	1,536,250.00	18,569.00

*Minus Agents' balances.

RECAPITULATION.

	(A)	(B)	(C)	(D)	(E)				
North ... Companies	4,406,034.13	49,314.35	439,000.19	390,755.83	1,829,832.48	----	1,150,788.84	271,302.46	275,039.98
...ies of other States (stock)	661,593,823.73	12,026,833.43	65,763,204.00	55,210,709.81	476,287,649.41	----	36,069,710.40	2,055,896.07	14,179,820.61
...ies of ther States ...	43,299,804.63	506,089.54	2,026,506.38	6,130,963.39	22,222,479.55	----	2,244,688.92	5,852.50	163,224.35
Companies of foreign countries	205,285,179.17	6,150,019.08	21,450,490.00	21,988,167.98	147,897,229.71	18,569.00	1,536,250.00	18,569.00	6,244,453.40
... tal totals	904,584,841.66	18,732,256.40	89,679,200.57	83,720,597.01	648,237,191.15	18,569.00	41,001,438.16	2,351,620.03	20,862,538.34

(xix)

TABLE No. IV—LIABILITIES.

SHOWING LIABILITIES OF FIRE, MARINE AND INLAND COMPANIES (LICENSED TO DO BUSINESS IN THIS STATE) FOR YEAR ENDING DECEMBER 31, 1918.

NORTH CAROLINA COMPANIES.

Name of Company	Net Unpaid Losses and Claims	Unearned Premiums, Fire	Unearned Premiums, Marine and Inland	Due for Commissions, Taxes Return and Reinsurance Premiums	Other Liabilities	Total	Cash Capital	Net Surplus	Total Liabilities
Alamance	$	$	$	$	$ 24.89	$ 24.89	$	$ 1,843.34	$ 1,868.23
......	5,700.45	100,137.05				105,837.50	200,000.00	62,269.57	368,107.07
Cabarrus Mutual	1,350.00					1,350.00		3,340.60	4,690.60
Carolina ...ity Mutual	1,706.00	33,685.58			1,500.00	36,891.58	50,000.00	60,407.58	147,298.58
Davidson ...ity Mutual								3,648.84	3,648.84
Dixie	68,053.00	341,190.84			14,841.31	424,085.15	500,000.00	252,875.31	1,176,960.46
...... (Raleigh)	4,454.34					4,454.34		52,508.61	56,962.95
Farmers Douglas								146.24	146.24
...... Mutual (Edgecombe County)								1,896.42	1,896.42
Gaston ...ity ...... Mutual								6,148.16	6,148.16
Hardware Mutual	3,003.94	8,198.47		342.12	190.55	11,735.08		13,671.68	25,406.76
1 ...rg Farmers Mutual								2,679.21	2,679.21
Methodist Mutual		2,488.91				2,488.91		9,646.97	12,135.88
N... Carolina	15,159.40	176,059.40			5,121.81	196,340.61	200,000.00	234,553.34	630,893.95
North Carolina State	1,000.00	4,305.90			627.50	5,933.40	50,000.00	12,127.19	68,060.59
......	6,452.45	162,136.35				168,588.80	100,000.00	344,776.33	613,365.13
......								1,399.21	1,399.21
Southern ...... Furniture	2,000.00	3,022.63				5,022.63		3,394.43	8,417.06
Southern Stock	9,537.00	130,746.42			11,833.00	152,116.42	179,700.00	38,899.87	370,706.29
Southern	10,659.00	150,042.44			12,000.00	172,701.44	200,000.00	75,889.61	448,591.05
Stanly ...ity Mutual					1,159.43	1,159.43		152.78	1,312.21
State	1,750.00				800.77	2,550.77		1,333.37	3,884.14
Underwriters ...... (...ky Mount)	4,586.86	35,909.45		717.69	10,000.00	51,214.00	51,500.00	57,205.36	159,919.36
Underwriters of	4,190.00	93,929.34			6,000.00	104,119.34	100,000.00	87,858.08	291,977.42
...... Farmers Mutual								717.75	717.75
Totals	139,602.44	1,241,852.78		1,059.81	64,153.26	1,446,668.29	1,631,200.00	1,329,379.27	4,407,247.56

Company										
Ætna	2,303,307.08	13,860,283.72	891,707.72	1,010,	0.00	105,446.94	18,170,745.46	5,0,	0.00	8,904,032.69	32,074,778.15
...gl	487,170.15	2,712,709.00	159,982.27	115,	0.00	262,700.00	3,737,561.42	500,	0.00	1,930,858.15	6,168,419.57
...al	451,861.56	1,063,338.08	153,364.69	75,	0.00	21,437.54	1,765,001.87	750,	0.00	1,316,943.88	3,331,945.75
American ...ie	97,232.00	842,016.02	2,190.59	35,	0.00	250.00	976,688.61	0,	0.00	1,044,519.29	3,021,207.90
American ...te	337,044.77	631,612.71	88,407.78	7,500.00		1,064,565.26	400,	0.00	483,262.77	1,947,828.03	
...n (Newark)	743,028.69	6,789,675.97	321,808.52	190,861.51		877,856.73	8,923,231.42	2,0,	0.00	2,700,512.15	13,623,743.57
...n Central (St. Louis)	280,717.00	1,869,497.65	105,927.89	65,	0.00	3,896.87	2,324,949.41	1,0,	0.00	1,237,978.78	4,562,928.19
...n Eagle	214,471.38	779,525.15	190,240.58	44,600.00		5,393.08	1,234,230.19	2,0,	0.00	900,572.17	3,134,802.36
Automobile	1,572,424.47	2,370,172.80	893,729.56	478,028.09		67,979.28	5,382,334.00	1,0,	0.00	1,833,866.73	9,216,200.73
Boston	1,791,947.86	3,627,240.22	1,040,620.68	188,700.00		175, 0.00	6,823,508.76	1,0,	0.00	3,224,137.88	11,047,646.64
Gas of Missouri	516,073.46	2,658,062.44	59,169.52	105,	0.00	33,927.89	3,372,233.31	1,0,	0.00	980,390.18	5,352,623.49
...sa Fire	47,713.07	252,146.84	190.99	399,819.74		699,870.64	200,	0.00	286,797.30	1,186,667.94	
...ian	54,952.36	19,067.28	226,093.66	10,	0.00	500.00	310,613.30	400,	0.00	748,485.85	1,459,099.15
...in National	47,878.35	203,039.73		6,	0.00	100.00	257,018.08	216,118.00		56,062.32	529,198.40
...al ion (New York)	105,659.50	548,264.87		14,200.00		604.16	668,728.53	976,675.00		120,069.07	1,765,472.60
Commonwealth	100,869.00	815,726.72	53,750.66	53,535.00		300.00	1,024,181.38	200,	0.00	383,397.56	1,607,578.94
Concordia	285,699.21	1,337,044.50	201,195.10	61,847.99		6, 0.00	1,891,786.80	500,	0.00	1,084,198.99	3,475,985.79
...di	181,561.55	1,890,630.76	14,883.13	65,	0.00	2,151,475.44	750,	0.00	503,367.64	3,404,843.08	
...al	76,556.50	364,650.66		10,450.80		742.27	452,400.23	839,580.00		370,232.34	1,662,212.57
Connecticut	646,420.00	5,146,374.78	323,728.87	268,	0.00	21,567.50	6,406,091.15	1,0,	0.00	2,051,743.86	9,457,835.01
Continental	1,243,502.58	12,491,640.12	620,801.07	767,555.80		1,161,872.32	16,285,371.89	10,0,	0.00	10,172,815.50	36,458,187.39
...el	52,313.45	243,160.14		25,500.00		163,543.54	484,517.13	400,	0.00	200,486.30	1,085,003.43
...le Fire and Marine	87,100.37	282,381.15		6,280.32		300.00	376,061.84	250,	0.00	185,155.47	811,217.31
...le (8th Carolina)	159,347.35	388,411.04	56,281.50	25,	0.00	1,621.54	630,661.43	500,	0.00	494,794.97	1,625,456.40
...l	9,710.93	166,371.31		31,067.12		207,149.36	200,	0.00	202,697.92	609,847.28	
Fidelity-Phenix	1,260,867.83	559,323.40	1,058,183.76	212,095.09		125, 0.00	3,215,470.08	1,000,	0.00	1,321,964.39	5,537,434.47
First	1,142,141.57	11,104,957.40	620,349.37	452,080.50		452, 0.00	13,771,528.84	2,500,	0.00	6,032,685.18	22,304,214.02
Fire ...n of Philadelphia	273,872.00	444,912.99		51,	0.00	905,361.51	1,675,146.50	0,	0.00	304,620.00	2,479,766.50
Fire ...hl	952,382.24	6,258,185.42	77,152.59	165,204.68		1,429,032.85	8,881,957.78	1,500,	0.00	3,599,623.24	13,481,581.02
...ns	2,849,039.90	6,527,660.76	2,047,759.08	900,	0.00	98,254.79	12,422,714.53	1,500,	0.00	4,017,108.05	17,939,822.58
Franklin (Newark)	773,953.48	3,931,803.82	210,339.85	102,	0.00	16,733.34	5,034,835.49	1,250,	0.00	2,246,144.07	8,530,979.56
...da	277,881.00	879,459.00	130,411.00	786,179.13		516,271.61	2,590,201.74	500,	0.00	682,212.41	3,772,414.15
Girard Fire and Marine	54,988.03	245,507.40		42,098.11		80, 0.00	422,593.54	200,	0.00	132,505.61	755,099.15
...Falls	121,182.30	1,333,822.12	271,517.33	29,	0.00	524,378.15	2,008,382.57	500,	0.00	373,035.34	2,881,417.91
...be National	888,898.45	3,298,025.83	1,880.16	160,357.83		205, 0.00	4,823,799.44	500,	0.00	2,560,353.72	7,884,153.16
...al Rutgers	2,409.00	33,289.93		1,500.00		200.00	39,279.09	1,0,	0.00	414,181.49	1,453,460.58
Granite State	3,910,338.00	9,173,903.37	2,327,219.87	1,065,	0.00	4,389, 0.00	20,865,461.24	700,	0.00	8,824, 0.31	30,389,461.55
Great	97,565.57	977,268.39		33,	0.00	3,909.94	1, 11,743.90	200,	0.00	336,590.27	1,648,334.17
Hanover	1,684,271.00	12,650,294.12	375,947.71	450,	0.00	71, 0.09	15,231,512.92	5,0,	0.00	10,484,934.13	30,716,447.05
...he Fire and Marine	713,750.40	3,150,012.70	195,357.18	104,820.49		36,052.77	4,199,993.54	1,2,	0.00	640,191.06	5,840,184.60
Hartford	2,729,811.94	22,491,533.90	678,282.70	1,950,	0.00	750, 0.00	28,600,228.54	0,	0.00	9,123,660.08	39,723,888.62
...he Fire and Marine	164,756.53	341,118.34	144,785.89	30,	0.00	2,500.00	683,160.76	500,	0.00	846,159.47	2,029,320.23

TABLE No. IV—LIABILITIES.

SHOWING LIABILITIES OF FIRE, MARINE AND INLAND COMPANIES (LICENSED TO DO BUSINESS IN THIS STATE) FOR YEAR ENDING DECEMBER 31, 1918.

COMPANIES OF OTHER STATES (STOCK)—CONTINUED.

Name of Company	Net Unpaid Losses and Claims	Unearned Premiums, Fire	Unearned Premiums, Marine and Inland	Due for Commissions, Taxes, Return and Reinsurance Premiums	Other Liabilities	Total	Cash Capital	Net Surplus	Total Liabilities
...e of New York	$3,431,654.98	$22,392,183.00	$1,167,766.00	$1,842,698.16	$200,000.00	$29,034,302.14	$6,000,000.00	$15,256,703.60	$50,291,005.74
...e of ...	90,261.58	377,499.13	----	16,000.00	----	483,760.71	300,000.00	881,386.09	1,665,146.80
...	49,307.00	497,955.42	----	26,500.00	1,000.00	574,762.42	200,000.00	810,972.76	1,585,735.18
...ny of North America	4,591,068.33	10,209,033.54	1,279,889.06	1,030,000.00	751,550.29	17,861,541.22	4,000,000.00	9,001,727.36	30,863,268.58
...	25,008.44	80,771.60	406.08	2,200.00	1,800.00	110,186.12	200,000.00	100,370.62	410,556.74
...	853,921.85	3,031,695.89	----	120,000.00	50,000.00	4,055,617.74	200,000.00	627,701.26	4,883,319.00
...	45,357.96	231,926.19	----	750.00	21,203.52	299,237.67	259,150.00	47,238.16	605,625.83
...va...	15,491.72	178,285.89	----	4,010.75	20.05	197,808.41	500,000.00	249,121.50	946,929.91
...	340,593.55	517,334.92	255,867.45	27,659.79	1,617.98	1,143,073.69	500,000.00	200,285.48	1,843,359.17
...	62,785.75	443,043.47	----	8,000.00	----	513,829.22	300,000.00	341,017.94	1,154,847.16
...nl Traders	94,441.50	777,187.51	----	17,500.00	320,296.01	1,209,425.02	250,000.00	311,705.23	1,771,130.25
...	83,395.67	756,309.25	----	34,000.00	2,500.10	876,205.02	300,000.00	762,838.41	1,939,043.43
...ure of ...	205,545.81	1,104,967.11	182,769.96	67,010.00	4,600.00	1,564,892.88	1,000,000.00	921,810.69	3,486,703.57
...	30,909.32	162,779.47	11,077.28	2,500.00	32,379.16	239,645.23	250,000.00	75,672.04	565,317.27
...	269,241.70	2,979,014.09	59,324.68	120,000.00	85,466.23	3,513,046.76	1,250,000.00	1,316,193.21	6,079,239.91
...	1,442,945.44	11,555,071.19	483,340.41	760,000.00	346,693.81	14,588,050.85	2,000,000.00	4,675,241.99	21,263,292.84
...nial Liberty	637,551.85	4,523,811.84	417,775.46	128,003.86	507,085.10	6,214,228.11	1,000,000.00	2,790,439.39	10,004,667.50
N... ...nn.	318,431.92	2,868,488.12	62,166.42	170,000.00	30,000.00	3,449,586.46	1,000,000.00	766,087.39	5,215,673.85
N... ...	168,420.20	1,332,829.59	92,082.65	75,000.00	15,616.10	1,683,948.54	500,000.00	560,053.36	2,744,001.90
New ...	467,052.75	3,576,515.62	70,530.37	190,000.00	70,009.00	4,374,107.74	1,500,000.00	2,137,302.08	8,011,409.82
Niagara	681,267.00	4,847,076.76	321,393.68	281,500.00	38,240.00	6,169,477.44	1,000,000.00	3,117,106.53	10,286,583.97
North River	541,112.13	2,583,803.20	64,521.63	120,000.00	5,246.25	3,314,683.21	600,000.00	1,407,481.58	5,322,164.79
North ...	139,686.68	501,961.81	55,714.54	31,500.00	2,000.00	730,863.03	500,000.00	161,693.41	1,392,556.44
...n Nati...	861,836.56	3,969,288.80	289,843.31	239,785.44	648,648.27	6,009,402.38	1,000,000.00	1,669,902.83	8,679,305.21
...n Fire and Marine	93,819.86	379,717.30	----	52,116.85	365,948.30	891,602.31	400,000.00	146,837.35	1,438,439.66
Old Colony	341,659.73	789,772.20	144,005.30	28,408.29	632.85	1,304,478.37	600,000.00	733,923.77	2,638,402.14
Orient	189,253.21	1,954,790.05	186,472.34	74,900.00	1,000.00	2,406,415.60	1,000,000.00	1,189,698.43	4,596,114.03
...o.	18,451.41	204,751.13	----	10,000.00	102.00	233,304.54	200,000.00	102,563.00	535,867.54
Pennsylvania	640,262.92	4,031,111.61	90,554.46	129,840.00	1,038,475.05	5,930,244.04	750,000.00	1,845,528.60	8,526,072.64
...s ...il	76,969.73	714,388.03	8,654.15	10,000.00	78,550.48	888,562.39	1,000,000.00	284,027.74	2,172,590.13
Petersburg	9,424.57	143,218.78	----	----	3,776.67	156,420.02	200,000.00	132,820.04	489,240.06
Phœnix (Hartford)	1,083,744.99	7,187,401.36	413,612.68	460,000.00	55,026.50	9,199,795.53	3,000,000.00	7,506,412.32	19,706,197.85

n of America	866,766.16	2,734,615.26	430,751.99	171,450.00	5, 0.00	4,208,583.41	1,000,000.00	2,142,188.25	7,350,771.66
Rhode	989,574.90	5,592,470.34	569,891.38	607,638.60	37,125.03	7,796,700.25	2,000,000.00	4,660,450.04	14,457,150.29
St. El He rl Marine	147,846.30	1,149,068.19	—	156,556.83	12,542.04	1,453,471.32	500,000.00	409,133.68	2,362,605.00
	1,323,553.16	6,010,648.00	744,369.46	631,290.22	—	8,722,407.88	1,000,000.00	4,304,535.95	14,026,943.83
Security	385,194.01	3,333,667.48	10,419.72	125,340.48	6,453.42	3,861,075.11	1,000,000.00	962,600.32	5,823,675.43
South Ga	17,344.91	81,222.71	147,214.28	255,000.00	20, 0.00	98,567.62	200,000.00	131,014.59	429,582.21
Springfield Fire and	832,465.49	7,909,661.77	—	15, 0.00	1,533.70	9,164,341.54	2,500,000.00	3,078,360.38	14,742,701.92
	88,743.70	618,522.26	20,638.98	40, 0.00	7,500.00	723,799.66	500,000.00	326,527.84	1,550,327.50
Str of	76,018.00	522,217.07	—	—	—	666,374.05	400,000.00	511,194.08	1,577,568.13
Sterling	144,862.79	512,141.45	705.98	39,850.00	150.00	697,710.22	850,000.00	476,639.64	2,024,349.86
Unil Sales	751,811.53	4,206,880.46	94,858.83	145, 0.00	12,973.84	5,211,524.66	1,400,000.00	2,025,136.01	8,636,660.67
Wia Fire and Marine	01,981.13	996,557.81	—	113, 0.00	28, 0.00	1,239,538.94	250,000.00	956,350.28	2,445,889.22
	828,090.56	5,034,386.80	171,096.73	165, 0.00	25, 0.00	6,223,574.09	1,000,000.00	1,339,506.02	8,563,080.11
	54,248,310.43	278,359,566.02	21,391,576.53	19,138,291.47	17,351,406.46	390,489,150.91	96,291,523.00	174,813,149.82	661,593,823.73

ES OF OTHER STATES (L).

me M	31,739.76	1,790,444.13	—	34,001.85	—	1,856,185.74	—	1,769,272.15	3,625,457.89
title tAl	365.43	62,185.66	—	1,800.00	2,500.00	66,851.09	—	73,738.07	140,589.16
tithe	16,664.17	1,097,792.18	—	15,158.30	520.67	1,130,135.32	—	843,260.32	1,973,395.64
rme	588,257.49	268,051.19	—	—	66,078.90	922,387.58	—	745,767.36	1,668,154.94
Cn rl W dn	6,778.04	458,670.37	6,931.03	—	495.96	472,875.40	—	462,387.44	935,754.84
Druggists Indemnity Exchange	320.80	61,322.47	—	160.00	960.90	62,764.17	—	68,681.84	131,446.01
Hs	27,218.80	1,483,521.38	—	30, 0.00	385.00	1,541,125.18	—	1,459,327.37	3, 0. 452.55
ig Mual	21,121.51	193,857.38	—	5,353.97	2,887.57	223,220.43	—	72,246.60	295,467.03
Ha ln's	8,725.08	548,008.29	—	12,165.30	622.65	569,521.32	—	424,881.83	994,403.15
	20,458.00	318,255.79	—	15, 0.00	3,245.51	356,959.30	—	597,416.91	954,376.21
l Underwriters	150.00	237,328.21	—	—	594,499.51	831,977.72	—	114,653.18	946,630.90
tMl	3,174.92	258,481.10	—	4,204.21	292.49	266,152.72	—	326,417.11	592,569.83
Sae tl	22,731.58	277,411.38	—	2,599.32	915.47	303,657.75	—	228,044.55	531,702.30
Lumber	153,763.25	86,453.74	—	—	18,004.78	258,221.77	—	72,850.45	331,072.22
Hir	19,234.75	340,143.17	—	18,477.65	200,676.11	578,531.68	—	727,259.99	1,305,791.67
	44,689.00	507,651.56	—	15,500.00	28,908.36	596,748.92	—	568,186.82	1,164,935.74
	28,550.00	484,965.97	—	—	43,415.01	556,930.98	—	847,209.00	1,404,139.98
n's Underwriters	22,657.64	254,173.06	—	2,343.23	881.90	280,055.83	—	209,490.96	489,546.79
	48,950.00	476,417.36	—	—	26,615.06	551,982.42	—	593,590.42	1,145,572.84
	205,004.41	97,487.66	—	—	3,158.24	305,650.31	—	32,877.23	338,527.54
	9,592.80	604,552.18	—	8,256.09	311.02	622,712.09	—	458,103.98	1,080,816.07
	1,500.00	214,764.30	—	5, 0.00	300.00	221,564.30	—	166,105.94	387,670.24
	6,540.95	360,244.33	—	3, 0.00	131,013.13	500,798.41	—	216,386.54	717,184.95
an al	123,658.76	788,458.75	—	31,950.00	593,446.44	1,537,513.95	—	610,148.11	2,147,662.06
Millers al	9,082.00	—	—	9, 0.00	209,522.45	227,604.45	—	409,574.69	637,179.14
Mrs rlity	123,004.98	9,033.72	—	—	33,393.08	165,431.78	—	193,148.16	358,579.94

TABLE No. IV—LIABILITIES.

SHOWING LIABI LTIES OF FIRE, MARINE AND INLAND COMPANIES (LICENSED TO DO BUSINESS IN THIS STATE) FOR YEAR ENDING DECEMBER 31, 1918.

COMPANIES OF ' OR STATES (MUTUAL)—CONTINUED.

Name of Company	Net Unpaid Losses and Claims	Unearned Premiums, Fire	Unearned Premiums, Marine and Inland	Due for Commissions, Taxes Return and Reinsurance Premiums	Other Liabilities	Total	Cash Capital	Net Surplus	Total Liabilities
Narragansett	$ 600.00	$ 89,713.55	$ ---	$ 2,500.00	$ 200.00	$ 93,013.55	$	$ 82,155.46	$ 175,169.01
	13,385.91	87,483.22	---	94.27	320.29	102,113.69		94,124.88	196,238.57
	55, 0.00	68,608.60	---	---	---	123,608.66		7,569.15	131,177.75
	13,027.69	323,028.39	---	14,489. 4	85,598.77	436,144.26		754,578.65	1,190,722.91
Mutual	10,260.28	500,411.30	---	5,296.41	837.01	516,805.00		425,238.25	942,043.25
	22,500.00	239,969.53	---	16,503.00	17,034.72	296,007.25		426,825.62	722,832.87
Southern	5,527.94	421,875.81	---	6,844.61	460.05	434,708.41		467,519.25	902,227.66
	6,873.97	38,843.90	---	6,056.45	16,094.94	67,869.26		17,855.22	85,724.48
	60,647.93	38,355.47	---	---	12,471.32	111,474.72		59,805.87	171,280.59
	15,379.44	86,959.89	---	12,498.75	653.66	102,992.99		42,379.05	145,372.04
Warners	8,847.24	567,171.87	---	1,816.39	622.66	589,140.52		452,898.63	1,042,039.15
(Int.)	---	106,099.41	---	---	---	107,915.80		187,980.92	295,896.72
Totals	1,755,984.52	13,848,196.27		287,830.24	2,097,343.63	17,989,354.66		15,310,449.97	33,299,804.63

COMPANIES OF OR STATES (STOCK).

Name of Company	Net Unpaid Losses and Claims	Unearned Premiums, Fire	Unearned Premiums, Marine and Inland	Due for Commissions, Taxes Return and Reinsurance Premiums	Other Liabilities	Total	Cash Capital	Net Surplus	Total Liabilities
e	52,688.36	301,509.30	33,486.68	46,687.97	---	400,885.63		420,664.27	821,549.90
A	231,901.17	2,386,110.51	20,905.64	75, 0.00	2,308.44	2,728,806.80	200, 0.00	1,228,278.77	3,957,085.57
h America	271,717.41	1,279,924.96	246,298.91	71,136.40	2, 0.00	1,645,684.41	200, 0.00	616,497.83	2,462,182.24
n	241,009.08	1,591,326.01	4,849.03	30,000.00	12, 0.00	2,120,634.00	200, 0.00	879,971.95	3, 0,605.95
Gy	50,198.52	229,123.64		15, 0.00		299,171.19		227,199.50	726,370.69
Ga	193,686.00	1,468,071.16		3,500.00	500.00	1,665,757.16	200, 0.00	678,717.23	2,544,474.39
l in he ue	1,330,339.11	6,836,682.26	478,948.51	484,172.15	103,478.78	9,233,620.81	200, 0.00	3,211,026.84	12,444,647.65
gle Sar ad h Do rn	142,476.35	723,742.47		20,032.01	1,500.00	887,750.83	200, 0.00	618,775.47	1,506,526.30
Re	331,306.00	1,501,373.09		16,750.00	5,188.75	1,854,617.84	200, 0.00	541,391.43	2,596,009.27
Et	361,667.00	1,662,818.06		39,490.83		2,063,975.89		434,901.86	2,698,877.75
Jakor	645,880.69	2,383,497.72		95, 0.00	25, 0.00	3,149,378.41	200, 0.00	643,682.53	3,993,060.94
rl London nd Globe	1,726,575.87	9,318,138.39	63,790.31	479,357.24	215,328.40	12,203,190.21		4,881, 7.17	17,084,397.38
n he	998,832.44	2,542,513.38	249,880.22	187,454.96	12,319.90	3,991, 0.90		2,102,134.65	6,093,135.55
n d Me	227,289.56	3,037,737.48	236,480.78	119, 0.00	1,800.00	3,622,307.82	200, 0.00	2,823,403.53	6,445,711.35
d	394,336.00	1,986,622.12		63,183.93		2,444,142.05	400, 0.00	518,007.75	3,162,149.80
M (	323,999.45	1,116,668.13	166,234.00	64,781.29	11, 0.00	1,682,682.87		710, 95.83	2,793,078.70

Me (Paris) ... Fire ... Life	79,032.60	452,263.97		70,031.96	3,522.64	601,328.53		525,704.51	1,127,033.04
... Fire	84,129.85	625,926.97		20,000.00	22,123.14	733,579.46	200,000.00	734,734.43	1,336,313.89
Norske Lloyd	489,842.44	2,119,932.64		5,000.00	22,898.22	2,636,998.22	200,000.00	267,743.26	3,104,641.48
North British ... Mercantile	937,743.85	5,604,928.07	205,955.09	234,465.00	70,083.50	7,053,175.51	400,000.00	2,920,294.62	10,373,470.13
Mn	659,828.65	4,028,818.74	100,398.97	231,696.20	16,337.49	5,037,080.05	200,000.00	1,895,288.33	7,132,368.38
Mn	216,526.15	742,144.31		13,000.00	12,000.00	983,670.46		440,780.98	1,424,451.44
Norwegian	168,125.75	929,015.56		3,000.00	23,382.06	1,123,523.37	200,000.00	436,621.22	1,760,144.59
... U nin	455,644.47	2,219,855.08	202,952.22	122,116.40	57,563.99	3,058,132.16		1,203,040.91	4,261,173.07
Paternelle	196,087.80	1,079,541.09		40,000.00		1,315,628.89		379,766.60	1,695,395.49
... Fire	79,032.60	452,263.97		70,031.96		601,328.53		420,262.40	1,021,590.93
Palatine	265,781.00	2,249,182.72	83,646.83	110,668.00	1,000.00	2,710,278.55		1,265,855.91	3,976,134.46
Phenix (London)	353,483.56	2,701,305.89	151,853.15	118,000.00	6,340.15	3,330,982.75		2,028,608.42	5,359,591.17
Prudential G. ad	121,274.55	653,788.11		12,224.41	250.00	787,532.07		888,953.72	1,676,485.79
Rossia	2,269,565.00	5,788,257.98	505,944.38	73,450.00	27,300.00	8,664,517.36	200,000.00	2,603,887.85	11,468,405.21
Royal	1,632,226.88	9,504,265.40	785,256.99	766,539.54	115,847.11	12,804,135.90	662,000.00		18,269,657.00
Royal Exchange	1,555,485.02	1,891,198.63	249,021.18	103,213.06	5,134.42	2,804,052.31	400,000.00	1,015,913.27	4,219,965.58
Russian Reinsurance	275,436.00	1,357,192.92	166,628.46	39,490.74	13,500.42	1,672,119.66	200,000.00	584,830.62	2,456,950.28
Salamandra	662,010.67	2,462,773.64		75,000.00	31,009.80	3,213,284.73		966,656.32	4,179,941.05
... in ad	406,788.00	3,191,373.51		160,000.00	575.60	3,955,799.77	200,000.00	3,728,495.50	7,884,295.27
Second	259,169.14	998,772.35		20,000.00		1,278,517.09	330,000.00	537,572.15	1,816,089.24
Sa...	279,747.44	1,068,624.26		19,529.55		1,387,901.25		468,042.08	2,185,943.33
Scandinavia	541,735.47	3,035,947.81	30,139.85	14,935.85	31,373.97	3,654,132.95	400,000.00	438,687.93	4,492,820.88
Sun	547,021.24	3,412,913.68	398,781.08	130,000.00	4,717.69	4,493,433.69	200,000.00	1,168,873.89	5,862,307.58
Svea Fire	125,108.09	1,321,702.20		31,500.00	2,000.00	1,480,310.29	200,000.00	821,093.33	2,501,403.62
Swiss	239,947.40	1,609,657.71		40,000.00	350.00	1,789,955.11		672,817.97	2,462,773.08
... Marine ... Fire	291,756.05	480,026.98	165,040.10	70,854.92	1,514.51	1,009,192.56	530,000.00	1,719,810.55	3,259,003.11
U nin	131,533.00	937,760.06	34,415.69	41,250.00	250.00	1,145,208.75		1,111,924.77	2,257,133.52
Union and Phenix Espagnol	362,947.11	1,864,953.19		25,000.00	35,000.00	2,287,900.32		509,914.44	2,797,814.76
... Hispano	21,488.06	153,278.00		104,629.75	4,717.69	174,766.06	510,000.00	92,039.09	776,805.15
... of Paris	100,117.58	620,298.27		71,763.44		825,045.60		598,527.85	1,423,573.45
... ne	445,861.07	2,350,860.24		10,500.00	16,432.50	2,884,917.25		1,005,271.50	3,890,188.75
Warsaw Fire	126,704.56	543,035.40			6,500.00	686,739.96	400,000.00	400,132.29	1,086,872.25
Western	1,050,670.48	1,541,654.76	243,711.45	122,427.51	1,500.00	2,959,964.20	400,000.00	1,333,616.33	4,693,580.53
Yorkshire	190,964.69	806,863.23	61,285.02	61,000.00	1,000.00	1,121,112.94	200,000.00	823,459.75	2,144,572.69
Ts	22,146,719.23	107,066,231.02	5,285,904.54	4,861,865.07	899,033.26	140,259,753.12	7,432,000.00	59,017,000.50	206,708,753.62

RECAPITULATION.

North	139,602.44	1,241,852.78	1,059.81		64,153.26	1,446,668.29	1,631,200.00	1,329,379.27	4,407,247.56
... of ... r States	54,248,310.43	278,359,566.02	21,391,576.53	19,138,291.47	17,351,406.46	390,489,150.91	96,291,523.00	174,813,149.82	661,593,823.73
... of foreign	1,755,984.52	13,848,196.37		287,830.24	2,097,343.63	17,989,354.66		15,310,444.97	33,299,804.63
...	22,146,719.23	107,066,231.02	5,285,904.54	4,861,865.07	899,033.26	140,259,753.12	7,432,000.00	59,017,000.50	206,708,753.62
Ts	78,290,616.62	400,515,846.09	26,677,481.07	24,289,046.59	20,411,936.61	550,184,926.98	105,354,723.00	250,469,979.56	906,009,629.54

RISKS IN FORCE AT BEGINNING OF YEAR, WRITTEN DURING YEAR AND GROSS PREMIUMS RECEIVED, RISKS TERMINATED DURING YEAR, RISKS IN FORCE AT END OF YEAR, AND PREMIUMS THEREON, AMOUNT REINSURED AND PREMIUMS THEREON, AND LOSSES INCURRED AND LOSSES INCURRED DURING THE YEAR 1918.

NORTH CAROLINA

Name of Company	Risks in Force at Beginning of Year	Risks Written During Year	Gross Premiums on Risks Written	Terminated During Year	Risks in Force at End of Year	Gross Premiums Thereon	Premiums on Amount Reinsured	Losses Paid
	$ 939,580.00	$ 90,610.00	$ 2,677.72	$ 55,490.00	$ 15,159,343.00	$ 2,677.72	$	$ 26,779.02
	12,948,125.00	12,555,173.00	504,346.82	10,343,958.00	995,445.00	301,046.42	105,014.30	533.05
Carolina	1,228,876.00	68,175.00	2,491.36	30,606.00	5,049,000.42	995,332.82		11,808.67
	3,257,867.21	3,815,318.00	123,819.54	2,024,184.79	850,682.00	91,332.82	27,403.90	964.00
	850,682.00		4,684.56			4,684.56		
Fire	47,507,212.00	61,284,043.00	1,269,074.32	51,802,447.00	56,999,308.00	747,600.68	137,635.23	152,164.87
	20,842,530.00	2,554,156.00	68,817.65	2,233,549.35	21,162,846.65	68,817.65		40,124.64
	68,182.00	2,135.50	355.97	16,472.00	54,845.50	355.97		
	496,292.00	41,545.00	2,027.39	8,425.00	729,412.00	2,027.39		774.67
an County Mutual	1,038,548.00	78,214.00	3,050.41	75,214.00	1,041,628.00	3,050.41		690.61
Fire	746,250.00	845,950.00	29,069.16	749,250.00	842,950.00	16,312.95	36.00	5,350.64
Farmers Mutual	778,832.00	116,848.00	3,792.24	3,528.00	879,152.00	3,792.24		2,781.97
Mutual	500,850.00	133,950.00	7,590.61	3,500.00	631,300.00	7,548.11	3,519.67	6.40
Carolina Fire	27,863,798.20	33,035,656.45	789,825.54	24,100,562.78	36,798,891.87	509,408.66	174,942.34	64,059.40
North Carolina Home		516,760.00	11,015.15	88,875.00	427,885.00	9,189.46	2,402.86	
	13,093,501.00	15,499,349.00	529,009.00	9,029,950.00	19,552,800.00	412,503.29	94,675.24	46,474.16
	2,000,000.00	100,000.00	8,960.14	270,100.00	2,100,000.00	8,960.14		7,005.04
Furniture	279,650.00	314,450.00			324,000.00	6,044.05		214.14
Stock	18,122,880.00	17,088,343.00	552,481.11	13,994,353.00	21,246,870.00	354,789.39	101,595.05	27,451.89
	23,888,778.00	19,433,576.00	648,020.72	16,414,908.00	26,907,446.00	426,395.17	136,699.94	41,331.20
Mutual	409,336.00	224,975.00	1,464.99	320,406.00	224,975.00	1,464.99	1,464.99	576.00
State Mutual	530,684.00	530,684.00	9,222.30	3,258,799.00	619,414.00			2,674.50
ers of	4,802,265.38	3,816,603.00	155,412.11	9,340,945.00	5,360,069.38	100,677.57	31,658.65	4,438.56
County	12,139,834.00	11,001,354.00	360,313.20	8,652.00	13,800,243.00	230,898.05	50,809.52	31,752.53
Mutual	742,025.00	88,240.00	1,112.38		821,613.00	1,112.38		333.79
Totals	194,746,173.79	183,236,107.95	5,088,634.39	144,458,294.92	233,514,889.82	3,313,181.43	867,857.69	468,289.75

Etna	2,551,357,703.00	1,968,657,655.00	20,901,584.38	1,677,236,611.00	2,461,471,580.00	26,434,232.57	3,292,349.50	8,807,806.19
gtl	619,876,300.00	488,779,400.00	4,832,300.25	405,369,400.00	554,200,200.00	5,217,304.00	1,478,686.00	1,635,845.16
rd	223,833,765.00	263,232,908.00	2,493,489.91	198,780,562.00	208,592,205.00	1,992,925.50	797,656.21	1,017,578.38
Alliance	643,741,703.00	598,288,693.00	5,268,765.18	481,989,303.00	194,565,547.00	1,486,024.22	4,991,007.37	422,801.96
In		115,951,145.00	1,078,151.85	28,124- 87.00	87,713,657.00	975,11.60	732.31	193,823.91
An W	1,348,748,181.00	02,99,508.00	8,21,16.56	774,045,619.00	1,252,711,594.00	12,801,567.22	2,146,843.28	2,763,004.63
Gil (St. Louis)	85,99,498.00	60,739,107.00	6,21,91.33	563,570,820.00	365,786,315.00	3,657,323.92	5,305,357.81	1,173,752.49
An	438,249,493.00	471,647,386.00	4,52,60.26	295,093,370.00	614,803,509.00	5,874,563.25	4,461,269.44	411,672.65
Automobile	348,684,305.00	822,436,859.00	7,18,942.16	484,765,987.00	686,355,177.00	6,299,256.07	1,789,355.21	3,271,568.87
3	23,87,637.00	787,375,040.00	7,043,15.18	542,220,929.00	726,308.	6,932,632.29	2,220,937.58	2,552,760.06
Gs of	500,085,766.00	60,65,701.00	5,248,058.29	87,931,466.00	504,641,820.00	5,058,309.11	1,092,561.36	1,589,936.30
	217,491,088.00	349,967,510.00	3,655,597.27	47,802,368.00	44,856,755.00	455,463.57	4,947,451.08	161,092.46
Columbia	36,102,463.00	41,431,387.00	444,81.36	30,715,090.00	36,766,361.00	85,461.18	118,791.31	43,683
An N io	115,744,500.00	123,724,183.00	1,429,20.45	96,947,286.00	92,807,496.00	1,07,81.60	584,123.86	465,488.59
Gil ation (New Ok)	199,827,208.00	180,623,519.00	1,703,605.72	147,558,314.00	166,616,285.00	1,540,603.90	670,712.96	404,840.92
	399,450,456.00	385,846,012.00	3,126,543.82	309,590,972.00	312,304,812.00	2,553,124.43	1,332,730.22	724,668.22
Ga	358,353,553.00	254,787,788.00	2,817,751.41	209,919,620.00	348,142,995.00	3,599,942.37	598,727.67	853,009.26
Cleveland National	71,896,378.00	123,162,009.00	1,01,939.90	75,225,903.00	76,870,688.00	684,818.58	391,281.40	215,231.01
	1,023,838,598.00	767,965,045.00	8,018,663.55	153,359,994.00	996,091,101.00	9,854,151.38	1,610,657.77	2,170,844.35
Gil	2,511,637,783.00	1,853,390,268.00	17,829,420.96	1,463,031,218.00	2,469,933,835.00	23,768,979.62	3,907,227.31	4,871,308.34
Gv	122,663,333.00	102,788,909.00	1,030,708.03	83,107,031.00	54,067,163.00	469,172.00	891,394.13	157,818.28
He Fire and M	110,722,513.00	151,596,257.00	1,470,531.71	140,142,737.00	50,273,100.00	539,330.41	774,543.01	242,644.44
He (South Carolina)	313,571,216.00	254,140,680.00	2,467,813.88	240,091,561.00	78,369,837.00	758,184.95	2,494,338.10	231,101.32
	27,016,984.00	22,850,254.00	375,691.81	22,435,255.00	18,812,073.00	333,507.66	155,549.75	57,270.36
al	2,067,65,011.00	94,856,472.00	917,176.36	23,766,134.00	71,090,338.00	743,99.28		60,715.12
t Reinsurance	58,452,191.00	70,590,239.00	15,288,082.83	1,239,792,323.00	2,013,240,238.00	20,597,87.64	3,372,494.44	4,135,497.68
Fire tion of ia	1,210,780,618.00	1,049,797,248.00	970,164.61	61,034,755.00	68,042,537.00	840,61.11		505,471.03
	1,131,235,237.00	1,013,811,025.00	11,263,602.82	899,795,583.00	1,171,098,540.00	11,856,93.95	1,948,601.18	3,276,366.98
			10,995,137.93	768,345,790.00	1,085,340,879.00	12,208,06.93	2,805,537.74	2,980,243.40
Firemen's of Newark	926,183,449.00	88,983,843.00	6,658,413.79	598,778,466.00	756,334,283.00	7,651,301.21	2,045,983.53	1,837,5 1.85
Franklin	480,967,319.00	82,897,887.00	5,131,608.56	417,081,265.00	185,102,692.00	1,601,616.00	4,613,122.00	373,445.64
Georgia Home	45,605,080.00	64,262,623.00	737,292.40	49,389,630.00	36,382,326.00	474,063.97	312,648.50	112,913.33
Girard e nd M	297,529,761.00	29,570,320.00	2,261,558.86	103,728,047.00	252,035,592.00	2,324,961.92	991,870.61	453,070.78
Gs	778,772,189.00	85,072,124.00	5,718,050.16	485,633,389.00	701,154,607.00	6,402,622.49	1,538,788.49	1,638,563.48
Ge		7,145,536.00	58,625.06	521,237.00	6,624,299.00	59,850.00		1, . 0
Ge nd	1,373,217,657.00	1,798,318,489.00	20,988,733.09	1,344,743,142.00	1,562,090,224.00	18,430,479.44	3,995,561.63	4,870,594.00
Ge S	180,897,748.00	148,048,510.00	1,792,292.87	120,131,432.00	208,628,826.00	2,493,491.25	656,385.67	473,378.14
Great	2,956,413,338.00	2,438,778,985.00	24,385,629.15	2,179,136,833.00	2,557,352,437.00	24,446,791.19	5,125,749.55	7,952,555.89
	731,549,500.00	488,675,992.00	5,107,773.03	437,929,460.00	631,157,208.00	6,235,216.98	1,464,483.89	1,644,528.27
Home Fire and Marine	4,453,188,473.00	3,715,556,817.00	40,870,744.22	4,813,100,592.00	4,005,343,568.00	43,213,119.74	6,894,396.33	12,880,493.34
		76,763,914.00	806,924.08	13,124,985.00	48,293,275.00	489,332.11	175,905.26	41,440.79

TABLE No. V—RISKS AND PREMIUMS, FIRE, 1918.

SHOWING RISKS IN FORCE AT BEGINNING OF YEAR, WRITTEN DURING YEAR, AND GROSS PREMIUMS RECEIVED, RISKS TERMINATED DURING YEAR, RISKS IN FORCE AT END OF YEAR, AND PREMIUMS THEREON, AMOUNT REINSURED AND LOSSES INCURRED DURING THE YEAR 1918.

COMPANIES OF STATES (STOCK)—CONTINUED.

Name of Company	Risks in Force at Beginning of Yr	Risks Written During Year	Gross Premiums on Risks Written	Risks Terminated During Yr	Risks in Force at End of Yr	Gross Premiums Thereon	Premiums on Amount Reinsured	Losses Paid
...de of New York	$4,674,933,664.00	$3,583,420,428.00	$39,445,600.06	$3,252,262,323.00	$4,368,396,413.00	$43,481,155.00	$ 5,865,729.00	$12,687,120.07
...de of Uth	32,990,204.00	72,785,545.00	879,498.64	32,377,949.00	57,233,276.00	675,701.19	212,161.30	119,221.23
...e G. of ...th America	167,891,85.00	175,590,364.00	1,359,510.69	143,408,830.00	123,933,566.00	949,289.82	665,457.29	248,297.46
...e.	2,024,328,467.00	1,905,021,751.00	18,229,410.46	1,498,825,835.00	1,908,074,062.00	19,416,217.03	4,319,519.07	4,882,751.94
...rine	21,638,83.00	35,679,216.00	279,853.35	33,599,246.00	16,426,731.00	167,688.78	65,200.39	85,270.50
...nal.	840,212,540.00	71,246,426.00	6,313,654.37	62,550,246.00	577,700,474.00	5,999,983.98	872,992.28	2,643,105.64
...Ms	62,044,86.00	29,179,941.00	658,040.45	73,564,197.00	41,266,89.00	448,826.95	160,231.89	234,614.48
...Ms nl Marine	11,735,25.00	88,242,672.00	323,849.45	10,208,133.00	26,273.00	277,075.25	67,979.30	52,640.71
...Ns Ml	118,785,645.00	82,611,966.00	924,887.23	83,633,873.00	100,087.00	1,020,579.35	238,997.27	317,997.93
wa			918,807.25	35,795,780.00	72,685.00	759,935.57	241,036.62	160,684.28
...Es nl	142,86,69.00	131,797,905.00	1,335,248.13	92,743,114.00	145,144,599.00	1,402,208.62	395,734.56	347,153.31
...Es	641,81.00	204,505,317.00	2,074,997.96	168,526,172.00	144,691,950.00	1,457,036.32	1,006,783.27	461,286.25
...Ms lis. G. of ...merica	327,180,61.00	339,341,401.00	2,705,198.83	259,433,814.00	265,894,504.00	2,048,166.05	1,065,363.17	559,283.04
...Ns Ml	16,698,83.00	34,609,572.00	391,044.68	2,485,521.00	25,864,824.00	301,127.16	27,415.58	126,531.00
...le	579,661,89.00	325,508,894.00	3,567,469.39	298,192,918.00	560,590,319.00	5,767,038.71	457,279.98	1,195,160.11
...l ...ly	2,864,807,094.00	2,084,628,437.00	21,157,039.05	1,93,91.00	2,39,121,86.00	22,145,129.40	7,640,158.59	5,712,520.49
...Ml Un	1,001,030,052.00	659,410,328.00	6,766,982.24	50,51,463.00	92,554,499.93	8,779,094.93	1,809,334.24	1,002,601.74
...Ml	1,756,653,672.00	561,474,231.00	6,045,521.09	56,104,624.00	39,097.00	5,537,275.12	2,648,314.76	1,758,767.38
...e	281,110,170.00	330,400,689.00	3,236,812.71	85,09,88.00	264,595,480.00	2,554,073.44	1,196,656.78	764,058.67
Nw ...e	764,883,081.00	536,159,363.00	5,845,198.26	450,83,414.00	63,957,042.00	6,885,782.81	1,400,654.04	1,747,558.15
Niagara.	1,06,243,569.00	951,377,743.00	9,513,724.65	85,30,62.00	941,839,05.00	11,964,732.26	2,734,680.53	2,500,648.30
Nh ...r.	591,628,141.00	599,468,217.00	6,226,332.19	534,99,87.00	478,058,82.00	5,040,016.87	1,762,914.53	1,391,487.16
Nh ...h.	88,862,364.00	147,418,02.00	1,770,550.02	15,65,642.00	77,229,39.00	944,681.05	569,008.39	460,140.99
...n ...fe nd ...e.	916,844,952.00	462,694,989.00	4,493,107.71	405,09,85.00	85,796,81.00	7,672,687.27	1,087,223.20	1,350,681.13
...rn ...fe nd ...e.	148,765,104.00	2,600,395.85	174,31,27.00	68,735,33.00	694,863.74	1,306,216.60	289,688.34
Od ...y	176,341,01.00	165-874,941.00	1,617,965.18	10,90,39.00	61,988,11.00	1,477,804.20	573,281.75	410,547.14
...tt.	99,66,399.00	481.00	3,512,210.74	33,548,473.00	96,554,85.00	3,737,980.46	1,373,946.01	826,733.46
...o. ...ia.	14,819,599.00	36,213,273.00	559,684.51	20,641,82.00	22,497,82.00	392,927.19	145,782.78	51,228.90
...Rs ...g	974,837,788.00	6,473,510.09	614,549,86.00	87,411,90.00	7,989,066.32	1,671,195.95	2,298,939.47
...Ms	173,753,245.00	196,045,480.00	1,905,737.97	69,92,480.00	25,67.00	1,313,326.41	771,928.35	381,121.52
...ix (Hartford)	16,448,283.00	5,496,887.00	85,904.52	3,496,354.00	17,046,36.00	282,045.00	23,331.50	9,069.51
	900.00	1,268,418,712.00	12,426,935.89	1,87,63,25.00	1,437,347.69.00	13,756,745.87	3,778,614.09	3,240,297.40

[redacted]Washington	700,198,875.00	629,730,030.00	6,465,070.69	572,588,213.00	520,654,960. 0	5,270,597.20	2,277,543.86	1,876,615.36
[redacted]n of [redacted]	1,185,479,994. 0	997,330,804.00	9,794,328.60	839,597,591.00	1,076, 41,460.00	10,792,836.95	2,276, 49.89	2,764,941.28
[redacted]e [redacted]	340,258,602.00	361,791,727.00	3,400,970.81	287,251,649.00	246, 14,207. 0	2,135,279.57	1,573,631.64	627,783.24
St. Paul Fire nd Marine	1, 66,713,213. 0	907,560,260.00	10,488,009.14	807,794,616. 0	1,097,753,816.00	11,856,731.45	1,708,885.33	3,560,702.53
Security	689,138 372.00	601,823,298. 0	6,691,588.83	484,988,302.00	618,155,936. 0	6,227,645.31	1,753,389.93	1,796,229.37
[redacted]h [redacted]	15,396 074.00	53,579,986.00	622,278.72	51,701,479.00	11,058,076.00	162,210.47	94, 74.08	25,211.83
[redacted]d [redacted]e nd Marine	1,562,310,070. 0	1,306,457,314. 0	13,163,152.86	1,079,843,483.00	1,448,013,388. 0	15,062,265.30	2,943,035.22	3,906,338.16
[redacted]	187,176,221.00	131,452,631.00	1,214,846.18	125,936,799. 0	136,061,249. 0	1,201,484.85	488,522.18	340,046.43
[redacted]r of America	165,027,277.00	178,316,437.00	1,740,989.72	152,764, 47.00	93,846,215.00	950, 11.40	974,895.90	222,381.78
Sterling	239,207,275.00	195,126,844.00	1,933,729.29	1 0182,618.00	90, 64,736.00	984,723.41	2,414,382.14	379,728.71
[redacted]d [redacted]s	889,542,298.00	788, 97,937. 0	8,264,338.31	690,581,153.00	755,597,465. 0	8,078,900.46	2,323,478.73	2,006,994.75
[redacted]a Fire and Marine	151,992,836.00	123,746,852. 0	1,718,127.97	110,212,362.00	134,356,672. 0	1,934,704.97	445,433.70	438,148.06
Westchester	1,181,786,058.00	918,006,503.00	10,434,224.27	797,498,578.00	964,137,602.00	9,596,082.44	3,044,733.65	2,920,551.92
[redacted]	60,293,714,436.00	51,698,557,722.00	522,519,823.10	43,535,919 519.00	53,440 144,215.00	542,354,352.51	150,479,272.76	147,940.295.22

[redacted]S OF [redacted]R [redacted]S [redacted]).

Arkwright [redacted]	430,519,238.00	406,834,899. 0	2,898,155.99	342, 79,523.00	495, 74,614. 0	3,488,449.56		163,348.02
Baltimore [redacted]	11,896,794.00	14,454,305.00	122,794.32	11,841,665. 0	14,509,434. 0	121, 67.52	1,602.94	6,937.66
Blackstone [redacted]	246,790,363.00	201,825,707. 0	1,471,303.51	64,839, 61. 0	83, 76, 69.00	2,041,025.14		172,745.73
[redacted]d [redacted]			2,352,989.01			2,206,184.37	379,321.23	1,192,729.89
[redacted]n nd [redacted]n t[redacted]ers	93,232,612.00	100, 47,568. 0	800,721.08	79,378,947. 0	14, 21, 23.00	899,802.55		64,335.74
Druggists [redacted] Exchange	10,268,960.79	12,036,006.61	188,097.10	11,579,816.61	10,725, 44.79	163,526.58	40,881.64	40,592.85
[redacted]s [redacted]	345,391,561.00	281,631,646.00	2,121,654.12	235,879,086.00	398, 44,121.00	2,883,363.49		233,563.76
[redacted]	33,471,382.00	34,325,610. 0	449,148.32	30,508,546.00	37,288,446.00	493,954.97	116,841.37	140,593.15
Hope [redacted]tual	111,066,781.00	04,258,749. 0	828,259.11	85,859,172.00	129,466,358. 0	1,018,643.43		87,262.63
[redacted]a [redacted]n's Mutual	29,159,864.00	37,246,365. 0	724,551.17	33,154,865.00	33,251,364. 0	641.645.38	5,133.80	248, 40.36
[redacted]l Underwriters	60,218,324. 0	75 136,311. 0	500,529.84	67,226,559.00	68,128,076.00	474,656.41		166,804.78
[redacted]	56,064,238.00	56,928,616.00	462,333.87	48,539,525. 0	64,453,329.00	515,553.21		38,813.99
[redacted]e Mutual	58,422,238. 0	59,481,527. 0	517,860.20	54,167,874. 0	63,735,891. 0	542,167.58		53,389.69
[redacted]r [redacted]s. [redacted]	23,185,221.00	23, 97,337.00	494,375.82	30,483,076.00	16, 69,482.00	317,763.90	102,502.06	297,628.17
[redacted]r [redacted]	29,682,833.00	37,604,078.00	779,693.97	34,443,427.00	32,843,484.00	680,286.33		282,252.73
[redacted]s [redacted]	57,637,483.00	68,706,816. 0	1, 17,140.84	61,394,400.00	64,949,899.00	995,019.94	9,025.43	401, 91.60
Lumbermen's Underwriters [redacted]nce	49,292,357.00	81,076,867.00	1,521,461.66	67,549,798.00	62,819,426. 0	1,212,414.92		670,296.78
[redacted]n [redacted]	54,224,261.00	55,672, 01. 0	488,472.27	51,129,729.00	58,767,233.00	504,805.42		44,473.98
[redacted]. [redacted]s [redacted]s	48,885,770.84	73,903,710.18	1,463,293.46	62,699,669.40	60,089,811.62	1,191,043.40		789,556.08
[redacted]fg [redacted]s [redacted]iters	12,355,134. 0	17,992,138. 0	335,324.84	15, 79,878. 0	14,567,394.00	266,035.67	71,060.35	156,185.86
[redacted]ts [redacted]	134, 64,296. 0	107,953,708. 0	789,309.38	86,682,412. 0	155,885,592.00	1,122,012.62		103,570.59
[redacted]e [redacted]	43,734,175.00	45,901,932.00	379,703.69	39, 41,069.00	50,195,038.00	408,884.42		34,597.98
[redacted]k [redacted]	56,124,598.00	23,580 005. 0	366,780.21	20,544,130.00	59,160,473. 0	880,625.60	186,274.67	78,573.31
[redacted]n Millers [redacted]	153,502,778. 0	187,638,612. 0	1,731, 94.05	61,324,520. 0	179,816,870. 0	1,945,458.37	3,010.81	816,085.13
Millers Mutual	10, 94,850. 0	5,115,048. 0	82,006.71	3,376,310. 0	12,533,588.00	230,863.29		115,103.72
[redacted]s [redacted]ity [redacted]ers								127,445.16

TABLE No. V—RISKS AND PREMIUMS, ΉE, 1918.

SHOWING RISKS IN FORCE AT BEGINNING OF YEAR, WRITTEN DURING YEAR, AND GROSS PREMIUMS RECEIVED, RISKS TERMINATED DURING YEAR, RISKS IN FORCE AT END OF YEAR, AND PREMIUMS THEREON, AMOUNT REINSURED, AND LOSSES INCURRED ΉG THE YEAR 18.

COMPANIES OF OTHER STATES (MUTUAL)—Continued.

Name of Company	Risks in Force at Beginning of Year	Risks Written During Year	Gross Premiums on Risks Written	Risks Terminated During Year	Risks in Force at End of Year	Gross Premiums Thereon	Premiums on Amount Reinsured	Losses Paid
Narragansett Mutual	$ 16,080,339. 0	$ 19,579,394.00	$ 163,924.67	$ 15,393,411. 0	$ 20,266,322.00	$ 168,444.09	$	$ 9,494.64
National Mutual	18,490,170.00	20,394,454.00	183,337.19	19,469,596.00	19,415,028.00	172,841.04		18,234.13
National ᴸber Manufacturers	9,114,137.23	11,398,118.25	191,911 34	10,377,612.40	10,135,143.08	171,558.76	1,177.33	85,601.67
Penn Lumbermen's ᴹᵘᵗ	28,427,207.00	34,587,867. 0	714,228.07	31,572,875.00	31,442,199.00	646,221.33	164.55	251,999.44
Philadelphia Manufacturers Mutual	103,239, 14.00	105,427,877.00	822,338.89	84,743,771.00	123,923,820.00	952,470.27		59,210.01
Reciprocal Exchange	53,577,229.00	69,883,123.00	921,209.21	65,320,431.00	58,139,921.00	771,143.43	293,137.84	272,157.47
Rubber Manufacturers Mutual	87,987,349.00	92,089,843.00	739,866.81	74,898,557.00	105,178,635.00	833,137.43		60,567.77
Southern Lumber Underwriters	1,358,630.00	6,477,910.00	145,753.10	6,110,146.00	1,726,394.00	38,843.98	6,849.06	56,268.04
ᵁᵗⁱᵉˢ Indemnity Exchange	11, 71,950.00	25,343,450.00	219,597.26	19,970,550.00	17,144,850.00	347,233.75		127,064.54
Western Reciprocal Underwriters	15,332,138.00	108,358,006.00	390,114.88	88,857,142.00	134,833,002.00	248,456.83	74,537.05	106,280.89
ᵂᵃᵗ ᴳⁱᵈᵉʳ Mutual	11,153,975.00	24,656,937.50	857,294.92	13,122,3627 3	22,688,549.77	1,046,987.27		89,113.38
ᵂⁱʳˢ Interins. (Grocers' Dept.)			291,093.45			265,250.78	53,049.96	103,425.06
Totals	617,068,950.86	2,631,837,241.54	28,627,824.33	2,229,840,212.14	3,026,066,474.26	30,907,913.03	1,344,570.09	7,766,686.38

COMPANIES OF FOREIGN COUNTRIES.

Name of Company	Risks in Force at Beginning of Year	Risks Written During Year	Gross Premiums on Risks Written	Risks Terminated During Year	Risks in Force at End of Year	Gross Premiums Thereon	Premiums on Amount Reinsured	Losses Paid
ᵀⁱᵗˡᵉ	$ 48,884,989. 0	$ 60,888,300.00	$ 530,847.50	$ 51,572,851.00	$ 58,200,438. 0	$ 576,127.46	$ 1,968,671.54	$ 195,787.28
Atlas	552,122,884.00	561,780,369.00	5,460,699.69	417,326,329.00	456,72,258.00	6,546,660.56		1,278,253.62
British ᴸᵃ	320,299,735.00	308,280,850.00	2,836,878.00	291,829,915.00	251,565,295.00	3,276,934. 0	728,809.00	845,282.02
Caledonian	389,999,320.00	280,377,385.00	3,033,193.49	274,629,267.00	299,854,489.00	3,110,874.00	1,036,928.16	821,184.48
Century	87,491,971.00	111,766,001.00	812,351.06	94,180,387.00	66,066,635.00	461,022.75	313,966.36	204,306.42
Christiana General	1,594,671,631.00	278,631,551. 0	2,548,583.42	60,687,799. 0	217,943,752.00	2,037,829.54		265,914.10
ᴳⁱᵃˡ Union Assurance	83,497,017.00	1,326,215,852.00	12,006,413.00	1,169,498,277.00	1,377,608,584.00	13,207,393.00	3,223,803.00	3,874,223.37
Eagle Star and British Dominion	304,714,560.00	201,889,246. 0	1,938,836.79	130,392,336.00	124,145,314.00	1,280,418.60	324,108.21	434,026.37
Fire Reassurance	311,826,278.00	442,665,600. 0	4,666,752.04	376,367,640.00	253,344,510.00	2,833,313.39	1,304,789.36	1,542,886.27
First Russian	1,058,771,951.00	359,381,893.00	3,235,682.08	339,725,033.00	331,483,138. 0	3,201,316.64		1,221,549.67
Jakor	2,677,957,853. 0	937,318,308.00	8,684,924.90	1,098,210,939.00	481,666,191. 0	4,736,458.08	4,188,648.81	2,391,296.93
Liverpool and London and Globe	543,103,789.00	2,157,874,723.00	21,648,332.41	2,003,698,447.00	1,877,062,267. 0	17,973,999.78	9,555,607.28	5,060,308.59
London Assurance	869,285,443.00	460,792,893.00	4,976,383.90	386,067,617. 0	458,394,492.00	4,931,200.07	1,745,315.16	1,102,771.04
ᴸondon and Lancashire	438,761,732.00	671,728,147.00	5,803,210.94	597,772,179. 0	4,377,125.61	5,874,877.22	2,440,999.40	1,196,437.81
National (Denmark)	60,133,724.00	414,722,908.00	3,805,407.38	461,107,639.00	392,377,001.00	3,870,690.67		1,647,436.25
		253,351,478.00	2,596,402.16	124,909,860.00	188,575,342.00	2,119,405.21		713,714.58

Financial summary table (rotated landscape). Company names at left; eight value columns.

Company	Col 1	Col 2	Col 3	Col 4	Col 5	Col 6	Col 7	Col 8
...le (Paris)	154,246,301.00	168,640,452.00	1,635,785.94	141,299,823.00	181,586,930.00	1,817,698.92	953,507.73	293,680.98
...s Fire and Life	169,966,534.00	168,668,669.00	1,869,667.25	135,271,306.00	203,363,897.00	2,208,067.17	1,007,801.71	332,228.00
...ds	239,524,198.00	453,897,819.00	4,228,139.13	293,608,565.00	399,813,452.00	4,056,450.83		1,618,162.30
...ish and ...ttle	1,612,410,275.00	1,412,913,949.00	11,254,840.48	1,295,824,529.00	1,729,499,695.00	14,449,332.33	3,581,514.32	3,015,726.15
Northern Assurance	928,139,695.00	803,926,133.00	8,054,698.88	687,100,919.00	752,659,512.00	7,742,615.31	2,661,106.63	2,195,663.88
...n (...)	182,735,577.00	185,599,984.00	1,763,659.91	160,995,287.00	137,283,850.00	1,375,176.89	608,683.30	712,875.45
Norwegian ...ance	39,198,710.00	224,758,292.00	2,018,560.48	110,533,621.00	153,423,381.0	1,653,236.87		473,776.91
...th Union	568,130,033.00	492,980,117.00	4,847,281.01	409,657,623.00	438,622,932.00	4,298,090.33	1,856,270.35	1,257,764.30
Paternelle	152,849,519.00	198,043,787.00	2,007,355.60	163,473,160.00	187,420,146.00	2,022,224.91		731,560.00
...nix Fire	147,662,796.00	166,245,203.00	1,606,971.49	134,765,045.00	87,300,655.0	864,191.19	892,283.34	293,680.98
Palatine (London)	518,716,172.00	476,288,211.00	4,613,453.01	396,662,204.00	419,397,710.00	4,305,434.14	1,601,952.57	1,150,817.83
...nix ...an	960,509,659.00	921,438,757.00	7,717,855.51	828,794,470.00	459,981,665.0	3,665,064.40	3,665,064.40	1,556,141.68
Prudentia G...ad Reinsurance	1,033,793,496.00	131,098,465.00	969,897.40	18,432,599.00	112,665,866.00	1,056,057.05	766,366.77	67,517.51
Rossia	2,301,221,590.00	1,124,800,275.00	11,853,322.82	1,079,465,717.00	1,004,606,037.00	10,928,765.87	5,898,581.23	51,833.05
Royal	1,688,396,320.00	1,688,396,320.00	17,092,810.51	1,522,348,652.00	1,855,217,173.00	18,440,594.85		4,446,820.21
Royal Exchange Assurance	505,872,261.00	397,291,359.00	3,720,475.04	357,183,470.00	391,797,243.00	3,671,566.33	1,248,934.39	1,109,104.75
Russian Reinsurance	327,361,622.00	277,926,329.00	2,558,397.89	334,733,299.00	270,554,652.00	2,683,721.04	5,618,960.75	1,230,984.95
Salamandra	1,409,426,418.00	1,114,623,869.00	10,049,121.29	1,440,638,583.00	500,549,507.00	4,860,657.19	3,420,351.35	2,404,460.05
Scottish Union and National	1,032,660,762.00	835,741,774.00	7,449,362.61	744,918,247.00	702,215,741.00	6,147,892.66		1,474,828.61
Second Russian	288,368,496.00	215,320,402.00	2,032,061.44	287,585,71.0	196,064,177.00	1,954,816.11		849,678.59
Scandia	154,170,487.00	208,413,947.00	1,988,436.29	179,960,754.00	182,623,680.00	1,993,639.88	5,368.37	699,877.17
Sa.	152,985,650.00	593,667,567.00	5,575,093.77	276,884,330.00	469,768,887.00	4,913,127.53		1,290,681.62
Sun Insurance Office	4,533,394.00	655,701,318.00	6,313,469.00	529,818,893.00	716,201,298.00	6,508,375.00	2,277,921.00	1,571,473.44
Sea Fire ad Life	235,160,353.00	256,341,000.00	2,920,646.00	198,304,294.00	209,997,565.00	2,536,868.00	913,220.00	695,883.76
Swiss Reinsurance	186,942,306.00	372,560,035.00	3,168,251.98	264,767,943.00	294,734,398.00	2,859,759.05		964,570.53
...o ...e ad ...		219,578,856.00	1,000,904.60	75,287,71.00	135,654,04.00	1,253,195.07	81,844.87	89,582.56
Union	91,770,735.00	232,861,710.00	2,090,417.00	172,242,424.00	180,436,573.00	1,733,417,30	597,134.02	370,283.79
Union of Paris	137,728,034.00	134,966,223.00	1,421,904.89	17,924,091.0	118,270,309.00	1,184,663.78	408,255.98	394,598.01
Union ...d Phenix Espagnol	260,250,049.00	384,676,833.00	3,550,085.97	280,209,571.00	364,717,311.0	3,527,466.51		1,282,921.41
Union Hispano Ame ...na		30,293,580.00	330,085.97	2,770,375.00	27,523,205.00	283,238.00		4,740.60
Urbaine	14,209,038.00	560,760,749.00	5,062,180.52	254,417,989.00	397,378,981.00	3,926,119.79	224,191.99	888,850.97
...w Fire ...ance	91,228,413.00	109,015,852.00	1,134,612.93	98,355,021.0	91,889,244.00	1,102,439,91		540,937.66
Yorkshire	478,174,866.00	463,211,249.00	4,056,705.00	430,828,91.00	312,511,91.00	3,030,002.97	1,698,339.42	965,195.34
	208,490,222.00	282,997,482.00	2,754,717.54	21,81,530.00	47,91,37.00	1,553,831.14	1,008,602.61	505,703.53
Totals	26,975,960,538.01	7,...00	233,295,818.18	21,554,523,232.00	20,683,361,895.61	210,646,326.29	67,827,903.38	58,328,185.37

II N

...th ... (...tok)	194,746,173.79	183,236,107.95	5,088,634.39	144,458,294.92	233,514,889.82	3,313,181.43	867,857.69	468,289.75
...of other ...ties ...(Mutual)	60,293,714,436.00	51,698,557,722.00	522,519,823.10	43,535,919.00	53,440,144,215.00	542,354,352.51	150,479,272.76	147,940,295.22
...of ther ...ties	2,617,068,950.86	2,631,837,241.54	28,627,824.33	2,229,840,212.14	3,026,066,474.26	30,907,913.03	1,344,570.09	7,766,636.38
...of r...n ...ies	26,975,960,538.01	24,794,313,071.00	233,295,815.61	21,	20,682,361,585.61	210,646,326.29	67,827,903.38	58,328,185.37
	90,081,490,098.66	79,307,943,142.49	789,532,101.00	23,971,357,658.06	77,382,087,474.69	787,221,773.26	220,519,603.92	214,503,456.72

TABLE No. VI—RISKS AND PREMIUMS, MARINE AND INLAND, 1918.

SHOWING RISKS IN FORCE AT BEGINNING OF YEAR, WRITTEN DURING YEAR, AND GROSS PREMIUMS RECEIVED, RISKS TERMINATED DURING YEAR, RISKS IN FORCE AT END OF YEAR, AND PREMIUMS THEREON, AMOUNT REINSURED AND LOSSES PAID DURING THE YEAR 1918.

COMPANIES OF OTHER STATES.

Name of Company	Risks in Force at Beginning of Year	Risks Written During Year	Premiums on Risks Written in 1918	Risks ... During Year	Risks in Force at End of Year	Gross Premiums Thereon	Premiums on Amount Reinsured	Losses Paid
Aetna	$120,009,_97.00	$1,229,802,808.00	$9,654,442.21	1,212,364,557.00	$85,840,620.00	$1,605,683.66	$1,042,295.67	$2,232,746.67
A_____	16,_96,_61.00	89,_22,_82.00	1,435,531.32	345,758,573.00	14,787,300.0	294,599.77	167,865.00	366,773.87
American Alliance	2,_94,005.00	8,_45,_08.00	155,604.77	5,889,490.00	145,995.00	4,381.17	85,509.89	165.86
__an Eagle	6,834,184.00	90,_97,_79.00	699,717.25	75,759,723.00	17,291,498.0	204,147.12	141,885.45	170,642.69
American of Newark	21,171,607.00	52,732,_52.00	1,228,438.51	43,654,564.00	24,187,723.00	643,617.06	80,598.13	333,203.96
__ Gl	19,440,_99.00	33,856,463.00	561,966.81	25,299,115.00	13,973,925.00	211,855.78	216,855.78	124,642.81
__ive	19,_69,_36.00	95,480,100.00	798,523.95	98,074,992.00	16,569,924.0	296,729.38	296,348.00	459,899.71
__an Equitable Assurance		152,547,303.0	1,778,362.20	141,350,173.00	2,883,394.00	57,803.67	160,199.00	101,611.49
__le	145,556,396.00	3,387,120,808.00	10,716,404.42	2,771,989,238.00	134,328,284.00	1,707,172.41	516,787.06	579,291.45
Boston	71,_32,_65.00	453,220,626.00	5,957,648.19	453,144,796.0	63,312,163.00	1,864,952.13	351,925.38	1,896,023.40
Camden	7,_32,720.00	536,028,472.00	667,843.79	526,692,907.00	16,246,059.00	83,067.05	4,477.01	275,614.60
__ies of Mi	3,_09,_96.00	5,189,213.00	85,423.38	4,782,324.00	25,513.00	381.99	64,429.28	
Columbia __ Union	31,470,_28.00	78,488,177.00	810,214.05	74,988,881.00	27,258,216.00	487,228.67	92,683.11	241,511.56
Gl		5,584,885.00	159,181.22	1,436,118.00	3,960,742.00	107,501.32	4,075.95	51,616.61
_	26,431,702.00	34,621,400.00	666,208.42	40,761,548.00	15,152,350.0	402,123.91	98,990.24	345,334.55
Gl		4,412,888.00	76,820.35	3,211,564.00	1,201,324.00	24,077.28		6,989.00
Gt Fire	19,568,838.00	401,578,982.00	1,108,968.73	394,695,261.00	25,915,331.00	627,211.39	6,678.08	456,899.08
__in	51,182,548.00	471,878,280.00	3,464,297.17	456,170,517.00	60,228,718.00	819,026.42	212,100.20	865,789.93
_	888,018.00	6,426,386.00	117,831.24	7,014,404.00	10,052,399.00	118,791.31		59,057.22
Equitable Fire __ M	8,947,606.00	192,491,702.0	419,_61.08	194,137,119.00	3,576,949.00	102,535.22	101,056.29	149,362.39
Fidelity— HP	40,103,091.00	305,922,214.00	2,350,826.21	279,471,175.00	58,384,540.00	819,282.03	209,345.20	815,715.34
Fire __h		135,281,_63.0	621,306.65	122,488,279.00	10,214,015.00	139,818.36	32,504.66	116,006.31
Firemen's Fund	298,_ 328.00	5,018,440,_03.00	16,142,379.18	5,041,663,099.00	196,797,540.00	3,958,654.14	1,928,158.33	5,231,043.48
Firemen's of Newark	3,_6,814.00	29,462,_36.00	825,150.80	17,848,632.00	12,_02,066.00	420,679.70	77,973.05	144,406.90
Franklin	12,_6,353.00	113,693,452.00	1,775,_51.96	99,490,884.00	9,084,693.00	232,023.00	516,741.00	175,351.71
Federal	313,479,486.00	9,359,282,763.00	12,514,442.94	8,504,299,873.00	33,_03,_05.00	1,946,224.37	1,763,575.55	2,297,_28.58
Great American	17,416,583.00	81,393,812.00	1,638,934.89	64,812,010.00	33,_82,430.00	716,722.60	26,162.31	513,_94.63
G__s Falls	41,826,121.00	146,_09,406.00	1,575,202.52	450,790,386.00	30,_82,_69.00	543,034.66	137,172.04	531,404.81
Girard Fire __ M		1,154,922.00	34,414.10	176,241.00			29,281.25	
G__e __ Rutgers	74,217,225.00	94,170,224.00	9,337,359.37	702,598,659.00	165,788,790.00	3,026,384.05		4,468,_29.01

Company								
Gl be National	33,631,991.00	505,232.00	4,228.75	367,433.00	137,799.00	2,506.88		
Han ver	56,512,390.00	124,376,946.00	845,212.58	133,055,892.00	21,446,595.00	389,691.00	69,410.79	344,247.14
Hartford	73,775,878.00	385,067,830.00	4,299,441.22	373,848,431.00	65,411,988.00	1,322,237.63	25,419.71	1,505,912.38
He of New York		1,884,769,710.00	4,724,706.69	1,865,555,597.00	76,428,734.00	1,927,901.00	411,300.00	2,296,730.52
Home Fire and Marine		210,194,783.00	1,132,572.06	186,844,233.00	12,798,339.00	276,333.55	203,065.72	126,688.41
Insurance Co. of North America	200,065,608.00	1,974,343,076.00	12,076,749.41	1,958,400,052.00	207,428,028.00	2,368,161.01	75,023.87	5,746,664.51
Massachusetts Fire and Marine	41,762,372.00	110,807,628.00	1,394,433.37	126,323,479.00	20,910,742.00	503,296.33	123,917.84	480,340.55
Mercantile Is. Co. of Ame oi	28,560,688.00	105,663,610.00	541,478.26	95,931,360.00	35,176,344.00	364,729.07	65,625.92	265,833.13
Merchants National	918,912.00	14,987,083.00	222,765.63	14,408,145.00	1,497,850.00	22,154.56		153,321.86
Milwaukee Mechanics	2,915,793.00	11,682,390.00	183,797.30	10,087,222.00	4,496,890.00	111,199.49	379.40	76,609.82
National	48,966,957.00	206,801,270.00	2,226,415.19	193,759,193.00	57,408,704.00	967,429.72	121,200.08	545,997.85
Natl Union	13,111,921.00	88,114,400.00	675,937.42	91,663,557.00	7,240,548.00	116,943.54	91,057.57	225,655.90
Newark Fire	6,155,333.00	24,743,147.00	341,655.85	20,859,347.00	9,952,746.00	177,173.84	1,783.83	112,984.17
New Hampshire	463,124.00	11,751,001.00	228,518.16	8,042,714.00	4,112,666.00	113,517.58	974.26	39,973.80
Niagara	15,744,433.00	48,945,514.00	1,027,014.89	40,741,135.00	23,409,785.00	620,136.08	12,376.80	476,233.99
North River	39,554.00	115,781,057.00	650,051.94	145,861,068.00	7,363,595.00	114,414.12	52,349.83	134,544.92
Northwestern National	23,665,208.00	135,622,863.00	1,606,152.32	132,281,523.00	18,770,322.00	560,568.71	161,393.15	354,963.62
North Branch		19,493,137.00	411,994.95	15,493,072.00	4,410,065.00	111,429.08		67,724.08
Northwestern Fire nd Mari n	953,006.00	2,384,675.00	36,499.72	1,766,829.00			24,391.14	
Old Colony	12,034,265.00	112,735,411.00	874,851.22	112,553,817.00	8,581,909.00	281,642.34	113,059.06	269,358.43
Orient	27,724,941.00	58,683,046.00	594,346.70	54,456,450.00	26,938,193.00	372,404.52	60,321.98	183,880.04
Pennsylvania		10,848,464.00	237,063.16	2,376,905.00	8,355,946.00	181,108.93	1,592.48	93,321.86
Peoples National	1,834,459.00	11,049,982.00	95,491.62	11,538,794.00	1,345,737.00	17,308.29		18,221.50
Phenix of Hartford	55,459,937.00	1,194,812,848.00	3,485,520.57	1,199,712,183.00	29,330,635.00	795,914.67	401,198.09	700,759.35
Provident-Washington	45,290,431.00	643,192,643.00	4,462,950.80	612,882,765.00	37,281,797.00	845,538.92	303,100.20	1,762,266.35
Queen of America	84,831,901.00	676,981,909.00	2,774,313.15	18,012,446.00	110,047,457.00	1,077,753.48	30,564.31	804,349.41
St. Paul Fire and Marine	129,192,353.00	2,139,506,935.00	6,769,266.92	2,167,149,671.00	78,010,813.00	1,353,938.68	176,361.48	2,819,268.60
Security		10,714,438.00	202,380.90	10,020,479.00	692,959.00	10,419.72	41.25	18,640.64
Springfield Fire and Marine	28,071,367.00	233,499,653.00	468,207.14	211,792,847.00	36,956,646.00	294,428.56	63,420.92	34,106.66
Star of	5,759,777.00	8,932,924.00	230,488.74	9,752,199.00	1,744,582.00	41,277.97	122,156.35	19,039.02
South Carolina	3,311,711.00	2,891,687.00	229,367.34	6,203,398.00		1,411.97	16,107.02	53,094.73
S..ng	664,497.00	1,128,069.00	33,228.68	1,305,490.00	85,841.00	169,697.56	134,672.39	10,371.33
United S.	18,354,863.00	427,436,374.00	1,496,049.41	423,681,410.00	11,340,115.00			292,660.89
Westchester	16,556,188.00	518,826,525.00	976,256.69	519,901,893.00	14,328,149.00	330,381.07	27,866.06	395,551.48
	2,349,482,815.00	35,413,188,097.00	142,938,616.43	32,902,698,133.10	2,514,962,774.00	37,398,759.49	10,999,804.41	43,441,028.56

SHOWING RISKS IN FORCE AT BEGINNING OF YEAR, WRITTEN DURING YEAR, AND GROSS P EMIBMS RECEIVED, RISKS TERMI AND DURING YEAR. 1SKS IN FORCE AT END OF YEAR, AND P EMRIMS THEREON, AMOUNT REINSURED AND LOSSES PAID I ING THE YEAR 1918,

COMPANIES OF FOREIGN COUNTRIES.

Name of	Risks in Force at Beginning of Year	Risks Written During Year	Premiums on Risks Written in 1918	Risks Terminated During Year	Risks in Force at End of Year	Gross Premiums Thereon	Premiums on Amount Reinsured	Losses Paid
Atlas	$ 9,128,825.00	$ 5,376,064.00	$ 97,255.24	$ 11,119,545.00	$ 3,385,344.00	$ 69,707.35	$ 2,734.00	$ 36,059.04
British America	2,665,303.00	10,442,821.00	68,753.26	11,524,074.00	1,584,050.00	43,418.97	2,328.73	53,778.56
Caledonian	3,494,883.00	17,734,314.00	778,486.51	7,433,044.00	13,796,153.00	558,715.02	66,117.21	211,442.53
Century	1,460,087.00	1,611,159.00	10,741.08	1,147,140.00	1,924,106.00	10,266.18	568.12	708.88
...al Union Assurance	34,315,552.00	7,558,829,836.00	3,454,153.55	7,468,191,502.00	124,953,886.00	851,886.82	12,194.85	723,232.85
Liverpool and London and the	56,549,217.00	293,264,890.00	2,476,769.43	289,892,249.00	59,921,858.00	1,252,852.22	343,177.80	583,602.25
London ...	70,871,986.00	571,543,634.00	3,270,150.03	581,796,044.00	60,619,576.00	504,628.95	96,415.46	1,256,468.84
London and Lancashire	35,880,379.00	104,606,721.00	868,750.95	102,150,402.00	38,336,698.00	553,839.58	80,878.01	1,246,300.32
North British and Mercantile	35,728,520.00	48,056,108.00	846,672.48	58,884,026.00	24,900,602.00	577,801.67	166,810.16	397,277.31
N...ern Assurance	8,094,271.00	12,032,690.00	254,708.61	11,457,807.00	8,669,154.00	203,263.91	2,465.98	92,180.86
Norwich Union	22,212,665.00	749,015,325.00	1,161,189.13	711,604,062.00	59,523,928.00	419,498.16	51,660.72	317,560.62
Phoenix of London	17,594,923.00	99,990,598.00	600,566.39	95,257,195.00	22,328,326.00	373,985.67	74,328.00	164,609.95
R...yal	104,683,117.00	1,257,151,293.00	4,111,715.89	1,213,600,526.00	148,233,884.00	1,548,623.34	43,673.47	1,218,320.51
Royal Exchange Assurance	46,411,730.00	701,073,678.00	2,295,169.02	698,831,405.00	48,654,003.00	852,230.48	367,461.76	577,910.77
Russia	43,133,975.00	3,451,371,531.00	5,131,032.23	3,455,182,867.00	39,322,639.00	1,007,799.26	8,417.30	2,767,782.50
Scottish Union	11,485,027.00	33,582,562.00	452,933.50	21,266,920.00	23,800,669.00	344,843.45	11,586.53	92,448.93
Skandinavia	1,581,765.00	1,000,655,480.00	414,200.46	1,000,223,728.00	2,013,517.00	44,354.66	410.00	240,785.71
Sun Insurance Office	1,732,021.00	26,075,293.00	1,034,077.94	6,869,939.00	20,937,375.00	810,351.30	58,434.15	264,248.38
Tokio Fire and Marine	35,743,147.00	695,176,553.00	2,937,819.52	692,292,625.00	38,627,075.00	493,446.31	201,986.37	801,627.76
Union Assurance		3,156,620.00	93,735.54	774,043.00	2,382,577.00	70,362.11	1,530.74	51,616.61
Y...n Assurance	45,674,754.00	331,866,562.00	2,805,714.17	308,103,217.00	69,438,099.00	698,001.95	284,240.16	839,533.86
Y...re	1,227,553.00	5,825,909.00	159,523.18	2,568,679.00	4,484,783.00	126,155.49	3,585.44	29,728.81
Totals	589,669,700.00	16,978,439,611.00	33,324,121.18	16,750,171,039.00	817,838,272.00	11,416,535.85	1,881,004.96	10,967,225.85

RECAPITULATION.

	Risks in Force at Beginning of Year	Risks Written During Year	Premiums on Risks Written in 1918	Risks Terminated During Year	Risks in Force at End of Year	Gross Premiums Thereon	Premiums on Amount Reinsured	Losses Paid
Companies of ...r States (stock)	2,349,482,815.00	35,413,188,097.00	142,938,616.43	32,902,698,133.00	2,514,962,774.00	37,398,759.49	10,999,804.41	43,441,028.56
Companies of foreign countries	589,669,700.00	16,978,439,611.00	33,324,121.18	16,750,171,039.00	817,838,272.00	11,416,535.85	1,881,004.96	10,967,225.85
Grand totals	2,939,152,515.00	52,391,627,708.00	176,262,737.61	49,652,869,172.00	3,332,801,046.00	48,815,295.34	12,880,809.37	54,408,254.41

TABLE No. VII—NORTH CAROLINA BUSINESS, 1918.

SHOWING RISKS WRITTEN, PREMIUMS RECEIVED, LOSSES INCURRED IN NORTH CAROLINA FOR THE YEAR ENDING DECEMBER 31, 1918, BY FIRE, MARINE AND INLAND INSURANCE COMPANIES.

NORTH CAROLINA COMPANIES.

Name of Company	Fire Business					
	Gross Risks Written	Gross Premiums Received	Net Risks Written	Net Premiums Received	Net Losses Paid	Net Losses Incurred
Alamance	$ 90,610.00	$ 2,224.68	$ 90,610.00	$ 2,224.68	$ 1,685.90	$ 1,685.90
[illegible]	12,555,173.00	251,103.47	5,672,178.00	118,291.48	20,832.53	26,440.48
Cabarrus M[utual]	68,175.00	2,491.36	68,175.00	2,491.36	533.05	533.05
Carolina [illegible]	3,815,318.00	64,236.84	1,727,710.00	31,472.87	11,808.67	10,195.67
Davidson Cunty M[utual]	850,682.00	119.29	850,682.00	119.29	964.00	964.00
Dixie	14,353,328.00	241,779.92	9,366,998.00	155,857.09	35,510.43	35,917.63
Farmers Mutual (Raleigh)	2,554,156.00	60,618.95	2,554,156.00	60,618.95	40,124.64	40,124.64
Farmers Douglas	2,135.50	288.16	2,135.50	288.16		
Farmers [illegible] (Edgecombe)	41,545.00	1,824.66	41,545.00	1,824.66	774.67	774.67
[illegible] unty Farmers Mutual	78,214.00	2,659.34	78,214.00	2,659.34	690.61	690.61
Hard[ware] [illegible] Farmers M[utual]	915,600.00	9,056.75	484,350.00	7,224.28	4,823.50	7,823.50
[illegible] West Mutual	116,848.00	3,208.00	116,848.00	3,208.00	2,781.97	2,781.97
North Carolina Home	14,629,209.45	232,382.09	6,318,905.14	113,847.10	6.40	6.40
North [Carolina] Ste	516,760.00	11,015.15	314,964.00	6,786.60	37,543.37	36,386.16
[illegible]						1,000.00
Piedmont	14,144,493.00	248,975.61	6,798,077.00	133,788.41	29,659.28	35,579.34
Rowan [illegible]	100,000.00	8,960.14	100,000.00	8,960.14	7,005.04	7,005.04
Southern [illegible]	108,000.00	2,032.67	108,000.00	1,845.67	214.14	2,000.00
Southern Stock	8,569,980.00	138,582.24	4,824,946.00	83,530.21	13,230.90	17,115.90
Southern Underwriters	7,861,719.00	127,138.16	4,140,064.00	73,492.81	17,217.07	20,124.07
[illegible] M[utual]	224,975.00	318.25	224,975.00	318.25	576.00	576.00
State M[utual]	530,684.00			9,196.16	2,674.50	1,750.00
Underwriters (Rocky [Mount])	3,816,603.00	69,574.67	2,056,095.00	38,608.19	4,438.56	9,025.42
Underwriters of [illegible]	5,743,285.00	94,706.37	3,480,350.00	62,593.09	17,031.82	17,760.82
Union Cunty F[armers] Mutual	88,240.00	1,112.38	88,240.00	1,112.38	333.79	333.79
Total	91,780,782.95	1,574,409.15	49,508,217.64	920,359.17	250,460.84	276,595.05

TABLE No. VII—NORTH CAROLINA BUSINESS, 1918.

SHOWING RISKS WRITTEN, PREMIUMS RECEIVED, LOSSES PAID, LOSSES INCURRED IN NORTH CAROLINA FOR THE YEAR ENDING DECEMBER 31, 1918, BY FIRE, MARINE AND WIND INSURANCE COMPANIES.

COMPANIES OF OTHER STATES (STOCK).

Name of Company	Fire Business					
	Gross Risks Written	Gross Premiums Received	Net Risks Written	Net Premiums Received	Net Losses Paid	Net Losses Incurred
Ætna	$41,557,824.00	$463,548.24	$27,918,932.00	$383,243.00	$105,644.13	$107,757.56
Agricultural	7,535,600.00	38,137.06	3,411,700.00	25,412.39	11,725.00	13,597.00
[illegible]	2,748,228.00	27,240.82	1,503,191.00	13,636.91	5,259.48	6,183.37
American Alliance	7,499,452.00	77,573.57	1,851,216.00	11,665.33	5,730.93	3,971.93
American Equitable	963,781.00	9,531.93	763,605.00	7,259.30	291.34	299.34
American (Newark)	5,386,159.00	70,868.18	2,813,898.00	44,997.97	19,118.90	22,808.57
American Central (St. Louis)	4,519,410.00	25,920.40	1,503,161.00	6,093.59	4,676.76	5,087.80
American Eagle	9,557,874.00	85,886.15	2,201,768.00	19,509.03	1,379.59	2,966.96
Automobile	13,524,916.00	84,572.04	6,225,556.00	48,750.85	21,719.96	22,129.39
Boston	12,194,656.00	107,251.34	5,559,142.00	58,942.09	15,366.10	18,433.51
Camden	9,219,077.00	42,998.48	5,168,003.00	28,524.89	10,822.17	13,221.79
Citizens of Missouri	2,357,629.00	28,827.66	1,848,730.00	22,466.71	4,642.47	3,483.00
Columbian	154,525.00	849.25	107,043.00	649.18.	845.95	824.93
Columbian National	70,879.00	394.99	63,962.00	362.20	------	------
Commercial Union (New York)	1,599,052.00	9,725.09	965,227.00	5,627.82	1,467.17	2,023.17
Commonwealth	2,646,991.00	22,653.26	956,592.00	12,098.34	4,072.60	6,062.14
Concordia	2,282,065.00	33,664.80	1,288,510.00	20,919.02	3,927.62	2,672.62
[...]nd National	334,728.00	1,698.50	151,858.00	835.22	------	------
Connecticut	6,794,601.00	63,711.73	4,104,247.00	42,162.68	7,593.96	6,294.08
Continental	22,480,224.00	181,157.75	11,722,166.00	117,166.13	20,623.87	25,053.47
[illegible]	679,790.00	7,144.95	408,890.00	6,041.18	1,486.90	1,935.73
Eagle	1,262,477.00	7,019.79	116,732.00	1,085.74	3,137.74	1,795.38
Equitable Fire and Marine	2,878,403.00	33,392.49	639,640.00	5,880.85	590.57	590.57
[...]le (South Carolina)	1,597,738.00	28,280.72	1,029,516.00	19,211.54	3,294.60	3,197.31
Federal	16,842,676.00	163,748.94	11,232,154.00	120,156.23	24,532.81	21,041.19
Fidelity-Phenix	------	------	------	------	------	------
First Reinsurance	------	------	------	------	------	------
Fire Association of [Philadel]phia	16,460,511.00	141,135.83	10,482,573.00	92,261.72	32,861.74	36,618.24
Firemen's Fund	21,386,614.00	120,919.46	14,487,128.00	76,745.28	27,937.60	19,365.55

Firemen's of Newark	4,848,720.00	58,655.31	2,755,464.00	39,822.40	1,957.60	7,760.39
Franklin	3,222,292.00	51,740.70	2,922,082.00	47,026.22	6,758.66	10,068.97
Georgia Home	1,901,517.00	25,910.16	919,557.00	14,724.33	1,349.29	1,993.01
Girard Fire and Marine	753,513.00	10,560.55	450,813.00	6,686.39	1,569.80	1,575.81
Glens Falls	7,075,087.00	55,629.39	3,443,146.00	33,078.25	14,861.78	16,363.31
Globe National	123,733.00	330.44	123,733.00	330.44		
Globe and Rutgers	6,250,069.00	103,309.50	4,142,633.00	74,392.78	38,722.42	40,752.31
State	2,853,776.00	41,849.24	1,523,401.00	24,551.86	5,748.30	7,056.48
Great American	33,885,273.00	346,483.34	20,113,261.00	249,024.34	80,953.49	84,438.49
Hanover	4,955,786.00	63,425.20	3,212,159.00	45,801.78	12,008.25	8,134.82
Hartford	34,098,534.00	415,205.32	27,832,733.00	361,694.77	170,763.92	154,354.32
Home Fire and Marine	250,883.00	2,140.97	217,650.00	1,796.90	834.27	836.06
Home of New York	36,836,854.00	320,560.63	32,836,643.00	320,560.63	139,248.02	116,250.01
Home of Utah	1,010,340.00	3,092.21	809,163.00	2,537.96	1,214.64	1,513.64
Imperial Insurance Co. of Gr. Brit.	18,912,601.00	174,702.88	10,454,734.00	107,082.97	39,459.15	46,197.23
Independence	1,883,891.00	21,714.55	1,143,866.00	13,968.55	732.47	4,940.05
International	8,236,616.00	56,718.68	4,814,033.00	38,141.34	39,665.96	35,850.86
Interstate	207,223.00	1,155.54	91,913.00	563.40	1,426.70	989.65
Iowa National	94,694.00	536.55	87,277.00	477.21	100.28	491.73
Massachusetts Fire and Marine	1,757,498.00	21,675.12	1,016,049.00	13,345.43	7,381.19	7,481.76
Marquette National	124,884.00	1,298.04	106,198.00	1,098.61		1,125.00
Mechanics	747,655.00	11,157.96	424,706.00	6,421.16	.65	1,360.65
Mechanics and Traders	4,494,126.00	36,862.59	2,460,965.00	18,663.48	10,177.93	4,491.16
Mercantile Insurance Company of America						
Merchants National	154,525.00	849.25	107,043.00	649.18	845.95	828.07
Milwaukee Mechanics	1,791,386.00	30,197.65	1,319,664.00	24,769.19	7,088.90	11,429.90
National	27,903,594.00	118,478.97	14,321,689.00	118,478.97	42,765.74	32,737.44
National Liberty	4,930,242.00	78,822.45	2,750,943.00	50,347.46	19,605.96	18,843.70
National Union	3,058,648.00	35,249.21	1,750,799.00	16,521.14	6,806.39	7,867.14
Newark	3,535,681.00	35,512.49	1,868,727.00	19,433.90	7,215.80	6,372.46
New Hampshire	17,424,959.00	81,858.90	12,484,782.00	56,703.79	24,930.29	23,568.78
Niagara	7,533,848.00	71,017.12	4,407,499.00	48,675.47	17,040.96	14,424.06
North River	3,536,016.00	43,459.21	2,113,290.00	31,691.40	10,388.64	13,113.64
North Branch	183,198.00	1,045.09	101,753.00	666.86	1,005.14	1,056.08
Northwestern National	1,540,312.00	24,615.27	996,053.00	17,418.62	4,162.64	3,704.47
Northwestern Fire and Marine						
Old Colony	2,938,411.00	37,088.77	1,868,788.00	21,635.52	4,342.52	6,046.62
Orient	7,660,437.00	37,305.28	4,246,423.00	23,539.28	9,312.59	10,940.46
Palmetto	707,542.00	9,443.22	557,659.00	7,276.77	82.78	1,084.28
Pennsylvania	8,538,357.00	52,958.36	3,353,995.00	33,236.26	16,545.97	14,983.09
Peoples National	261,418.00	3,350.47	220,866.00	2,982.10	317.44	1,379.00
Petersburg	1,289,372.00	24,429.47	929,492.00	18,868.29	2,138.14	4,029.05
Phœnix (Hartford)	24,412,511.00	146,688.31	12,915,943.00	89,611.51	23,209.24	18,826.47

TABLE No. VII—NORTH CAROLINA BUSINESS, 1918.

SHOWING [RIS]KS WRITTEN, P[RE]MI[U]MS RECEIVED, LOSSES PAID, LOSSES INCURRED IN NORTH CAROLINA FOR THE YEAR ENDING D[ECEMB]ER 31, 1918, BY FIRE, MARINE AND INLAND INSURANCE COMPANIES.

COMPANIES OF OTHER STATES (STOCK)—Continued.

[Na]me of Company	Fire Business					
	Gross Risks Written	Gross Premiums Received	Net Risks Written	Net Premiums Received	Net Losses Paid	Net Losses Incurred
Providence-Washington	$ 11,772,634.00	$ 67,636.64	$ 4,961,594.00	$ 43,312.17	$ 17,853.34	$ 14,145.01
[Qu]een of [Ameri]ca	10,676,603.00	78,378.00	5,946,736.00	51,379.28	20,477.72	15,043.72
Rhode Island	5,367,436.00	60,345.09	2,778,856.00	35,632.53	12,377.89	13,819.24
St. Paul Fire and Marine	10,543,425.00	66,991.88	9,347,534.00	49,053.52	13,446.92	18,358.32
Security	8,379,786.00	36,452.29	2,973,870.00	23,388.12	6,099.24	7,729.67
South Carolina						
Springfield Fire and Marine	9,287,636.00	104,934.68	4,936,575.00	66,260.33	53,834.14	41,607.88
Standard	6,012,209.00	33,446.11	2,900,017.00	19,218.13	1,365.65	1,919.87
Star of America	3,500.00	40.36	3,500.00			
Sterling						
United States	1,470,089.00	10,761.73	608,255.00	5,410.59	6,441.13	2,730.64
Virginia Fire and [Mar]ine	6,169,938.00	119,737.56	4,459,359.00	92,846.90	18,518.78	21,053.47
Westchester	12,499,501.00	84,042.25	6,965,907.00	47,626.11	24,025.21	24,478.74
Totals	588,644,659.00	5,197,684.37	352,644,900.00	3,630,129.68	1,285,929.84	1,253,561.58

COMPANIES OF OTHER STATES (MUTUAL).

[Na]me of Company	Gross Risks Written	Gross Premiums Received	Net Risks Written	Net Premiums Received	Net Losses Paid	Net Losses Incurred
Arkwright Mutual	2,134,564.00	18,416.11	2,066,264.00	11,556.97	72.21	14.15
Baltimore Mutual	526,924.00	4,626.06	454,885.00	1,451.79	234.29	234.29
Blackstone Mutual	907,439.00	7,673.52	857,239.00	5,495.13	43.75	9.55
Consolidated Underwriters				62,804.19	48,601.02	
Cotton and Woolen Manufacturers	2,919,956.00	62,804.19	2,617,176.00	2,700.17	239.62	239.62
Druggists Indemnity Exchange	306,526.00	3,102.47	250,226.00	1,467.04		
Firemen's Mutual	1,621,941.00	13,563.15	1,490,017.00	13,212.95	64.58	4.50
Fitchburg Mutual	354,566.00	7,860.63	304,472.00	7,331.18	2,163.38	2,163.38
Hope Mutual	2,174,275.00	20,808.87	1,915,551.00	19,600.39	240.63	241.98
Indiana Lumbermen's Mutual	908,725.00	28,729.02	815,025.00	17,928.19	4,005.76	4,005.76
Individual Underwriters	306,225.00	3,206.49	301,725.00	1,714.48		

Industrial Mutual	237.34	237.34	1,581.50	1,567,016.00	17,460.20	1,774,612.00
Keystone Mutual	146.53	146.53	2,845.14	1,321,157.00	22,095.18	1,741,197.00
Lumber Manufacturers Interinsurance	775.59	775.59	6,848.12	150,750.00	11,017.33	398,500.00
Lumber Mutual	4,897.62	4,894.38	25,627.41	1,141,546.60	42,216.97	1,330,989.60
Lumbermen's Mutual	2,553.06	2,549.82	28,549.48	901,762.00	30,564.91	1,066,129.00
Lumbermen's Underwriters Alliance	761.27	761.27	23,418.73	1,173,928.34	31,118.80	1,381,478.34
Manton Mutual	146.52	146.52	2,871.03	1,328,557.00	22,142.53	1,722,996.00
...ing Lumbermen's Underwriters	27,077.38	27,077.38	33,047.27	1,962,384.95	51,156.43	2,310,822.95
Manufacturing Woodworkers Underwriters	243.60	243.60	8,916.71	322,000.00	13,691.81	450,500.00
Merchants Mutual	5.53	27.22	2,934.13	466,729.00	4,215.52	495,729.00
Mercantile Mutual	257.50	257.50	5,488.00	1,594,646.00	15,597.79	1,784,470.00
Middlesex Mutual	13.18	13.18	6,522.36	516,791.00	8,378.79	659,028.00
Michigan Mrs Mutual	2,211.72	2,173.24	5,294.24	1,066,556.00	6,995.14	1,450,308.00
Mrs Mutual	7,000.00	7,000.00	20,223.50	91,500.00	24,183.50	111,500.00
Millers Indemnity Underwriters	4,014.42	3,056.41	13,853.69		15,405.29	
Naragansett Mutual	90.20	90.20	2,532.35	9,354.18	8,688.17	1,029,090.00
National Mutual	58.62	58.62	1,057.78	484,423.00	8,502.02	669,552.00
National ...her Manufacturers		109.48	8,752.60	399,150.00	9,466.45	439,150.00
Penn Lumbermen's Mutual	6,779.57	6,779.57	35,794.73	1,158,310.00	38,158.22	1,235,160.00
Philadelphia Manufacturers Mutual	223.20	223.20	7,726.15	1,833,561.00	21,102.18	2,212,597.00
Reciprocal Exchange	2,379.35	2,407.26	7,642.74	596,250.00	11,911.13	725,300.00
Rubber ... Mrs Mutual	239.62	239.62	2,599.69	2,517,149.00	27,713.09	2,833,429.00
Southern Lumber Underwriters		382.32	7,374.99	326,160.00	10,400.70	475,750.00
Utilities Indemnity Exchange		15.00	729.10		967.29	
Western Reciprocal Underwriters	2,112.48	2,112.48	3,979.93	281,260.00	9,163.37	374,810.00
...ber Mutual	241.98	240.63	19,985.45	1,977,133.00	21,078.59	2,222,057.00
Mrs ...rs (Grocers' Dept.)	7,500.00	7,500.00	5,674.01	489,200.00	8,273.60	542,700.00
Totals	76,879.51	125,183.60	437,133.31	34,750,194.07	789,687.20	41,598,995.89

COMPANIES OF FOREIGN COUNTRIES.

Al ...lle	4,588.23	4,393.97	10,500.94	919,720.00	12,210.42	1,162,505.00
...las	18,159.06	16,783.54	37,241.47	5,257,854.00	62,158.81	10,996,947.00
British America	18,568.63	20,855.09	33,473.89	2,223,352.00	45,165.61	3,273,630.00
Caledonian	5,717.11	5,110.23	7,963.56	586,708.00	11,913.32	1,032,320.00
Century	9,914.21	5,239.27	17,971.00	1,204,965.00	26,284.30	1,991,707.00
Christiania General	11,458.00	7,831.99	25,869.26	4,844,519.00	28,159.05	5,354,199.00
...al Union Assurance	28,208.96	26,646.93	60,660.81	4,724,462.00	96,179.25	9,482,945.00
Eagle Star and British Dominion						
Fire Reassurance	17,278.79	17,970.79	21,593.32	1,797,656.00	36,085.10	4,168,137.00
First Russian	37,580.59	21,339.59	38,060.27	4,321,105.00	45,435.64	5,735,364.00

TABLE No. VII—NORTH CAROLINA BUSINESS, 1918.

SHOWING RISKS WRITTEN, PREMIUMS RECEIVED, LOSSES PAID, LOSSES INCURRED IN NORTH CAROLINA FOR THE YEAR ENDING D██ ██ER 31, 1918, BY FIRE, MARINE AND INLAND INSURANCE COMPANIES.

COMPANIES OF FOREIGN COUNTRIES—Continued.

Name of ██ ██y	Gross Risks Written	Gross Premiums Received	Net Risks Written	Net Premiums Received	Net Losses Paid	Net Losses Incurred
Jakor	$ 11,187,936.00	$ 68,957.65	$ 3,967,948.00	$ 28,130.84	$ 32,817.25	$ 30,147.87
██ol and London and Globe	35,326,996.00	390,667.39	18,085,579.00	246,816.47	92,264.45	130,110.45
London Assurance	5,333,069.00	89,142.54	3,515,955.00	64,986.95	12,866.50	10,852.92
London and Lancashire	11,054,636.00	61,292.25	6,256,455.00	42,871.15	20,180.30	15,648.63
██w	6,471,071.00	54,787.38	4,900,363.00	47,154.42	25,096.96	49,968.96
National (Denmark)	2,445,372.00	18,908.39	1,804,776.00	15,226.60	11,756.77	11,494.02
Nationale (Paris)	4,375,200.00	43,167.26	1,379,575.00	15,751.44	6,590.97	6,882.37
Netherlands Fire and Life	522,997.00	8,557.15	185,232.00	3,461.19	3,512.28	3,522.21
Norske Lloyd	4,591,772.00	34,538.32	3,757,888.00	28,047.62	11,049.38	22,508.20
██th ██sh ██rd Mercantile	19,062,528.00	86,875.74	10,215,167.00	47,436.32	23,869.10	32,464.49
Northern Assurance	15,200,398.00	105,614.82	7,192,147.00	59,897.43	32,420.72	30,821.67
Northern (Moscow)	1,965,708.00	14,136.59	1,021,845.00	8,238.80	6,961.00	9,262.40
██n Assurance	3,021,030.00	18,497.24	1,941,369.00	13,506.06	5,867.72	7,947.41
██h Union	10,334,436.00	46,799.58	4,711,861.00	26,313.71	9,632.03	9,071.18
Paternelle	2,123,954.00	16,778.29	1,613,407.00	13,445.92	6,398.83	4,072.83
██hix Fire	2,717,385.00	29,846.60	1,379,575.00	15,751.44	6,590.97	6,882.37
Palatine (London)	7,129,356.63	31,984.86	3,631,349.41	18,596.26	3,293.26	8,505.26
Phoenix (London)	13,832,462.00	62,911.64	4,372,115.00	27,389.28	10,269.50	9,919.04
Prudentia G. and Reinsurance	18,173.27	8,510.63	17,707.02	8,268.17	3,267.43	4,036.09
Rossia	13,999,583.00	148,610.29	10,244,473.00	115,603.09	69,813.72	66,471.72
Royal	16,641,581.00	120,621.28	9,667,158.00	87,210.15	36,226.85	18,492.46
Royal Exchange Assurance	8,532,946.00	47,498.62	4,128,418.00	28,171.78	8,711.89	10,594.89
Russian Reinsurance	4,268,616.00	35,523.01	3,135,424.00	30,345.67	17,211.73	34,363.73
Salamandra	13,493,640.00	83,389.31	4,532,100.00	32,230.53	32,149.07	29,822.78
Scottish Union and National	11,160,221.00	61,800.57	4,588,418.00	33,956.39	18,260.52	17,116.02
Second Russian	2,527,100.00	15,451.44	1,677,897.00	11,807.95	12,379.76	11,385.10
Sca██dia						
Scandinavia	6,737,108.00	46,604.97	5,255,399.00	38,531.48	26,178.71	25,731.77
Sun Insurance Office	8,786,071.00	90,893.16	2,748,685.00	49,052.04	21,370.91	23,090.97
Svea Fire and Life	2,964,247.00	34,330.54	1,593,570.00	19,381.25	8,237.38	10,310.44

RECAPITULATION.

North Carolina Companies	91,780,782.95	1,574,409.15	49,508,217.64	920,359.17	250,460.84	276,595.06
Companies of other States (stock)	588,644,659.00	5,197,684.37	352,644,900.00	3,630,129.68	1,285,929.84	1,253,561.58
Companies of other States (mutual)	41,598,995.89	789,687.20	34,750,194.07	437,133.31	125,183.60	76,879.51
Companies of other countries	324,016,011.90	2,527,832.88	177,976,535.43	1,641,935.73	796,052.79	896,084.00
Grand totals	1,046,040,449.74	10,089,613.60	614,879,847.14	6,629,557.89	2,457,627.07	2,503,120.15

STATISTICAL TABLES

RELATING TO LIFE INSURANCE COMPANIES

SHOWING THE INCOME OF LIFE INSURANCE COMPANIES (LICENSED

Name of Company	Premiums
Ætna Life	$ 19,109,507
Atlantic Life	1,490,922
American Central	1,331,149
American National	2,701,417
Business Men's Mutual	77,706
Columbian National	2,792,434
Connecticut Mutual	9,120,645
Durham Life	442,203
Equitable Life	67,473,860
Federal Life	800,810
Fidelity Mutual	5,566,876
Gate City Life and Health	217,768
George Washington Life	382,890
Guardian Life	6,901,887
Home Life of New York	5,224,037
Home Security	121,127
Imperial Mutual Life and Health	258,118
Jefferson Standard	2,775,457
LaFayette Mutual Life	45,012
Life Insurance Company of Virginia	4,890,432
Life and Casualty	2,048,163
Manhattan Life	1,669,511
Maryland Life	463,444
Maryland Assurance	18,351
Massachusetts Mutual	16,078,456
Metropolitan	154,564,347
Michigan Mutual	1,760,495.
Missouri State	5,757,817.
Morris Plan Life	69,234.
Mutual Benefit Life	34,673,985.
Mutual Life	67,146,992.
National Life of America	3,133,386.
National Life of Vermont	8,245,266.
New England Mutual	13,387,305.
New York Life	110,154,139.
North Carolina Mutual and Provident	800,393.
Northwestern Mutual Life	57,261,501.
Pacific Mutual	7,469,920.
Pan-American Life	1,723,343.
Penn Mutual	29,083,897.
Philadelphia Life	1,249,368.
Phœnix Mutual Life	7,788,506.
Provident Life and Trust	14,864,259.
Prudential of America	124,459,656.
Reliance Life	3,315,781.
Reserve Loan	1,146,916.
Security Mutual	1,929,791.
Southern Life and Trust	909,080.
Standard Life (Atlanta)	339,327.
State Life	3,255,120.
State Mutual of Massachusetts	8,294,550.
Travelers Life	19,666,973.
Union Central Life	19,402,817.
Union Mutual Life and Health	1,280.
United Life and Accident	312,180.
Volunteer State Life	911,564.
Totals	855,081,400.

INCOME.

Interest and Rents	All Other Sources	Total Income	Income Over Disbursements	Disbursements Over Income
$ 6,158,118.44	$ 723,380.92	$ 25,991,006.45	$ 4,877,802.61	$...............
267,088.96	23,454.39	1,781,466.25	610,716.18	....
359,883.56	19,886.67	1,710,919.55	230,358.79	....
324,743.90	633,680.63	3,659,841.59	706,443.36	....
10.75	7,550.00	85,267.39	1,465.28	....
713,173.06	410,964.09	3,916,572.00	1,266,475.54	....
3,891,925.05	649,250.45	13,661,821.31	2,522,981.83	....
6,551.32	15,789.73	464,544.87	21,775.80	....
26,261,834.24	26,076,840.26	119,812,535.42	34,316,155.63	....
248,597.74	66,422.31	1,115,830.86	165,760.40	....
1,867,488.28	1,072,247.43	8,506,611.74	392,135.58	....
4,335.50	7,601.00	229,705.23	....	17,511.26
93,880.00	216,750.75	693,521.12	372,352.41	....
2,744,979.09	463,556.39	10,110,423.31	1,011,935.59	....
1,699,589.21	191,636.75	7,115,263.67	1,617,042.44	....
2,950.34	....	124,077.84	....	15,011.44
1,810.00	8,193.50	268,122.25	....	967.07
508,353.38	34,092.61	3,317,903.49	1,192,934.00	....
2,830.54	23,468.44	71,311.08	28,197.59	....
964,288.04	400,675.84	6,255,396.53	1,761,233.96	....
37,265.88	64,677.77	2,150,107.30	72,653.10	....
1,089,393.23	128,651.83	2,887,556.19	182,434.72	....
189,204.23	22,392.64	675,041.39	97,222.29	....
52,339.24	2,120,014.56	2,190,705.26	615,811.38	....
4,938,749.65	5,443,195.92	26,460,401.58	11,472,741.35	....
35,204,486.35	10,449,929.83	200,218,763.48	68,342,078.31	....
666,067.43	19,887.15	2,446,450.53	400,217.14	....
1,076,182.45	773,941.83	7,607,941.55	2,364,113.76	....
6,963.95	66.80	76,265.57	12,350.83	....
10,813,384.97	16,024,103.34	61,511,474.14	30,156,139.37	....
29,935,965.92	26,814,736.60	123,897,694.70	38,581,836.71	....
765,987.68	571,622.51	4,470,996.74	1,264,231.86	....
3,421,605.30	137,776.58	11,804,648.87	2,087,112.36	....
3,886,735.60	386,947.59	17,660,988.53	4,971,809.17	....
41,500,876.98	27,231,363.26	178,886,379.40	56,186,172.40	....
16,920.85	2,456.61	819,771.09	86,956.79	....
19,344,961.06	1,422,043.61	78,028,516.05	20,239,247.81	....
2,308,985.76	171,623.54	9,950,529.69	3,178,093.54	....
331,601.71	189,285.72	2,244,231.06	280,009.00	....
9,099,507.34	13,610,705.59	51,794,110.25	20,775,380.76	....
334,945.99	357,777.86	1,942,092.84	624,600.51	....
2,435,137.47	598,660.19	10,822,304.15	2,922,759.41	....
4,650,682.14	323,255.62	19,838,197.73	4,984,693.78	....
23,390,148.28	43,147,319.05	190,997,123.91	79,274,870.61	....
368,367.62	219,579.31	3,903,728.09	1,165,435.00	....
190,402.72	33,048.22	1,370,367.75	8,537.64	....
434,545.43	19,792.96	2,384,129.78	614,158.96	....
117,765.93	2,819.42	1,029,665.60	238,091.74	....
17,748.82	25,045.80	382,122.39	120,170.47	....
1,098,642.47	52,369.15	4,406,132.58	1,425,554.68	....
2,672,535.51	342,706.39	11,309,792.74	3,366,377.88	....
4,848,210.95	830,685.26	25,345,869.42	8,501,356.27	....
7,584,861.88	1,075,115.17	28,062,795.01	6,505,316.36	....
1,795.18	....	3,075.40	1,191.28	....
70,250.20	31,088.19	413,518.96	122,442.72	....
239,544.50	32,085.47	1,183,194.81	463,524.09	....
259,265,202.07	183,722,213.55	1,298,068,816.48	422,801,461.04	33,489.77

SHOWING THE DISBURSEMENTS OF LIFE INSURANCE COMPANIES (LICENSED TO

Name of Company	Death and Endowment Claims	Annuities Surrender Values, Dividends, etc., Paid to Policy-holders	Total Paid to Policy-holders
Ætna Life	$11,602,707.56	$ 4,055,377.84	$ 15,658,085.40
Atlantic Life	369,651.97	203,431.81	573,083.78
American Central	618,092.89	336,273.74	954,366.63
American National	922,027.83	113,286.01	1,035,313.84
Business Men's Mutual	33,602.56		33,602.56
Columbian National	925,544.12	339,250.99	1,264,795.11
Connecticut Mutual	5,816,910.94	2,833,267.06	8,650,178.00
Durham Life	218,267.88		218,267.88
Equitable Life	38,652,522.46	26,759,967.72	65,412,490.18
Federal Life	308,808.58	223,153.24	531,961.82
Fidelity Mutual	2,515,617.02	1,758,388.71	4,274,005.73
Gate City Life and Health	96,835.28		96,835.28
George Washington Life	104,811.85	49,147.74	153,959.59
Guardian Life	4,131,242.71	2,267,798.42	6,399,041.13
Home Life of New York	2,473,316.54	1,635,005.83	4,108,322.37
Home Security	63,356.00		63,356.00
Imperial Mutual Life and Health	114,588.27		114,588.27
Jefferson Standard	743,698.37	240,267.28	983,965.65
LaFayette Mutual Life	11,046.23	660.73	11,706.96
Life Insurance Company of Virginia	2,232,902.52	143,316.23	2,376,218.75
Life and Casualty	818,671.13	2,792.13	821,463.26
Manhattan Life	1,497,100.62	755,421.59	2,252,522.21
Maryland Life	278,165.47	136,248.59	414,414.06
Maryland Assurance	1,000.00		1,000.00
Massachusetts Mutual	6,263,911.02	4,752,510.27	11,016,421.29
Metropolitan	66,464,661.74	15,926,482.58	82,391,144.32
Michigan Mutual	1,070,549.25	389,813.15	1,460,362.40
Missouri State	1,811,100.95	653,943.39	2,465,044.34
Morris Plan Life	6,200.00		6,200.00
Mutual Benefit Life	14,275,332.68	10,402,120.44	24,677,453.12
Mutual Life	34,323,233.52	35,328,196.29	69,651,429.81
National Life of America	1,449,910.25	614,236.16	2,064,146.41
National Life of Vermont	4,227,850.66	3,584,480.79	7,812,331.45
New England Mutual	6,148,803.36	3,726,720.16	9,875,523.52
New York Life	50,975,450.59	46,724,405.61	97,699,856.20
North Carolina Mutual and Provident	341,628.32	4,754.79	346,383.11
Northwestern Mutual Life	26,175,389.50	20,820,964.74	46,996,354.24
Pacific Mutual	2,626,000.15	1,662,845.47	4,288,845.62
Pan-American Life	420,983.40	651,232.31	1,072,215.71
Penn Mutual	12,953,424.73	9,103,291.29	22,056,716.02
Philadelphia Life	535,845.57	179,948.22	715,793.79
Phœnix Mutual Life	3,677,451.96	2,122,894.89	5,800,346.85
Provident Life and Trust	7,697,975.56	3,861,290.58	11,559,266.14
Prudential of America	53,331,421.53	17,701,200.88	71,032,622.41
Reliance Life	933,320.64	251,771.47	1,185,092.11
Reserve Loan	286,189.54	696,616.26	982,805.80
Security Mutual	781,247.23	339,846.81	1,121,092.04
Southern Life and Trust	282,248.82	118,054.07	400,302.89
Standard Life (Atlanta)	79,733.47	320.99	80,054.46
State Life	1,065,256.84	895,323.03	1,960,579.87
State Mutual of Massachusetts	3,384,889.47	2,599,658.08	5,984,547.55
Travelers Life	8,651,370.07	1,594,237.70	10,245,607.77
Union Central Life	9,529,074.35	6,309,044.96	15,838,119.31
Union Mutual Life and Health	330.80		330.80
United Life and Accident	110,800.79	14,773.48	125,574.27
Volunteer State Life	272,730.77	85,521.13	358,251.90
Totals	394,704,806.33	232,969,553.65	627,674,359.98

DISBURSEMENTS.

DO BUSINESS IN THIS STATE) FOR THE YEAR ENDING DECEMBER 31, 1918.

Supplementary Contracts, Dividends to Stockholders, etc.	Commissions, Agency Expenses, Medical Examiners' Fees, etc.	Salaries, Rents, Advertising, Printing, etc.	License, Fees and Taxes	Miscellaneous Items	Total Disbursements
$ 740,122.93	$ 2,495,285.27	$ 1,075,852.83	$ 758,077.12	$ 385,780.29	$ 21,113,203.84
9,640.44	388,337.55	97,429.18	45,211.29	57,047.83	1,170,750.07
13,341.47	262,607.11	148,144.14	34,085.46	68,015.95	1,480,560.76
52,436.56	935,463.94	204,289.67	61,878.19	664,016.03	2,953,398.23
------------	39,236.40	7,220.00	630.96	3,112.09	83,802.01
81,788.07	539,740.27	211,687.76	76,500.86	475,584.39	2,650,096.46
375,396.87	1,059,949.05	457,626.72	409,547.08	186,141.76	11,138,839.48
2,000.00	177,716.25	32,608.91	4,033.31	8,142.72	442,769.07
1,353,987.78	8,024,215.33	2,881,247.39	1,741,397.44	6,083,041.67	85,496,379.79
16,392.22	189,183.15	123,053.31	28,313.89	61,166.07	950,070.46
68,030.22	813,011.30	379,666.68	148,254.30	215,779.09	5,898,747.32
27,000.00	84,468.04	24,103.40	6,444.74	8,365.03	247,216.49
11,617.50	93,342.22	45,838.80	7,609.96	8,800.64	321,168.71
82,800.28	1,108,331.57	425,276.87	182,075.89	900,961.98	9,098,487.72
34,783.69	804,394.50	339,032.88	117,578.01	94,109.78	5,498,221.23
------------	61,777.00	9,206.00	806.45	3,943.83	139,089.28
------------	126,955.08	23,102.88	1,599.48	2,843.61	269,089.32
69,586.47	757,626.60	167,047.81	87,047.03	59,695.93	2,124,969.49
------------	13,345.47	2,827.31	203.00	15,030.75	43,113.49
184,011.35	1,300,704.32	407,468.13	120,673.81	105,086.21	4,494,162.57
60,000.00	1,005,909.93	110,194.45	36,843.25	43,043.31	2,077,454.20
19,476.99	175,185.25	212,848.90	156,490.11	253,467.45	3,069,990.91
8,076.90	84,479.85	40,493.73	12,884.70	17,469.86	577,819.10
------------	20,787.30	14,081.70	8,306.51	1,530,718.37	1,574,893.88
561,501.87	2,096,518.25	704,443.00	373,148.58	235,627.24	14,987,660.23
316,473.71	29,635,657.77	8,741,111.16	3,209,435.16	7,582,863.05	131,876,685.17
46,561.46	238,126.55	138,068.60	44,712.92	118,401.46	2,046,233.39
127,047.18	1,340,997.57	323,036.44	164,925.78	822,776.48	5,243,827.79
------------	29,756.78	21,946.23	4,412.60	1,599.13	63,914.74
799,852.71	3,730,599.92	886,037.84	918,902.06	342,489.12	31,355,334.77
657,242.08	8,187,087.64	3,190,993.47	2,061,406.51	1,567,698.48	85,315,857.99
64,671.40	691,356.75	249,417.09	69,866.63	67,306.60	3,206,764.88
55,242.09	1,074,355.96	390,767.60	255,522.77	129,316.64	9,717,536.51
130,177.51	1,727,857.14	508,712.16	322,698.70	124,210.43	12,689,179.46
1,146,257.18	11,946,611.73	3,889,757.63	2,578,177.87	5,439,546.39	122,700,207.00
------------	311,557.10	47,902.93	16,624.48	10,346.68	732,814.30
808,865.22	5,884,082.08	1,571,480.09	1,471,939.68	1,056,546.93	57,789,268.24
100,535.72	1,356,038.66	581,754.87	250,233.04	195,028.24	6,772,436.15
89,847.08	438,119.97	156,829.20	65,119.62	142,090.48	1,964,222.06
512,515.17	3,580,439.21	1,107,060.38	583,402.78	3,178,595.93	31,018,729.49
36,273.28	213,096.09	134,861.14	38,954.34	178,513.69	1,317,492.33
147,458.33	1,125,950.57	376,649.90	254,561.72	194,577.37	7,899,544.74
143,413.00	1,636,232.66	881,759.79	438,788.47	194,043.89	14,853,503.95
1,154,664.70	26,310,953.64	6,404,654.91	2,748,706.77	4,070,650.87	111,722,253.30
83,673.46	1,009,434.92	163,106.54	93,701.23	203,284.83	2,738,293.09
11,348.43	216,943.07	109,315.00	26,933.79	14,482.02	1,361,828.11
9,821.51	362,549.26	165,685.46	55,974.64	54,847.91	1,769,970.82
36,544.33	231,387.43	108,622.21	14,841.64	9,875.36	791,573.86
7,500.00	117,458.02	37,132.53	8,733.54	12,073.37	262,951.92
122,199.60	626,533.95	227,200.05	82,141.73	61,922.70	2,980,577.90
192,370.11	1,088,314.40	326,303.33	228,947.59	122,931.88	7,943,414.86
690,810.16	3,369,810.78	1,153,628.19	798,285.47	586,370.78	16,844,513.15
344,657.06	2,475,900.00	975,683.15	1,127,669.58	795,449.55	21,557,478.65
------------	281.50	628.30	568.52	75.00	1,884.12
250.00	73,020.14	50,045.37	14,089.90	28,096.56	291,076.24
19,069.33	180,613.08	65,937.30	35,575.46	60,223.65	719,670.72
11,517,333.42	131,869,695.34	41,130,881.31	22,405,496.41	38,853,227.35	873,450,993.81

SHOWING THE ASSETS OF LIFE INSURANCE COMPANIES (LICENSED T

Name of Company	Value of Real Estate	Mortgage Loans	Collateral Loans	Premi Notes Policy I
Ætna Life	$ 1,113,876.63	$ 58,041,501.59	$12,779,723.16	$ 65,8
Atlantic Life	7,495.93	3,419,491.80	719,847.10	56,7
American Central	502,642.83	3,784,331.32	1,180,270.84	
American National	844,300.00	2,790,930.11	568,898.26	
Business Men's Mutual		2,000.00		
Columbian National	1,030,122.75	2,293,902.09	2,224,106.60	181,7
Connecticut Mutual	2,277,669.93	38,059,418.19	8,991,636.53	97,9
Durham Life	19,554,367.20	110,596,766.00	90,422,075.59	
Equitable Life	20,303.89	54,160.00	897.50	6,6
Federal Life	540,414.03	1,654,269.50	1,246,468.24	20,0
Fidelity Mutual	1,576,663.55	15,066,106.27	6,630,689.16	510,2
Gate City Life and Health		74,740.00		
George Washington Life	95,976.04	860,764.00	385,254.53	36,3
Guardian Life	4,777,279.08	25,579,117.20	7,204,105.47	
Home Life of New York	1,500,000.00	7,003,177.00	5,409,433.84	786,1
Home Security		49,800.00		
Imperial Mutual Life and Health				
Jefferson Standard	239,991.57	5,615,819.61	1,789,499.61	344,9
LaFayette Mutual Life	16,575.49	42,639.33	5,346.65	18,0
Life Insurance Company of Virginia	510,962.50	14,240,237.36	655,382.00	1,4
Life and Casualty	97,300.00	340,775.00		139,0
Manhattan Life	4,682,239.07	5,510,560.91	3,814,669.46	
Maryland Life	232,500.00	185,600.11	501,321.93	14,4
Maryland Assurance				
Massachusetts Mutual	1,142,138.33	39,103,083.95	14,995,678.56	1,426,2
Metropolitan	27,108,516.02	277,937,310.29	48,871,272.83	7,324,6
Michigan Mutual	102,967.95	10,497,016.15	1,788,588.77	56,9
Missouri State	758,635.78	12,352,000.13	2,923,175.04	167,2
Morris Plan Life				
Mutual Benefit Life	2,863,842.98	103,089,721.05	43,904,482.12	
Mutual Life	17,486,999.93	106,410,090.17	87,744,651.91	
National Life of America	64,130.92	6,669,319.24	2,671.419.13	230,3
National Life of Vermont	251,000.00	31,774,807.45	8,368,077.27	2,069,9
New England Mutual	1,908,416.00	16,280,385.61	13,632,458.15	1,053,9
New York Life	13,449,600.00	166,053,804.71	151,724,113.81	4,124,5
N. C. Mutual and Provident	76,650.00	40,025.39	8,280.90	
Northwestern Mutual Life	4,474,084.09	210,450,715.93	58,174,182.32	1,674,7
Pacific Mutual	2,078,758.50	21,768,303.68	9,878,016.15	959,3
Pan-American Life	117,432.10	3,729,811.92	696,381.57	39,5
Penn Mutual	2,251,795.92	76,141,319.52	26,702,507.63	6,890,8
Philadelphia Life	678,822.23	2,346,350.00	1,114,837.46	36,7
Phœnix Mutual Life	710,000.00	27,565,033.34	6,442,432.12	30,8
Provident Life and Trust	909,690.85	26,695,145.73	13,549,270.05	1
Prudential of America	19,548,923.17	131,916,627.20	42,949,980.28	
Reliance Life	194,852.54	1,007,469.98	834,295.27	558,9
Reserve Loan	97,250.00	2,591,505.90	1,035,272.54	15,4
Security Mutual	862,000.00	2,920,875.00	1,610,727.26	45,2
Southern Life and Trust		1,457,863.00	434,426.38	
Standard Life (Atlanta)		81,476.43	18,813.98	
State Life	1,235,811.47	11,193,006.38	4,622,702.22	51,3
State Mutual of Massachusetts	1,738,000.00	18,422,396.00	8,251,371.89	11,1
Travelers Life	4,871,443.15	41,796,884.48	13,906,959.42	
Union Central Life	2,666,460.87	93,744,042.28	18,441,293.31	1,984,7
Union Mutual Life and Health		23,530.33		
United Life and Accident	19,000.00	687,238.57	105,027.32	6
Volunteer State Life	471,062.40	1,306,477.15	746,125.61	10,1
Totals	147,758,965.69	1,741,319,744.35	730,676,447.74	31,042,6

*Minus.

Value of Bonds and Stocks	Cash in Office, Banks, and Deposited with Trust Companies	Accrued Interest and Rents Due	Unpaid and Deferred Premiums	Other Assets Less Deductions	Total Admitted Assets
$ 48,194,152.76	$ 4,012,168.77	$ 2,642,142.70	$ 1,682,529.62	$ 805.17	$ 128,532,419.78
292,651.86	215,957.56	60,371.00	65,537.62	2,537.50	4,840,638.03
396,400.00	139,485.28	105,305.52	105,670.26	258,245.20	6,472,351.25
720,627.03	686,008.75	239,354.29	80,955.25	73,255.24	6,004,328.93
----------	1,797.41	35.00	182.79	----------	4,015.20
8,687,873.37	237,047.33	251,888.17	244,762.83	43,389.29	15,194,862.32
29,416,638.00	560,361.75	1,700,566.81	987,621.16	289,642.21	82,381,485.03
370,753,021.43	4,827,840.10	7,848,654.08	7,361,867.87	449,327.56	611,813,919.83
57,900.00	6,926.39	2,915.34	2,047.28	----------	151,797.46
737,352.00	18,459.53	62,048.71	70,449.14	10,968.39	4,360,517.36
12,101,174.18	484,631.50	478,256.53	466,042.61	*67,342.91	37,246,478.33
7,828.00	2,595.78	1,003.95	28.83	8,433.99	94,630.55
430,762.00	47,643.90	16,396.60	30,265.58	*681.93	1,902,742.84
14,710,026.61	554,752.12	816,663.48	1,587,974.15	460,582.61	55,690,500.72
20,382,330.00	143,300.45	320,571.72	567,336.96	*15,277.44	36,097,016.81
6,000.00	954.49	533.57	997.15	2,473.35	60,758.56
38,500.00	1,804.61	1,005.00	1,810.70	----------	43,120.31
762,110.00	586,472.50	127,976.62	243,766.57	*7,336.57	9,703,224.95
2,600.00	4,592.99	1,653.78	1,311.34	*56.59	92,712.99
1,908,522.00	620,865.11	276,258.76	144,276.39	4,926.32	18,362,862.75
99,570.00	23,745.63	5,772.91	----------	826.70	567,990.24
4,030,594.00	495,055.72	381,108.90	134,220.31	24,728.57	19,212,265.21
2,688,306.50	62,992.20	41,592.51	37,462.61	*2,122.44	3,762,147.69
1,039,495.60	88,541.91	8,794.01	1,546.06	254,990.14	1,393,393.22
50,819,268.58	1,257,414.71	1,858,588.92	2,046,503.74	12,927.09	112,661,852.34
381,461,500.26	1,757,863.42	11,852,432.77	15,218,925.58	3,922,265.95	775,454,698.28
260,834.00	580,028.20	192,804.43	135,713.46	2,760.45	13,617,668.99
1,670,492.55	970,024.19	488,074.50	570,838.01	*4,792.36	19,895,653.58
156,326.00	46,152.67	2,767.94	473.38	----------	205,719.99
89,270,278.40	2,167,202.71	4,538,935.98	3,298,683.44	*6,853.95	249,126,292.73
444,264,898.62	2,252,542.46	8,702,744.11	5,704,087.39	1,148,279.23	673,714,293.82
6,209,991.06	261,116.50	205,388.94	283,716.74	40,551.93	16,635,957.21
25,459,759.94	517,438.52	1,635,402.53	957,916.57	*547.18	71,033,766.19
53,698,362.00	619,841.09	1,155,829.36	817,390.78	----------	89,166,637.66
609,717,288.86	20,290,834.88	15,105,402.62	13,647,771.41	973,886.00	995,087,284.86
288,800.00	1,850.24	6,165.10	54,007.02	917.00	476,695.65
125,706,735.26	2,112,867.53	6,612,921.18	5,029,810.61	601,405.51	414,837,471.74
5,649,042.89	1,196,420.09	735,378.82	706,316.86	3,076.17	42,974,634.00
1,481,667.16	137,659.91	138,164.43	112,853.35	16,103.80	6,469,616.63
83,282,926.41	848,616.63	2,845,653.63	3,877,290.73	22,024.98	202,862,994.87
1,630,106.27	330,896.44	92,328.72	73,354.00	*14,691.16	6,288,728.38
11,798,323.20	868,114.35	858,329.15	608,757.02	----------	48,881,385.13
57,623,875.60	31,340.07	1,383,487.01	1,898,555.59	24,901.33	102,116,387.99
352,477,420.70	7,253,067.19	7,080,195.38	9,811,074.49	425,021.03	571,462,309.44
5,097,302.15	585,403.85	115,024.26	364,712.76	33,010.89	8,790,974.65
199,194.20	146,779.05	98,524.40	68,175.68	*4,263.74	4,247,870.62
3,310,302.25	254,882.55	164,787.20	217,054.17	7,620.48	9,393,453.04
188,173.39	174,836.94	37,245.99	70,189.87	708,169.43	3,070,905.00
258,969.29	45,069.03	5,439.05	77,494.13	*8,528.82	478,781.02
2,358,030.00	499,451.43	228,014.13	191,283.82	*14,904.20	20,364,663.57
26,926,975.75	1,221,174.54	826,893.04	1,097,876.03	2,872.56	58,498,695.81
42,633,249.59	1,126,466.11	1,687,014.47	2,681,145.26	74,081.34	108,777,243.82
4,626,996.00	1,582,646.03	4,265,554.04	852,758.78	----------	128,164,484.46
1,850.00	1,246.68	----------	----------	----------	26,627.01
524,371.00	21,041.67	24,747.89	26,993.63	----------	1,409,117.55
771,099.16	152,527.00	56,601.16	72,924.41	*1,734.38	3,585,279.36
2,907,288,845.88	63,136,818.46	88,391,711.11	84,393,311.79	9,755,813.74	5,803,764,325.75

SHOWING THE LIABILITIES OF LIFE INSURANCE COMPANIES LICENSED TO

Name of Company	Net Reserve	Value Supplementary Contracts and Liability on Canceled Policies	Unpaid Policy Claims	Premiums, Interest and Rents Paid in Advance and Dividends left with Company
Ætna Life	$ 106,760,277.00	$ 1,783,020.14	$ 1,360,471.45	$1,780,052.29
Atlantic Life	3,894,585.01	23,151.23	71,640.92	183,955.15
American Central	5,581,021.78	31,054.64	83,800.21	40,826.22
American National	4,573,819.43	48,461.25	123,744.57	19,269.48
Business Men's Mutual	3,444.00			388.40
Columbian National	12,929,318.00	162,619.00	263,862.14	70,187.55
Connecticut Mutual	72,930,157.14	713,888.62	587,123.83	2,388,953.95
Durham Life	478,434,050.00	5,452,389.48	8,365,193.07	4,584,582.90
Equitable Life	94,173.00		564.00	17,805.44
Federal Life	3,603,589.00	58,989.06	68,209.87	31,096.65
Fidelity Mutual	30,967,251.00	522,468.86	512,448.95	369,907.04
Gate City Life and Health	32,432.00		702.00	6,331.35
George Washington Life	1,376,861.91	9,072.85	15,028.31	13,868.02
Guardian Life	48,602,072.00	228,014.06	1,009,580.94	205,280.20
Home Life of New York	33,568,403.00	310,372.00	417,668.73	359,729.93
Home Security	8,333.09			1,895.15
Imperial Mutual Life and Health	30,855.00		275.50	1,996.80
Jefferson Standard	7,669,794.27	147,515.22	251,980.48	66,836.05
LaFayette Mutual Life	69,315.00		99.00	453.51
Life Insurance Company of Virginia	15,510,563.00	49,630.00	250,928.41	113,853.78
Life and Casualty	197,138.32		8,766.95	48,981.68
Manhattan Life	18,144,380.00	155,970.87	192,224.93	99,867.09
Maryland Life	3,274,408.89	1,098.68	44,043.11	8,926.48
Maryland Assurance	8,352.82	203.07		
Massachusetts Mutual	95,161,662.00	1,635,555.01	919,995.78	3,294,687.94
Metropolitan Life	720,376,455.00	2,722,039.64	4,162,645.71	2,700,688.40
Michigan Mutual	12,290,106.46	61,458.76	78,219.53	32,102.90
Missouri State	15,876,852.00	199,309.80	490,055.64	196,025.93
Morris Plan Life	9,166.52		4,700.00	14,512.85
Mutual Benefit Life	211,066,452.00	5,256,091.00	1,479,952.71	480,844.52
Mutual Life	536,113,077.00	5,137,785.19	10,827,980.39	2,045,542.66
National Life of America	14,149,123.67	135,351.33	344,146.89	72,417.42
National Life of Vermont	59,492,522.50	464,031.52	370,315.20	66,995.50
New England Mutual	79,802,229.68	1,158,078.84	844,518.13	194,244.02
New York Life	755,699,522.00	7,987,794.75	17,447,200.60	7,466,370.04
N. C. Mutual and Provident	386,243.00		2,405.30	2,421.08
Northwestern Mutual Life	366,258,457.00	7,441,342.41	3,490,783.41	299,975.96
Pacific Mutual	37,319,594.00	431,516.00	516,218.14	390,052.85
Pan-American Life	4,353,437.80	49,665.47	129,013.25	15,138.86
Penn Mutual	161,710,461.00	4,860,981.19	2,215,285.38	879,249.89
Philadelphia Life	5,041,500.67	25,799.40	73,702.00	96,012.23
Phœnix Mutual Life	43,310,152.60	472,729.79	405,848.26	1,480,289.50
Provident Life and Trust	91,701,527.00	1,135,259.99	628,557.32	640,991.20
Prudential of America	468,042,561.00	3,931,850.08	6,006,190.65	3,283,375.11
Reliance Life	7,231,352.00	72,349.22	92,310.47	44,036.72
Reserve Loan	3,631,803.12	14,245.81	71,570.41	43,569.01
Security Mutual	8,759,356.00	60,077.35	180,285.16	65,757.65
Southern Life and Trust	2,185,532.36	13,012.73	60,947.00	6,982.97
Standard Life (Atlanta)	291,033.88	1,782.32	6,324.85	285.00
State Life	16,541,724.66	165,145.81	194,086.20	197,783.68
State Mutual of Massachusetts	51,405,121.00	600,521.38	442,876.00	987,618.74
Travelers Life	95,783,743.00	5,697,861.70	1,630,601.72	480,869.58
Union Central Life	105,693,983.00	1,475,847.00	1,033,587.97	256,780.88
Union Mutual Life and Health	437.06			
United Life and Accident	604,280.00	22,954.76	23,375.72	3,016.26
Volunteer State Life	3,044,276.00	46,407.75	85,270.52	22,629.49
Totals	4,821,598,339.64	60,974,765.03	67,887,327.68	36,176,313.95

(1)

LIABILITIES.

Commissions, Salaries, Cost of Collections, Taxes and Unpaid Dividends to Stockholders	Dividends Due and Apportioned to Policy-holders (Including Provisional Assignment for Deferred Dividends)	All Other Liabilities	Capital Stock	Surplus	Total Liabilities
$ 895,785.37	$ 2,368,468.73	$ 974,466.74	$ 5,000,000.00	$ 7,609,878.06	$ 128,532,419.78
11,039.76	163,108.90	1,000.00	300,000.00	192,157.06	4,840,638.03
32,045.21	1,950.28	352,771.50	137,000.00	211,881.41	6,472,351.25
60,040.00	187,637.09	49,499.75	250,000.00	691,857.36	6,004,328.93
114.98	----------	----------	----------	67.82	4,015.20
58,312.22	220,221.56	257,871.66	1,000,000.00	232,470.19	15,194,862.32
408,106.07	158,965.16	1,838,786.30	----------	3,355,503.96	82,381,485.03
1,791,593.64	98,710,153.27	1,449,144.89	100,000.00	12,926,812.58	611,813,919.83
11,500.00	----------	----------	25,000.00	2,755.02	151,797.46
21,874.92	96,967.64	161,782.36	300,000.00	18,007.86	4,360,517.36
1,150,394.32	2,628,073.89	12,743.65	----------	1,083,160.62	37,246,448.33
2,550.31	----------	----------	50,000.00	2,614.89	94,630.55
23,025.00	7,301.03	177,585.72	250,000.00	30,000.00	1,902,742.84
110,796.86	3,928,764.23	51,991.15	200,000.00	1,354,001.28	55,690,500.72
83,600.72	403,946.68	29,674.68	----------	923,621.07	36,097,016.81
168.28	----------	----------	50,000.00	362.04	60,758.56
8,362.10	----------	----------	----------	1,630.91	43,120.31
67,338.45	524,322.36	400,538.12	350,000.00	225,000.00	9,703,324.95
433.55	10,100.00	27.52	----------	12,284.41	92,712.99
433,762.53	258,848.11	9,238.95	800,000.00	936,037.97	18,362,862.75
105,174.78	----------	----------	200,000.00	7,928.51	567,990.24
50,932.52	210,921.51	76,248.09	100,000.00	181,720.20	19,212,265.21
11,191.29	152,385.88	3,918.00	100,000.00	166,175.36	3,762,147.69
2,034.86	----------	865,711.36	500,000.00	17,091.11	1,393,393.22
4,531,876.20	1,796,641.12	3,379.47	----------	5,318,054.82	112,661,852.34
10,458,668.68	5,758,977.72	2,226,309.09	----------	27,048,914.04	775,454,698.28
41,494.02	257,011.62	----------	250,000.00	607,275.70	13,617,668.99
131,944.30	902,144.81	13,445.29	1,000,000.00	1,085,875.81	19,895,653.58
4,364.10	----------	----------	100,000.00	72,976.52	205,719.99
16,088,206.08	8,268,805.56	6,485,940.86	----------	----------	249,126,292.73
27,482,808.29	75,650,622.39	16,456,477.91	----------	----------	673,714,293.83
669,905.45	439,782.35	160,913.32	500,000.00	164,316.88	16,635,957.31
332,856.40	6,291,558.44	133,808.07	----------	3,881,678.56	71,033,766.19
368,410.41	3,041,744.22	150,000.00	----------	3,607,412.36	89,166,637.66
26,417,993.36	135,712,589.39	44,355,814.72	----------	----------	995,087,284.86
10,098.47	----------	----------	----------	75,527.80	476,695.65
1,557,378.86	16,241,997.24	48,760.03	----------	19,498,776.83	414,837,471.74
169,989.43	3,213,576.79	182,935.08	1,000,000.00	2,208,813.32	45,432,695.61
46,894.01	79,496.60	356,728.18	1,000,000.00	439,242.46	6,469,616.63
10,923,675.71	18,348,534.46	3,924,807.24	----------	----------	202,862,994.87
244,536.61	64,713.54	----------	560,320.00	182,143.93	6,288,728.38
144,050.76	1,461,395.74	1,606,918.48	----------	----------	48,881,385.13
522,449.82	2,637,262.13	253,000.00	2,000,000.00	2,597,340.53	102,116,387.99
43,714,442.35	32,017,028.29	1,042,577.50	2,000,000.00	11,424,284.46	571,462,309.44
43,965.06	146,712.81	82,241.20	1,000,000.00	78,007.17	8,790,974.65
35,205.17	9,245.79	181,768.05	100,000.00	160,481.26	4,247,888.62
68,764.19	89,619.48	8,671.31	----------	160,921.90	9,393,453.04
22,273.45	72,251.77	202,365.87	400,000.00	107,538.85	3,070,905.00
11,003.95	----------	25,045.80	125,000.00	18,305.22	478,781.02
129,865.35	361,469.35	160,467.75	----------	2,614,120.77	20,364,663.57
183,044.02	2,019,773.93	73,198.36	----------	2,786,542.38	58,498,695.81
669,017.78	493,944.73	29,192,853.35	6,000,000.00	8,619,548.33	148,568,440.19
651,302.43	11,051,048.57	2,059,292.51	2,000,000.00	3,942,642.10	128,164,484.46
----------	----------	----------	25,000.00	1,189.95	26,627.01
4,395.07	66.00	868.47	500,000.00	250,161.27	1,409,117.55
14,460.46	54,656.70	47,805.79	200,000.00	69,772.65	3,585,279.36
151,035,517.98	436,514,807.86	116,149,394.14	28,472,320.00	127,204,885.56	5,846,013,671.84

(ji)

EXHIBIT OF POLICIES OF LIFE INSURANCE COMPANIES (LICENSED TO DO

Name of Company	Policies in Force at Beginning of Year		Policies Issued, Revived, and Increased During Year	
	Number	Amount	Number	Amount
Ætna Life	214,814	$ 572,916,282.45	23,630	$218,251,456.34
Atlantic Life	19,967	36,513,647.00	4,888	10,863,411.00
American Central	21,635	46,855,818.00	5,211	15,134,046.00
American National	19,333	26,462,988.00	6,699	8,715,522.00
Business Men's Mutual	5,921	254,309.00	6,004	235,888.00
Columbian National	32,514	82,059,851.25	5,733	17,907,312.00
Connecticut Mutual	113,935	270,243,227.37	1,133	32,003,096.34
Durham Life	79,303	4,784,035.00	59,555	3,161,539.00
Equitable Life	665,414	1,754,868,908.00	75,826	350,460,925.00
Federal Life	13,269	25,101,635.00	2,310	5,710,011.00
Fidelity Mutual	67,017	142,022,569.00	6,339	19,566,470.00
Gate City Life and Health	30,241	1,146,328.00	32,821	1,579,709.00
George Washington Life	5,399	10,356,491.00	1,594	2,634,114.00
Guardian Life				
Home Life of New York	69,526	146,050,145.00	8,445	24,510,677.00
Home Security	18,309	1,013,779.00	22,614	1,116,317.50
Imperial Mutual Life and Health				
Jefferson Standard	37,349	62,414,222.00	12,054	26,734,268.00
LaFayette Mutual Life	1,178	741,719.00	234	208,304.00
Life Insurance Company of Virginia	27,950	32,171,826.00	5,361	7,906,023.00
Life and Casualty	203,999	8,989,974.00	366,360	18,622,037.00
Manhattan Life	31,410	57,467,120.00	1,689	4,388,160.00
Maryland Life	8,680	13,834,731.00	1,177	1,795,128.00
Maryland Assurance			207	1,073,943.00
Massachusetts Mutual	195,679	450,212,181.00	18,843	64,588,393.00
Metropolitan Life (Ordinary)	1,782,223	1,773,207,811.00	381,405	463,008,744.00
Metropolitan Life (Industrial)	16,480,710	2,162,974,087.00	2,858,599	419,331,865.00
Michigan Mutual	38,660	60,129,374.04	3,847	8,650,627.80
Missouri State	86,762	156,948,542.11	18,418	41,370,082.15
Morris Plan Life	1,428	167,800.00	20,817	2,988,925.00
Mutual Benefit Life	365,249	915,297,422.00	33,127	113,197,286.00
Mutual Life	783,899	1,773,411,526.00	66,655	208,920,389.00
National Life of America	56,990	97,179,897.00	7,315	16,042,186.00
National Life of Vermont	110,447	223,593,866.00	9,330	26,104,481.00
New England Mutual	153,538	375,494,658.00	13,971	47,352,794.00
New York Life	1,301,969	2,673,334,336.00	147,741	356,993,266.00
N. C. Mutual and Provident (Ordinary)	5,273	2,891,112.00	4,917	3,681,226.00
N. C. Mutual and Provident (Industrial)	111,043	8,265,860.00	63,108	5,432,832.00
Northwestern Mutual Life	604,580	1,604,426,324.00	40,131	151,346,127.00
Pacific Mutual	95,192	185,958,459.00	14,716	36,957,884.00
Pan-American Life	21,455	45,803,114.00	5,691	12,847,655.00
Penn Mutual	270,012	757,732,514.00	23,861	95,478,047.00
Philadelphia Life	14,182	35,117,202.00	3,288	8,671,277.00
Phœnix Mutual Life	98,777	197,097,509.00	10,291	29,167,773.00
Provident Life and Trust	151,411	389,073,549.00	16,735	52,564,622.00
Prudential of America	1,174,040	1,418,670,438.00	245,922	337,808,018.00
Reliance Life	46,285	86,563,717.00	12,390	27,344,027.00
Reserve Loan	16,906	29,629,580.00	3,075	6,289,763.00
Security Mutual	36,232	54,616,218.00	5,145	8,153,525.00
Southern Life and Trust	12,338	22,195,563.00	4,210	8,686,321.00
Standard Life (Atlanta)	6,172	5,174,491.00	6,512	6,041,501.00
State Life	41,481	86,536,246.00	6,474	13,674,614.00
State Mutual of Massachusetts	88,354	222,508,273.00	8,920	30,221,387.00
Travelers Life	202,756	617,239,004.00	38,132	214,079,457.00
Union Central Life	225,086	522,340,427.00	21,759	76,602,166.00
Union Mutual Life and Health	116	8,000.00	53	26,500.00
United Life and Accident	5,495	7,762,401.00	1,552	2,501,219.00
Volunteer State Life	14,807	28,812,894.00	3,173	8,032,370.00
Totals	26,286,610	20,286,644,000.00	4,770,007	3,632,735,704.13

No. XII.

Policies Terminated During Year		Policies in Force at End of Year		Increase		Decrease	
Number	Amount	Number	Amount	Number	Amount	Number	Amount
18,463	$117,996,271.25	219,814	$ 673,171,467.54	5,000	$100,255,185.09		$
1,758	3,107,395.00	23,097	44,325,827.00	3,130	7,812,180.00		
3,027	7,958,284.00	23,819	54,031,580.00	2,184	7,175,762.00		
4,040	5,450,123.00	21,992	29,627,387.00	2,659	3,164,399.00		
		11,925	490,197.00	6,004	235,888.00		
2,844	7,771,338.00	35,403	92,195,825.25	2,889	10,139,974.00		
6,891	17,124,890.02	118,077	285,121,433.69	4,142	14,878,206.32		
36,440	1,846,214.00	102,418	6,099,360.00	3,115	1,315,325.00		
45,757	180,791,255.00	695,483	1,924,538,578.00	30,069	169,669,670.00		
2,196	4,803,381.00	13,383	26,008,265.00	114	1,006,630.00		
4,977	12,293,489.00	68,379	149,295,550.00	1,362	7,272,990.00		
24,662	1,008,607.00	38,400	1,717,430.00	8,159	571,102.00		
756	1,293,802.00	6,238	11,701,804.00	839	1,345,313.00		
5,315	11,850,530.00	72,656	158,710,292.00	3,130	12,660,147.00		
16,010	790,445.00	24,913	1,339,651.50	6,604	325,872.50		
		55,667	2,619,161.00				
4,149	7,503,496.00	45,254	81,644,994.00	7,905	19,230,772.00		
		1,412	950,023.00	234	208,304.00		
2,205	2,633,948.00	31,106	37,443,981.00	3,156	5,272,155.00		
246,839	11,510,841.00	246,839	11,510,841.00	42,840	2,520,867.00		
2,328	5,414,247.00	30,771	56,441,033.00			629	1,026,087.00
785	1,237,475.00	9,072	14,392,384.00	392	557,653.00		
2	4,000.00	205	1,069,943.00				
9,154	24,007,193.00	205,368	490,793,291.00	10,289	40,581,110.00		
145,212	152,208,917.00	2,018,416	2,054,007,638.00	236,193	310,799,827.00		
1,573,464	236,801,774.00	17,765,845	2,345,504,178.00	1,285,135	182,530,091.00		
3,608	6,202,595.20	38,899	62,577,406.64	239	2,448,032.60		
11,510	21,581,988.26	93,670	176,746,636.00	6,908	19,798,093.89		
4,919	692,250.00	17,326	2,464,475.00	15,898	2,296,675.00		
16,869	41,012,921.00	381,507	987,481,787.00	16,258	72,184,365.00		
48,188	120,449,962.00	802,366	1,861,881,953.00	18,467	88,470,427.00		
6,727	12,641,649.00	57,578	100,580,434.00	588	3,400,537.00		
7,448	16,273,971.00	112,329	233,424,376.00	1,882	9,830,510.00		
7,420	19,237,584.00	160,089	403,609,868.00	6,551	28,115,210.00		
89,277	191,497,800.00	1,360,433	2,838,829,802.00	58,464	165,495,466.00		
1,070	725,625.00	9,119	5,846,713.00	3,847	2,955,601.00		
42,832	3,448,683.00	131,328	10,250,009.00	20,285	1,984,149.00		
28,487	74,835,905.00	616,224	1,680,936,546.00	11,644	76,510,222.00		
6,804	14,268,823.00	103,104	208,647,520.00	7,912	22,689,061.00		
3,628	8,182,862.00	23,518	50,467,907.00	2,063	4,664,793.00		
17,275	50,984,774.00	276,598	802,225,787.00	6,586	44,493,273.00		
1,782	4,570,640.00	15,692	39,217,839.00	1,510	4,100,637.00		
5,995	12,785,317.00	103,073	213,479,965.00	4,296	16,382,456.00		
9,503	28,804,470.00	158,643	412,833,701.00	7,232	23,760,152.00		
89,769	114,268,811.00	1,330,193	1,642,209,645.00	156,153	223,539,207.00		
6,265	11,066,481.00	52,510	102,841,263.00	6,225	16,277,546.00		
3,101	6,054,517.00	16,880	29,864,826.00		235,246.00	26	
3,656	5,501,925.00	37,721	57,267,818.00	1,489	2,651,600.00		
1,558	3,062,358.00	14,990	27,719,526.00	2,652	5,523,963.00		
3,466	3,007,272.00	9,218	8,208,720.00	3,046	3,034,229.00		
3,483	6,891,403.00	44,472	93,319,457.00	2,991	6,783,211.00		
4,403	12,575,527.00	92,871	240,152,133.00	4,517	17,643,860.00		
13,668	77,027,379.00	227,220	754,291,082.00	24,464	137,052,078.00		
15,301	35,513,929.00	231,544	563,428,654.00	6,458	41,088,227.00		
		69	34,500.00	53	26,500.00		
991	1,456,719.00	6,056	8,806,631.00	561	1,044,230.00		
1,920	3,813,551.00	16,060	33,031,713.00	1,253	4,218,819.00		
2,618,197	1,723,845,606.73	28,427,252	22,237,430,807.62	2,066,036	1,948,227,799.40	655	1,026,087.00

Name of Company	By Death	
	Number	Amount
Ætna Life	3,318	$ 9,095,766.!
Atlantic Life	249	455,989.(
American Central	263	616,476.(
American National	217	285,988.(
Business Men's Mutual		
Columbian National	· 418	1,091,235.(
Connecticut Mutual	2,082	5,510,240.
Durham Life		
Equitable Life	9,912	30,495,095.(
Federal Life	154	315,306.(
Fidelity Mutual	1,001	2,492,284.(
Gate City Life and Health		
George Washington Life	71	120,808.(
Guardian Life	1,265	2,708,322.(
Home Life of New York	863	1,793,735.(
Home Security		
Imperial Mutual Life and Health		
Jefferson Standard	423	734,353.(
LaFayette Mutual Life		
Life Insurance Company of Virginia	459	533,932.(
Life and Casualty		
Manhattan Life	539	1,350,080.(
Maryland Life	139	281,703.(
Maryland Assurance	1	1,000.(
Massachusetts Mutual	2,564	6,557,126.(
Metropolitan Life	25,210	23,417,660.
Michigan Mutual	565	829,334.
Missouri State	1,166	2,300,851.
Morris Plan Life		
Mutual Benefit Life	4,545	12,550,243.
Mutual Life	11,742	30,508,011.
National Life of America	830	1,472,677.
National Life of Vermont	1,397	2,956,623.
New England Mutual	2,148	5,869,154.
New York Life	18,394	40,348,878.
North Carolina Mutual and Provident	93	52,075.
Northwestern Mutual Life	7,196	19,854,962.
Pacific Mutual	1,227	2,599,305.
Pan-American Life	236	479,572.
Penn Mutual	3,830	11,879,674.
Philadelphia Life	231	580,802.
Phœnix Mutual Life	1,408	2,827,994.
Provident Life and Trust	1,761	4,679,056.
Prudential of America	15,651	18,498,575.
Reliance Life	470	950,670.
Reserve Loan	210	325,751.
Security Mutual	523	833,480.
Southern Life and Trust	119	287,480.
Standard Life (Atlanta)	64	71,500.
State Life	534	1,113,136.
State Mutual of Massachusetts	1,106	3,040,181.
Travelers Life	2,706	8,593,829.
Union Central Life	2,784	6,483,464.
Union Mutual Life and Health		
United Life and Accident	81	114,599.
Volunteer State Life		
Totals	210,465	267,958,975.

ERMINATED DURING THE YEAR 1918—MODE OF TERMINATION.

By Maturity		By Disability		By Expiry	
Number	Amount	Number	Amount	Number	Amount
2,022	$ 2,963,711.83		$	2,246	$ 1,811,904.00
2	1,500.00			55	107,876.00
3	69,241.00			191	489,378.00
		13	18,500.00	72	51,023.00
8	21,600.00			19	85,670.00
186	421,617.16			154	327,209.11
4,407	11,322,179.00			4,775	19,201,227.00
40	35,400.00			36	165,260.00
203	301,896.00			390	1,117,880.00
				3	8,000.00
1,435	2,087,722.00			304	1,030,862.00
269	710,675.00			167	380,465.00
4	18,700.00	14	32,260.00	161	226,333.00
9	7,500.00	2	3,000.00	191	101,934.00
102	199,495.00			171	405,380.00
24	58,808.00			25	49,291.00
182	392,716.00			361	885,776.00
8,153	5,598,891.00			2,682	2,469,257.00
171	324,032.35			86	132,240.03
24	38,918.00			725	1,213,312.36
969	2,118,016.00			4,687	8,976,998.00
3,401	6,473,421.00			4,261	12,694,793.00
227	220,777.00	2	11,000.00	3,500	6,187,409.00
763	1,375,248.00			745	1,314,575.00
395	760,563.00			396	977,133.00
10,513	17,536,338.00		31,136.00	10,005	26,797,594.00
3,508	8,244,555.00			4,105	11,288,672.00
236	343,549.00	6	19,786.00	1,768	3,268,867.00
2	3,500.00			142	273,018.00
1,202	2,548,287.00			2,356	6,517,331.00
2	2,095.00			51	78,070.00
675	1,147,592.00			1,103	1,807,262.00
1,311	3,192,123.00			15	46,384.00
2,438	2,517,885.00	146	239,365.00	32,622	37,890,445.00
1	5,000.00			341	775,739.00
2	2,000.00			151	264,000.00
31	44,099.00			146	255,484.00
2	5,000.00			11	30,500.00
7	16,102.00			246	394,080.00
318	687,864.00			167	430,905.00
582	1,285,299.00	9	25,300.00	950	2,811,715.00
1,640	2,581,905.00			1,823	3,699,409.00
				1	2,000.00
45,469	75,685,820.34	192	380,347.00	82,406	157,042,660.50

SHOWING POLICIES OF LIFE INSURANCE COMPANIES

Name of Company	By Surrender	
	Number	Amount
Ætna Life	4,948	$ 11,688,534.66
Atlantic Life	207	491,137.00
American Central	360	767,009.00
American National	252	430,662.00
Business Men's Mutual		
Columbian National	377	1,002,601.00
Connecticut Mutual	1,852	5,095,923.58
Durham Life		
Equitable Life	9,621	26,799,419.00
Federal Life	98	213,110.00
Fidelity Mutual	1,220	2,739,197.00
Gate City Life and Health		
George Washington Life	150	280,180.00
Guardian Life	1,504	2,788,214.00
Home Life of New York	1,583	3,365,718.00
Home Security		
Imperial Mutual Life and Health		
Jefferson Standard	317	524,848.00
LaFayette Mutual Life		
Life Insurance Company of Virginia	490	541,533.00
Life and Casualty		
Manhattan Life	804	1,704,893.00
Maryland Life	83	132,295.00
Maryland Assurance		
Massachusetts Mutual	2,834	7,890,728.00
Metropolitan Life	22,758	27,934,715.00
Michigan Mutual	797	1,023,534.37
Missouri State	1,149	2,495,683.34
Morris Plan Life		
Mutual Benefit Life	3,346	9,040,891.00
Mutual Life	14,051	40,485,067.00
National Life of America	655	1,068,380.00
National Life of Vermont	1,364	3,418,496.00
New England Mutual	1,428	3,205,233.00
New York Life	18,041	39,562,149.00
North Carolina Mutual and Provident	13	4,300.00
Northwestern Mutual Life	6,029	14,739,237.00
Pacific Mutual	1,405	3,352,437.00
Pan-American Life	742	1,689,480.00
Penn Mutual	3,090	10,014,372.00
Philadelphia Life	165	408,325.00
Phœnix Mutual Life	1,095	2,898,332.00
Provident Life and Trust	2,710	8,832,213.00
Prudential of America	7,312	8,686,011.00
Reliance Life	190	323,862.00
Reserve Loan	598	1,463,616.00
Security Mutual	349	565,229.00
Southern Life and Trust	33	45,554.00
Standard Life (Atlanta)	6	5,000.00
State Life	638	1,594,217.00
State Mutual of Massachusetts	1,178	2,347,188.00
Travelers Life	2,386	6,547,867.00
Union Central Life	4,045	10,175,334.00
Union Mutual Life and Health		
United Life and Accident	113	156,945.00
Volunteer State Life		
Totals	122,388.00	268,539,669.95

*Minus.

TERMINATED DURING THE YEAR 1918—MODE OF TERMINATION.

By Lapse		By Decrease		Total Terminated	
Number	Amount	Number	Amount	Number	Amount
5,929	$ 20,180,159.00	----	$ 72,256,194.89	18,463	$ 117,996,271.25
1,242	1,983,469.00	3	67,424.67	1,758	3,107,395.67
2,207	5,439,784.00	3	576,396.00	3,027	7,958,284.00
3,486	4,632,714.00	----	31,236.00	4,040	5,450,123.00
2,022	4,961,233.00	----	608,999.00	2,844	7,771,338.00
2,617	5,185,219.00	----	584,681.00	6,891	17,124,890.02
17,042	36,913,895.00	----	56,059,440.00	45,759	180,791,255.00
1,788	3,905,113.00	80	169,192.00	2,196	4,803,381.00
2,154	5,210,324.00	9	431,908.00	4,977	12,293,489.00
				24,662	*1,008,607.00
532	884,814.00	----	----	756	1,293,802.00
2,515	5,273,467.00	----	----	7,023	14,646,115.00
2,433	5,249,717.00	----	350,220.00	5,315	11,850,530.00
3,230	5,766,572.00	----	200,430.00	4,149	7,503,496.00
1,054	1,373,144.00	----	72,905.00	2,205	2,633,948.00
712	1,539,052.00	----	215,347.00	2,328	5,414,247.00
514	700,042.00	----	15,336.00	485	1,237,475.00
1	3,000.00	----	----	2	4,000.00
3,213	6,604,397.00	----	1,676,450.00	9,154	24,007,193.00
86,409	82,243,641.00	----	10,544,753.00	145,212	152,208,917.00
1,989	3,732,764.56	----	160,689.49	3,608	6,202,595.20
8,446	15,291,644.59	----	241,578.57	11,510	21,581,988.26
3,316	7,260,314.00	6	1,066,459.00	16,869	41,012,921.00
14,630	29,193,212.00	103	1,095,458.00	48,188	120,449,962.00
1,512	3,306,164.00	1	375,242.00	6,727	12,641,649.00
1,737	3,370,073.00	1,446	3,838,956.00	7,448	16,273,971.00
3,053	6,686,930.00	----	1,738,571.00	7,420	19,237,584.00
32,324	60,264,400.00	----	6,957,305.00	89,277	191,497,800.00
964	669,250.00	----	----	1,070	725,625.00
7,649	19,147,356.00	----	1,561,123.00	28,487	74,835,905.00
2,162	4,245,237.00	----	----	6,804	14,268,823.00
2,506	5,477,384.00	----	259,908.00	3,628	8,182,862.00
5,060	12,001,857.00	1,737	8,023,253.00	17,275	50,984,774.00
1,333	3,234,064.00	----	267,284.00	1,782	4,570,640.00
1,714	3,673,191.00	----	430,946.00	5,995	12,785,317.00
3,706	9,579,748.00	----	2,474,946.00	9,503	28,804,470.00
31,600	42,126,479.00	----	4,310,051.00	89,769	114,268,811.00
5,256	8,792,621.00	7	218,589.00	6,265	11,066,481.00
2,140	3,911,525.00	----	87,625.00	3,101	6,054,517.00
2,607	3,759,541.00	----	44,092.00	3,656	5,501,925.00
1,380	2,608,062.00	13	85,762.00	1,558	3,062,358.00
3,396	2,930,772.00	----	----	3,466	3,007,272.00
2,045	3,425,465.00	13	348,403.00	3,483	6,891,403.00
1,535	3,734,183.00	99	2,335,206.00	4,403	12,575,527.00
6,979	18,245,240.00	56	39,518,129.00	13,668	77,027,379.00
5,009	11,636,062.00	----	937,755.00	15,301	35,513,929.00
796	1,180,751.00	----	----	991	1,456,719.00
293,944	487,534,046.15	3,576	220,238,243.62	1,114,248	1,479,587,964.40

Name of Company	Whole Life Policies	
	Number	Amount
Ætna	38,258	$ 138,903,01:
Atlantic Life	18,622	35,675,45
American Central	17,657	34,765,34
American National (Ordinary)	20,198	27,874,18
American National (Industrial)	275,151	39,183,10
Business Men's Mutual	1,283	68,51
Columbian National	26,592	65,752,03
Connecticut Mutual	60,777	155,303,12
Durham Life	33,083	3,769,32:
Equitable Life	497,160	1,296,608,51
Federal Life	9,713	18,733,10:
Fidelity Mutual	34,890	75,527,68:
Gate City Life and Health	4,809	360,44
George Washington Life	4,807	9,201,69
Guardian Life	49,034	103,899,29
Home Life of New York	55,631	115,777,31
Home Security	5,939	592,03
Imperial Mutual Life and Health		
Jefferson Standard	42,431	75,063,30
LaFayette Mutual Life	834	570,06:
Life Insurance Company of Virginia (Ordinary)	27,917	33,450,97
Life Insurance Company of Virginia (Industrial)	636,919	92,625,25
Life and Casualty	304,813	14,395,50:
Manhattan Life	26,028	47,762,70
Maryland Life		
Maryland Assurance	153	437,75
Massachusetts Mutual	175,452	425,407,72
Metropolitan Life (Ordinary)	995,732	1,121,184,29
Metropolitan Life (Industrial)	9,960,944	1,390,024,84
Michigan Mutual	26,341	39,506,03
Missouri State	77,062	145,797,17
Morris Plan Life		
Mutual Benefit Life	337,361	879,546,22
Mutual Life	665,329	1,538,748,31
National Life of America	30,507	47,241,53
National Life of Vermont	72,373	157,182,71
New England Mutual	121,497	302,538,06
New York Life	915,983	2,030,830,98
North Carolina Mutual and Provident (Ordinary)	9,119	5,846,71
North Carolina Mutual and Provident (Industrial)	131,328	10,250,00
Northwestern Mutual Life	483,365	1,318,459,154
Pacific Mutual Life	67,687	130,347,36
Pan-American Life	19,465	38,241,20
Penn Mutual	210,103	622,118,32
Philadelphia Life	10,395	22,925,834
Phœnix Mutual Life	10,391	20,623,98
Provident Life and Trust	24,575	84,679,497
Prudential of America	936,758	1,147,747,065
Reliance Life	43,422	81,264,331
Reserve Loan	15,925	27,503,176
Security Mutual	26,031	38,275,805
Southern Life and Trust	12,975	23,471,550
Standard Life (Atlanta)	6,117	5,655,250
State Life	35,164	73,987,688
State Mutual of Massachusetts	69,340	184,158,972
Travelers Life	158,521	441,464,228
Union Central Life	191,182	474,112,871
Union Mutual Life and Health (Ordinary)	37	18,500
Union Mutual Life and Health (Industrial)	18	4,898
United Life and Accident	5,442	7,531,876
Volunteer State Life	14,191	28,018,839
Totals	1,805,277,855	15,251,014,806

FORCE DECEMBER 31, 1918.

Endowment Policies		Term and Other Policies, Including Return Premium Additions		Additions to Policies by Dividends	Total Numbers and Amounts	
Number	Amount	Number	Amount	Amount	Number	Amount
147,309	$290,274,034.00	34,247	$ 243,794,422.00	$ 199,996.54	219,814	$ 673,171,467.54
3,720	6,815,958.00	755	1,834,415.00	------------	23,097	44,325,827.00
2,135	4,151,470.00	4,027	15,045,666.00	69,100.00	23,819	54,031,580.00
1,382	1,395,763.00	412	256,404.00	101,040.00	21,992	29,627,387.00
59,708	6,243,804.00	660	45,494.00		335,519	45,472,405.00
93	7,606.00	10,549	414,075.00	------------	11,929	490,197.00
5,401	10,535,210.00	3,410	15,709,365.00	199,214.00	35,403	92,195,825.00
53,436	118,278,794.00	3,864	11,410,765.00	128,753.97	118,077	285,121,434.00
999	80,943.00	68,336	2,249,095.00	------------	102,418	6,099,360.00
148,199	284,110,328.00	50,124	328,353,112.00	15,466,622.00	695,483	1,924,538,578.00
1,494	2,358,114.00	2,176	4,917,049.00	------------	13,383	26,008,265.00
26,263	55,342,267.00	7,226	18,055,713.00	369,788.00	68,379	149,295,550.00
299	14,753.00	33,292	1,342,228.00	------------	38,400	1,717,430.00
1,233	1,705,650.00	198	718,411.00	76,043.00	6,238	11,701,804.00
38,156	67,212,893.00	1,647	7,190,798.00	818,365.00	88,837	179,121,354.00
11,585	19,418,987.00	5,440	19,888,709.00	3,625,285.00	72,656	158,710,292.00
18,974	747,616.00	------------	------------		24,913	1,339,652.00
------------					55,667	2,619,161.00
1,503	3,025,724.00	1,320	3,541,139.00	14,827.00	45,254	81,644,994.00
578	379,958.00	44	57,000.00	------------	1,412	950,023.00
284	2,251,597.00	905	1,734,865.00	6,542.00	31,106	37,443,981.00
155,129	18,956,474.00	5,749	144,601.00	------------	797,797	111,726,339.00
18,707	1,705,668.00	------------	------------		323,520	16,101,170.00
3,526	5,026,584.00	1,217	3,576,598.00	75,142.00	30,771	56,441,033.00
------------					9,072	14,392,384.00
19	49,500.00	33	582,693.00	------------	205	1,069,943.00
22,703	38,222,449.00	7,213	24,875,287.00	2,287,826.00	205,368	490,793,291.00
990,319	800,780,458.00	32,365	159,552,143.00	2,490,742.00	2,018,416	2,084,007,638.00
7,376,905	915,373,626.00	427,996	40,044,730.00	60,974.00	17,765,845	2,345,504,178.00
8,821	13,390,011.00	3,737	9,543,555.00	137,806.00	38,899	62,577,407.00
11,115	14,867,839.00	5,493	16,051,528.00	30,095.75	93,670	176,746,636.00
		17,326	2,464,475.00		17,326	2,464,475.00
30,648	65,161,098.00	13,498	31,725,342.00	11,049,122.00	381,507	987,481,787.00
107,004	185,970,301.00	30,033	102,388,929.00	34,774,406.00	802,366	1,861,881,953.00
15,282	26,850,121.00	11,789	26,473,549.00	15,255.00	57,578	100,580,434.00
26,580	43,264,332.00	13,376	32,000,997.00	976,331.00	112,329	233,424,376.00
28,667	57,048,796.00	9,925	39,449,732.00	4,753,280.00	160,089	403,609,868.00
402,761	682,658,968.00	41,689	109,214,945.00	16,124,906.00	1,360,433	2,838,829,802.00
------------					9,119	725,625.00
------------					131,328	10,250,009.00
85,650	174,645,143.00	47,209	160,482,910.00	27,349,339.00	616,224	1,680,936,546.00
22,172	40,449,557.00	13,245	34,206,521.00	3,644,074.00	103,104	208,647,520.00
2,745	7,826,400.00	1,308	4,400,299.00	------------	23,518	50,467,907.00
36,262	71,355,051.00	30,233	105,545,210.00	3,207,204.00	276,598	802,225,787.00
2,274	4,049,482.00	3,023	12,158,117.00	84,406.00	15,692	39,217,839.00
82,532	161,267,780.00	10,150	29,801,826.00	1,786,379.00	103,073	213,479,965.00
119,893	265,832,831.00	14,175	58,048,594.00	4,272,779.00	158,643	412,833,701.00
308,238	276,433,495.00	85,197	216,122,461.00	1,906,624.00	1,330,193	1,642,209,645.00
6,996	11,358,294.00	2,092	10,024,239.00	194,399.00	52,510	102,841,263.00
168	327,316.00	787	2,004,532.00	9,802.00	16,880	29,864,826.00
5,856	7,744,517.00	5,834	11,162,795.00	84,701.00	37,721	57,267,818.00
1,378	2,151,927.00	637	2,081,622.00	14,427.00	14,990	27,719,536.00
3,101	2,553,470.00	------------	------------		9,218	8,208,720.00
4,905	7,603,407.00	4,403	11,682,155.00	46,207.00	44,472	93,319,457.00
19,073	40,080,947.00	4,458	13,277,177.00	2,635,037.00	92,871	240,152,133.00
45,849	82,895,157.00	22,850	229,576,926.00	354,771.00	227,220	754,291,082.00
30,254	53,160,659.00	10,108	30,128,874.00	6,026,250.00	231,544	563,428,654.00
------------		------------			37	18,500.00
------------					18	4,898.00
516	637,882.00	98	617,473.00	19,400.00	6,056	8,806,631.00
610	1,200,423.00	1,259	3,800,203.00	12,248.00	16,060	33,031,713.00
10,501,409	4,955,250,632.00	1,107,137	2,269,769,763.00	145,499,509.26	29,726,076	22,573,209,054.54

EXHIBIT OF POLICIES, LOSSES INCURRED, LOSSES PAID AND PREMIUMS RECEIVED

Name of Company	Policies in Force December 31, 1917		Policies Issued During 1918	
	Number	Amount	Number	Amount
Ætna Life	4,439	$ 9,266,174.38	675	$3,738,351.73
Atlantic Life	3,748	6,351,917.00	1,119	2,205,032.00
American Central	382	587,761.00	86	181,223.00
American National (Ordinary)	1,708	1,132,939.00	101	139,000.00
American National (Industrial)	15,213	1,540,571.00	5,151	553,813.00
Business Men's Mutual	5,921	254,309.00		
Columbian National	1,311	2 265,811 00	338	592,301.00
Connecticut Mutual	1,329	2,907,877.00	160	322,887.00
Durham Life (Ordinary)	417	132 400.00	140	55,350.00
Durham Life (Industrial)	79,303	4,784,035.00	58,652	3,125,023.00
Equitable Life	8,234	15,179,105.00	1,308	2,575,444.00
Federal Life			2	10,000.00
Fidelity Mutual	1,617	3,049,722.00	127	345,122.00
Gate City Life and Health*	30,241	1,146,328.00	32,821	1,579,709.00
George Washington Life	37	41,268.00	238	341,897.00
Guardian Life	1,224	2,537,540.00	286	871,336.00
Home Life of New York	816	1,246,683.00	53	227,008.00
Home Security*	18,309	1,013,779.00	22,614	1,116,317.50
Imperial Mutual Life and Health*				
Jefferson Standard	20,593	31,846,574.00	4,605	8,725,570.00
LaFayette Mutual Life	1,178	741,719.00		
Life Insurance Company of Virginia (Ordinary)	5,635	5,848,253.00	1,039	1,220,957.00
Life Insurance Company of Virginia (Industrial)	156,152	21,056,641.00	33,914	5,250,361.00
Life and Casualty*			43,877	2,237,727.00
Manhattan Life	636	776,560.00	106	252,959.00
Maryland Life	1,318	1,871,141.00	265	305,081.00
Maryland Assurance				
Massachusetts Mutual	1,602	3,414,627.00	156	603,894.00
Metropolitan Life (Ordinary)	13,654	16,219,345.00	3,904	4,744,403.00
Metropolitan Life (Industrial)	150,832	19,157,949.00	37,682	5,077,590.00
Michigan Mutual	1,555	2,332,537.69	230	357,096.99
Missouri State	1,498	2,207,237.00	446	707,922.00
Morris Plan Life*			181	22,875.00
Mutual Benefit Life	12,206	20,990,287.00	1,279	3,094,437.00
Mutual Life	11,837	20,614,622.00	1,299	3,072,890.65
National Life of America	324	520,654.40	394	686,559.80
National Life of Vermont	3,864	6,490,875.69	533	1,329,937.78
New England Mutual	2,050	3,840,394.00	351	725,562.00
New York Life	10,418	19,119,685.00	1,542	3,281,593.00
North Carolina Mutual and Provident (Ordinary)	1,877	1,000,175.00	1,587	1,146,146.00
North Carolina Mutual and Provident (Industrial)	46,654	3,010,214.00	19,007	1,298,707.00
Northwestern Mutual Life	4,163	8,361,948.00	151	397,900.00
Pacific Mutual	1,182	1,622,695.00	405	822,077.00
Pan-American Life	641	983,338.00	538	1,046,200.00
Penn Mutual	6,012	11,477,120.00	371	932,093.00
Philadelphia Life	1,546	2,649,052.00	693	1,108,040.00
Phœnix Mutual Life	2,370	3,473,646.15	306	472,284.00
Provident Life and Trust	901	1,867,051.00	261	612,607.00
Prudential of America	5,271	10,576,720.00	238	601,535.00
Reliance Life	964	1,411,272.00	342	641,250.00
Reserve Loan	229	278,000.00	53	149,500.00
Security Mutual	980	1,398,940.01	161	252,335.00
Southern Life and Trust	8,260	14,035,096.00	2,891	5,770,876.00
Standard Life (Atlanta)			238	200,750.00
State Life	731	1,703,882.00	67	253,941.00
State Mutual of Massachusetts	1,728	3,259,667.00	211	509,461.00
Travelers Life	1,618	4,456,845.00	310	1,105,466.00
Union Central Life	6,770	10,517,180.00	477	980,009.00
Union Mutual Life and Health (Ordinary)	16	8,000.00	53	26,500.00
Union Mutual Life and Health (Industrial)	4	684.00	14	4,241.00
United Life and Accident	1,744	2,218,891.00	244	467,708.00
Volunteer State Life	730	1,821,576.00	218	616,936.00
Totals	663,992	316,619,313.32	284,460	79,093,792.45

*Industrial. (lx)

OF LIFE INSURANCE COMPANIES FOR THE YEAR ENDING DECEMBER 31, 1918.

Policies Ceased During 1918		Policies in Force December 31, 1918		Losses Unpaid December 31, 1917	Losses Incurred During 1918	Losses Paid During 1918	Premiums Received
Number	Amount	Number	Amount				
358	$2,246,891.00	4,756	$10,757,635.11	$ 911.00	$ 143,650.00	$ 142,635.00	$ 268,077.33
257	423,753.00	4,610	8,133,196.00	----------	92,501.91	79,501.91	329,657.59
109	156,238.00	359	612,746.00	----------	7,033.00	7,033.00	18,750.64
154	284,720.00	1,665	987,219.00	1,256.00	17,438.00	17,694.00	34,005.25
4,600	445,250.00	15,764	1,649,134.00	----------	30,587.99	29,413.19	82,824.51
		11,925	490,197.00	----------	----------	33,602.56	77,706.64
131	192,018.00	1,518	2,666,094.00	3,000.00	23,000.00	20,500.00	78,904.83
162	351,225.00	1,327	2,879,539.00	10,361.00	57,380.00	62,741.00	98,771.58
78	26,800.00	479	160,950.00	----------	2,900.00	2,900.00	5,069.66
36,342	1,342,181.00	101,613	6,066,877.00	251.50	76,902.17	76,589.67	436,099.76
589	1,154,863.00	8,953	16,599,686.00	18,485.90	281,730.10	243,517.39	558,801.87
		2	10,000.00	----------	----------	----------	126.11
132	296,007.00	1,612	3,098,837.00	2,000.00	79,348.00	76,536.00	114,332.32
24,662	1,008,607.00	38,400	1,717,430.00	110.00	96,835.23	96,243.28	217,768.73
14	16,000.00	261	367,165.00	----------	----------	----------	11,802.52
158	436,008.00	1,352	2,972,868.00	----------	34,696.97	27,093.60	102,434.03
83	150,165.00	786	1,323,526.00	4,000.00	39,179.49	26,179.49	38,597.96
16,010	790,445.00	24,913	1,339,651.50	----------	21,398.00	21,398.00	121,127.50
		55,667	2,619,161.00	208.00	113,921.15	113,853.65	258,118.75
1,931	3,141,335.00	23,267	37,430,809.00	14,045.00	420,133.60	339,233.60	94,945.00
		1,412	950,023.00	2,000.00	9,145.23	11,046.23	45,012.10
551	649,815.00	6,123	6,419,395.00	1,156.00	100,308.56	89,464.56	181,299.90
21,289	2,670,867.00	168,777	23,636,135.00	2,741.40	378,241.57	372,865.52	76,846.54
20,855	1,067,949.00	23,022	1,169,778.00	----------	6,037.50	5,663.00	107,329.13
50	67,824.00	692	961,695.00	----------	11,476.00	9,466.00	31,472.61
186	261,790.00	1,410	1,935,432.00	1,000.00	15,149.26	14,149.26	69,834.40
126	309,429.00	1,632	3,709,092.00	----------	----------	26,070.00	115,511.54
1,350	1,544,477.00	16,208	19,419,271.00	14,000.00	291,213.04	264,005.04	577,199.25
19,147	2,460,190.00	169,367	21,775,349.00	2,807.00	353,883.23	351,752.23	765,477.72
225	336,584.63	1,560	2,353,050.05	----------	33,202.48	33,202.48	67,640.12
239	361,728.00	1,705	2,553,431.00	14.00	19,980.00	12,994.00	80,640.97
3	250.00	178	22,625.00	----------	250.00	150.00	588.43
643	1,069,649.00	12,782	23,015,875.00	15,000.00	308,517.00	289,517.00	756,128.57
665	1,266,724.65	12,471	22,420,788.00	906.00	404,037.79	394,718.79	771,437.35
86	165,500.00	632	1,041,714.20	----------	5,000.00	3,000.00	34,451.24
275	465,770.39	4,122	7,355,043.08	10,000.00	94,579.13	103,579.13	253,114.67
181	349,679.00	2,220	4,216,277.00	1,000.00	137,736.00	115,696.00	153,472.68
767	1,400,837.00	11,193	21,000,441.00	12,594.00	417,245.15	374,598.68	752,031.72
423	289,475.00	3,002	1,856,846.00	----------	22,175.00	22,175.00	57,097.82
16,135	975,700.00	49,526	3,333,221.00	492.00	39,363.96	39,892.66	243,524.97
191	463,092.00	4,123	8,296,756.00	10,330.00	223,926.00	207,210.00	225,129.02
106	140,361.00	1,481	2,304,411.00	5,000.00	26,238.00	23,155.00	74,032.03
190	323,331.00	989	1,706,207.00	----------	7,000.00	7,000.00	43,825.84
258	587,006.00	6,125	11,822,207.00	13,026.00	203,768.76	193,268.76	387,866.23
221	368,677.00	2,018	3,388,415.00	10,000.00	34,049.02	40,049.02	121,687.60
136	199,452.55	2,540	3,746,477.60	1,000.00	47,540.87	41,540.87	119,114.99
122	228,583.00	1,040	2,251,075.00	----------	24,133.00	23,133.00	63,699.15
205	428,322.00	5,304	10,749,933.00	10,000.00	143,495.69	127,184.09	325,891.57
124	167,973.00	1,182	1,884,549.00	----------	18,978.70	16,978.70	65,388.15
514	86,500.00	228	341,000.00	----------	1,997.18	981.74	11,859.95
113	152,171.00	1,028	1,499,104.01	1,000.00	11,500.00	9,000.00	50,439.71
791	1,439,187.00	10,360	18,366,785.00	----------	190,472.85	149,408.45	596,980.14
28	26,500.00	210	174,250.00	----------	----------	----------	3,339.30
67	220,201.00	731	1,737,622.00	1,000.00	39,152.00	37,152.00	43,703.81
134	312,048.00	1,805	3,457,080.00	4.00	52,764.08	49,281.08	106,822.39
130	255,040.00	1,798	5,307,271.00	----------	38,004.54	36,004.54	139,848.10
557	937,018.00	6,690	10,560,171.00	2,140.00	277,883.65	234,544.83	342,267.50
		69	34,500.00	----------	----------	----------	466.10
1	80.00	17	4,818.00	----------	----------	----------	----------
140	187,683.00	1,848	2,498,916.00	4,000.00	34,922.00	32,422.00	82,826.40
136	318,381.00	812	2,120,131.00	----------	15,000.00	14,000.00	62,026.58
172,670	35,518,351.20	837,661	362,279,080.55	175,838.80	5,577,002.90	5,192,985.00	11,361,062.99

STATISTICAL TABLES

RELATING TO MUTUAL LIFE ASSESSMENT ASSOCIATIONS

Name of Association	Income		
	From Members	All Other Sources	Total
Afro-American Mutual	$ 6,284.05	$ 799.00	$ 7,083.05
Catawba Benevolent	1,642.72		1,642.72
Citizens Mutual	26,593.36	15,426.49	42,019.85
Cumulative Coffin Club	291.25		291.25
International Mutual	24,740.23	210.00	24,950.23
Toilers Mutual	3,092.95	120.00	3,212.59
Winston Mutual Life	28,620.06	663.53	29,283.59
Totals	91,264.62	17,219.02	108,483.64

MENT LIFE ASSOCIATIONS.

LIABILITIES FOR THE YEAR ENDING DECEMBER 31, 1918.

Disbursements			Total Admitted Assets	Total Liabilities
To Members	All Other Payments	Total		
$ 2,634.54	$ 4,767.56	$ 7,402.10	$ 9,914.32	$ 1,098.00
1,375.00	232.33	1,607.33	368.57	270.00
9,466.21	30,965.75	40,431.96	2,207.50	2,207.50
153.50	275.67	329.17	205.13	109.00
13,053.41	11,428.03	24,581.44	6,148.86	500.00
1,754.20	1,342.85	3,097.05	3,220.95	--------------
17,371.64	10,682.43	28,054.07	7,081.11	300.00
45,808.50	59,694.62	105,503.12	29,146.44	4,484.50

SHOWING LIFE ASSESSMENT ASSOCIATIONS,

Name of Association	Certificates in Force December 31, 1917		Certificates Written During 1918	
	Number	Amount	Number	Amount
Afro-American Mutual	8,709	$ 449,612.05	335	$ 11,240.00
Catawba Benevolent	280			
Citizens Mutual			11,105	600,891.50
Cumulative Coffin Club	199	19,900.00	20	2,525.00
International Mutual	8,272		4,003	
Toilers Mutual	707	19,415.00	211	6,913.00
Winston Mutual Life	8,180	316,160.00	6,140	148,780.00
Totals	26,347	805,087.05	21,814	770,349.50

No. XVII.

BUSINESS IN NORTH CAROLINA DURING 1918.

Certificates Terminated During 1918		Certificates in Force December 31, 1918		Premiums or Assessments Received	Losses Incurred	Losses Paid	Losses Unpaid
Number	Amount	Number	Amount				
124	$ 4,047.50	8,924	$ 457,044.55	$ 6,284.05	$ 833.50	$ 833.50	$--------
10	-------------	270	-------------	1,642.72	1,085.00	1,375.00	270.00
8,304	449,329.44	3,111	168,336.21	26,593.36	1,429.88	1,168.85	168.75
20	-------------	199	-------------	291.25	153.50	153.50	-----------
3,540	-------------	8,955	358,200.00	24,740.23	3,941.00	3,941.00	-----------
134	3,886.00	784	22,442.00	3,092.95	498.00	498.00	-----------
2,000	50,000.00	12,422	416,100.00	28,620.06	4,104.00	4,104.00	-----------
14,132	507,262.94	34,665	1,422,122.76	91,264.62	12,044.88	12,073.85	438.75

STATISTICAL TABLES

RELATING TO ACCIDENT, CASUALTY, FIDELITY, SURETY AND LIVE-STOCK COMPANIES

SHOWING INCOME OF FIDELITY AND CASUALTY COMPANIES (LICENSED TO

Name of Company	Premiums		
	Accident	Health	Liability
Ætna Casualty and Surety	$ 18,536.78	$ 2,591.92	$ 1,112,559.40
Ætna Life (Accident)	2,514,114.97	857,863.73	6,559,539.43
American Automobile			
American Credit Indemnity			
American National Life (Accident)	221,202.24	181,653.28	
American Surety			
Belt Automobile			
Columbian National Life (Accident)	193,443.10	165,068.02	
Continental Casualty	3,051,213.56	1,181,182.59	589,599.02
Employers Liability	365,116.23	149,068.04	5,576,803.06
Fidelity and Casualty	1,666,882.02	1,324,639.73	2,846,525.26
Fidelity and Deposit	191,628.58	135,289.52	315,269.88
General Accident	743,808.91	421,225.71	1,657,855.70
Georgia Casualty	37.21	50.84	1,614,601.37
Hartford Accident and Indemnity	182,737.73	77,422.19	1,543,469.80
Hartford Steam-boiler			
Lloyd's Plate-glass			
London Guarantee and Accident	194,539.51	96,155.71	2,643,812.27
Maryland Assurance (Accident)	1,271,446.40	845,274.93	
Maryland Casualty	*344,993.90	*202,661.65	5,140,900.03
Massachusetts Bonding	1,907,494.59		1,126,645.79
Metropolitan Casualty	128,344.50	48,951.74	
National Surety			
National Casualty	698,911.14		
National Life of America (Accident)	1,474,181.03		
New Amsterdam Casualty	246,364.87	67,476.29	990,690.56
New York Plate-Glass			
North American Accident	1,518,578.32		
Ocean Accident and Guarantee	371,464.03	119,897.12	3,195,364.58
Pacific Mutual Life (Accident)	1,445,271.48	596,850.63	
Provident Life and Accident	742,106.03		
Preferred Accident	935,947.26	298,030.68	1,269,870.19
Reliance Life (Accident)	82,296.20	54,659.83	
Royal Indemnity	198,140.21	69,608.40	2,140,548.14
Standard Accident	1,533,316.89	412,891.27	1,970,304.02
Travelers (Accident)	4,777,022.14	1,525,414.39	9,077,266.17
United States Casualty	464,977.20	283,945.97	1,653,043.66
U. S. Fidelity and Guaranty*	295,219.24	142,156.69	4,010,610.79
Western Live Stock			
Totals	26,706,091.31	8,584,128.53	54,404,739.36

*Altered check indemnity.

INCOME.

Received

Workmen's Compensation	Fidelity	Surety	Plate-glass	Steam-boiler	Burglary and Theft	Credit
$ 742,292.15 9,760,474.30	$ 344,474.68	$ 1,496,335.80	$ 324,976.80	$............	$ 554,895.08	$............
						870,324.13
	2,062,799.94	2,514,056.53			67,164.05	
823,601.80 12,237,815.87	85,581.51	13,515.77	139,161.57	73,764.57	356,438.12	
3,900,481.98 6,268.43 1,116,241.61 303,257.70 2,242,827.15	523,238.24 1,394,721.55 247,676.08	657,251.22 2,387,909.27 380,125.95	573,826.57 133,489.70 52,139.96 165,574.57	644,086.87	833,943.51 276,921.29 63,842.68 14,097.40 233,550.19	
6,864,027.49			789,500.67	2,366,560.81 30,850.17	185,970.99	485,582.44
7,603,920.66	256,494.06	934,919.52	420,079.33	412,812.79	527,921.72	
149,850.62	309,991.97 2,163,981.15	540,518.88 3,043,297.38	267,705.64 771,184.96		312,881.95 63,741.00 646,082.97	
1,142,742.86	251,009.31	460,446.05	213,183.27 1,164,778.02		182,832.81	
6,038,181.75	83,883.77		183,470.79	161,418.81	363,855.38	500,797.01
*122.40	61,372.72	83,560.47			190,276.58	
2,281,487.49 2,570,694.71	299,927.35	311,798.61	189,701.84	106,528.39	353,493.20	
20,109,750.78 1,147,723.29 5,083,717.42	1,808,116.00	3,441,034.10	106,692.84 288,843.98	15.68 605,026.86	114,872.47	
84,125,235.66	9,893,268.33	16,264,769.55	5,517,331.11	4,401,064.95	5,342,781.39	1,856,703.58

TABLE No. XVIII—

SHOWING INCOME OF FIDELITY AND CASUALTY COMPANIES (LICENSED TO

| | | | | Premiums |
Name of Company	Sprinkler	Physicians' Defense	Fly-wheel	Automobile and Team Property Damage
Ætna Casualty and Surety	$ 228,323.43	$	$ 14,437.95	$ 1,932,881.99
Ætna Life (Accident)				
American Automobile				2,482,261.75
American Credit Indemnity				
American National Life (Accident)				
American Surety				
Belt Automobile				441,200.40
Columbian National Life (Accident)				
Continental Casualty				148,071.14
Employers Liability			27,387.54	896,309.99
Fidelity and Casualty			125,419.35	518,140.07
Fidelity and Deposit				80,431.87
General Accident				434,510.35
Georgia Casualty				339,873.30
Hartford Accident and Indemnity				418,879.41
Hartford Steam-Boiler			156,271.59	
Lloyds Plate-Glass				
London Guarantee and Accident				445,761.03
Maryland Assurance (Accident)				
Maryland Casualty	220,670.07		41,234.85	711,432.92
Massachusetts Bonding				169,421.91
Metropolitan Casualty				
National Surety				
National Casualty				
National Life of America (Accident)				
New Amsterdam Casualty				196,649.64
New York Plate-Glass				
North American Accident				
Ocean Accident and Guarantee			29,504.75	519,391.48
Pacific Mutual Life (Accident)				
Provident Life and Accident				
Preferred Accident				433,199.73
Reliance Life (Accident)				
Royal Indemnity			57,134.12	552,761.35
Standard Accident				459,213.09
Travelers (Accident)				
United States Casualty				213,075.93
U. S. Fidelity and Guaranty*				552,883.02
Western Live Stock				
Totals	448,993.50		451,390.15	11,785,486.03

*Altered Check Indemnity.

INCOME—Continued.

Received						
Workmen's Collective	Marine	Live Stock	Total Premiums	Interest, Dividends and Rents	All Other Items	Total Income
$...........	$2,216,871.98	$...........	$ 8,989,177.96	$ 363,623.70	$ 2,525.00	$9,355,326.66
28,795.55	....	....	19,720,787.98	551,249.71	39,401.80	20,311,439.49
....	....	....	2,482,261.75	56,795.18	104.45	2,539,161.38
....	....	....	870,324.13	83,845.17	9,629.87	963,799.17
....	....	....	402,855.52	....	3,256,986.07	3,659,841.59
....	....	....	4,644,020.52	718,298.65	78,682.45	5,441,001 62
....	....	....	441,200.40	3,335.82	227,391.93	671,928.15
....	....	....	358,511.12	....	....	358,511.12
8,244.26	....	....	5,801,912.37	92,140.45	88,665.99	5,982,718.81
22,202.73	....	....	19,943,165.00	516,526.55	184,190.04	20,643,881.59
763.47	....	....	13,615,198.29	725,298.51	80,616.28	14,421,113.08
....	....	....	3,209,710.99	530,463.61	551,714.68	4,291,889.28
....	....	....	4,437,484.96	99,873.22	643,580.04	5,180,938.22
25,308.00	....	....	2,349,365.78	82,659.80	....	2,432,025.58
....	....	463,150.81	5,955,413.88	172,203.80	300,000.00	6,427,617.68
....	....	....	2,522,832.40	327,300.63	60,388.23	2,910,521.26
....	....	....	789,500.67	49,848.54	154.25	839,503.46
18,287.87	....	....	10,964,987.48	365,593.88	256,001.92	11,586,583.28
....	....	....	2,116,721.33	....	115.99	2,116,837.32
43,405.88	....	19,565.59	15,785,701.87	570,370.11	316,593.59	16,672,665.57
....	....	....	4,784,511.35	173,517.62	152,173.37	5,110,202.34
....	....	....	1,012,222.20	32,560.88	17.00	1,044,800.08
....	....	....	5,853,361.50	613,969.56	1,018,144.86	7,485,475.92
....	....	....	698,911.14	16,293.11	26,434.65	741,638.90
....	....	....	1,474,181.03	17.76	63,655.00	1,537,853.79
41,290.97	....	....	3,792,686.63	147,884.47	94,452.99	4,035,024.09
....	....	....	1,164,778.02	30,108.08	344.72	1,195,230.82
....	....	....	1,518,578.32	40,798.43	102,872.44	1,662,249.19
4.31	....	....	11,567,233.78	365,153.41	15,147.08	11,947,534.27
....	....	....	2,042,122.11	130,670.22	26,208.60	2,199,000.93
....	....	....	742,106.03	22,026.05	128,431.52	892,563.60
....	....	....	3,272,135.23	189,576.59	....	3,461,711.82
....	....	....	136,956.03	....	3,940,727.00	4,077,683.03
523.00	....	....	6,561,652.10	237,794.86	2,642.49	6,802,089.45
4,038.39	....	....	6,950,458.37	346,840.13	79,389.60	7,376,688.10
20,892.89	....	....	35,510,346.37	1,098,764.65	81,008.32	36,690,119.34
9,684.50	....	....	3,994,031.54	176,490.92	226,648.59	4,397,171.05
49,553.03	*1,251.25	....	16,278,412.38	600,608.26	37,416.85	16,916,437.49
....	....	151,482.09	151,482.09	23,592.34	31.32	175,105.75
272,994.85	2,218,123.23	634,198.49	232,907,300.62	9,556,094.67	12,092,488.98	254,555,884.27

SHOWING DISBURSEMENTS OF FIDELITY AND CASUALTY COMPANIES (LICENSED

Name of Company	Losses			
	Accident	Health	Liability	Workmen's Compensation
Ætna Casualty and Surety	$ 11,505.60	$ 492.57	$ 424,962.39	$ 159,874.70
Ætna Life (Accident)	998,136.72	460,063.62	2,364,322.91	3,707,397.99
American Automobile				
American Credit Indemnity				
American National Life (Accident)	64,377.23	109,097.68		
American Surety				
Belt Automobile				
Columbian National Life (Accident)	87,190.87	104,696.88		
Continental Casualty	972,685.07	783,414.36	139,096.27	246,310.08
Employers Liability	105,505.48	86,709.46	1,599,870.09	4,251,115.66
Fidelity and Casualty	647,828.26	829,580.38	871,803.91	1,406,525.48
Fidelity and Deposit	99,679.29	87,467.64	364,025.56	149,724.43
General Accident	313,562.41	236,832.49	880,508.15	487,547.75
Georgia Casualty	7,135.79	1,345.09	580,923.50	186,171.83
Hartford Accident and Indemnity	68,852.60	45,133.69	482,896.81	865,797.40
Hartford Steam-Boiler				
Lloyds Plate-Glass				
London Guarantee and Accident	93,737.17	72,780.24	777,908.36	2,444,174.65
Maryland Assurance (Accident)	287,012.73	330,610.79		
Maryland Casualty	111,079.96	63,758.89	1,876,747.93	2,505,487.61
Massachusetts Bonding	867,554.73		450,290.59	172,910.97
Metropolitan Casualty	53,665.23	30,782.28		
National Surety				
National Casualty	312,271.73			
National Life of America (Accident)	520,484.10			
New Amsterdam Casualty	112,720.38	57,557.93	260,836.10	442,726.30
New York Plate-Glass				
North American Accident	720,007.56			
Ocean Accident and Guarantee	162,452.16	71,448.51	1,140,692.93	2,188,795.97
Pacific Mutual Life (Accident)	516,066.17	328,391.68		
Provident Life and Accident	402,210.15			
Preferred Accident	323,872.20	158,449.71	312,618.24	
Reliance Life (Accident)	34,758.87	30,565.78		
Royal Indemnity	123,193.69	39,191.16	694,528.65	825,464.10
Standard Accident	686,187.98	254,379.82	520,443.33	815,454.72
Travelers (Accident)	1,827,360.25	883,593.55	2,721,087.01	6,500,648.98
Travelers Indemnity	46,834.18	56,193.12	18,531.18	158,439.07
United States Casualty	161,193.47	183,098.77	546,511.90	473,390.19
U. S. Fidelity and Guaranty	125,658.43	85,543.51	1,577,708.48	2,133,324.89
Western Live Stock				
Totals	10,864,780.46	5,391,179.60	18,606,314.29	30,121,373.77

TO DO BUSINESS IN THIS STATE) FOR THE YEAR ENDING DECEMBER 31, 1918.

Paid

Fidelity	Surety	Plate-glass	Steam-boiler	Burglary and Theft	Credit	Sprinkler
$ 78,909.79	$ 397,625.68	$ 154,855.47	$----	$ 178,961.48	$----	$ 150,674.81
					72,577.19	
476,611.23	299,870.18	----	----	1,573.00	----	----
23,095.96	404.67	75,993.39	3,181.29	128,766.44	----	
103,943.23	72,004.53	247,888.19	91,055.28	256,191.79		
255,518.44	629,126.16	68,041.70	----	119,997.17		
				35,603.24		
----	1,442.91	35,018.08	----	10,787.36	----	
45,124.95	39,821.17	84,174.09		87,992.61		
			200,200.53	----		
		330,749.83				
			2,135.48	83,477.74	51,862.26	----
40,807.81	99,538.91	193,229.04	32,669.87	162,187.04	----	194,017.54
51,222.41	169,066.90	132,933.91	----	115,616.16		----
		345,687.09		14,612.21		
609,449.97	625,217.21			238,584.60		
79,736.25	169,147.15	91,180.03	----	72,701.11	----	----
		496,609.68				
11,822.94	----	88,481.05	15,450.25	103,245.50	36,713.74	----
17,291.34	5,610.10	----		67,964.68	----	----
77,060.44	22,151.66	99,222.47	6,009.13	94,579.20		----
----	----	138,456.61	38,809.91	130,201.58	----	----
		55,418.43		43,399.34		
601,789.80	1,284,815.36	136,101.91	----	215,463.22		
2,472,384.56	3,815,842.59	2,774,040.97	389,511.74	2,162,005.47	161,153.19	344,692.35

SHOWING DISBURSEMENTS OF FIDELITY AND CASUALTY COMPANIES (LICENS

Name of Company	Fly-wheel	Automobile and Team Property Damage	Workmen's Collective
Ætna Casualty and Surety	$	$ 1,003,916.14	$ 1,013,267.
Ætna Life (Accident)			10,898.
American Automobile		1'000,212.75	
American Credit Indemnity			
American National Life (Accident)			
American Surety			
Belt Automobile		287,204.38	
Columbian National Life (Accident)			
Continental Casualty		57,394.69	3,169.0
Employers Liability	5,005.41	331,337.54	14,492.8
Fidelity and Casualty	34,220.50	225,841.32	
Fidelity and Deposit		64,014.50	
General Accident		222,236.40	
Georgia Casualty		164,634.64	10,789.8
Hartford Accident and Indemnity		175,386.66	
Hartford Steam-Boiler	14,232.82		
Lloyds Plate-Glass			
London Guarantee and Accident		162,783.34	15,088.2
Maryland Assurance (Accident)			
Maryland Casualty	21,611.49	288,821.35	19,486.8
Massachusetts Bonding		58,968.21	
Metropolitan Casualty			
National Surety			
National Casualty			
National Life of America (Accident)			
New Amsterdam Casualty		81,037.83	19,451.1
New York Plate-Glass			
North American Accident			
Ocean Accident and Guarantee	1,173.38	215,689.33	
Pacific Mutual Life (Accident)			
Provident Life and Accident			
Preferred Accident		149,940.02	
Reliance Life (Accident)			
Royal Indemnity	5,170.99	187,698.98	
Standard Accident		185,686.51	1,916.3
Travelers (Accident)			9,851.1
Travelers Indemnity	876.34	795,346.98	
United States Casualty		90,593.46	1,529.2
U. S. Fidelity and Guaranty		237,298.55	23,114.8
Western Live Stock			
Totals	82,290.93	5,986,043.58	1,143,055.7

DISBURSEMENTS—Continued.

TO DO BUSINESS IN THIS STATE) FOR THE YEAR ENDING DECEMBER 31, 1918.

Paid Live Stock	Total Losses Paid	Investigation and Adjustment of Claims and Commissions	Dividends	Salaries of Officers and Agents	All Other Expenditures	Total Disbursements
$	$ 3,575,045.98	$1,989,900.20	$ 240,000.00	$ 792,595.26	$ 794,907.60	$ 7,392,449.04
	7,540,820.07	4,780,931.76	250,000.00	1,243,242.31	2,024,419.77	15,839,413.91
	1,000,212.75	770,236.26	36,000.00	138,396.27	170,018.67	2,114,863.95
	72,577.19	239,472.86	70,000.00	87,425.75	115,931.46	585,407.26
	173,474.91	373,486.24		21,529.70	2,384,907.38	2,953,398.23
	778,054.41	852,782.34	400,000.00	1,449,744.92	875,730.88	4,356,312.55
	287,204.38	252,938.75		8,765.24	20,768.69	569,677.06
	191,887.75	97,695.79		32,155.61	26,348.87	348,088.02
	2,202,069.47	1,768,023.37	60,000.00	596,979.03	743,743.49	5,370,815.36
	6,625,478.20	4,917,575.11	475,924.63	712,948.72	1,268,310.70	14,000,237.36
	4,786,882.87	3,971,789.99	250,000.00	1,288,423.07	1,556,324.09	11,853,420.02
	1,837,594.89	1,343,066.61	480,000.00	862,685.16	775,499.28	5,298,845.94
	2,176,290.44	1,506,955.91	310,000.00	303,888.82	373,395.99	4,670,531.16
	998,249.00	811,374.30	21,037.80	74,558.28	171,606.18	2,076,825.56
306,391.80	2,201,571.78	1,640,247.62		520,582.71	462,315.54	4,824,717.65
	214,433.35	381,027.10	200,000.00	417,468.98	981,447.40	2,194,376.83
	330,749.83	244,482.13	50,000.00	85,508.72	118,162.03	828,902.71
	3,703,947.52	2,614,759.26	182,283.44	682,314.19	601,553.22	7,784,857.63
	617,623.52	739,722.29		73,185.90	93,489.17	1,524,020.88
14,069.73	5,623,513.98	3,650,025,08	349,862.50	1,022,146.64	2,230,853.51	12,876,401.71
	2,018,563.88	1,608,401.65		672,606.87	338,703.88	4,638,276.28
	444,746.81	333,079.34	36,000.00	122,913.15	66,132.07	1,002,871.37
	1,473,251.78	1,462,017.63	479,964.00	986,702.67	816,789.46	5,218,725.54
	312,271.73	279,566.47	16,000.00	80,728.53	62,282.96	750,849.69
	520,484.10	467,158.80		442,781.80	93,564.12	1,523,988.82
	1,387,160.27	1,165,485.55	120,000.00	261,760.59	292,143.64	3,226,550.05
	496,609.68	423,090.31	40,000.00	86,930.67	64,958.21	1,111,588.87
	720,007.56	581,669.48	30,000.00	190,714.00	118,835.86	1,641,226.90
	4,035,965.76	2,659,519.36		686,726.37	1,217,257.80	8,599,469.29
	844,457.85	728,576.86	150,000.00	200,944.04	215,884.49	2,139,860.24
	402,210.15	218,260.73	30,239.58	78,467.61	148,012.03	877,190.10
	1,035,746.29	947,287.63	175,000.00	206,858.40	205,909.19	2,660,801.51
	65,324.65	45,679.24		37,687.01	2,589,602.19	2,738,293.09
	2,174,270.47	1,730,907.47		435,125.10	435,118.75	4,775,421.79
	2,464,068.74	1,957,367.52	100,000.00	470,155.24	553,701.52	5,545,293.02
	11,942,540.93	7,194,903.15	960,000.00	1,218,584.75	4,414,629.51	25,730,658.34
	1,383,688.97	1,061,376.39	80,000.00	348,708.28	485,480.66	3,359,254.30
	1,555,234.82	1,110,307.29	99,920.00	263,765.92	307,660.31	3,336,888.34
	6,420,819.04	3,521,576.11	450,000.00	2,142,033.05	1,446,793.60	13,981,221.80
135,216.81	135,216.81	47,470.56	11,250.00	14,921.04	14,789.84	223,648.25
455,678.34	84,770,322.58	60,490,194.51	6,153,481.95	19,453.660.37	29,677,981.01	200,545,640.4 2

(lxxvii)

SHOWING ASSETS OF FIDELITY AND CASUALTY COMPANIES (LICENSED TO

Name of Company	Real Estate	Loans on Mortgages	Loans on Collaterals
Ætna Casualty and Surety	$	$ 1,442,100.00	$ 605,815.05
Ætna Life (Accident)	9,618.93	3,108,950.00	267,300.00
American Automobile			
American Credit Indemnity		25,000.00	
American National Life (Accident)			
American Surety	3,166,047.91		
Belt Automobile		22,500.00	
Columbian National Life (Accident)			
Continental Casualty	75,000.00	761,370.00	
Employers Liability			
Fidelity and Casualty	1,218,833.45		45,192.78
Fidelity and Deposit	2,558,284.09	120,744.00	
General Accident	180,000.00		
Georgia Casualty	375,000.00	658,316.72	3,135.63
Hartford Accident and Indemnity		190,000.00	
Hartford Steam-Boiler	90,000.00	1,493,900.00	12,000.00
Lloyds Plate-Glass	275,000.00	23,250.00	
London Guarantee and Accident		11,000.00	
Maryland Assurance (Accident)			
Maryland Casualty	1,577,845.32	49,401.33	63,826.08
Massachusetts Bonding	18,500.00		
Metropolitan Casualty			
National Surety	105,253.92	69,339.46	72,052.18
National Casualty		30,000.00	750.00
National Life of America (Accident)			
New Amsterdam Casualty	147,251.66	63,000.00	
New York Plate-Glass		41,000.00	
North American Accident		298,800.00	12,000.00
Ocean Accident and Guarantee		96,000.00	
Pacific Mutual Life (Accident)	42,158.40	1,479,267.48	109,000.00
Provident Life and Accident		147,315.00	15,500.00
Preferred Accident		82,000.00	
Reliance Life (Accident)			
Royal Indemnity			
Standard Accident		295,550.00	59,494.22
Travelers (Accident)			1,159,574.93
Travelers Indemnity		413,999.97	27,900.00
United States Casualty	250.00	166,500.00	
U. S. Fidelity and Guaranty	710,567.14	21,800.00	111,795.56
Western Live Stock		125,350.00	30,000.00
Totals	10,549,610.82	11,236,453.97	2,595,336.43

*Minus Agents' balances.

ASSETS.

DO BUSINESS IN THIS STATE) FOR THE YEAR ENDING DECEMBER 31, 1918.

Bonds and Stocks	Cash in Office and Banks	Interest and Rents Due and Accrued	Outstanding Premiums	All Other Assets	Total Assets
$ 6,645,415.44	$ 2,094,271.96	$ 131,330.82	$ 1,498,223.70	$ 64,994.54	$ 12,482,151.51
11,011,423.19	3,762,271.62	199,533.71	2,892,910.90	3,672.26	21,255,680.61
1,409,103.75	238,336.98	23,319.78	565,677.15	63,868.65	2,300,306.31
1,853,588.29	131,109.65	20,249.99		53,087.67	2,083,035.60
			11,825.19	5,992,503.74	6,004,328.93
6,918,483.19	533,483.67	61,514.42	564,684.75	122,012.25	11,366,226.19
39,375.00	123,109.90	1,470.51	25,534.60	30,834.00	242,824.01
			79,688.97	8,546.95	88,235.92
1,566,868.26	177,405.41	31,591.27	1,216,351.55	138,239.65	3,966,826.14
16,203,507.50	606,449.96	192,573.82	4,141,127.74	38,192.00	21,181,851.02
12,797,375.60	634,056.44	127,252.86	2,099,760.30	353,160.17	17,275,631.60
6,257,041.12	1,071,096.00	5,504.68	645,667.08	122,608.46	10,780,945.43
2,640,118.00	182,328.49	29,234.70	945,086.30	3,249.53	3,980,017.02
406,011.60	214,323.49	14,015.60	521,589.46	5,273.19	2,197,665.69
4,317,010.00	906,334.38	52,695.24	1,239,921.27	127,016.62	6,832,977.51
5,121,486.85	361,295.49	108,152.83	654,112.42		7,840,947.59
455,878.15	36,760.27	5,022.13	146,482.38		942,392.93
8,432,625,57	701,134.18	125,348.08	2,385,448.06	370,210.43	12,025,766.32
			235,624.68	19,718.98	255,343.66
11,649,726.12	736,380.78	89,700.42	2,670,862.77	42,360.93	16,880,103.75
4,133,450.26	390,157.19	46,624.75	704,775.63	95,854.97	5,389,362.80
689,974.16	44,836.49	6,901.96	218,495.88	2,050.34	962,258.83
13,242,261.84	816,630.45	141,348.69	1,218,476.03	420,010.32	16,085,372.89
309,815.80	12,278.23	5,712.97	6,800.00	8,154.86	373,511.86
1,900.00	375.00	20.14	7,926.05	16,625,736.12	16,635,957.31
2,731,464.40	396,399.39	21,544.85	871,128.58	104,565.98	4,335,354.86
662,111.00	72,903.83	4,285.38	243,625.61		1,023,925.82
458,179.48	52,475.80	13,252.68	63,587.94		898,295.90
9,664,867.96	585,464.38	146,985.20	1,728,618.62	368,085.41	12,590,021.57
414,336.21	36,250.26	33,168.73	354,637.06	*10,756.53	2,458,061.61
175,198.00	36,725.86	4,565.72	90,284.23	18,370.31	487,959.12
4,299,135.00	166,577.36	52,351.87	756,583.50	215.28	5,356,863.01
			33,401.49	8,757,573.16	8,790,974.65
5,924,783.63	909,009.73	79,885.48	1,250,176.81	99,315.78	8,263,171.43
7,516,959.00	412,521.86	135,780.98	740,516.40	123,990.67	9,284,813.13
27,608,759.00	4,671,996.94	277,750.84	6,071,958.41	1,156.25	39,791,196.37
3,726,361.39	153,894.98	52,878.10	693,517.48		5,068,551.92
3,986,825.00	70,036.63	37,773.29	559,252.57	73,456.23	4,894,093.72
12,390,431.57	1,679,202.81	167,916.73	2,927,818.68	545,181.45	18,554,713.94
201,092.00	33,501.74	5,366.69	29,430.22		424,740.65
195,862,943.33	23,051,387.60	2,452,625.91	41,111,590.46	34,792,510.62	321,652,459.13

SHOWING LIABILITIES OF FIDELITY AND CASUALTY COMPANIES (LICENSED

Name of Company	Unpaid Claims and Expense of Settlement	Unearned Premiums
Ætna Casualty and Surety	$ 3,054,672.54	$ 3,496,180.54
Ætna Life (Accident)	9,812,241.30	5,488,794.10
American Automobile	574,533.06	1,072,479.48
American Credit Indemnity	720,073.84	447,799.97
American National Life (Accident)	12,937.18	
American Surety	1,291,030.86	2,892,332.49
Belt Automobile	39,812.00	139,398.84
Columbian National Life (Accident)	51,414.19	144,102.45
Continental Casualty	816,368.23	1,737,278.04
Employers Liability	9,698,629.00	6,007,483.03
Fidelity and Casualty	5,724,651.32	6,728,604.23
Fidelity and Deposit	2,364,439.74	2,566,693.66
General Accident	1,465,935.41	1,490,415.52
Georgia Casualty	690,832.43	835,497.52
Hartford Accident and Indemnity	2,516,376.48	2,302,157.80
Hartford Steam-Boiler	153,378.80	3,429,363.68
Lloyds Plate-Glass	84,099.89	412,873.53
London Guarantee and Accident	5,772,327.76	3,037,827.95
Maryland Assurance (Accident)	142,034.26	626,109.82
Maryland Casualty	5,931,198.23	5,748,601.18
Massachusetts Bonding	1,424,778.22	1,720,033.85
Metropolitan Casualty	68,454.08	503,080.10
National Surety	1,863,969.98	3,536,076.72
National Casualty	29,940.00	20,363.00
National Life of America (Accident)	43,753.66	40,801.02
New Amsterdam Casualty	1,440,988.48	1,433,247.62
New York Plate-Glass	88,277.66	535,420.44
North American Accident	183,999.51	273,598.33
Ocean Accident and Guarantee	5,020,713.48	3,572,023.05
Pacific Mutual Life (Accident)	283,992.08	841,300.53
Provident Life and Accident	43,065.00	71,993.31
Preferred Accident	1,040,628.12	1,600,028.83
Reliance Life (Accident)	9,769.26	69,059.64
Royal Indemnity	2,942,525.00	2,628,498.38
Standard Accident	3,961,313.14	2,440,686.00
Travelers (Accident	16,838,880.78	9,477,455.67
United States Casualty	1,577,927.60	1,637,737.04
U. S. Fidelity and Guaranty	6,239,525.73	6,032,425.42
Western Live Stock	14,793.32	83,048.12
Totals	94,034,281.62	85,120,870.90

LIABILITIES.

Other Liabilities	Total Liabilities Except Capital and Surplus	Cash Capital	Surplus	Surplus to Policyholders	Total Liabilities, Including Capital and Surplus
$ 690,591.36	$ 7,241,444.44	$ 2,000,000.00	$ 3,240,707.07	$ 5,240,707.07	$ 12,482,151.51
117,322,411.06	132,623,446.46	5,000,000.00	12,164,653.93	17,164,653.93	149,788,100.39
185,861.20	1,832,873.74	300,000.00	167,432.57	467,432.57	2,300,306.31
139,592.73	1,307,466.54	350,000.00	425,569.06	775,569.06	2,083,035.60
5,049,534.39	5,062,471.57	250,000.00	691,857.36	941,857.36	6,004,328.93
1,003,176.97	5,186,540.32	5,000,000.00	1,179,685.87	6,179,685.87	11,366.226.19
4,700.00	183,910.84	-------------------	58,913.17	58,913.17	242,824.01
40,905.47	236,422.11	-------------------			236,422.11
513,179.87	3,066,826.14	600,000.00	300,000.00	900,000.00	3,966,826.14
2,883,625.56	18,589,737.59	200,000.00	2,392,113.43	2,592,113.43	21,181,851.02
1,618,773.58	14,072,029.13	1,000,000.00	2,203,602.47	3,203,602.47	17,275,631.60
1,127,794.42	6,058,927.83	3,000,000.00	1,722,017.60	4,722,017.60	10,780,945.43
340,150.08	3,296,501.01	250,000.00	433,516.01	.683,516.01	3,980,017.02
167,703.01	1,694,032.96	300,540.00	203,092.73	503,632.73	2,197,665.69
383,100.61	5,201,634.89	800,000.00	831,342.62	1,631,342.62	6,832,977.51
367,147.68	3,949,890.16	2,000,000.00	1,891,057.43	3,891,057.43	7,840,947.59
71,322.28	568,295.70	250,000.00	124,097.23	374,097.23	942,392.93
2,147,110.94	10,957,266.65	250,000.00	818,499.67	1,068,499.67	12,025,766.32
108,158.03	876,302.11	500,000.00	17,091.11	517,091.11	1,393,393.22
1,721,523.24	13,401,322.65	2,000,000.00	1,478,781.10	3,478,781.10	16,880,103.75
291,617.85	3,436,429.92	1,500,000.00	452,932.88	1,952,932.88	5,389,362.80
87,883.29	659,417.47	200,000.00	102,841.36	302,841.36	962,258.83
1,819,426.30	7,219,473.00	4,000,000.00	4,865,899.89	8,865,899.89	16,085,372.89
13,500.00	63,803.00	200,000.00	109,708.86	309,708.86	373,511.86
15,887,085.75	15,971,640.43	500,000.00	164,316.88	664,316.88	16,635,957.31
352,893.96	3,227,130.06	1,000,000.00	108,224.80	1,108,224.80	4,335,354.86
94,703.74	718,401.84	200,000.00	105,523.98	305,523.98	1,023,925.82
69,155.27	526,753.11	200,000.00	171,542.79	371,542.79	898,295.90
2,644,045.42	11,236,781.95	250,000.00	1,103,239.62	1,353,239.62	12,590,021.57
42,481,651.29	43,606,943.90	1,000,000.00	825,751.71	1,825,751.71	45,432,695.61
133,705.10	248,763.41	200,000.00	39,195.71	239,195.71	487,959.12
1,016,206.06	3,656,863.01	700,000.00	1,000,000.00	1,700,000.00	5,356,863.01
7,634,138.58	7,712,967.48	1,000,000.00	78,007.17	1,078,007.17	8,790,974.65
512,985.51	6,084,008.89	1,000,000.00	1,179,162.54	2,179,162.54	8,263,171.43
422,913.32	6,824,912.46	1,000,000.00	1,459,900.67	2,459,900,67	9,284,813.13
107,632,555.41	133,948,891.86	6,000,000.00	8,619,548.33	14,619,548.33	148,568,440.19
503,429.08	3,719,093.72	500,000.00	675,000.00	1,175,000.00	4,894,093.72
1,135,501.36	13,407,452.51	3,000,000.00	2,147,261.43	5,147,261.43	18,554,713.94
11,379.06	109,220.50	225,000.00	90,520.15	315,520.15	424,740.65
318,631,138.84	497,786,291.36	46,725,540.00	53,642,609.20	100,368,149.20	598,154,440.56

SHOWING PREMIUMS IN FORCE OF FIDELITY AND CASUALTY COMPANIES (LICENSED

Name of Company	Accident	Health
Ætna Casualty and Surety	$ 19,053.23	$ 2,791.90
Ætna Life (Accident)	2,351,374.87	796,906.91
American Automobile		
American Credit Indemnity		
American National Life (Accident)	39,035.22	
American Surety		
Belt Automobile		
Columbian National Life (Accident)	162,653.27	125,302.51
Continental Casualty	1,902,210.56	527,123.47
Employers Liability	342,648.81	133,896.47
Fidelity and Casualty	1,721,632.21	1,384,598.93
Fidelity and Deposit		
General Accident	288,463.85	125,730.45
Georgia Casualty		
Hartford Accident and Indemnity	168,944.55	70,096.79
Hartford Steam-Boiler		
Lloyds Plate-Glass		
London Guarantee and Accident	168,097.33	77,313.83
Maryland Assurance (Accident)	741,979.58	510,240.06
Maryland Casualty	41,665.14	21,378.97
Massachusetts Bonding*	190,444.96	
Metropolitan Casualty	119,672.26	41,101.65
National Surety		
National Casualty*	36,926.00	
National Life of America (Accident)*	63,849.24	
New Amsterdam Casualty	228,944.70	63,217.51
New York Plate-Glass		
North American Accident	511,292.32	
Ocean Accident and Guarantee	335,393.32	96,416.58
Pacific Mutual Life (Accident)	1,233,273.05	446,525.14
Provident Life and Accident*	136,048.74	
Preferred Accident	852,100.51	285,086.54
Reliance Life (Accident)	83,701.82	54,417.46
Royal Indemnity	188,373.67	61,668.65
Standard Accident	1,089,073.15	372,093.15
Travelers (Accident)	4,060,785.53	1,265,880.67
Travelers Indemnity	133,761.50	114,390.19
United States Casualty	433,491.83	247,644.71
U. S. Fidelity and Guaranty	277,230.25	129,263.71
Western Live Stock		
Totals	18,222,121.42	6,953,085.89

*Accident and Health.

EXHIBIT OF PREMIUMS.

TO DO BUSINESS IN THIS STATE) FOR THE YEAR ENDING DECEMBER 31, 1918.

Liability	Workmen's Compensation	Fidelity	Surety	Plate-glass	Steam-boiler
$ 1,093,740.94 4,506,282.54	$ 284,278.72 4,415,845.70	$ 323,996.10	$ 1,465,737.71	$ 337,724.97	$
		2,263,720.97	3,251,199.83		
479,263.19 4,574,535.90	406,286.06 5,096,376.40	86,361.29	14,144.54	139,160.99	193,241.92
2,571,684.56 17,694.42	2,436,224.12	490,458.79 1,428,027.71	725,053.60 2,912,813.41	580,304.17 18,499.41	1,503,352.66
1,459,228.30 1,127,264.59 1,376,254.21	580,014.94 144,874.51 1,030,120.99	238,704.67	449,535.19	53,483.62 160,056.97	
				819,069.86	5,989,629.45 93,653.72
2,039,647.05	2,661,905.39				
3,393,602.55	3,180,230.46	246,305.83	1,049,856.48	426,563.41	1,066,789.75
1,134,632.76	75,025.64	348,665.94	504,828.84	272,372.96 767,121.45	
		2,288,677.13	3,761,419.33		
795,952.33	542,173.56	233,644.07	358,468.47	217,944.99 1,070,714.40	
2,163,000.36	2,236,345.10	90,938.58		180,648.15	484,105.96
1,212,645.02		61,002.18	115,439.72		
1,933,425.16 1,720,750.62	851,904.22 1,242,723.44	282,877.85	355,818.83	189,716.42	293,572.76
6,693,642.39 71,071.11 1,380,776.97 2,749,379.66	7,891,823.32 274,703.30 734,103.75 1,492,926.61	1,757,027.35	3,918,883.54	285,041.44 112,229.60 289,098.52	1,005,343.45
42,494,474.63	35,577,886.23	10,140,408.46	18,883,199.49	5,919,751.33	10,629,689.67

SHOWING PREMIUMS IN FORCE OF FIDELITY AND CASUALTY COMPANIES (LICENSED

Name of Company	Burglary and Theft	Credit	Sprinkler
Ætna Casualty and Surety	$ 736,319.66	$	$ 336,100.57
Ætna Life (Accident)			
American Automobile			
American Credit Indemnity		833,316.44	
American National Life (Accident)			
American Surety	73,000.56		
Belt Automobile			
Columbian National Life (Accident)			
Continental Casualty			
Employers Liability	437,357.50		
Fidelity and Casualty	1,067,268.00		
Fidelity and Deposit	358,871.67		
General Accident	70,352.81		
Georgia Casualty	15,543.16		
Hartford Accident and Indemnity	293,328.26		
Hartford Steam-Boiler			
Lloyds Plate-Glass			
London Guarantee and Accident	226,072.77	361,633.75	
Maryland Assurance (Accident)			
Maryland Casualty	716,529.45		446,233.71
Massachusetts Bonding*	397,514.18		
Metropolitan Casualty	72,356.67		
National Surety	871,044.89		
National Casualty*			
National Life of America (Accident)*			
New Amsterdam Casualty	214,591.62		
New York Plate-Glass			
North American Accident			
Ocean Accident and Guarantee	504,144.89	425,185.32	
Pacific Mutual Life (Accident)			
Provident Life and Accident*			
Preferred Accident	247,992.80		
Reliance Life (Accident)			
Royal Indemnity	416,220.12		
Standard Accident			
Travelers (Accident)			
Travelers Indemnity	686,109.54		
United States Casualty	150,702.82		
U. S. Fidelity and Guaranty	744,053.56		
Western Live Stock			
Totals	8,299,374.93	1,620,135.51	782,334.28

*Accident and Health.

TO DO BUSINESS IN THIS STATE) FOR THE YEAR ENDING DECEMBER 31, 1918.

Fly-wheel	Automobile and Team Property Damage	Workmen's Collective	Live Stock	Physicians' Defense	Altered Check Indentures
$ 33,238.09	$ 1,794,646.57	$ 351,686.41 10,137.93	$	$	$
	2,144,958.96				
	278,797.68				
	128,159.85				
82,644.91	867,184.32	4,487.94			
312,377.18	502,838.04	660.20			
	401,655.26				
	325,010.58	1,974.26			
	389,489.65		395,827.04		
424,915.37					
	418,950.12	8,579.54			
120,385.49	649,750.79	14,641.04		17,231.18	
	159,613.18				
	185,082.66	2,412.00			
60,126.11	469,536.77	270.12			
	416,639.84				
139,085.57	502,616.58	530.00			
	421,629.72	2,847.18			
		4,186.03			
38,477.11	1,687,294.26				
	196,390.28	8,775.45			
	526,514.38	7,667.51			1,251.25
			166,096.24		
1,211,249.83	12,466,759.49	418,855.61	561,923.28	17,231.18	1,251.25

SHOWING PREMIUMS COLLECTED AND LOSSES PAID OF FIDELITY AND CASUALTY COMPANIES

Name of Company	Accident	Losses Paid	Health	Losses Paid	Liability
Ætna Casualty and Surety	$	$	$	$	$ 3,339.48
Ætna Life (Accident)	13,753.90	4,227.67	11,047.93	4,733.22	75,257.67
American Automobile					
American Credit Indemnity					
American National Life (Accident)	1,801.27	113.49	1,801.28	522.64	
American Surety					
Belt Automobile					
Columbian National Life (Accident)	200.56	34.28	324.94	157.50	
Continental Casualty	56,100.46	17,442.16	19,622.40	16,909.48	
Employers Liability	2,375.10	1,735.54	1,571.25	1,296.16	74,528.60
Fidelity and Casualty	8,178.40	2,904.17	6,910.08	4,213.04	41,549.55
Fidelity and Deposit	2,589.56	2,781.97	2,593.90	7,042.64	1,234.74
General Accident	9,540.43	4,526.84	7,516.33	4,979.56	28,650.08
Georgia Casualty	8.81	88.33	12.55	405.66	70,548.33
Hartford Accident and Indemnity	697.51	158.50	592.25	174.14	20,534.59
Hartford Steam-Boiler					
Lloyds Plate-Glass					
London Guarantee and Accident					
Maryland Assurance (Accident)	19,101.16	9,702.88	19,618.02	13,388.69	
Maryland Casualty	743.26	1,843.72	957.03	3,790.17	250,756.22
Massachusetts Bonding*	23,802.68	11,591.95			5,194.16
Metropolitan Casualty					
National Surety					
National Casualty*	8,111.83	3,408.90			
National Life of America (Accident)*	11,377.66	4,560.96			
New Amsterdam Casualty	4,973.05	1,326.90	3,567.91	3,073.61	35,285.82
New York Plate-Glass					
North American Accident	3,905.43	1,863.23			
Ocean Accident and Guarantee	1,620.07	836.32	1,742.62	1,246.26	16,004.54
Pacific Mutual Life (Accident)	6,075.05	2,156.95	2,992.99	2,067.49	
Provident Life and Accident*	41,870.17	21,907.59			
Preferred Accident	2,369.98	467.67	1,397.57	921.04	
Reliance Life (Accident)	1,975.12	2,675.53	3,397.29	865.72	
Royal Indemnity	3,829.30	7,994.28	3,285.57	1,659.09	7,141.27
Standard Accident	49,657.43	22,829.89	19,469.82	20,313.19	4,018.76
Travelers (Accident)	15,055.57	4,290.00	7,675.76	5,901.94	60,139.48
Travelers Indemnity	214.54	17.50	17.50	17.14	
United States Casualty	6,981.09	1,453.75	6,990.64	114,957.04	29,690.04
U. S. Fidelity and Guaranty	2,900.16	2,445.33	2,823.24	578.03	49,824.27
Western Live Stock					
Totals	299,809.55	135,386.30	125,928.87	209,213.45	773,697.60

*Accident and Health.

IN NORTH CAROLINA.

(LICENSED TO DO BUSINESS IN THIS STATE) FOR THE YEAR ENDING DECEMBER 31, 1918.

Losses Paid	Fidelity	Losses Paid	Surety	Losses Paid	Plate-glass	Losses Paid	Steam-boiler	Losses Paid
$_____ 32,731.64	$ 2,587.15	$_____	$ 3,638.21	$7,164.26	$ 1,894.92	$ 498.81	$_____	$_____
_____	11,209.62	7,964.86	14,604.98	24.71				_____
18,287.79	40.02	_____			670.62	529.24		
21,581.59	3,230.35	_____	2,717.19	_____	5,058.56	1,620.22	7,673.24	113.59
4,812.35	23,476.51	17,803.96	18,624.74	6,881.54	87.89	1,237.76	_____	
18,720.38								
15,665.55					597.51	398.99		
4,350.39	1,533.52	_____	4,041.47	_____	1,469.81	866.07		
							34,925.30	1,282.69
_____	_____	_____	_____	_____	3,476.18	1,403.81		
121,046.52	3,844.53	500.00	8,926.54	1,600.78	4,187.84	1,814.71	8,446.67	562.51
5,417.88	2,390.13	40.00	6,291.14	5,443.11	1,208.98	558.10	_____	
					3,776.01	1,502.50		
_____	17,510.91	1,931.61	14,054.77	2,719.60				
3,423.77	3,112.34	65.00	3,165.81	1.80	696.42	194.60		
					5,221.32	3,486.47	_____	
12,651.62	377.50	_____	_____	_____	1,167.96	909.86	460.85	_____
563.62	3,901.64	100.00	1,202.86	_____	1,675.69	833.81	1,329.93	_____
5.00	_____	_____						
28,738.27								
_____	_____	_____	_____		436.74	155.70	64.70	_____
					1,765.94	801.72		
14,376.10	20,470.25	2,447.19	36,168.58	39,181.97	1,813.25	517.77	_____	
302,372.47	93,684.47	30,852.62	113,436.29	63,017.77	35,205.64	17,331.14	52,900.69	1,958.79

SHOWING PREMIUMS COLLECTED AND LOSSES PAID OF FIDELITY AND CASUALTY COMPANIES

Name of Company	Burglary and Theft	Losses Paid	Credit	Losses Paid	Sprinkler	Losses Paid
Ætna Casualty and Surety	$ 882.16	$	$	$	$ 102.32	$
Ætna Life (Accident)						
American Automobile						
American Credit Indemnity			15,467.25	20.02		
American National Life (Accident)						
American Surety	235.42					
Belt Automobile						
Columbian National Life (Accident)						
Continental Casualty						
Employers Liability	908.04	40.25				
Fidelity and Casualty	3,179.14					
Fidelity and Deposit	4,863.73					
General Accident	136.95					
Georgia Casualty	63.06					
Hartford Accident and Indemnity	1,115.88	320.00				
Hartford Steam-Boiler						
Lloyds Plate-Glass						
London Guarantee and Accident			51,794.61	1,402.38		
Maryland Assurance (Accident)						
Maryland Casualty	7,532.67	116.85			1,024.53	50.15
Massachusetts Bonding*	386.56					
Metropolitan Casualty						
National Surety	1,462.62					
National Casualty*						
National Life of America (Accident)*						
New Amsterdam Casualty	396.65					
New York Plate-Glass						
North American Accident						
Ocean Accident and Guarantee	1,142.12	63.85	1,700.00	61.62		
Pacific Mutual Life (Accident)						
Provident Life and Accident*						
Preferred Accident						
Reliance Life (Accident)						
Royal Indemnity	1,444.70	69.64				
Standard Accident						
Travelers (Accident)						
Travelers Indemnity	427.07					
United States Casualty	1,715.66					
U. S. Fidelity and Guaranty	4,480.35	39.22				
Western Live Stock						
Totals	30,372.78	649.81	68,961.86	1,484.02	1,126.85	50.15

*Accident and Health.

(LICENSED TO DO BUSINESS IN THIS STATE) FOR THE YEAR ENDING DECEMBER 31, 1918.

Fly-wheel	Losses Paid	Auto and Team Property Damage	Losses Paid	Work-men's Col-lective	Losses Paid	Live Stock	Losses Paid	Phy-sicians' Defense	Losses Paid
$ 85.96	$ _____	$3,903.38	$ 851.99	$ _____	$ _____	$ _____	$ _____	$ _____	$ _____
		15,646.89	851.34						
		142.50							
		2,828.47	640.26	22.31					
1,431.75		3,338.20	829.77						
		103.43	81.25						
		4,134.74	840.34						
		6,275.00	1,588.64						
		3,668.95	695.67			2,421.11	360.00		
5,659.17									
3,970.35		9,519.52	1,659.89					370.16	
		1,110.76	216.90						
		1,536.90	328.83						
		402.80	1,709.80						
160.34		1,550.34	180.60						
		765.98	126.95						
		3,104.20	116.98						
		1,641.62	312.85						
3,391.59	1,134.86								
						1,057.31	7,655.00		
14,699.16	1,134.86	59,673.68	11,031.96	22.31	_____	12,478.42	8,015.00	370.16	_____

STATISTICAL TABLES

RELATING TO FRATERNAL ORDERS

———

Name of Order	Income	
	Paid by Members	All Other Sources
American Knights Ethiopian	$ 293.75	$ 133.50
Atlantic Coast Line Relief Department	190,639.58	58,058.19
Ben Hur, Supreme Tribe	1,564,440.26	99,278.85
Benefit Association of all Railway Employees	485,310.49	3,237.70
Brothers and Sisters Aid Society	353.60	33.91
Brothers and Sisters Union of America	1,919.70	
District Household of Ruth, No. 10	22,820.09	180.20
Eastern Star	21,780.29	20.00
Funeral Benefit Association	533,573.56	64,277.55
Fraternal Mystic Circle	413,295.36	29.125.11
Gates Mutual Burial		
Grand Court of Calanthe	4,345.98	3,816.07
Grand United Order of Abraham		
Grand United Order of Brothers and Sisters of Love and Charity	11,362.60	160.00
Grand United Order of Odd Fellows (colored)	56,982.34	1,104.77
Household of David	294.85	
Independent Order of Good Samaritans (Raleigh)	722.45	
Independent Order of Good Samaritans (Kinston)	1,501.95	
Independent Order of True Reformers		
Independent Order of Good Samaritans and Daughters of Samaria		
Independent Order of St. Luke	129,845.38	25,012.11
Independent Order of J. R. Giddings and Jollifee Union	19,786.25	964.00
Independent Order of Brith Sholom	304,009.51	75,660.39
Junior Order of United American Mechanics (Beneficiary Degree)	198,099.48	24,425.46
Knights of Gideon Mutual Society	53,261.56	4,675.70
Knights of Columbus	2,209,546.33	380,388.86
Knights of the Guiding Star of the East	960.00	
Knights of King Solomon	887.79	609.07
Knights of Pythias, Supreme Lodge	2,486,212.95	505,638.41
Knights of Pythias, (colored)	35,000.81	4,107.39
Lincoln Benefit Society	5,012.85	700.00
Loyal Order of Moose	754,023.27	792,427.56
Masons Annuity	214,722.80	49,872.99
Masonic Benefit Fund (colored)	62,950.89	511.74
Masonic Mutual Life	415,031.85	258,777.51
Modern Brotherhood of America	1,345,002.58	200,956.59
Modern Woodmen of America	19,967,056.24	762,138.95
Mutual Life and Indemnity	1,101.20	
Oasis and Omar Temple	64,171.80	2,603.33
Order of the Golden Seal	237,522.30	36,753.99
Order United Commercial Travelers	965,288.50	70,171.14
North Carolina Camp, Patriotic Order Sons of America	10,230.23	4,771.71
Norfolk and Western Relief Department	338,909.70	68,846.67
Patriotic Order Sons of America	22,296.16	965.94
Pink Hill Fraternal	229.85	
Peoples Independent Order True Reformers	686.76	520.42
Raleigh Union Society		
Red Men's Benefit	14,692.61	1,045.62
Royal Arcanum	7,175,627.06	212,481.51
Royal Fraternal Association	5,999.84	60.00
Royal Knights of King David	50,304.70	2,879.90
Sons and Daughters of Peace	1,067.76	429.00
Tent Sisters, Grand United Order	440.85	31.00
The Maccabees	6,540.058.17	897,706.53
Travelers Protective Association	554,359.37	14,362.97
United Order of J. R. Giddings and Jollifee Union	4,843.44	846.80
Woodmen of the World, Sovereign Camp	14,687,601.72	2,026,446.32
Woodmen Circle, Supreme Forest	2,455,761.25	320,308.06
Woman's Association of the Maccabees	2,415,646.75	580,026.46
Woman's Union Burial Association	10,527.78	
Totals	67,068,915.19	7,587,543.95

| Total Income | Disbursements | | | Total Assets | Total Liabilities |
	Paid for Claims	All Other Disbursements	Total Disbursements		
$ 427.25	$ 160.00	$ 239.22	$ 399.22	$ 28.03	$ 293.75
248,697.77	233,105.28	53,415.87	286,521.15	1,769.15	55,253.60
1,663,719.11	1,269,232.87	351,295.79	1,620,528.66	1,778,886.54	183,212.52
488,548.19	236,650.43	218,643.44	455,293.87	157,131.07	42,745.43
387.51	75.00	161.83	236.83	361.65	75.00
1,919.70	1,562.50	397.81	1,960.31	169.80	1,275.00
23,000.29	20,556.08	1,850.98	22,407.06	7,522.68	2,470.82
21,800.29	19,532.05	998.24	20,530.29	5,091.39	4,000.00
597,851.11	652,250.00	20,631.59	672,881.59	193,455.15	86,207.55
442,420.47	319,270.50	79,580.44	398,850.94	584,464.82	495,590.36
		81.00	81.00	294.70	
8,162.05	4,141.50	1,438.90	5,580.40	2,881.65	500.00
11,522.60	14,670.00	1,149.18	15,819.18	10,089.67	
58,087.11	53,261.90	4,486.32	57,748.22	42,648.88	11,458.30
294.85	375.00	60.75	435.75	90.29	
722.45	600.00	180.00	780.00	4,607.99	
1,501.95	1,021.25	586.61	1,607.86	1,384.70	575.00
154,857.49	68,374.10	66,003.47	134,377.57	126,518.56	7,750.00
20,750.25	19,705.00	1,764.42	21,469.42	23,760.41	1,425.00
379,669.90	211,151.31	93,882.19	305,033.50	410,887.82	165,100.00
222,524.94	106,267.20	57,980.39	164,247.59	529,269.10	57,561.83
57,937.26	52,631.00	8,559.35	61,190.35	21,307.65	750.00
2,589,935.19	1,543,559.44	380,202.15	1,923,761.59	8,889,204.29	618,492.86
960.00	600.00	268.00	868.00	261.65	100.00
1,496.86	201.00	295.76	496.76	1,000.10	809.07
2,991,851.36	1,835,018.00	378,748.21	2,213,766.21	10,459,458.47	9,474,184.22
39,108.20	23,250.00	10,736.46	33,986.46	10,603.70	3,500.00
6,212.85	3,795.50	1,834.96	5,630.46	1,802.73	800.00
1,546,450.83	828,140.58	340,027.24	1,168,167.82	1,981,046.13	2,743,173.51
264,595.79	196,947.65	50,837.60	247,785.25	1,010,804.47	1,036,117.33
63,462.63	56,700.00	4,075.28	60,775.28	27,408.24	3,328.05
673,803.36	203,807.36	198,770.20	402,577.56	1,680,775.54	1,665,362.65
1,545,959.17	868,294.53	204,560.45	1,072,854.98	4,086,829.07	295,262.70
20,729,195.19	18,383,422.85	1,761,447.97	20,144,870.82	15,892,763.36	6,366,113.72
1,101.20	900.00	139.20	1,039.20	201.61	
66,775.13	58,500.00	5,833.80	64,333.80	10,220.33	2,329.90
274,276.29	112,646.99	159,827.99	272,474.98	721,778.22	117,357.90
1,035,459.64	776,989.49	188,180.31	965,169.80	975,251.33	272,101.44
15,001.94	11,300.00	1,366.52	12,666.52	4,179.82	1,000.00
407,756.37	390,990.97	65,965.90	456,956.87	28,623.54	28,000.00
23,262.10	23,000.00	1,028.29	24,028.29	31,596.78	5,622.30
229.85	125.00		125.00	193.60	50.00
1,207.18	583.00	529.50	1,112.50	94.68	325.00
15,738.23	18,776.50	1,030.77	19,807.27	21,832.98	2,300.00
7,388,108.57	6,008,348.74	434,538.24	6,442,886.98	6,395,650.53	1,034,605.00
6,059.84	5,002.10	2,511.43	7,513.53	8,295.89	1,256.00
53,184.60	24,695.00	17,011.12	41,706.12	38,146.22	3,500.00
1,496.76	450.00	194.00	644.00	2,682.51	925.00
471.85	64.00	296.20	360.20	111.65	231.70
7,437,764.70	6,396,264.77	996,826.48	7,393,091.25	15,127,983.16	2,445,211.98
568,722.34	454,268.48	93,976.12	548,244.60	327,964.53	98,203.62
5,690.24	3,225.00	21,467.10	24,692.10	41,914.46	875.00
16,714,048.04	10,997,668.82	1,876,941.51	12,874,610.33	39,329,309.52	9,045,553.50
2,716,069.31	1,591,844.46	537,818.01	2,129,662.47	7,493,806.94	800,465.03
2,995,673.21	1,669,023.49	437,529.99	2,106,553.48	12,410,777.71	378,342.04
10,527.78	9,774.57	768.00	10,542.57	559.35	509.89
74,656,459.14	55,782,771.26	9,138,972.85	64,921,744.11	130,915,754.81	48,217,653.57

Name of Order	Certificates in Force December 31, 1917		Certificates Issued During 1918	
	Number	Amount	Number	Amount
American Knights Ethiopian		$	4,116	$
Atlantic Coast Line Relief Department	11,168		4,116	
Ben Hur, Supreme Tribe	85,224	83,431,065.00	12,393	12,503,855.00
Benefit Association of all Railway Employees	33,676	504,000.00	21,017	536,500.00
Brothers and Sisters Aid Society	149		38	
Brothers and Sisters Union of America	946		199	
District Household of Ruth, No. 10	7,582	476,419.00	625	31,250.00
Eastern Star	8,829	956,475.00	918	45,900.00
Funeral Benefit Association				
Fraternal Mystic Circle	16,652	13,377,705.00	3,919	1,080,678.00
Gates Mutual Burial				
Grand Court of Calanthe				
Grand United Order of Abraham				
Grand United Order of Brothers and Sisters of Love and Charity	3,987			
Grand United Order of Odd Fellows (colored)	17,000		2,124	
Household of David	297		18	
Independent Order of Good Samaritans (Raleigh)	289	22,900.00	232	23,200.00
Independent Order of Good Samaritans (Kinston)	575	27,750.00	185	9,250.00
Independent Order of True Reformers				
Independent Order of Good Samaritans and Daughters of Samaria				
Independent Order of St. Luke	34,058	3,659,167.85	7,147	691,825.00
Independent Order of J. R. Giddings and Jollifee Union	8,163	702,100.00	562	56,200.00
Independent Order of Brith Sholom	52,596	25,788,650.00	4,285	2,134,750.00
Junior Order United American Mechanics (Beneficiary Degree)	10,287	10,454,000.00	3,218	3,481,500.00
Knights of Gideon Mutual Society			2,111	
Knights of Columbus	123,979	131,679,400.33	12,554	13,597,000.00
Knights of the Guiding Star of the East	350	35,000.00	24	2,400.00
Knights of King Solomon	310	31,000.00		
Knights of Pythias, Supreme Lodge	72,461	96,508,135.00	3,969	5,293,000.00
Knights of Pythias (colored)				
Lincoln Benefit Society	4,579	739,800.00	937	94,700.00
Loyal Order of Moose				
Masons Annuity	4,940	1,721,700.00	784	234,800.00
Masonic Benefit Fund (colored)	8,000	2,400,000.00	500	15,000.00
Masonic Mutual Life	13,246	19,809,512.00	3,890	7,247,000.00
Modern Brotherhood of America	58,428	69,209,750.00	2,563	2,649,250.00
Modern Woodmen of America	1,047,011	1,638,899,500.00	76,427	80,661,500.00
Mutual Life and Indemnity				
Oasis and Omar Temple	1,552	310,400.00	446	89,200.00
Order of the Golden Seal	9,546	12,751,425.57	4,983	6,486,700.00
Order United Commercial Travelers	76,619	383,095,000.00	5,323	26,615,000.0
N. C. Camp, Patriotic Order Sons of America				
Norfolk and Western Relief Department				
Patriotic Order Sons of America	887	925,500.00	18	18,000.0
Pink Hill Fraternal				
Peoples Independent Order True Reformers	141	176,250.00	4	500.00
Raleigh Union Society				
Red Men's Benefit				
Royal Arcanum	145,568	246,382,161.88	2,065	2,261,000.0
Royal Fraternal Association	689	112,756.00	147	22,880.0
Royal Knights of King David	14,686	975,850.00	11,004	975,850.0
Sons and Daughters of Peace	272	27,200.00	70	7,000.0
Tent Sisters, Grand United Order				
The Maccabees	300,061	359,824,687.82	17,970	18,141,000.0
Travelers Protective Association	65,201	326,005,000.00	12,168	60,840,000.0
United Order of J. R. Giddings and Jollifee Union	6,755		1,208	
Woodmen of the World, Sovereign Camp	842,546	1,122,930,200.00	109,882	137,285,545.0
Woodmen Circle, Supreme Forest	183,424	183,307,900.00	37,880	39,621,000.0
Woman's Association of the Maccabees	178,228	134,439,965.46	17,081	12,169,650.0
Woman's Union Burial Association	2,888		414	
Totals	3,453,845	4,871,704,325.91	385,418	434,922,883.0

Certificates Terminated During 1918		Certificates in Force December 31, 1918		Increase		Decrease	
Number	Amount	Number	Amount	Number	Amount	Number	Amount
	$		$		$	547	$
4,663		10,621				8,704	7,467,356.00
21,097	19,971,211.00	76,520	75,963,709.00				
18,378	139,500.00	36,315	901,000.00	2,639	364,500.00		
4		183		34			
						89	
301		857					
303	27,916.68	7,979	483,502.32	397	7,083.32		
348	42,150.00	9,434	961,975.00	805	5,500.00		
3,319	1,650,902.00	17,252	12,807,481.00	600			570,224.00.
						86	14,670.00
86	14,670.00	3,901	585,150.00				
333		18,791		1,791			
						25	
43		272					
6	600.00	515	51,500.00	226	22,600.00		
50	2,500.00	715	34,750.00	140	7,000.00		
4,881	476,324.10	37,008	3,941,118.75	2,950	281,950.90		
187	18,700.00	8,567	856,700.00	404	154,600.00		
5,643	2,740,750.00	51,238	25,182,650.00			1,358	606,000.00
1,131	1,167,500.00	12,378	12,825,000.00	2,091	2,371,000.00		
542		26,475		1,569			
7,598	8,061,966.00	128,935	137,214,434.33	4,956	5,535,034.00		
2	200.00	308	308,000.00			2	200.00
4,927	6,769,664.00	72,547	96,365,445.00	86	142,690.00		
3,763	648,700.00	1,785	189,000.00			2,794	550,800.00
456	153,100.00	5,302	1,803,400.00	382	81,700.00		
165	49,500.00	8,335	2,365,500.00	335			45,500.00
1,787	3,048,150.00	15,372	24,044,612.00	2,132	4,235,100.00		
12,718	16,149,654.75	50,216	58,184,345.25			8,212	11,025,404.75
56,277	75,922,000.00	1,067,161	1,644,662,000.00	20,150	5,762,500.00		
293	58,600.00	2,017	403,400.00	465	93,000.00		
4,683	6,049,086.90	9,846	13,189,038.67	300	437,613.10		
9,676	48,380,000.00	74,641	373,205,000.00			1,978	9,890,000.00
		12,469	12,327,750.00				
46	45,000.00	861	900,500.00			86	24,000.00
		305	7,575.00				
38	4,750.00	107	13,375.00			34	162,875.00
12,763	23,983,987.50	135,751	228,009,531.01			9,817	18,372,730.87
213	28,140.23	623	107,495.77			66	5,260.23
6,829	617,150.00	18,861	1,388,700.00	4,175	358,700.00		
30	2,950.00	312	31,250.00	40	4,050.00		
4		82					
23,231	23,711,528.19	294,800	354,254,159.63			5,261	5,570,528.19
12,180	60,900,000.00	66,242	331,210,000.00	1,041			5,205,000.00
		7,963		1,208			
74,147	92,638,104.00	893,615	1,187,718,754.00	51,069	64,788,554.00		
13,033	12,052,300.00	208,271	210,876,600.00	24,847	27,568,700.00		
11,749	8,117,094.80	183,560	138,492,520.66	5,332	4,052,555.20		
538		2,778				110	
18,461	413,644,350.15	3,582,086	4,951,866,922.39	130,164	116,274,430.52	39,169	59,510,549.04

Name of Order	Certificates in Force December 31, 1917		Certificates Issued During 1918	
	Number	Amount	Number	Amount
American Knights Ethiopian		$		$
Atlantic Coast Line Relief Department	11,168		4,116	
Ben Hur, Supreme Tribe	20	29,000.00		
Benefit Association of all Railway Employees	318	500.00	792	10,00(
Brothers and Sisters Aid Society	149		38	
Brothers and Sisters Union of America	946		199	
District Household of Ruth, No. 10	7,582	476,419.00	625	31,25(
Eastern Star	8,829	956,475.00	918	45,90(
Funeral Benefit Association				
Fraternal Mystic Circle	573	740,741.00	5	6,50(
Gates Mutual Burial				
Grand Court of Calanthe				
Grand United Order of Abraham				
Grand United Order of Brothers and Sisters of Love and Charity	3,987			
Grand United Order of Odd Fellows (colored)	17,000		2,124	
Household of David				
Independent Order of Good Samaritans (Raleigh)	289	28,900.00	232	23,20(
Independent Order of Good Samaritans (Kinston)	575	27,750.00	185	9,25(
Independent Order of True Reformers				
Independent Order of Good Samaritans and Daughters of Samaria				
Independent Order of St. Luke	1,473	158,560.00	490	49,07&
Independent Order of J. R. Giddings and Jollifee Union	8,163	702,100.00	562	56,20(
Independent Order of Brith Sholom				
Junior Order United American Mechanics (Beneficiary Degree)	2,832	3,011,000.00	1,000	1,200,50(
Knights of Gideon Mutual Society			2,111	
Knights of Columbus	150	171,000.00		
Knights of the Guiding Star of the East	350	35,000.00	24	2,40(
Knights of King Solomon				
Knights of Pythias, Supreme Lodge	2,781	3,706,708.00	155	205,50(
Knights of Pythias (cloored)				
Lincoln Benefit Society	4,579	739,800.00	937	94,70(
Loyal Order of Moose				
Masons Annuity				
Masonic Benefit Fund (colored)	8,000	2,400,000.00	500	15,00(
Masonic Mutual Life	1,325	1,726,700.00	78	105,00(
Modern Brotherhood of America				
Modern Woodmen of America	6,064	8,017,500.00	2,330	2,472,00(
Mutual Life and Indemnity				
Oasis and Omar Temple	1,552	310,400.00	446	89,20(
Order of the Golden Seal	38	47,000.00	1	1,00(
Order United Commercial Travelers	734	3,670,000.00	41	205,00(
N. C. Camp, Patriotic Order Sons of America				
Norfolk and Western Relief Department				
Patriotic Order Sons of America	2	2,000.00		
Pink Hill Fraternal			103	
Peoples Independent Order True Reformers	141	176,250.00	4	50(
Raleigh Union Society				
Red Men's Benefit				
Royal Arcanum	2,252	4,476,251.00	3	4,00(
Royal Fraternal Association	620	105,196.00	98	18,45(
Royal Knights of King David	6,206	444,510.00	4,347	
Sons and Daughters of Peace	272	27,200.00	70	7,00(
Tent Sisters, Grand United Order			84	
The Maccabees	679	1,020,000.00	101	135,50(
Travelers Protective Association	2,591	12,955,000.00	519	2,595,00(
United Order of J. R. Giddings and Jollifee Union	6,755		1,208	
Woodmen of the World, Sovereign Camp	27,563	34,689,600.00	3,063	3,877,68(
Woodmen Circle, Supreme Forest	1,887	1,793,700.00	454	448,40(
Woman's Association of the Maccabees	273	215,000.00	47	40,75(
Woman's Union Burial Association	2,888		414	
Totals	141,606	82,860,260.00	28,424	12,057,83&

Certificates Terminated During 1918		Certificates in Force December 31, 1918		Received from Members During the Year	Claims Incurred During the Year	Claims Paid During the Year	Claims Unpaid December 31, 1918
Number	Amount	Number	Amount				
4,663	$ ----------	10,621	$ ----------	$ 293.75	$ ----------	$ 160.00	$ ----------
				190,639.58	117,000.00	96,902.50	39,497.50
20	29,000.00						
237	----------	873	10,500.00	10,714.66	5,722.40	4,779.90	1,177.42
4	----------	183		353.60	150.00	75.00	75.00
301		857		1,919.70			
303	27,916.68	7,979	483,502.32	22,820.09	21,912.50	20,416.68	2,470.82
348	42,150.00	9,434	961,975.00	21,780.29	19,525.00	19,525.00	4,000.00
				21,577.00		29,937.50	
45	65,300.00	533	681,941.00	17,073.99	9,300.00	7,487.62	6,800.00
				4,345.98			
86		3,901		11,362.60	14,670.00	14,670.00	
333		18,791		56,982.34	61,900.00	53,253.49	11,458.30
				294.85	375.00	375.00	
6	600.00	515	51,500.00	722.45	600.00	600.00	
50	2,500.00	715	34,750.00	1,501.95	925.00	990.00	300.00
305	30,500.00	1,703	181,635.00	5,321.50	2,700.00	2,300.00	400.00
187	18,700.00	8,567	856,700.00	19,786.25	18,700.00	19,700.00	1,025.00
346	420,000.00	3,490	3,822,000.00	61,033.89	38,000.00	22,375.00	12,500.00
542	----------	26,475		53,261.56	52,631.00	52,631.00	750.00
6	7,000.00	144	164,000.00	2,542.83	4,000.00	3,000.00	2,000.00
				960.00	600.00	600.00	100.00
		308	308,000.00	887.71	400.00	200.00	200.00
179	256,354.00	2,805	3,712,854.00	89,370.37	59,608.00	60,608.00	8,000.00
3,763	648,700.00	1,785	189,000.00	5,512.85	3,507.50	3,682.50	500.00
165	49,500.00	8,335	2,365,500.00	62,950.89	46,500.00	46,500.00	3,000.00
96	123,400.00	1,307	1,708,300.00	46,605.54	20,000.00	16,750.00	3,250.00
1,245	1,397,500.00	7,268	9,249,500.00	101,086.18	126,000.00	94,000.00	32,500.00
				1,101.20			
293	58,600.00	2,017	403,400.00	64,171.80	58,500.00	58,500.00	
9	14,000.00	30	34,000.00	543.54	350.00	350.00	
98	490,000.00	708	3,540,000.00	8,704.00	6,300.00	10,850.00	650.00
				10,230.23	10,750.00	11,300.00	1,000.00
		12,469	12,327,750.00	338,909.70	183,242.80	156,742.80	28,000.00
		2	2,000.00	64.80			
		305	7,575.00	229.85			50.00
38	4,750.00	107	13,375.00	686.76	750.00	550.00	
				14,692.61		18,776.50	
168	368,265.00	2,102	4,166,225.00	123,872.66	123,165.00	117,087.95	25,500.00
125	22,051.00	578	101,595.00	5,999.84	4,266.73	3,508.23	1,160.00
325	296,350.00	7,235	457,043.00	50,304.70	11,500.00	10,850.00	1,150.00
30	2,950.00	312	31,250.00	1,067.76	300.00	450.00	50.00
4		82		440.85	25.00	25.00	
62	81,500.00	718	1,074,000.00	13,041.49	3,500.00	3,454.55	
598	2,990,000.00	2,584	12,920,000.00	27,742.00	18,000.00	13,500.00	8,000.00
		7,963		4,843.44	18,875.00		875.00
430	2,961,344.00	29,136	36,786,936.00	479,698.73	491,300.00	269,683.54	237,272.22
216	192,600.00	2,125	2,049,500.00	23,883.13	25,600.00	13,716.65	6,416.66
30	20,500.00	290	235,250.00	3,868.70	1,000.00	2,000.00	
538		2,778		10,527.78			
188	10,622,030.68	188,130	98,931,556.32	1,996,328.05	1,582,150.93	1,262,864.41	440,127.92